SPANISH
FRONT

SPANISH FRONT
WRITERS ON THE CIVIL WAR

EDITED BY
VALENTINE CUNNINGHAM

Oxford   New York
OXFORD UNIVERSITY PRESS
1986

Oxford University Press

Oxford   New York   Toronto
Delhi   Bombay   Calcutta   Madras   Karachi
Petaling Jaya   Singapore   Hong Kong   Tokyo
Nairobi   Dar es Salaam   Cape Town
Melbourne   Auckland

and associated companies in
Beirut   Berlin   Ibadan   Nicosia

Oxford is a trade mark of Oxford University Press

Introduction and selection © Valentine Cunningham 1986

First published in the United States in 1986 by Oxford University Press,
Inc., 200 Madison Avenue, New York, New York 10016

British Library Cataloguing in Publication Data
Spanish front: writers on the civil war.
1. Spain—History—Civil War, 1936–
1939—Personal narratives
I. Cunningham, Valentine
946.081′092′2   DP269.9
ISBN 0-19-212258-4
ISBN 0-19-282006-0 Pbk

Library of Congress Cataloging in Publication Data

Spanish front.
Includes index.
1. Spain—History—Civil War, 1936–1939—
Literary collections.   I. Cunningham, Valentine.
PN6071.S6S63   1986   808.8′0358   86-8728
ISBN 0-19-212258-4
ISBN 0-19-282006-0 (pbk.)

2 4 6 8 10   9 7 5 3 1
Printed in the United States of America

For
J. V. A. and W. B. R. B. Cunningham

CONTENTS

WRITERS' CONGRESS

I-WITNESSES

PRIVATE FACES IN THAT PUBLIC PLACE

SECOND THOUGHTS

THE LAST FIGHT

I REMEMBER SPAIN

LOOKING BACK

'   ' have been used for the title in the original text. No inverted commas have been used where the anthology title does not occur in the original.

LIST OF ILLUSTRATIONS

INTRODUCTION

Introductions, by their nature, pose initial problems. But an introduction to a gathering of writing about the Spanish Civil War thrusts one into an intensified version of those usual initial difficulties. For the Spanish Civil War is, initially and throughout, an affair of initials. It was a war of initial letters, initial letters that are still as provoking and deterring to the unprepared reader as they were to the naïve visitor to wartime Spain or the uninitiated volunteer for the fighting who came from overseas. 'As for the kaleidoscope of political parties and trade unions, with their tiresome names— PSUC, POUM, FAI, CNT, UGT, JCI, JSU,* AIT—they merely exasperated me'. Thus George Orwell, reflecting wryly in *Homage to Catalonia* on his own untutored simplicity, the innocence of the straightforward good-willed English leftist bloke about to have his political blank sheets scribbled on all over by the tangling alphabetical factions of Republican Spain. My own student astonishment and dismay over Orwell's book is still a vivid memory. After two terms of Milton the discovery one hot summer afternoon that the twentieth century did in fact exist for Oxford University's English Faculty, even if its texts were tucked away in obscurity behind a vast dummy wall of earlier tomes in the old temporary Faculty Library upstairs in the Examination Schools, was cheering enough. But joy soon got stifled by disappointment mounting to incredulity that the book I'd carried off with me by the famously biddable author of *Nineteen Eighty Four* and *Animal Farm*, by the look of it an enticing Spanish War Book, should be devoted so extensively to a confusing play of sigla—all those initial capitalised and capitalised-on letters of the alphabet. What on earth was the Spanish Civil War all about? The *alphabet?*

Nowadays, though, that clamant capitalised alphabeticism seems one of the most instructive things of all about the nature of the Spanish War.

---

* *Partit Socialista Unificat de Catalunya* (effectively the Catalan Communist Party); *Partido Obrero de Unificación Marxista* (a dissident Communist Party at odds with the Comintern); *Federación Anarquista Ibérica* (a militant federation of Anarchist groups); *Confederación Nacionas del Trabajo* (the anarcho-syndicalist trade union); *Union General de Trabajadores* (the Socialist trade union); *Juventud Communista Ibérica* (the youth movement of the POUM); *Juventudes Socialistas Unificadas* (the united socialist youth organisation, formed in 1936 by a fusion of the Socialist and Communist youth organisations).

For it asserts and brings home the pre-eminence, the prominence of language stuff, the stuff of writing, and so inevitably the centrality of writing itself, that is utterly apt to what happened in, and to, this conflict.

Good people used, rightly, to feel they had to protest against the grotesque distortion and specialisation of the Spanish Civil War into a Poets' War—and a foreign, non-Spanish Poets' War at that. Literary critics were, very properly, put in their place for being so preoccupied with the handful of poets and writers who exploded like bombs, with the famous artists and filmstars and intellectuals who wrote and sang and danced for the benefit of the Republic or even dropped in from time to time at some battle-front or casualty clearing-station. Forget Shirley Temple, Errol Flynn and Paul Robeson, or even Hemingway and Auden, was the going advice: concentrate rather on the thousands of anonymous Spanish militiamen and the hundreds of unsung foreign volunteers, on the German exiles who carried their fight against Hitler from the streets of Berlin to the streets of Madrid, on the American and British proletarians, the doctors from Canada and Cambridge, the London nurses, the ambulance drivers from Glasgow and the stretcher bearers from Dublin, the ordinary people who laid down their lives fighting among the olive groves for the political beliefs that animated them or who came back home not at all in one piece, those people who stare out at the photographer from silent group photographs, nameless people, most of them unnameable now, teetering right on the edge of a historical annihilation that the writers, the poets, the photogenic stars have not had to suffer. And the advice was good; and an imbalance of emphasis and focus got itself in some measure redressed. The so-called Poets' War took on the more historically instructed, alert texture of a Workers' War, a war fought in and supported by some workers of brain, alright, but engaged in mainly by workers of hand, and supported largely by donations from proletarian work-places, by door-to-door collections in mean streets, by the pennies of workers' children in run-down industrial areas, by the sacrificial purchasers of sixpenny Co-op milk tokens for starving Spaniards—by charitable people who could, in fact, often have done with an extra sixpenn'orth of nourishment for their own families. And this sense of the Spanish War as a People's War, as the most potent and most emotionally engaging focus of thirties democratic struggles and progressive working-class ambitions, hopes and fears must never again be lost sight of.

But, for all that, the Spanish Civil War was also a war in which writing, text, image, and writers, artists, photographers, film-makers, poster-designers, print-workers played central and essential parts. In no war before this one had the means of propaganda been used on so massive a scale. This was the war in which the military importance of forces not visible on battlefields got open recognition. Mola invented the Fifth Columnist, in name if not in practice, when he boasted that his Four Columns advancing on Madrid were backed by a Fifth Column secretly waiting in the city to rise in Franco's favour. The propagandists became in this war a sort of open Fifth Column—a vital set of extra troops, an essential troupe of military extras. Never before had wartime printing presses worked so hard or printing-works turned out so many propaganda posters. Multi-colour printing techniques, still in their infancy, were exploited for the first time extensively in political warfare. The art of political photomonatage had been developed in pre-Hitler Germany by people like John Heartfield just in time, you might say, for use in Spain. The documentary film, only recently brought to birth, mainly in England, found its apogee in propaganda movies, especially the Hemingway-Joris Ivens documentary film, *Spanish Earth.* In earlier times the occasional intellectual or writer had volunteered to travel abroad and fight in someone else's domestic cause. But this war had, as it were, numerous Byrons, even if some of them did only write for the newspapers. Many writers and artists fought and were wounded and killed in the First World War and some of them had been volunteers and not conscripts. But that was in an extremely large-scale conflict and most of the fighting writers had been coerced by their governments into taking part. What was startling and special about Spain was that this relatively small-scale war had so many voluntary writer-participants in it— whether they were doing medical work or actually fighting, were engaged in propaganda or political activities, or had gone to Spain simply to report events.

It is indeed extraordinary and quite distinctive that an Orwell or a Malraux, a Hemingway, an Auden, a Spender, a Claude Simon, a Simone Weil, should have wished to have done anything at all in this foreign conflict. It is characteristic of this extraordinary situation that at least one writer, the awful rightwing Roy Campbell, who in actuality got out of the country of his temporary residence as fast as he could when the war broke out, should have felt he must pretend he had been in the thick of the fighting and fake up quite untrue stories about how he had toted a rifle on behalf of his new-found Catholic faith and General Franco. It is indeed notable that in this war so many writer-volunteers should have got themselves killed for their decision to put aside their pens and books in order to bear arms or carry stretchers in Spain. Ralph Fox, John Cornford, Charley Donnelly, Christopher St John Sprigg (or Caudwell),

Julian Bell—to name only the British and Irish writers who were killed in Spain—all had much still to prove about their quality as poet or critic or novelist. Cornford, Bell and Donnelly in particular were only fledgeling writers. Each of them became, as Borges has put it of Byron, 'more important for his image than his work'. But on any reckoning they make an arresting group. And merely making catalogues of the names of writers and artists who did something for the Republican side does bear out one of the major and distinctive claims of that side, that the forces of the legally elected Spanish government were struggling not just in the name of freedom and democracy against the forces of repression and Fascism, but were fighting for the survival of art and culture in free societies. Franco's men shot Garcia Lorca; and most of the Spanish poets were in the Republican ranks. Things were that simple; and nothing, not even the intervention of the darker proponents of Soviet cultural imperialism, can detract from the starkness of the fact. Anticlerical mobs did indeed sack and burn churches in Republican Spain —a fact which greatly exercised even extreme Leftists from overseas: for nobody on the British, American, French or German Left was greatly inclined to advocate firing churches, even in their wildest revolutionary programmes—but historic religious art objects were carefully stored and catalogued and exhibited as part of the Republic's dedicated campaign to preserve the national art and to make it available to the people. Nationalist clerics were bumped off, to be sure, but peasants and soldiers were taught to read by the Republic's teams of adult-educators and reading-matter was widely disseminated in the Republic's powerful drive for popular literacy. And of course Franco's bombers did not hesitate to bomb museums and churches. When he achieved dominance his agents not only hounded and silenced intellectuals and artists but burned the Spanish Bibles that the Republic had had printed by the thousand and sold openly in Barcelona literacy festivals.

In the Republican zones poetry became truly popular. Spanish poets like Rafael Alberti read to packed houses. Ordinary people on the Republican side were apparently much gladdened by the support they were getting from foreign writers. Poetry, as Spender argued in his Introduction to *Poems for Spain*, the anthology that he and John Lehmann brought out in 1939, achieved in Spain an extraordinary flowering, both among Republican Spaniards and in the ranks of the foreign militia-men. Writing was alive and well in the midst of the Spanish adversities (revolutions, especially in their early phases, have always been good for art). Some writers did, of course, support the Franco side, especially Roman Catholics such as Pierre Drieu La Rochelle, Evelyn Waugh, Roy

Campbell, Hilaire Belloc and Arnold Lunn, people who feared communism more than anything, even than regimes that would savagely kill a
Lorca, and who read Franco as the saviour of European Christianity
against Stalin's Asiatic hordes. But even when you grant all the Rightists
their due credit—and the anti-Republicans did include Ezra Pound and
(more or less) W. B. Yeats and T. S. Eliot—the collective force of
writers, artists and artistes supporting the Republic gives colour to the
notion that on one side was Franco and his German and Italian allies and
his Moorish mercenaries and on the other side was Sweetness and Light.
And if the Sweetness was not always or for the whole duration of the War
wholly unadulterated and the Light flickered and waned, at least there
were thronged against Franco's cause Eric Gill, Henry Moore, Paul
Nash, Ben Nicholson, Jacob Epstein, Pablo Picasso and Joan Miró
representing painting and sculpture, and Pablo Casals, Benjamin
Britten, Paul Robeson and Benny Goodman representing music, and
Charles Chaplin, Errol Flynn, Marlene Dietrich, Bette Davis, Joan
Crawford speaking for the movies, and Pablo Neruda, Thomas Mann,
Octavio Paz, Julien Benda, André Chamson and all the many, many
others, standing for the world of letters. 'The Sodomites are on your
side, The cowards and the cranks': so jeered Roy Campbell at the
Republic. But the Republic's column of cultural extras was not at all as
limited as that.

But even had many more thirties writers and artists been in favour of
Franco, the most important point hereabouts would have remained
unchanged. And that is that Spain deeply engaged the world's writers
and artists, their writing and their art, their words and images, in some
way or another, on one side or another. For the writers of the thirties
Spain was irresistible, magnetic, a very cynosure. Not surprisingly it
became for them a test, indeed *the* test. There was intense pressure upon
writers and writing to take sides, for or against the Republic. And sides
were taken. The *Left Review* symposium published in 1937 with the title
Authors Take Sides on the Spanish War not only managed to assemble an
enormous band of Republican sympathisers and to winkle out only a very
few Franco admirers, it also showed, and more crucially, just how few
there were among British writers who were prepared to stand aside or
back from the issue and profess themselves neutral. And other evidence,
either about those the survey labelled 'Neutral?' or about writers whose
names did not appear in *Authors Take Sides* or writers who we know
refused to contribute to it, supports this broad picture of general
engagement in the argument and aroused concern about Spain. If one
looks at the accumulating political and critical journalism of T. S. Eliot,

his fence-sitting position can be seen wobbling more and more towards the side of Franco and the Right. George Orwell described the whole exercise as 'bloody rot' in a private letter to Spender, but he had nonetheless almost lost his life fighting for the Republic. The absence of Graham Greene from the survey has long intrigued—but now we can add to the clearly pro-Republican despairs of this British Roman Catholic manifested in his novel *The Confidential Agent*, his much overlooked *Spectator* article, characteristically tangential and crab-wise, about some earlier taking of sides in Spanish politics by a youthful Cambridge poet called Alfred Tennyson and a bunch of enthusiastic nineteenth-century Cambridge Apostles. In common with almost everybody else Graham Greene was neither neutral nor disinterested.

'We are determined or compelled, to take sides', wrote the sponsors of the *Authors Take Sides* survey. And taking sides was not the only determination or compulsion around. Other compulsions vigorously converged in the matter of Spain. There was the compulsion to 'go over' to Spain and the cause of democracy and the working-class not just in your head or your texts but also (as Marx and Engels had suggested bourgeois intellectuals would in Capitalism's late phases) actually, physically. There was the compulsion to bear arms, or to attend the Second Congress of the International Association of Writers that was held in Valencia, Madrid and Barcelona in July 1937, the compulsion to bear some kind of first-hand witness to events in Spain (a compulsion felt strongly on the Right as well as on the Left: but then being an I-witness in that era of fraught selfhood and compulsive testimony, that time when almost every other book had a title beginning *I* . . . , did come rather naturally to writers). And Spain's test, its set of tests, was experienced widely, especially on the Left, as a set of necessities. It is noticeable how greatly the very word *necessary* irked some readers when it appeared in Auden's poem 'Spain'. Auden, like lots of other writers, had taken on the personal Spanish burden of 'The conscious acceptance of guilt in the necessary murder'. The burden seemed at the time a necessary one. (When later Auden rejected the idea of that necessity he also dropped that word from his poem, and eventually he discarded the stanza that had once carried it.) 'As an Englishman I am not in the predicament of choosing between two evils', Evelyn Waugh replied for *Authors Take Sides*. But he did choose, and choose, despite his resentment at being called a Fascist, for fascist Franco. His diary for 25 September 1936 shows him discussing the provision of 'relief' for the Insurgent side at a meeting of the Catholic Archbishop of Westminster's 'Spanish Association'. You might in the event, of course, fail to satisfy Spain's various tests—as Auden feared he might ('I shall probably be a bloody bad soldier') and in effect did, and as poem after poem of Spender presents his cowardly poetic persona as doing ('Port Bou' is a good example). Turning yourself into André Malraux, the most satisfying western example on the Left, of the writer as Man of Action would be for most writers next to impossible. But the invitation to put yourself in for the examination was widely felt as ineluctable.

And if Spain's necessities tested thirties writers in their lives, it also provided tests for their writing. Bluntly put, thirties writing's pre-occupation with questions of war, action, pacifism and the possibility of heroism in the light of the First World War, of Wilfred Owen's anti-war poetry and the absorbing failure of the 'self-conscious' man of action T. E. Lawrence, its fascination with placing and displacing, with map-making and map-reading, with frontier-anxieties, with exile and abroad, its alertness to issues of class, revolution and the popularity of art, its talk of the revolutionary hour of the knife and the apocalyptic moment of decisive struggle: all these recurrent obsessions came suddenly very sharply and nastily to life in Spain. And not just on the Left. 'Then Comrades come rally, And the last fight let us face', Leftists sang in The Internationale; John Cornford meditated on death 'On the last mile to Huesca'; and the proletarian novels *We Live* and *The Land of the Leal* (both 1939) contrived to end their stories of working-class struggle with deaths in Spain; but Drieu La Rochelle's right-wing novel *Gilles* evinces an even stronger craving to have its hero come to an end masochistically in the Spanish fight.

Some writers' writing never recovered from the testing Spain gave it. Auden, for example, found it difficult to go on praising bombing planes and helmeted airmen after his Spanish experiences. Spender's poems abandoned any claim on revolutionary enthusiasm and started going in for stories of physical cowardice while he was still in Spain. And Spain had instant effects on people's texts, not least because a clear and central part of its nature was textual. This was a war that had been given a kind of proleptic existence in huge tracts of post-First World War writing. It was a war that provided the tragic enactment and instructive apotheosis of much main thirties writing in English. In Spain, as Auden's 'Spain' has it, 'the menacing shapes of our fever / Are precise and alive'. There 'our faces . . . are projecting their greed as the firing squad and the bomb'. There 'our moments of tenderness blossom / As the ambulance and the sandbag; / Our hours of friendship into a people's army'. MacNeice made the same sort of point in his *Autumn Journal*: 'our spirit / would find its frontier on the Spanish front'. These writers perceived Spain as being dense with their own textualising. And when these textualised Spanish events got turned back into text by writers such as this it was scarcely surprising to find the shapes of the pre-Spanish fictions, the old metaphors, tones and themes still 'precise and alive', or at least still powerfully in play and in debate. Critics would note, for example, how much John Sommerfield's style of battle reportage owed to Hemingway's fiction style (and, of course, Hemingway was himself also in Spain testing out his own textualised paper-courage in battle-front situations that generated not only more text in the shape of his newspaper stories but, eventually, the most famous example of the Hemingway fictional manner in his Spanish novel *For Whom the Bell Tolls*).

Sommerfield had his eye on the movies as well as on his copies of Hemingway's stories. He gave one section of his book *Volunteer in Spain* (1937) the title 'War Picture'. Spender called one of his poems 'War Photograph'. And these labels weren't just signalling how easy it was in Spain to feel that you were acting in a war movie or to read scenes of horror as if they'd already been snapped and developed and turned out as one of those atrocity photographs that so upset Virginia Woolf in *Three Guineas*; though such feelings were evidently widespread. Nor was this only because of Isherwood's famous granting of camera-status to the text of reportage, the discourse of the I-witness or reporter ('I am a camera'), though this too is not irrelevant. Even more importantly, it has to do with that instant conversion of events into images that writing, like photography, inevitably achieves.

And, naturally, once it has been written down or photographed, even the most painfully awful battle or scene of suffering finds itself clamped into the stilling embrace of the aesthetic, into the literary, imagic hold of text. It is not, then—although it might at first appear so to the casual reader—the action of a dilettante or the pursuit of some obscene irrelevance that Cyril Connolly should in *Enemies of Promise* (1938) have chosen to reflect on the contributions to the *Authors Take Sides* survey in terms of their prose styles, or that so many responses to Picasso's Spanish drawings and his *Guernica* should have been built around the debates about social or socialist realism going on in the period. These reactions to textual matters, to manner, tone, style, this stress on cultural and critical relevance and on placings within the art-historical continuum were only acknowledging that Spain—so literary in any case to start with—existed for every reader of a book or an article about it, for everybody who saw the film *Spanish Earth*, for everyone who noticed a propaganda poster or cartoon or who heard a radio talk about the war, Spain existed *also* (and in most cases existed *only*) as text, as image. Every fighter, every ambulance-man, every commissar or observer or poet or journalist in Spain who wrote letters to loved-ones and friends back home, took photographs, wrote a Spanish poem, wrote a book about Spain or sent an article to *Left Review*, the *New Statesman*, *Life and Letters Today*, *New Writing*, or wherever, was, it should go without having to be said, turning the Spain that he was enduring and enacting into another kind of reality, the reality of text. And it is in their texts, it is as text, that Spain exists, by and large, for most of us, the belated readers of their text-making labours.

It is because of its profound realisation of this inevitable process of textualisation and the difficulties thus sponsored for the observer stuck with the task of reading, that the meditation in Claude Simon's novel *Les Géorgiques* (1981) on a photograph of some Spanish volunteers is so important. It is a meditation that refuses to allow the experience and knowledge even of a Spanish veteran like Simon himself to inspire any special insight or intimacy. Even the general reader's feeling that the photograph is one (s)he has come across before is not allowed to help. The description acts with painstaking naïvety, scanning the image with minute care as if for the first time, pretending to come to it as from the pen of the merest uninitiated reader. And in refusing to accept anything as pre-read it mightily illuminates the serious drawbacks and difficulties, the postures and clenched fists of men that would indeed puzzle the uninstructed, the mystifyingly cut-off parts of bodies, the marred bits of the photograph, the dirt and the smoke that obscure and only half-reveal —all those features obstructing epistemological progress and her-meneutic satisfaction. And these are, in fact, the sort of barriers that always get in the way of making sense of and tracing out the meaning in any writing or photograph, even in writing and photography that have to do with an event as real and historical as Spain, but that custom and conventions of reading and interpretation encourage us to overlook. In treating Spain as mere text, and in offering a new piece of writing about Spain as an engagement not with the unmediated events of the past but as an intertextual dialogue with precedent images, writings, texts (*Les Géorgiques* includes a reinterpretation of one of Simon's own earlier Spanish fictions *Le Palace* and a rewriting of the French version of *Homage to Catalonia*) Simon isn't being quirky or fanciful, nor even wilfully French and post-structuralist; he's simply being wise and instructive.

But, of course (as Roland Barthes's extraordinary and moving medi-tation on the death of his mother and on the photography that holds her memory for him as image, the book *Camera Lucida*, spells out with some vigour) photographs—and Barthes's point can be applied even to photographs described at second hand in novels—are not simply textual. They are textual, but they are also turned towards and tuned into history, they capture and preserve traces of the past, they testify to the inerasable presence of the real for all that they have textualised it. In effect, photographs have a dual existence, straddling the border between fact and image. So also do certain kinds of writing, not least writing about the Spanish Civil War. In consequence the Spanish Front/Frontier is also that border at which fact overlaps fiction, and *vice versa*. What is more, because of the peculiar distortions of the ordinarily paradoxical dualities of the fact-fiction border that are brought about by the special Spanish circumstances, this particular frontier of the image and the real is an extraordinarily animated and difficult one. It is perhaps even the ultimate apotheosis of the terrible border tensions that so pack thirties writing.

Fiction, of course, always seeps into so-called factual writing. The two discourses are hardly ever completely separable. No effort at reportage can ever be a mere transcription of the real. And nobody in the 1930s, when documentary techniques and theories in photography, film and writing were being invented and developed, ever believed it might be. This anthology's section-title 'War Stories', which contains self-professed fictions, could just as easily be applied to much Spanish War writing, especially the reportage. After all, novelists write stories, and journalists 'file' them. And this is a reflection whose implications might have saved some of Orwell's current detractors and defenders a deal of their trouble. The contributors to Christopher Norris's *Inside the Myth: Orwell; Views from the Left* (1984) make great, but unnecessary, play with mistakes of fact in *Homage to Catalonia*. Who does not make mistakes? Claude Simon, the apostle of Spain's textuality and narrativity, mounts a much more sophisticated attack. He accuses Orwell (and Orwell's readers) of the hypocritical pretence that *Homage to Catalonia* is telling the whole truth rather than composing a writing, arranging a narrative that, though it might contain some truth and even be essentially truthful, is by no means telling all the truth. Simon refers (in an interview in *The Review of Contemporary Fiction*, v, no. 1, 1984) to the suppressions and rearrangements implicit, if only to the alert critical intelligence, in *Homage*, a text that is, he declares, 'faked from the very first sentence' —that arresting opening line, 'In the Lenin Barracks, the day before I joined the militia, I saw an Italian militiaman standing in front of the officers' table'. 'If . . . critics', says Simon,

find, after analysing it, that this sentence is innocent (what it says, and above all what it carefully omits to say) it is because they are singularly ignorant of the political circumstances in Barcelona at that time, and, in general, of the circumstances in revolutionary movements in Europe at that same period. I shall restrict myself to informing them that one did not just wander casually into Republican Spain at that time, and that if there did exist in Barcelona something called the 'Lenin Barracks' (or rather a 'Cuartel Lenin'), there was also, not far away, a 'Cuartel Karl Marx', and another invoking the name of Bakunin. The respective occupants of these various barracks considered each other to be 'counter-revolutionaries' and thought only of the best way of eliminating them (as happened in May 1937 to the benefit of the Stalinists). To give an idea of the idyllic proletarian unanimity which then reigned in Barcelona, it should be recalled that the occupants of the Cuartel Karl Marx called the occupants of the Cuartel Lenin 'hitlero-trotskyites'. Finally, it was not 'by chance' that a foreigner made for one of these cuartels rather than another: thus it was because I had a communist party membership card in my pocket at that period (September 1936) that I went straight to the Hotel Colon, which was then the headquarters of the PSUC. All these things (including the motives which led him to the Cuartel Lenin) are carefully suppressed by Orwell, until he gets to the account of the May insurrection, about which the uninformed reader will understand very little.

But Orwell himself, who carefully and with self-conscious craft reworked the material of his notes and diaries into texts like *The Road to Wigan Pier*, and was always quite consciously suppressing things (and not always just for reasons of narrative polish) would, I am sure have been surprised at Simon's fuss. Everyone in the thirties documentary movement would have assumed that Simon's suggestions about story-tellers' fakings went really without saying. What, though, gives the issue of narrativity special resonance in Spanish writing is that we know there was continual conscious and unconscious pressure upon writers to go in for suppressions and re-arrangements of their material to make the truths of the report conform not just to conventional narrative ambitions, pleasing form, and the like, but to the less reputable and continually shifting demands of some political party line. The results of serving those kinds of demand are undoubtedly sniffable in, say, the praise for Soviet equipment that gets into Sommerfield's *Volunteer in Spain*, or the way James Barke's Communists in *The Land of the Leal* preach up the current Communist International political line of the Popular Front, or in the technique developed in Republican propaganda posters of attacking the POUM and other non-Communist revolutionaries but in coded phrases about the dangers of pursuing social innovations and experiments while a war with Franco was still going on. But the textual results here are by no means the same thing as lying. Deliberate liars like Roy Campbell, floating untruths to increase his image as the most macho poet around, or a Black Propagandist like Claud Cockburn in his persona as

Daily Worker Spain correspondent Frank Pitcairn inventing untruths to aid his own side, are relatively easy for readers to cope with. The case with a Capa photograph or an Orwell story is usually far less simple. It is the involvement of the would-be truthteller (such as Orwell clearly was) in the war of words, in the murky textual waters of propaganda and counter-propaganda inevitably tending to influence opinion and judgement, to colour narrative and handicap fact in its jockeying with fiction, which helps to make readers like Claude Simon so edgy.

And if Spanish propagandising exacerbated the normal fact-fiction problem, so also did the peculiarities of acquiring Spanish impressions. The rushed impressions of hasty visitors to any country are always unreliable and sketchy. And most writers about the Spanish War were essentially ignorant and short-term visitors, involved in an odd species of tourism. The acquaintance that a Hemingway or a V. S. Pritchett brought to his Spanish War writing was quite special and rare. And what the raw tourists were seeing was especially difficult to form impressions about. Spain in Civil War-time was no ordinary tourist spot. Civil War—Simone Weil makes the point as one of the writing-tourists, in a 'Fragment' she jotted down probably around the time of her own aborted visit to Spain (it was published in 1960 in her *Écrits Historiques et Politiques*)—civil wars will turn any place into a shifty, kaleidoscopic object of focus:

What is going on in Spain? Over there, everyone has his word to put in, his stories to tell, a judgement to pronounce. Right now, it's in fashion to go on a tour down there, to take in a spot of revolution, and to come back with articles bursting out of your pen. You can't open a newspaper or a magazine any more without coming across accounts of events in Spain. How can all this not be superficial? In the first place a social transformation can only be correctly appreciated as a function of what it means to the daily life of each of those who make up the population. It is not easy to get inside this daily life. Furthermore each day that passes brings new developments. Also, constraint and spontaneity, necessity and idealism are so mixed up that they generate inextricable confusion not only as to the facts, but also in the very consciousness of the actors and spectators in the drama. Right here lies the essential character and perhaps also the greatest evil of civil war. This is also the first conclusion to be drawn from a swift inspection of events in Spain, and what one knows about the Russian revolution confirms it only too amply. It is not true that revolution tallies automatically with an awareness of the social problem that is more elevated, more intense, clearer. It's the contrary that proves true, at least when revolution takes the form of civil war. In the howling gale of civil war, principles get completely out of phase with realities, every sort of criterion by which one might judge actions and institutions disappears, and social transformation is left completely to chance. So how can one report something coherently on the strength of a short stay and some fragmentary observations? The most one can hope for is to put together a few impressions, tug just a few lessons into the light of day.

Claude Simon accuses the 'idyllic description' of Barcelona in the first part of *Homage to Catalonia* of being 'little more than a comic tourist guide'. But after all we have to afforce Simone Weil's observations with Auden's powerful suggestions about the malleability of Spain. The war, suggests the poem 'Spain', is all things to all men (and women), it responds to whatever subjective needs the observer brings to bear on it. It's very like Hamlet's cloud formations, in fact, very like a whale if you want it to be:

> 'To you, I'm the
>
> 'Yes-man, the bar-companion, the easily-duped;
> I am whatever you do. I am your vow to be
> Good, your humorous story.
> I am your business voice. I am your marriage.
>
> 'What's your proposal? To build the just city? I will.
> I agree. Or is it the suicide pact, the romantic
> Death? Very well, I accept, for
> I am your choice, your decision. Yes, I am Spain.'

The point rings truer and truer the more the touristic reader travels through the hundreds of pieces of Spanish War writing. Spain does indeed seem to have possessed the multivalence Auden ascribes to it. And in the writings reprinted here from various angles, male and female, democratic and liberal, insistently Communist, or Roman Catholic, or pro-POUM (like Orwell), or Trotskyite (like, well, Leon Trotsky), Spain remains—for such is the powerful persistence of writing—like that.

'I am your choice, your decision'. And just as Spain came in the variety of readings that Auden suggested, so also those various readings have not remained an exclusive or static bunch of interpretations. Experience, the passage of time, the shifting realities of revolution and counter-revolution, the fluctuating political tides of the war, effected numerous changes in many individual readings. Powerful turns, dodges, shifts of perception and sympathy are the staple subject of many of the most impressive of the Spain texts: the loss of revolutionary faith manifested by Simone Weil's 'Letter to Georges Bernanos' or by Auden and Isherwood's *On the Frontier*; the anger over the behaviour of the Spanish Catholic hierarchy that is evinced by the French Catholic Bernanos's *A*

Diary of My Times; the marked turning away from the Communists and the British Left establishment in favour of the suppressed P O U M in *Homage to Catalonia* and in numerous other texts of Orwell's; the sadness at a revolution's fade-out in Franz Borkenau's *The Spanish Cockpit*; the turn away from the Communist Party line about André Gide in the renegade Dutch Communist Jef Last's report on the International Writers' Congress. Lapsing and failing relationships with the gods people started off by worshipping are all over the place in these writings. Furthermore, Spain is still capable of sustaining new readings, it is a still reinterpretable, revisable set of texts. One aspect stressed by this anthology's arrangement of material to which previous generations did not pay particular attention is the role of women in this war. On the Republican side women fought, wore trousers in public, went about unchaperoned; they could practice birth-control and in some circumstances obtain legal abortions. One of the most prominent of Republican leader-figures was the woman Dolores Ibarruri known as 'La Passionaria'. On the other side, Franco's armies, egged on by the Catholic hierarchy, sought to restore traditional Spanish womanliness and Catholic motherhood. And we are now in a position to perceive women in Spain in the wider context of the twentieth-century struggle for women's liberation. The fairly well-known male story of concerned male artists and writers has now to be supplemented by the story of engaged women writers and artists. At the heart of this newly tellable story are the artist and Communist Felicia Browne from London, first Briton to be killed fighting in Spain (in August 1936); a nurse like Nan Green; the lesbian poet and novelist Sylvia Townsend Warner who made at least two extended visits to wartime Spain with her fellow-poet and lover Valentine Ackland and wrote as much as anybody did about the war; and Simone Weil who travelled to Spain to fight, went to the Aragon front with Durutti's column and would have stayed longer had an accident with hot cooking-oil not supervened.

But though the still resonant multivalence of Spain helps us notice the role of these New Women of the thirties, and allows us to afford a new place of honour to them and to their particular Spanish texts, what is also brought home by attending to the women's writings of this war is the degree to which female participation in Spain continued also in quite traditional modes. In Spain the men were still, by and large, going off to fight, leaving their women behind them to grieve their absence and their loss and/or to question the necessities that took their lives. Virginia Woolf mourned the death of her beloved nephew Julian Bell and joined her interrogation of war's inevitabilities (in *Three Guineas*) with the pacifism

Vera Brittain voiced in *Authors Take Sides* (a pacifism sponsored by the loss of a beloved in the First World War). Margot Heinemann was left behind, the recipient of John Cornford's letters from the Front with the ancient womanly task of composing the dead fighter's epitaph. Nan Green, whose husband the musician George Green was killed on the Ebro in the International Brigade's very last engagement, was left in like condition. She had also done what women have always done—she followed her man to the war, a modern version of the traditional female camp-follower, working with the medicals (who were organised by another wife, Winifred Bates, whose husband the novelist Ralph Bates edited the Brigade's paper *Volunteer for Liberty* and engaged in other male political activities). Rosamond Lehmann stayed behind to organise help for International Brigaders and was mightily gladdened when her wounded husband and ambulance-man Wogan Phillips decided not to return to Spain. These were traditional motifs and routines surviving alongside innovativeness of role and action. But then, a mélange of old and new is what keeps on marking the Spanish experience and the Spanish writings. In the end Spain failed to satisfy the deep political and artistic cravings of the thirties that it had focussed so sharply and had initially appeared able to resolve. There would be no utter renewal, no clean break with the past, no utopian resolution. Spain and its texts did not rewrite or iron out the paradoxes of the Great War and its texts. They did not fully answer the old questions about heroism and the life of action. They did not prove Wilfred Owen wrong about the bewildering but necessary alliance in war between feelings of disgust and outrage at the evil and futility of it all and feelings of love and admiration for the bravery of the soldiers and their pathetically and nobly borne sufferings. For Spain and its texts certainly do not sustain the earliest lyrical and romantic readings of the war as the zone where the necessary evils and terrors of revolution and war might after a temporary outing prove the gateway to happy conclusions. 'Today the struggle': that was true. But tomorrow, after all, there still remained 'the private nocturnal terror'; and the post-War 'fun' that Auden hoped would eventuate from submission to purgatorial struggles 'under Liberty's masterful shadow' was as elusive as ever—for the winners even more than for the losers. 'There is', indeed, as Esmond Romilly said in his *Boadilla* (1937), thinking of his friends killed in the defence of Madrid, 'something frightening, something shocking, about the way the world does not stop because these men are dead.' History, in fact, could not manage much more than a grim Audenic 'Alas' for anybody, on any side, whether actor or writer or reader.

SPANISH
FRONT

GOING OVER

W. H. AUDEN

'Spain'

First publ. as a pamphlet, 1937

Yesterday all the past. The language of size
Spreading to China along the trade-routes; the diffusion
    Of the counting-frame and the cromlech;
Yesterday the shadow-reckoning in the sunny climates.

Yesterday the assessment of insurance by cards,
The divination of water; yesterday the invention
    Of cartwheels and clocks, the taming of
Horses. Yesterday the bustling world of the navigators.

Yesterday the abolition of fairies and giants,
The fortress like a motionless eagle eyeing the valley,
    The chapel built in the forest;
Yesterday the carving of angels and alarming gargoyles.

The trial of heretics among the columns of stone;
Yesterday the theological feuds in the taverns
    And the miraculous cure at the fountain;
Yesterday the Sabbath of witches; but to-day the struggle.

Yesterday the installation of dynamos and turbines,
The construction of railways in the colonial desert;
    Yesterday the classic lecture
On the origin of Mankind. But to-day the struggle.

Yesterday the belief in the absolute value of Greece,
The fall of the curtain upon the death of a hero;
      Yesterday the prayer to the sunset
And the adoration of madmen. But to-day the struggle.

As the poet whispers, startled among the pines,
Or where the loose waterfall sings compact, or upright
      On the crag by the leaning tower:
'O my vision. O send me the luck of the sailor.'

And the investigator peers through his instruments
At the inhuman provinces, the virile bacillus
      Or enormous Jupiter finished:
'But the lives of my friends. I inquire. I inquire.'

And the poor in their fireless lodgings, dropping the sheets
Of the evening paper: 'Our day is our loss, O show us
      History the operator, the
Organiser, Time the refreshing river.'

And the nations combine each cry, invoking the life
That shapes the individual belly and orders
      The private nocturnal terror:
'Did you not found the city state of the sponge,

'Raise the vast military empires of the shark
And the tiger, establish the robin's plucky canton?
      Intervene. O descend as a dove or
A furious papa or a mild engineer, but descend.'

And the life, if it answers at all, replies from the heart
And the eyes and the lungs, from the shops and squares of the city:
      'O no, I am not the mover;
Not to-day; not to you. To you, I'm the

'Yes-man, the bar-companion, the easily-duped;
I am whatever you do. I am your vow to be
      Good, your humorous story.
I am your business voice. I am your marriage.

'What's your proposal? To build the just city? I will.
I agree. Or is it the suicide pact, the romantic
      Death? Very well, I accept, for
I am your choice, your decision. Yes, I am Spain.'

Many have heard it on remote peninsulas,
On sleepy plains, in the aberrant fisherman's islands
      Or the corrupt heart of the city,
Have heard and migrated like gulls or the seeds of a flower.

They clung like burrs to the long expresses that lurch
Through the unjust lands, through the night, through the alpine tunnel;
      They floated over the oceans;
They walked the passes. All presented their lives.

On that arid square, that fragment nipped off from hot
Africa, soldered so crudely to inventive Europe;
      On that tableland scored by rivers,
Our thoughts have bodies; the menacing shapes of our fever

Are precise and alive. For the fears which made us respond
To the medicine ad. and the brochure of winter cruises
      Have become invading battalions;
And our faces, the institute-face, the chain-store, the ruin

Are projecting their greed as the firing squad and the bomb.
Madrid is the heart. Our moments of tenderness blossom
      As the ambulance and the sandbag;
Our hours of friendship into a people's army.

To-morrow, perhaps the future. The research on fatigue
And the movements of packers; the gradual exploring of all the
      Octaves of radiation;
To-morrow the enlarging of consciousness by diet and breathing.

To-morrow the rediscovery of romantic love,
The photographing of ravens; all the fun under
      Liberty's masterful shadow;
To-morrow the hour of the pageant-master and the musician,

The beautiful roar of the chorus under the dome;
To-morrow the exchanging of tips on the breeding of terriers,
    The eager election of chairmen
By the sudden forest of hands. But to-day the struggle.

To-morrow for the young the poets exploding like bombs,
The walks by the lake, the weeks of perfect communion;
    To-morrow the bicycle races
Through the suburbs on summer evenings. But to-day the struggle.

To-day the deliberate increase in the chances of death,
The conscious acceptance of guilt in the necessary murder;
    To-day the expending of powers
On the flat ephemeral pamphlet and the boring meeting.

To-day the makeshift consolations: the shared cigarette,
The cards in the candlelit barn, and the scraping concert,
    The masculine jokes; to-day the
Fumbled and unsatisfactory embrace before hurting.

The stars are dead. The animals will not look.
We are left alone with our day, and the time is short, and
    History to the defeated
May say Alas but cannot help nor pardon.

GEORGE ORWELL

In the Caserne Lenin

from *Homage to Catalonia*, 1938

In the Lenin Barracks in Barcelona, the day before I joined the militia, I saw an Italian militiaman standing in front of the officers' table.

He was a tough-looking youth of twenty-five or six, with reddish-yellow hair and powerful shoulders. His peaked leather cap was pulled fiercely over one eye. He was standing in profile to me, his chin on his breast, gazing with a puzzled frown at a map which one of the officers had open on the table. Something in his face deeply moved me. It was the face of a man who would commit murder and throw away his life for a friend—the kind of face you would expect in an Anarchist, though as likely as not he was a Communist. There were both candour and ferocity in it; also the pathetic reverence that illiterate people have for their supposed superiors. Obviously he could not make head or tail of the map; obviously he regarded map-reading as a stupendous intellectual feat. I hardly know why, but I have seldom seen anyone—any man, I mean—to whom I have taken such an immediate liking. While they were talking round the table some remark brought it out that I was a foreigner. The Italian raised his head and said quickly:

'*Italiano?*'

I answered in my bad Spanish: '*No, Inglés. Y tú?*'

'*Italiano.*'

As we went out he stepped across the room and gripped my hand very hard. Queer, the affection you can feel for a stranger! It was as though his spirit and mine had momentarily succeeded in bridging the gulf of language and tradition and meeting in utter intimacy. I hoped he liked me as well as I liked him. But I also knew that to retain my first impression of him I must not see him again; and needless to say I never did see him again. One was always making contacts of that kind in Spain.

I mention this Italian militiaman because he has stuck vividly in my memory. With his shabby uniform and fierce pathetic face he typifies for me the special atmosphere of that time. He is bound up with all my memories of that period of the war—the red flags in Barcelona, the gaunt trains full of shabby soldiers creeping to the front, the grey war-stricken towns farther up the line, the muddy, ice-cold trenches in the mountains.

This was in late December 1936, less than seven months ago as I write, and yet it is a period that has already receded into enormous distance. Later events have obliterated it much more completely than they have obliterated 1935, or 1905, for that matter. I had come to Spain with some notion of writing newspaper articles, but I had joined the militia almost immediately, because at that time and in that atmosphere it seemed the only conceivable thing to do. The Anarchists were still in virtual control of Catalonia and the revolution was still in full swing. To anyone who had been there since the beginning it probably seemed even in December or January that the revolutionary period was ending; but when one came straight from England the aspect of Barcelona was something startling and overwhelming. It was the first time that I had ever been in a town where the working class was in the saddle. Practically every building of any size had been seized by the workers and was draped with red flags or with the red and black flag of the Anarchists; every wall was scrawled with the hammer and sickle and with the initials of the revolutionary parties; almost every church had been gutted and its images burnt. Churches here and there were being systematically demolished by gangs of workmen. Every shop and café had an inscription saying that it had been collectivized; even the bootblacks had been collectivized and their boxes painted red and black. Waiters and shop-walkers looked you in the face and treated you as an equal. Servile and even ceremonial forms of speech had temporarily disappeared. Nobody said '*Señor*' or '*Don*' or even '*Usted*'; everyone called everyone else 'Comrade' and 'Thou', and said '*Salud!*' instead of '*Buenos días*'. Tipping was forbidden by law; almost my first experience was receiving a lecture from a hotel manager for trying to tip a lift-boy. There were no private motor-cars, they had all been commandeered, and all the trams and taxis and much of the other transport were painted red and black. The revolutionary posters were everywhere, flaming from the walls in clean reds and blues that made the few remaining advertisements look like daubs of mud. Down the Ramblas, the wide central artery of the town where crowds of people streamed constantly to and fro, the loudspeakers were bellowing revolutionary songs all day and far into the night. And it was the aspect of the crowds that was the queerest thing of all. In outward appearance it was a town in which the wealthy classes had practically ceased to exist. Except for a small number of women and foreigners there were no 'well-dressed' people at all. Practically everyone wore rough working-class clothes, or blue overalls, or some variant of the militia uniform. All this was queer and moving. There was much in it that I did not understand, in some ways I did not even like it, but I recognized it immediately as a state of affairs worth fighting for. Also I believed that things were as they appeared, that this was really a workers' State and that the entire bourgeoisie had either fled, been killed, or voluntarily come over to the workers' side; I did not realize that great numbers of well-to-do bourgeois were simply lying low and disguising themselves as proletarians for the time being.

Together with all this there was something of the evil atmosphere of war. The town had a gaunt untidy look, roads and buildings were in poor repair, the streets at night were dimly lit for fear of air-raids, the shops were mostly shabby and half-empty. Meat was scarce and milk practically unobtainable, there was a shortage of coal, sugar, and petrol, and a really serious shortage of bread. Even at this period the bread-queues were often hundreds of yards long. Yet so far as one could judge the people were contented and hopeful. There was no unemployment, and the price of living was still extremely low; you saw very few conspicuously destitute people, and no beggars except the gipsies. Above all, there was a belief in the revolution and the future, a feeling of having suddenly emerged into an era of equality and freedom. Human beings were trying to behave as human beings and not as cogs in the capitalist machine. In the barbers' shops were Anarchist notices (the barbers were mostly Anarchists) solemnly explaining that barbers were no longer slaves. In the streets were coloured posters appealing to prostitutes to stop being prostitutes. To anyone from the hard-boiled, sneering civilization of the English-speaking races there was something rather pathetic in the literalness with which these idealistic Spaniards took the hackneyed phrases of revolution. At that time revolutionary ballads of the naïvest kind, all about proletarian brotherhood and the wickedness of Mussolini, were being sold on the streets for a few centimes each. I have often seen an illiterate militiaman buy one of these ballads, laboriously spell out the words, and then, when he had got the hang of it, begin singing it to an appropriate tune.

STEPHEN SPENDER
'I Join the Communist Party'

from the *Daily Worker*, 19 February 1937

In January Victor Gollancz chose my book, *Forward from Liberalism*, as the book of the month for his Left Book Club. My aim in this book was to portray an attitude of mind which would be a common denominator among people who really care for progress rather than reaction, peace under international control rather than imperialist aggression, government in the interests of the whole people rather than fascism.

I believed that if the implications of this attitude of mind were clearly stated many liberal individualists would find themselves set on a path which would lead them ultimately to the idea of the classless international society and to an acceptance of the action necessary—such as the formation of a United Front—to achieve that society.

This book produced various reactions among the reviewers of the capitalist press, from the patronizing coos of *Punch* to the sadistic fury of Mr F. A. Voigt, of the *Manchester Guardian*, who found that I am lacking in all generous feeling and implied that I should be put in one of those fascist concentration camps which he has made his speciality, and now, it seems, his spiritual home.

But most of the reviewers confined themselves to pointing out that my prose is bad, just as when a boy stammers the schoolmaster has an excellent excuse for pointing out to him that he stammers and ignoring what he is saying.

It is not necessary to answer this criticism, which is simply fault-finding, but I think it is necessary to answer the article on my book by Comrade Campbell, which appeared in the *Daily Worker*.

First, it is very important that I should remove the misapprehensions for which I am alone responsible in my attitude to the Soviet Trial. When I wrote this book the Soviet Trial had only just begun; I realized that if I ignored it the critics in the capitalist press might use it as an argument to refute the latter part of my book about the new Soviet constitution. I therefore thought that it was necessary for me to prejudge the whole issue and prejudge it against the USSR as far as possible.

Some time before my book had appeared I had read the rest of the evidence and I became convinced that there undoubtedly had been a gigantic plot against the Soviet Government and that the evidence was true. However, it was too late for me to alter my book.

Some comrades will think that I ought to have assumed immediately that all actions taken by the Soviet Government were justified; but I explicitly stated at the beginning of my book that I was portraying an attitude of mind which was not communist but that of a liberal approaching communism; and I determined to make this portrait consistent throughout.

In the latter part of his article Comrade Campbell interpreted one of my remarks to mean that I was the sort of person who is unable to work within a political movement.

It is possible that there are inconsistencies in my book which would lead critics, who want to think the worst, to this conclusion. However, I made one remark which I myself imagined to be conclusive: that the only genuine criticism of a socialist movement is made by those who give their life to it, thus modifying it with the structure of their own being.

Anyhow, I do not think that there is much point in arguing about past words. In order to make my attitude as clear as possible, I have now joined the Communist Party, before going to Valencia in order to broadcast anti-fascist propaganda from the U G T station. I think a good many readers of my book will see that both these actions are a consistent development of my thesis there. Admittedly, to join the Communist Party is one thing, to be a good communist another. And I do not imagine that I can do anything—nor do I desire to do it—which will put my own political actions and writing beyond the pale of criticisms by other party members.

It was not merely as an answer to Comrade Campbell's review that I joined the Communist Party. A few weeks ago I went on a political tour which took me to Gibraltar, Tangiers, Oran and Marseilles—all of them towns on the border of the Spanish conflict.

Nothing could be clearer to me from seeing these towns than that the Spanish Civil War is the class war played out on an international scale, in which the small capitalist class is backed by international imperialism against the democratic will of at least 80 per cent of the Spanish people.

Everywhere I found that the sympathies of the official, ruling capitalist class were unconcealedly with Franco, while the Spanish population of all these towns passionately identified itself with the government. Everywhere I found that the best workers in these towns, the people with the most dignified standard of life, were Communist Party members.

I felt that it was necessary to make a choice between one international class representing imperialism, and the workers' international.

It seems to me that the most important political aim of our time should be the United Front, organized so that it has a common interest with the Soviet and the Popular Fronts of Spain and France. I wish to belong to the party which is most active in working towards this end, and so I have joined the Communist Party.

CARL A. MANZANI

'The Volunteers'

from the *Spectator*, 12 February 1937

The rendezvous was at Perpignan. Perpignan of Languedoc: the name has a Cyranoesque fragrance of musty chivalry and quixotic pride, an aroma of worn velvet, silent courtyards and empty stables, a certain mellifluous affinity to Gauthier's *Capitaine Fracasse*.

But we entered to no tune of spavined hoofbeats; the rhythmic wheels below us shifted their tempo, the steady chatter subsided into a more complacent cadence, the complacency became reluctance, the reluctance lassitude, the lassitude exhaustion. The train had stopped. I came out of my compartment into the narrow corridor and looked out of the window. The station platform was full of men with hardly any luggage: a small, cheap valise here and there, a few knapsacks, parcels wrapped in newspaper. The presence of such a crowd at this small station in a far-flung corner of France was illogical and puzzling. I felt the vague need of an explanation.

'More volunteers,' said a man beside me.

I hadn't noticed him before. He was rather young, short, with a friendly face under his dark blue *béret*. He wore a cheap overcoat of thick goods.

'Are you a volunteer, too?'

'Why, yes.' From the tone of my voice and the poverty of my French, he felt compelled to add, 'Volunteers to Spain.'

'Yes, yes, I know,' I said absently, as I saw more men in the corridor and realised that they, too, were volunteers. It is hard to define what they had in common: a certain alertness of eye, strength of features, poverty of clothing. They were all workers, workers and students that had assembled here or come in the Paris train from all parts of France. By twos and threes and fives they had come, fishermen of Calais, sailors of Marseilles, machinists from Toulouse, textile-workers from Lille, students from the Sorbonne, and here they were, in the little town of Perpignan in the region of Languedoc.

The few passengers descended and the volunteers filled the compartments, overflowing into the corridors and vestibules. Their organisers had not been idle. Little station wagons appeared with huge baskets of bread, golden fresh loaves that were tossed up to avid hands. Round red cheeses and tins of sardines were distributed; pocket knives were brought out, blades glinted, everyone set to with a will.

Came the squeak of the starting signal, the train pulled out and gathered speed, click-clicking its way to Spain. Soon it veered towards the coast and the Mediterranean came into view, a brilliant blue shading off into a cool green at the horizon. Then the foothills of the Pyrenees and glimpses of the sea below, wearily lapping the base of a rocky coast. Cerbère was the last town on the French side of the frontier. A French customs inspector perfunctorily walked through the train. A money-changer followed him, offering a hundred pesetas for a hundred francs. Hawk-nosed, indifferent to jibes and jokes, a strap over his shoulders supporting a leather pouch stuffed with banknotes, he seemed a mediaeval figure in quasi-modern dress as he made his way through the crowd, tenaciously patient.

A whistle, a toot, a jar, and, before we knew it, we had crossed the frontier and leisurely rolled into Port-Bou on Spanish soil. There were not many people about, a few men in the green uniform of the old frontier guard and a few militiamen. They had no uniform properly speaking; their clothes were heterogeneous, but they all had the same leather jacket and the same leather cap. Their pistols at their hips were obviously of many different makes. A few Russian boots of synthetic rubber could be seen. Over the station waved the handsome red-and-black flag of the anarchists, with the letters CNT-FAI, which are the initials of their trade unions. On the other side of the platform a train was in readiness for us. We detrained and I saw that we were a good-sized contingent, probably about six hundred men. We stood in groups for a few minutes before going to the other train, and I had a sudden sense of unreality. The sky above seemed such a gentle blue, while my surroundings struck me as incongruous. On one side we had a small, lovely church, with a delicate, dainty spire that proudly exhibited its exquisite tracery of white stone, while on the other side the grim granite mass of the foothills squatted mastiff-like across the railroad tracks, swallowing them up in the black gullet of its tunnel. A queer peristaltic motion I thought, and I had a feeling of being naked and exposed like John the Baptist's head on Salome's platter. I shook myself and was drawn in the movement towards the train.

In those few minutes the station had become alive. The villagers had turned out to greet us and their unnoticed filtration had been steady and effective. The platform we had just quitted was alive with them, mostly women and children. The whole atmosphere had changed, had become so charged with the feelings of friendship and gratitude of those people that it had almost a tactile quality. The feeling of unreality was transformed into one of life and animation. Little boys and girls ran along the train brandishing postcards and fishing stubby pencils from about their clothes so that the volunteers could send messages. A few bottles of wine appeared, the strong, acrid, unadulterated wine of the austere land. Money was laughed at and unoffensively but firmly refused. The volunteers reciprocated by giving out the cheese and bread that was left over. Somewhere someone started the 'Internationale,' and it was taken up here, there, everywhere, its powerful rhythm exalting and intoxicating. Then cheers. A stentorian voice shouted:

'*Viva España!*'

'*Viva!!*' It had the force of an explosion.

'Down with Franco!'

'*Bajo!!!*'

Then everyone was cheering. '*Viva la Francia, viva el comunismo, viva el frente popular, bajo Franco, bajo los fascistas,*' on and on, one long, mad, laughing, exuberant expression of solidarity.

There were no mock heroics, nor for that matter heroics of any kind. But underneath the surface was felt the seriousness of the people and of the times. It was that unspoken seriousness, that awareness of the significance of the struggle, that gave to the cheers, the songs and the laughter their peculiar exaltation, an exaltation which, though not hysterical, was vibrant with high tension. When the Spaniards say that they are fighting for the democracy of the world, they mean literally that. And in the faces of the old men and women I caught the spirit of the war in Spain. It was the expression of people who are witnessing a miracle and can't quite believe the evidence of things seen. It was something infinitely touching. These young people, the faces seemed to say, they don't know what it is they are witnessing. Born in a world of ferment and unrest it seems natural to them that they should be fighting for their rights, guns in hand, defending themselves and their ideals. But we, we the people of fifty and sixty and seventy, we who have lived through feudalism and industrialism in our lives, who have known repressions and the oppressive fears of unknown dangers, we tell you that it is something very unusual, something very much out of the ordinary indeed that workers should stand up and fight for themselves, their own very selves . . .

The siren hooted a long, encompassing blast. An old woman in the typical black dress and shawl hopped forward, swishing her skirt. Her withered face dominated by the little snapping eyes, one bony hand across her chest clutching the shawl, the other extended at the end of a pitifully thin arm, she began shaking hands with the volunteers perched out of the windows. As if at a signal the crowd surged forward and everyone was shaking hands, chattering in their own language, the words lost but the sense retained. In a woman's arms I saw a baby crowing and clapping his hands with the jerkiness of uncoordinated movements. The mother laughed and held it tightly, then raised its little fist to wave at us as the train hissed slowly away. The crowd stood shouting, 'Salud!' their fists raised. As the train gathered speed, the last person I saw was a big-boned workman, his hands and face grimy with streaks of black oil, standing at attention saluting us. He had just finished oiling the wheels of our train.

The train plunged into a tunnel, then into another. The countryside was a monotonous brown of rough-hewn landscape, a landscape every bit of which evidenced hard and patient toil. The prismatic hills were terraced tier on narrow tier so as not to waste an inch of space or a bit of dirt, and everything set to grape vines. Long wavy rows of close-cropped dark brown vines followed each other as far as the eye could see; each vine a rough, gnarled, terrifically misshapen dwarf; stubborn growth of a stubborn land tilled by stubborn men.

I saw them at work, those men, as we passed. Older men they were for the most part, in dark sombre corduroys, a black cloth sash around each waist; as we passed the bent backs straightened up from their task, the leathery faces smiled, the arm went up, the hand closed into a fist. 'Salud!' On and on clicked the train through a deep-cut ravine, and on the skyline of the embankment an old woman collecting firewood stood up, her arms raised, a black figure flung against the sky. 'Salud!' On and on through town after town, Figueras, Ciurona, Colomas, Gerona, where little crowds had collected to cheer as the train went by. 'Salud!'

Night fell, a rain drizzled. Tired men dozed off against windows and comradely shoulders. It was cold; hands disappeared into pockets, faces retreated between hunched shoulders and raised collars. Now and again the door would be flung open and a voice call, *'Responsable de Nantes! Responsable de Lille! Responsable de Toulouse!'* If the particular organiser was in our car he would disentangle himself and go out. Somewhere in one of the carriages, a big man bent over papers on his knees under the yellowish pallor of a small light, patiently organizing the men into sections. Tired men sleep, but organisation goes on, for Barcelona is getting nearer and nearer, and beyond Barcelona is Madrid, and Madrid must not fall.

JOHN SOMMERFIELD

'To Madrid'

from *New Writing*, Spring 1937

Under the echoing vault of the Quai D'Orsay Station people scurried like ants, intent upon departures and arrivals.

Headed by Gustave, a cheerful gnome-like little man who was in charge of us, we marched in, slung our packs, and sat down.

We looked at the big clock and the hurrying people, we heard the noise of trains, and mixed with the mounting pleasure and excitement of knowing that after so much difficulty and delay another stage of our long journey was beginning was the atmosphere of adventure which one inhales from the air of these great Continental railway-stations.

We looked around us and gradually we began to notice something curious. There was the ordinary crowd of passengers, the well-dressed characterless travellers, the middle-class families returning to the provinces, the prudently dissipated business men, the soldiers and the priests ... but also small groups of a different type were continually arriving —men with haversacks and cloth caps, men who were unmistakably working-class. They came in tens and dozens, inconspicuously, and gradually the great circulating area of the station took on quite a different character.

'Man!' exclaimed little Jock. 'There's hundreds of us, bluidy hundreds ...'

We stared at one another, puzzled, delighted and almost incredulous. We had not known it: but here the advance guard of the International Column was assembling itself. At this hour, in this place, under this echoing roof, before the staring electric clock-face, a moment of history was creating itself of which we, sharing in it, began to be obscurely aware.

A young man, wearing dark blue bell-bottomed trousers, a blue wind-jacket and scarf, his bright white cap jammed at a terrific angle on the side of his head, danced up to us.

'Two thousand Italians!' he exclaimed, his voice bubbling with excitement. 'There's two thousand Italians coming.' And overcome with excitement he broke into a little step-dance.

'D'you know which way we're going?' we asked him. (You could see that he was the sort of chap who would know the answers.)

'Marseilles,' he said. 'And then in a ship.'

'He looks a good sort of guy,' said John.

'Sure,' I said. 'Let's talk to him. Hey, Bernard, come and make some translations.' (Bernard was our linguist.)

His name, it turned out, was Antonio, and he was a sailor. We walked up and down chatting. Every now and then he would dart off and slap someone on the back, and then come rushing back to us again. A tremendous energy radiated from his slim strong figure, and manifested itself in his quick movements and the tremendous smile that exploded across his face which, in rare moments of stillness, was classic Italian, beautiful.

Being English we were something of a curiosity—so there are Communists in England: *c'est formidable!*—and by the time we moved off to the platform we had collected a number of friends. Our crowd led in the storming of the train. Six of us and Antonio and a not very sober Belgian and Gustave, our *responsable*, and two Paris lads called Marcel and Michel, packed into one compartment. Antonio, still overflowing with Latin vigour, was continually jumping up and rushing down the corridor to tell people about his 'Deux milles Italiens,' while the Belgian, who was small with a cheerful alcoholic's face, kept on standing up and starting a speech that no one would let him finish, about how he was a Belgian and an aviator and was going to Spain for various noble and important reasons.

Everyone felt good and talked at once, and you could hear them all down the corridor babbling excitedly in French and German and Polish and Italian. (There were quite a lot of Italians after all.)

Then the train began to move, and the noise rose to a clamour like some huge swarming flight of bees. And the Belgian aviator stood up and declaimed with great emotion, 'I am a Belgian, I am an aviator. I am going to Spain to fight for my class—' And everyone said, shut up, and the train jerked and they all fell on top of him as they were shoving him back to his seat.

The lights of Paris went sliding by in the darkness; the train gathered speed to pound through the night.

The Belgian slept, snoring a little. Antonio passed round a bottle of wine; sausages, with garlic in them, appeared, and the atmosphere grew hot and rich. Boots and coats began to be removed. Antonio took off his scarf and wind-jacket, revealing a blue shirt, and then he took that off and under it was a blue pullover. Soon that came off too, disclosing yet another and more dazzlingly blue shirt with white stripes. (All this of course was accompanied with theatricality and triumph.) Michel sat quite quietly; his threadbare clothes and horribly worn shoes, his emaciated face and sunken eyes told the story of his unemployment. There was something puzzlingly familiar to me in that face which was so haggard and yet so youthful: his whole air and appearance reminded me of something that I knew very well indeed and yet could not remember.

Next to him was Marcel, deep in conversation with Bernard, who was fascinated by his Place de la République slang. Marcel was a small dogged-looking person with a shock of reddish-brown hair, freckles, and a grin, a wide, large and friendly grin that every now and then suddenly became depreciating and rather unsure of itself. He was telling some great story of how he had been knifed by a fascist. I couldn't understand the finer and more savoury details, and Bernard was doing his best to translate in the manner of a running commentary at a football match.

The climax was reached when Marcel began to take down his trousers.

'*Regarde!*' he exclaimed, and pointed to a long, red, newly healed scar along the inside of his right thigh.

'So what happened?' we asked, after having been suitably impressed.

'Oh, I shot the swine,' he said, and roared with laughter.

We looked at him with a certain amount of respect; and then it occurred to us that we too would be shooting the swine pretty soon . . .

The train roared through the night, across the wide plain of Central France. Once more everyone had settled down, after having been wakened by Antonio's fall from the luggage-rack, where he had tried to compose himself for the night.

My eyes were closed, but I stayed awake, listening to the roaring engine song, the sound of the striding pistons that bore us southwards; and however fast they went they could not be fast enough for us now.

I gave up trying to sleep and lit a cigarette. Then I began to stare at Michel, trying to understnd the meaning of the strange familiarity of his face that, while he slept, was more emaciated and mournful than ever. I felt I had only to connect it with *something* for a whole forgotten region of past thought and feeling to be revealed.

Beside him Marcel dreamed with a child-like expression. And then there was Antonio, his face, in repose and without its vivacity and warm vulgarity, like a classic mask. Under his thin shirt was sketched the outline of a heroic Greek torso.

I looked at all of them in turn, and somehow in each different sleeping countenance was a certain dignity, a beauty, something which they had in common that was hard to understand or explain, but that made me glad that they were my comrades, beside whom I would be fighting.

And then my eyes closed again of their own accord; everything was lost in the roar of the train, that told of the flying telegraph-poles and departing landscapes, the endless movement of shattered calm that spread outwards like a wave into sleeping country-sides, trembling upon the windows of farmhouses and across shivering grass, briefly but continually touching remote and alien lives that dreamed or waked, in the huge darkness through which we rushed.

The train ran right through the night and out into day again. The pale sunrise showed a different country, a rich and southern landscape through which ran the turbulent, travelled waters of the Rhone. One by one we woke, rubbed the grit from our eyes, stretched, lit cigarettes, yawned with aching weariness of our unrestful night, and became aware.

'I feel like hell,' said John.

We headed for Spain; the endless rhythm of the jolting rail-joints had sung all night of the lessening miles to our dear objective. But now we were deaf to that song; soaked with the discomfort and foul air of the whole night we peered with bleary and unappreciative eyes at the lovely river.

'*Merde*,' said Michel unheatedly, about nothing in particular. And he sighed.

And as he sank back to sleep, letting his long arms fall trailingly at his sides, I recognized him. The shape of his haggard, wistful melancholy was the very copy of those unhappy circus boys that for a while Picasso had loved to paint. Unconsciously I had always considered those sad and strangely moving figures as his own creations. And here before me in the living flesh was that lank resignation, so truly the imitation of the painted images that now I could not look on him as an ordinary human being at all.

For a year a reproduction of one of these pictures had hung in my room. In that time I must have stared at it for many hours and shared so deeply of its melancholy that it had passed into my own experience. To encounter it now, on this journey, in this shabby compartment, filled me with those old forgotten feelings, so that for a little while I was altogether removed from *this* atmosphere, and relived the incongruous sensations and thoughts of a period which I had so long ceased to remember that it seemed to belong to the life of a stranger.

Then we ran into Avignon, and it was time to count the remaining miles.

The Marseilles taximen mobilized themselves for us. From the back rooms of cafés, from the dozen obscure rooms and cellars in which we had been hidden during the day, we were collected by a fleet of taxis and whirled through busy streets, past lights and neon signs and crowded pavements, glimpsing for a few moments the secret yet familiar life of an unknown city. Then there were long, dark, unpopulated roads, the lonely sound of trains and ships, the blank walls of warehouses, and then we came to the dock.

We got out. It was ill-lit, faintly sinister with the sound of lapping water and the peculiar dockside smell, the smell of ships and voyages and the outposts of land. Each of us felt compelled to walk softly, listen, looking all around as if we expected to be challenged.

The huge white prow of our ship reared before us. I could see faintly the letters of her name and port of registration.

'Look,' I said, 'It's Spanish.'

In a moment now we would have left French soil, and surely, before then, someone would challenge us, some official (armed behind cold eyes with the whole machine of prisons and denials) would stop us and demand papers that we did not possess. It did not seem possible that we would be able to leave so easily.

And when we stepped onto the gangplank I breathed a sigh of relief, as if we had come through some trial.

At the top of the gangway stood a sailor, an old man with a wrinkled kindly peasant's face. He looked at us and raised his hand, saluting with a clenched fist held in the air.

'*Salud, comaradas*,' he said.

And we felt that now, at last, the final stage of our journey was about to begin.

The ship moved cautiously through the Mediterranean night. That morning we had seen Barcelona, a smear of buildings and the smoke of factories low down on the horizon. But we had passed it by, heading still southwards, to a port whose name we did not know.

Now we were in a danger zone. The ship's name had been painted out, she flew no flag, and not a single light shone aboard. She was only a dim white shape, a muffled thud of powerful engines working slowly.

In the darkness there was a murmur of voices; down pitch-black alleyways cigarette-ends glowed like little stars. These were the signs that, between the night sky and the sea-bed, the ship bore eight hundred men within her iron bowels.

Somewhere one of the sailors was singing a *flamenco*. His voice was low, but pitched to the true *flamenco* note that sounds as if the singer was wailing of some great wrong at the top of his voice in an empty, echoing room.

Here was the ship and the night, the unknown danger and the urgent whisper of eight hundred lives packed close together, but the song was another thing, sounding of southern grief on lonely, arid hills; it was something very old, and it had the richness of music that has been distilled from centuries of a people's experience. It seemed strangely irrelevant to this iron ship, this night, this unknown danger, without meaning for the lives of these eight hundred. Here were factory workers, miners from Poland, men who had escaped from the concentration camps, exiles and political refugees, the men of cities, of the electrically lit nights, of the loud street corners, of the crowds at meetings and of the picket lines, the men whose song was the *Internationale*. They had carried the red banners through streets of great cities, the noises of machinery

and traffic had attended their birth, their lives had been moulded by the
struggles of classes, they were the vanguard of history. But the immemorial griefs and wrongs of this song were also theirs, and it was in the
age-long struggle against them that they had come together and so far.

GEORGE ORWELL
'Spanish Nightmare'

from a review of John Sommerfield's *Volunteer in Spain*, 1937—which contained the
previous piece—in *Time and Tide*, 31 July 1937; *Collected Essays, Journalism and
Letters of George Orwell*, ed. Sonia Orwell and Ian Angus, 1968

Mr Sommerfield was a member of the International Brigade and fought
heroically in the defence of Madrid. *Volunteer in Spain* is the record of his
experiences. Seeing that the International Brigade is in some sense
fighting for all of us—a thin line of suffering and often ill-armed human
beings standing between barbarism and at least comparative decency—it
may seem ungracious to say that this book is a piece of sentimental tripe;
but so it is. We shall almost certainly get some good books from members
of the International Brigade, but we shall have to wait for them until the
war is over.

CYRIL CONNOLLY
'Costa Brava'

from a review of *Volunteer in Spain*: *New Statesman & Nation*, 7 August 1937

John Sommerfield was there to fight for an idea . . . It is fortunate for us
that he is also an excellent writer. His book is short, modest, and
readable, and gives an admirable account of the sensations of fighting, a
true picture of what war feels like, of fear, the death of friends, the noise
of different kinds of projectiles, the dangers, and also the discomfort. He
has one fault, which is a very tiresome imitation of Hemingway, when he
is not being himself. Obviously Hemingway has mastered the art of
writing about war, for he is able exactly to catch the note of sentimental
heartiness which living an animal sort of life generates. But to write in the

same way now is a trick, especially when you lack altogether the cynical attitude which is its complement.

T. C. WORSLEY

'Propaganda in Spain'

review of Spanish books, including *Volunteer in Spain: Life and Letters Today*, Autumn 1937

Those who are actually fighting, especially the ordinary infantrymen, know too much about it to feel anything but envy for those who escape, whether they desert, or resign (where that is possible), or get appointed to the base, or seconded home for duties there. While those in command must use any and every method to keep those who are fighting at their posts; at the front they will, when necessary, use revolvers: at home, when necessary, lies. That is the ordinary condition of any war, and it seems that those who are prepared to embark on it, must be prepared to accept that condition.

The most tempting, because the most specious, of those lies is that 'this war is *different*', a lie which has probably been used in every war that has yet been waged, but which is particularly potent for socialists in this particular case, when their sympathies and passions are naturally aroused. This is one of the falsities which I find in Sommerfield's book in spite of its stressing of the horrors . . . Sommerfield is a writer rather than a journalist, and his book is reportage rather than journalism. It contains some very effective writing, for instance in the section called 'Natural History of the War', where, by listing the variety of kinds of Bullets, Aeroplanes, Shells, Wounds, Death, etc., he produces a really horrifying effect.

So long as the writer is generalizing other parts are equally effective. But as soon as he particularizes, as soon as he comes to deal with a scene involving horror, action, or violence, something happens.

'I began to feel fine, so did John. I must say it seemed against nature: it would have been more reasonable to have felt awful: the others did. When we told them how fine we felt they hated us. The lorry came, and there were buckets of hot coffee with brandy in it, plenty of it, and some biscuits.

'"This is a fine war,"' said John.

'"Sure," I said, "it's a fine war."'

I noticed that it was a quite common thing in Spain for people to behave not as if they were themselves in the Spanish war, but as if they were characters from Hemingway's forthcoming (?) novel on the Spanish war; and since some evasion from the intensity of suffering is essential in war-time for the mere preservation of sanity, perhaps relapsing into the sentimental toughness of a Hemingway character is as good a way as any other. But to continue to fake your feelings (whether consciously, or unconsciously) once you are out of it seems to me no part of a writer's business.

And if you do, you reach a position something like this:

'. . . I learned something about war that I would never forget—that its real vileness did not only lie in its physical horrors but also in what it could do to men's minds. We were lucky, we could remember what we were fighting for and it was something real; but ordinary wars were for a lie, and either one found out, or forgot, and in either case it would be too late and one would be lost.'

This point is put more explicitly later. When they had just come out of the line, dead to the world and soaking wet, the Thaelmann battalion going towards the line, marched past them singing: 'There was a big red flag at the head of the column and each company had a red banner. It was a brave sight. It had all the glamour and excitement that governments can use to make men forsake their homes and die on foreign soil for foreign markets, but it was *ours* and the glamour was real . . .

'It was good that there were moments like this to remind us why we were here and give point to what we were doing . . . I think that in ordinary wars soldiers only stick around because they can't get away, because they are trapped—in their minds I mean—so that they can't think beyond what is happening to them at the moment. But this was a different war; it was possible for things to happen to make you remember why you were in it and then all the other things didn't matter.'

The feelings which Sommerfield here describes are, of course, in no way *different*. They are exactly what in the first few months of any war any soldier might feel at the sight of his own flag. It is just what some of our fathers and uncles felt in 1914 when they were defending, as they thought, liberty, democracy, and right as against might.

To say that is not to belittle in any way those who are fighting in Spain. Far from that. It is simply to state the truth about war and the wideness of the gap between the real feelings of the actual combatants and the faked feelings of propaganda departments; a discrepancy which, as everyone knows, the combatants themselves usually resent. Whether it is the only way to conduct propaganda during a war, I don't know. Perhaps it is.

GUSTAV REGLER
Straying Buffalo

from *The Owl of Minerva*, transl. Norman Denny, 1959

It was a remarkable chance that at just that time, when we were in urgent need of a sympathetic world-opinion to explain our defeats, Ernest Hemingway should have appeared as a war-correspondent on our front. I at once took him to Pacciardi's battalion. I did so for a purpose. In *A Farewell to Arms* Hemingway had written about the disaster of Caporetto in 1917. He was convinced that the Italians always ran away when the fighting got too hot. It was in his nature to despise them for this, just as he despised men of letters and intellectuals because he caught in them the scent of cowardice. Courage was the quality by which he first judged a man. I took him to the muddy trenches by the Arganda bridge. He met Nenni, the parliamentary fox, who stamped into the attack as though he were on his way to the speaker's tribune; and Vittorio, who later became the head of the trade unions in de Gasperi's republic, and who at that moment was cleaning a machine-gun in view of the enemy. Then he saw the wounded Pacciardi, who was being helped on to a motor cycle, to be taken as quickly as possible to a first-aid post, so that the battalion should not be left too long without a commander. Hemingway was amazed to hear them all talking Italian.

Finally he saw Werner, the 'intellectual,' at work. 'Only the best bull-fighters,' he remarked, 'are so detached in the presence of death.' Werner was joking, making all those about him laugh. He greeted the visitor briefly, although he had been delighted on the previous day to hear that Hemingway was coming to us. 'He could have earned much more fame and dollars on the other side,' he said.

A wounded man was brought in; Werner invited him into his car. Shells were whistling down from the hillside. 'You can't go now,' said Hemingway. Werner got in and beckoned to me. He wanted me in the hospital. He was not sure of some of the nurses, who might be Fascists, and he wanted me to interrogate them. Another shell whistled past, exploding in a nearby tree. I took leave of Hemingway and got into the car. 'We shall be back in an hour,' said Werner in his most casual voice. 'You aren't afraid, are you?' Hemingway laughed. Like the work of evil magicians, the surrounding swamp erupted in chalices of mud under the shellfire.

We turned on to the lane which my Frenchmen called *l'avenue de la Mort*. Hemingway was climbing down the river-bank . . .

In the streets of Arganda I assembled the remains of the decimated French battalion. It was a wine town, and they kept returning to a deserted cellar and broaching the casks; they had much grief to drown.

Marty had heard through his spies about their looting forays, and he sent an express messenger to me to ask what I intended to do. In the innocence of his sergeant-major's soul, he had ordered that they should all be arrested and tried to trees, to sweat themselves sober in the sunshine. If there was any resistance I should shoot a few in the presence of the others, to make an example.

I was tempted to reply that we were no longer living in the days of Frederick the Great, but I did not do so. I had heard a few days before of the interpretation he put on my methods of education, and I still shuddered when I thought of it. It was a cynical tale. I told Hemingway about it as he accompanied me to the Town Hall, where the French had of their own accord offered to meet me for a discussion. Two volunteers had lost their heads in an engagement near the Escorial, seeing enemies everywhere in the mist, and had shouted to the others to run. I had had them arrested and brought to headquarters. They were professed anarchists, suffering from our lack of success and from the climate. I decided to send them to a sanatorium, and I reported this to Marty. He replied promptly that he knew of a suitable place, near Alcalá de Henares. They were taken there, and two days ago I had heard that they had been shot in the castle by a Russian execution squad.

'Swine!' said Hemingway, and spat on the ground.

The gesture made me his friend . . .

Hemingway had the calming effect of a buffalo straying shaggily over the tundra, knowing its water-holes and its pastures. For him we had the scent of death, like the bullfighters, and because of this he was invigorated in our company. We had achieved a certain familiarity with death and had gone beyond all normal calculations. Hemingway came from a country whose standard was material success, and whose consuls asked people applying for visas what they were 'worth,' meaning how much money they had in the bank. There could be no more absolute contradiction of this attitude than the one he now encountered, among the poorly clad volunteers from sixteen nations, under a bridge in a civil war. God knows, none of them carried life-insurance, and they were all tolerably sure of having to sacrifice their present so that Spain might have a future.

As early as the third day I came upon Hemingway lying in the mud beside a young Spaniard whom he was instructing in the use of his rifle against the *caprones*, the Fascists. If he had been captured in a sudden counter-attack he would have been stood up against the nearest olive-tree and shot, for no mercy was shown to members of the International Brigade.

His devotion to our cause has often been misrepresented. It has been called blood-thirstiness and worse. He loved the Communists, who were capable of rebelling against the stupid orders that came from Albacete. He loved the commander, Hans Kahle, for reasons which went so deep that he proposed to write a whole book about him. However, I have not mentioned Kahle solely for this reason, but because he played a great part in our victory at Guadalajara, and because he lessened my dislike for the self-assurance of German officers through the friendship which he inspired in everyone from the first moment they met him. He was a Communist, commanded the Eleventh Brigade, was precise in his orders, understood the unstable Spaniards, mingled the methods of Potsdam with those of Alcazar, obeyed his Party, because obedience flowed downwards to the troops, but leavened it at staff meetings and conferences with an almost French irony. He resisted onsets of melancholy with a formal bearing which dominated all staff activities and meals. He liked looting, but handed everything he found in the castles over to the legal Government, departing from this principle only with a big china vase which he took with him from one field headquarters to another in a packing-case. He wore silk shirts and during lulls in the fighting went to Madrid, where he slept in the Empire bed of a film-star who had fled, swam in her pool and slowly drank her cellar dry. During critical periods he scorned all feminine consolations, but as soon as things eased up he was to be seen again at Gaylord's or at the theatre, which was kept open despite the bombardment. Hemingway would have been hard put to it to say which he loved more, the towering German or the thick-set Hungarian, Lukacz, who mingled war and peace, self-sacrifice and pleasure, in quite other ways. Hemingway wrote later:

I think I cried when I heard Lukacz was dead. I don't remember. I cried once when somebody died. It must have been Lukacz because Lukacz was the first great loss. Everyone else who had been killed was replaceable . . . And about crying let me tell you something that you may not know. There is no man alive today who has not cried at a war if he was at it long enough. Sometimes it is after a battle, sometimes it is when someone that you love is killed, sometimes it is from a great injustice to another, sometimes it is at the disbanding of a corps or a unit that has endured and accomplished together and now will never be together again. But all men at war cry sometimes, from Napoleon, the greatest butcher, down.

A shy declaration of love! Of course it was for Lukacz, the son of the Russian Revolution, who had not let himself be frightened by it; the rider who appeared on the Castilian plateau like an emissary of the army which in 1919 fought another Franco. When Hemingway first visited us in the mess Lukacz sent a messenger to the village asking all the girls to come because he had a great writer as a guest. Twenty came, and Lukacz introduced them all to Hemingway. None of us wanted to choose, so they all stayed and waited on us. The meal was of the plainest kind, but they all wore their best clothes and served it as though it were a royal banquet. One of them, Paquita, fixed a high comb in her raven-blue hair and danced a tango after the tables had been pushed aside, and everything was human dignity and beauty, and the cries of *Olé!* were tomorrow's music and Hemingway was no longer a guest but the homecoming brother of everyone in the room.

In 1938 he gave up reporting the war, returned to his hurricane-proof house on the Gulf of Mexico, exercised with the punch-ball before breakfast, drank his bottle of Hennessy while he thumbed over his sheaf of 'true stories,' fished off the Florida keys, danced with fair-haired girls in Josie's Bar under the admiring gaze of his wise, polio-stricken friend, Canby, and pushed him home in a wheel-chair through the peaceful palm-avenues of Key West—was all this a final farewell to arms?

By that time I had been discharged from the Spanish service with severe wounds and was busy, in a beautiful castle in Brive-la-Gaillarde, writing my book on the Brigade, which had now, in conformity with international orders, been withdrawn from the fighting. But in the evening I switched on the radio and listened to news of Belchite and Madrid, the Ebro and Teruel. My wounds burned (it is no superstition, they share my feelings!) whenever a Republican counter-attack was bled to death—how else should one describe it? Did the world not understand that it was not merely a matter of Spain? Was the century bogged down in indifference?

Then one evening, when I was pacing up and down like an exile in front of the stove in the big dining-room, planning a manifesto (but who would read it without asking, 'Why is anyone still talking about Spain?') a brief announcement came from the radio:

'The writer, Ernest Hemingway, has suddenly left his home in Key West. He was seen in New York boarding a ship, without hat or baggage, to rejoin the Spanish Republican troops at the front.'

'Without hat or baggage.' I repeated the words in sudden wonderment as I stared into the fire. The gesture restored the feeling of certainty which for many months Madrid had given me. Not everything ended in banality and betrayal. 'Without hat or baggage.' Thus had Tolstoy walked through the darkness over the steppe. 'Without hat or baggage.'

Who thinks of a secure house while the people of Spain are in danger of being rendered voiceless by dictatorship? 'Without hat or baggage.' Who takes his Sunday suit with him? It is the hour of destiny, the frontiers are on the Ebro and all men are at the beginning of all things.

JEF LAST

Spanish Tragedy

from *The Spanish Tragedy*, 1939 (*De Spaansche Tragedie*, 1938, transl. David Hadett)

As we were marching from the University City to our new positions, a boy of fifteen acted as our guide. For the space of an hour we marched in darkness through suburbs where every house had been damaged more or less by the bombardment and abandoned. The poles of the electric trams had snapped. The wires were hanging low over the street; shells had dug deep craters in the pavement, and everywhere fragments of broken glass were glittering in the moonlight. Our young guide was from the south, and Pepe said to him, 'Antonio, sing something to us. The lieutenant would like to hear one of your flamencos.' As we were marching on to where the machine-guns were barking like mad dogs, the boy began to sing. All conversation in the company was stilled. His tender high-pitched boyish voice had the crystal purity of the moon. The melody put one in mind of Arab songs, and then again of an old Gregorian chant. The text, which he was improvising as he went along was very simple: 'Our brave militiamen, they will surely win; oh! how happy we shall be when our militiamen win!' I was reminded of a little bird at Getafe that had calmly settled upon a tree, while the battle was at its fiercest, unruffled by the bullets. We turned a corner in pitch darkness, and immediately the rattling of the machine-guns seemed closer, harsher, and more cruel. 'Bend down,' commanded the captain; 'extend to five paces, double march to the trench.' We were in the firing-line and the boy's song suddenly broke off like a bit of glass.

The enemy is about 800 metres away from us, in a trench running from the Military Hospital to the Estremadura road. He occupies the small village opposite, and we can clearly see the holes in the houses behind which he has installed his machine-gunners. His artillery, which must be somewhat farther back, engages our positions for a few hours every afternoon. The marksmanship is bad and most of the shells burst in the cemetery a hundred metres behind our line. It looks as if the dead were to be denied their peace; perhaps the Fascist slogan 'Spain, awake!' is for their benefit as well.

Great damage has been done to the workmen's houses that constitute our line together with the trench. Holes through which we can fire in the event of an attack have been bored in every wall; the moon peers through the broken tiles of the roofs; the smashed window-panes have been replaced by boards that shut out the light. In the evenings, by the reeking flame of an oil wick, dark shadows play upon the broken furniture and our quarters wear a spectral air. A bridal couple on the wall stares at us from out of a gilt frame half hidden in cobwebs, and a broken gramophone still testifies to a modest pretence at well-being. Two militiamen are busy chopping up an old chair for firewood. Some tattered books have been swept in a corner. Everything about us is filthy, dusty, broken, neglected. The husky yelping of hungry dogs left behind in the houses farther up echoes through the night.

We have been living in these ruins for the last twelve days. Everything we touch is dirty; even the water from the well is muddy and leaves a grey deposit in our glasses. It is too cold to have a good wash. The pavement in front of our house, the only bit of the street that is not in the line of fire, is impassable owing to the excrement of 140 soldiers. We haven't been out of our clothes these twelve days. Three times we have had to beat off a night attack, and we are on duty eight hours a day. Most of us have no decent boots left and throughout these two weeks we have not once had a warm meal, since the cook-wagon is unable to cross the line of fire. Nevertheless, I have not heard a single complaint. In the evenings, as we sit round the fire with running eyes, we tell each other stories from *Tyl Eulenspiegel* or *Ali Baba and the Forty Thieves*, and we often break into song. Nobody has any doubts of victory. Yesterday a bullet crushed the shoulder-blade of our little Manuel. Thomas has been hit in the thigh by a shrapnel splinter. 'Qué suerte!' the comrades say, 'our luck is in; here we've been a whole week and we're all alive!'

Often they come and say to me, 'Now tell us, *teniente*, what really made you come here?' I shrug my shoulders. 'You fellows should know the reason by this time. I came because the fight you are putting up also concerns us.'—'Yes,' they say, 'we know all about that, but that fellow over there comes from the village; you must explain it properly to him.' I then produce a map, and show them that, if the Fascists win in Spain, France will be encircled on all sides. 'With Spain as a jumping-off ground, Germany can cut England off from her colonies. That is the moment when the world war should break out under the most favourable conditions possible for Fascism. That is why we are defending here not only Spain, but democracy, and even the frontiers of the Soviet Union.' They then look at me with flashing eyes and say, 'Qué lucha!'—'What a struggle!'

ESMOND ROMILLY

Boadilla

from *Boadilla*, 1937

All this time I had the pleasant illusion that the bombing and shelling did not actively concern us. I somehow could never really believe the enemy were occupying themselves with *us*; we were only playing at soldiers, we were only amateurs. It seemed impossible that over there, beyond the outline of the fort, someone was scheming how *we* were to be destroyed, eliminated, or—the simplest and most expressive word of all—just killed. Delmer had said we were holding the most vital position; it was ridiculous that we should be doing this—who were surely concerned all the time only with seeing that we had the same food rations as the Flems and quarrelling among ourselves and holding Group Meetings. It was all wrong.

I thought about all this as we stood waiting, sometimes gazing over the parapet at the Italians ahead on the ridge, waiting for the attack. The next thing that happened that morning was over almost before we realised it. We thought nothing of the familiar words: '*Fliege, Decke!*'—as they were shouted down the line, until the three gigantic birds had swept right over us spraying machine-gun bullets into the valley below, and I saw someone raise his rifle to his shoulder as though to shoot, and then they were gone as swiftly as they had come. By great good luck, not one man was hit, as all the bullets from the aeroplanes went into the valley between the Thaelmann and Garibaldi lines.

The order was given for a general move down the road to the right, so that we should not be surprised by a tank attack from the White House. We moved into better dug-outs where the Germans had made proper firing positions. Jeans hurried from one to the other, seeing everyone was well placed, and shepherding Sid, who had found nowhere to go. I made a firing step with my haversack and an empty ammunition box. Then I sat down and read my book about snobbery in the United States of America.

The shelling was dying down now, but there was an increasing racket of rifle and machine-gun fire. A man who required to relieve himself was forced to do so in his own dug-out, as the road behind was under fire.

The tempo of the firing grew and I abandoned my book and sat with my rifle on my knees. I wondered what the time was. There was a lull in the battle just before we heard the first rumours, whispered from mouth to mouth—'Spanish troops on our right are in full retreat.'

We were in a bad position. It was impossible to move more than a quarter of a mile down the road—to retreat to the ridge behind brought us under direct fire of the White House and the fort. We knew nothing of what was happening. Jeans had gone to find out. We could only remain—and wait. I felt frightened.

The firing started again—now it was much louder and nearer—one was more conscious of the bullets. They thudded into the bank below our barricades. The Garibaldi men came back—some wounded, some dragging machine-guns. Singly and in groups we saw them descend the slope into the valley. Volunteers scrambled down the bank with stretchers and brought some of the wounded. There was nothing to be done with them; they could only be left in the trenches. To have attempted to get them back by the road would have been madness; some were left in the open.

All I got was a blurred picture from occasional quick glances over the top; then, with the last mad scramble of men as the Italians joined us on the road, we knew the front line was evacuated. They had held it against bombs, trench mortars, and a continual machine-gun fire from close range. Then the fire had come from the right, infiltrating their narrow trench. It made evacuation and *sauve qui peut* the only policy. They crowded into our dugouts. There was no panic, no sign of disorderly retreat. Now that the danger was definite, now rumour was fact, now the attack was a reality, everyone was calm. There was even an exaggerated calmness in the passing on of orders, in remarks about how we should all stand to or the amount of ammunition we possessed.

Jeans came back—and about forty men were grouped behind him. The sloping ground to the right was difficult to hold. It was all quite plain now—we were going to make a stand on that four hundred yard stretch of level road.

'Keep your heads down,' said Jeans. 'No one is to fire till the order is given. There are four machine-guns behind us. If an enemy tank comes down, no one is to move while the anti-tank squad deals with it.'

In answer to breathless questions, he told us: 'Our line has been broken half a mile down, but our machine-guns are still commanding the road. Sixteen Russian tanks are on the way' (cheers from everyone, 'About time them fellows showed up, heard enough about them,' from Joe); 'if we have to retire to the other road behind we shall be protected by them.'

There were about two hundred of us, all bunched close together. Perhaps half an hour elapsed—perhaps more; it started with two men falling dead from close-range bullets in a dug-out near by. Then the real hailstorm of lead came at us. I was lying flat on my stomach. We shoved in clip after clip of cartridges until the breaches and barrels of our guns were red hot. I never took aim. I never looked up to see what I was firing at. I never heard the order to open fire. I never saw the enemy—never knew for certain where they were—these things were talked over afterwards. My head was in a whirl—I was almost drunk with the smell of powder. I remember a young Spaniard next to me, wondering what he was doing and how he got there; but there was no time to work it all out. It was a mad scramble—pressing my elbows into the earth, bruising them on the stones, to get my rifle to my shoulder, pressing the trigger, rasping back the bolt, then shoving it home, then on to my elbows again.

We never learned how long it had all been—how long before Alex shouted 'Forward,' and stumbled down the bank first, waving a muddy bayonet in his hand. Jock and Birch and Messer never stopped talking for days afterwards about the Moors they'd picked up—I was not on that job—and they all had an odd assortment of knives and scarves and boots.

'Ah was goin' to have his beard and dress meself like a Moor to give ye all a fright,' Jock told us, 'only Alex woudna let me, he said you boys'd all be on the run at the first sight of that beard.'

I foresaw there would be calls on volunteers to dig a grave for the Moors, so I busied myself with other jobs. Ray and I went round collecting ammunition—and later on we went to the ridge ahead and returned in triumph with three boxes we had found hidden in one of the dug-outs. When the lorry brought us up hot soup and meat, and tins of chicken and eggs and cheese and coffee with milk that night, we were too tired, too excited to eat and sleep. We just wanted to talk about it all.

The fascist attack had failed. The Moors had never crossed the road. The presence of the Russian tanks may have been a deterrent (we never saw or heard anything more of these, and more than one sceptic among us cast doubts upon their existence); but at any rate, at no point could they cross the road. In several places they reached the Government lines on the other side of the reservoir, then attempted a direct attack on our positions to clear the way for an advance down the road, and at the same time surround the hospital building. They had occupied the Italians' line (three hundred yards away), but they were never able to get established in their trenches or to attempt to cross the valley. All who scrambled over the parapet had to face a withering fire from our lines. Time and again the accurate range of their marksmen claimed a victim among the machine-gunners behind us; each time we would redouble our fire while someone else slipped back to take the dead man's place.

I have seen accounts of attacks in newspapers which tell you about men, yielding ground 'inch for inch', and everything sounds romantic and spectacular. It may seem like that afterwards. At the time all is blurred and confused. You do not know what is happening—probably your one thought is to keep your head down.

T. A. R. HYNDMAN
Volunteer in Trouble

from *The Distant Drum: Reflections on the Spanish Civil War*, ed. Philip Toynbee, 1976

I was in Portugal with my employer, a journalist, when the Popular Front took over in Spain. We had planned to leave for Greece and on our way stayed in Madrid for a week. There was considerable tension. Some newspapers predicted an uprising by the army. In the Puerta del Sol, on several cold evenings, we were stopped by the Civil Guard. Passports were examined; after protests, a warning was given. We should not keep our hands out of sight, in our coat pockets. We bought gloves.

On a Greek island a book for the Left Book Club was completed. We returned to London for its publication. It did well. My employer, whom I called Stephen, joined the Communist Party which, aided by the left wing of the labour movement, controlled the main thrust of the Popular Front against fascism. I joined also. The vital issue was Spain. A group of British volunteers were already fighting there, including John Cornford and Esmond Romilly. All our spare time was taken up by this cause —marches, rallies, meetings, selling the *Daily Worker* in the streets of London. I noticed that Stephen always returned from meetings with the intellectuals of the party in a slight state of irritation.

Esmond returned from Spain on a recruiting mission. Casualties had been heavy; volunteers were needed, many of them. There was a plan to form a British Battalion of an International Brigade. Esmond, nephew of Winston Churchill, was in the news, the man for the job. He was hardly eighteen years old. John Cornford was reported killed in action. He became symbolic of all we believed in: a poet, romantic, young, a hero.

During all the activities I met Giles, Esmond's brother. He was up at Oxford and hated it. We became friends, and whenever he was in London we met. Not quite so forceful as Esmond, he was, I am sure, a very lonely young man. He telephoned me from Oxford. By some arrangement he was going to leave, for the time being—or something like that. However, the main reason for the call was Spain. Should we join the International Brigade? All over the country hundreds were being enrolled. I arranged to meet him in Hyde Park the next day.

We walked slowly along the main footpath. I told him I would go with him as soon as possible, that once decided it was fatal to hang around, letting friends and families intervene. He had already joined the Communist Party in Oxford; our passports were up to date. He became elated, in full flight. This was a different Giles. 'They will take us on. I have been trained in an O T C, you are an ex-Guardsman. Both of us can now fight in a militia. We shall have the right to question any orders with which we don't agree.' He shook his fist at Mayfair where his mother was playing bridge.

I got Giles to move on. A small crowd was collecting. We were not far from Speaker's Corner. We went to his home for tea. Mrs Romilly arrived by taxi. I knew her quite well, and liked her. She changed her gown. Fresh tea was served. Giles told her of our plans. She lit a cigarette, sipped her tea, staring above our heads. Mrs Romilly had an engaging sense of drama, of theatre. 'Two sons,' she said. 'Both in the same war. I must speak to the Colonel.'

She reached for the telephone. 'My father,' said Giles. 'He lives in the country, for health reasons. Have some more walnut cake.' His mother was now listening to her husband. 'Yes, my dear. Of course. You are quite right. I will tell Giles, and his friend. He was in the Guards, you know. No; I don't think he was an officer. See you next weekend. My dear, goodbye.' Mrs Romilly turned to us. 'The Colonel has given me a message for both of you. As soon as you have been accepted, you must both go to the Army and Navy, get yourselves well kitted out with the best boots they have, besides a good supply of their warmest underwear. All on his account. Please do as he says. He is an old soldier. You have his blessing. Now wait a moment.' She went upstairs and came down with the longest scarf I have ever seen. She gave it to me. 'I knitted this myself, for my husband during the war. It is to be worn next to your skin, around your stomach, to keep you warm.' She gave me a kiss. 'Now, some sherry.'

The party recruiting office was crowded. Giles and I were soon accepted, but others were an obvious puzzle. Plenty of enthusiasm but hardly one who could fire a weapon. All were taken on. They would be taught. I had a strange meeting with Bert Overton, who had been a close friend of mine in the Guards. I had not seen him for nearly four years. He had been a brilliant Guardsman, but that was in peacetime. However, he still looked the part. Over some tea in a Lyons we talked of our army days, and now Spain. It did not seem to me that Bert's political motives amounted to much; there were personal reasons, but that could be said of any of us. We agreed to meet in Paris. The night before I left, all I owned was stacked away, my pack was ready. I was Romilly shod, lined, and belly-banded. After some protests, Stephen was very quiet, writing. He was resigned. I was scared. Why and what the hell was I doing?

At Victoria Station the next morning, there was a small crowd to see us off. Mrs Romilly, Communist Party friends, Oxford friends, my family. Stephen handed me thirty one-pound notes, in case, he said, I changed my mind and wanted to get back home. Then the whistle went. The train moved. We hung out of the windows, fists clenched. 'Viva España!' All clenched fists now, including Nellie Romilly, fur-coated. Some heads were high, some were down. Press cameras flashed.

Paris now, and a 'certain address' for another ticket for Perpignan, with food, smokes and cash for the journey. We linked up with Bert. Quietly, I answered Bert's questions on the politics and ideology of the Civil War. He said he understood and agreed. We ate our food, drank a lot of wine, and slept. Suddenly, there was Perpignan. We were met by French communists who checked our names and loaded us into trucks. Altogether we made a total of about forty men. A proper meal at a field kitchen, then darkness. A coach arrived; we stumbled in. The coach began to climb, very slowly. No smoking. No talking. High up in the Pyrenees came the French frontier. We sat very still. The driver produced a list of names, all Spanish, I learned. Over the Spanish frontier. We could talk and smoke. On to Figueras, where we slept for the night in what might have been a church. Anyway, it was now a shelter for men on straw, field kitchens and trucks. The next day came Barcelona, then a train to Albacete, International Brigade headquarters. Finally trucks to Madrigueras, the village a few miles out which was to be our training ground before going into action. A tall young man approached us and checked our names. He then sorted out Giles and myself and said, 'I've been here for two weeks. My name is John Lepper. Welcome to the biggest shambles in Europe.'

John was a liberal anti-fascist. Although the Popular Front included liberals, he had had some difficulties with the communists over getting to Spain. A product of a public school and O T C, he could fire a rifle, a pistol, even machine-guns. He told me that he had met a Conservative who had got to Spain with the perfectly logical reason that since the Nazis and Italian fascists would have to be destroyed one day, he might as well start now. The Communist Party had been somewhat suspicious of him, so he joined the Anarcho-Syndicalists, who liked him. The last John heard of him, he was fighting successful battles on the front near Catalonia with the F A I. We were all placed in billets for sleeping, and the local church, the largest building in the village, was used as a communal eating place for the villagers and troops. It was all arranged very well by a committee made up from a few workmen and peasants. I was told that about half of the people of Madrigueras had moved out during the early days of the uprising. There had been many executions of leading socialists by Spanish army officers. With fresh volunteers arriving almost every day, the British Battalion was now several hundred strong. By February, with the arrival of a large group of Irishmen, we were almost a complete unit of 400 men. Yet no rifles were issued. At first our commander was Wilfred Macartney. He left under a cloud, literally—of gunpowder. There was a shooting accident in a hotel room in Albacete. Now came Tom Wintringham, almost a founder member of the British Communist Party. He was the man we needed. It took him only a few days to win the respect and loyalty of all under his command. He was cool, quick in deciding who did what, with a wry sense of humour. He took us into action when our turn came.

Giles worked in the orderly room with John Lepper. I called in to talk to them often. 'I wonder what happened to that militia we heard about,' I said. 'There is no such thing around here,' said John. 'A reasonable commander is the best we can expect, and we now have one.' He told Giles that if he still wanted to fight in a militia he should join the anarchists, the ones in the red and black. He had got to know them well in Barcelona, and they fascinated him. When he asked them who gave the orders they said, 'Nobody. We know what to do.' Since all ranks dressed alike, how could they pick out the men in charge? 'No trouble about that,' was the F A I answer. 'We can tell by the looks on their faces.' Some carried guitars only. 'We can't shoot guns, some of us, so we play and sing Flamencos. It scares the shit out of the fascists. They've never heard anything like it.' Until now, neither had we.

Suddenly there were rumours. There was a big push near Madrid.

The fascists had to be stopped; their objective was control of the Valley of Jarama: if they succeeded, the capital—still open—could be surrounded, engulfed, cut off. We were issued with rifles and uniforms; I left my civilian clothing with a friendly little family near my billet. Their mother wept. I left her kneeling before her tiny, chipped madonna. All our arms were Russian. They looked good. Any oil, or grease? All in good time, comrade. Trucks, trains, then more trucks. We were there. This battle and its many disasters, terrors and heroism has been described elsewhere by myself and many others. One thing I know. The heavy losses of the first day's fighting could have been avoided. The machine-gun coverage was missing. By early afternoon the lorry which carried them was found. It had overturned. The only way to reach it was to go quickly down a pathway, and drag the guns and ammunition boxes across two sloping ploughed fields, the shortest way. I was glad to be called upon for this rescue job. My rifle was useless, even dangerous, without oil. It could blow up in my face. The enemy fire was increasing. Dive-gunning planes swooped on us. The dead and wounded were everywhere. No stretchers, no food, no water. Most of us got to the guns. Any casualties on our way had to be left; time was precious. I reckon there were about a dozen guns. It is hard to remember exactly. I know they were on small metal wheels, and each gun had a red star. Each man in our team used one hand for his side of a gun, the other hand for a case of ammunition. We were spotted. I lost my partner; bullets got him in an almost straight line down his back. I pushed him off the gun, moved forward a few feet with it and went back for the cases. The planes whirled, ready for another dive. I curled up, convinced they would get me this time. Some instinct concerning my manhood made me put the two metal cases across my middle parts. It was ridiculous. One bullet into either of those cans and away I'd go, balls and all. Help came; the sunken road was reached with all the guns intact, mine still bloody. Before dark they were on the job, in full blast. They bubbled over with heat, drying up. For the final burst we all urinated into a steel helmet. Some liquid was poured into each gun as the light of the day ended. We cheered. We shouted abuse. The other side was silent, strangely silent. A field kitchen appeared and fed cold boiled rice into our muddy hands. We ate, then raised them for more—and more. Our water bottles were filled. The guns drank also. Suddenly there was silence. I sat, leaning against the wall, carefully lighting a cigarette. What I dreaded most was not happening. There were no tears yet.

John Lepper wrote a poem about that day. He had survived. Parts of it still tug my memory.

The sun warmed the valley
But no birds sang
The sky was rent with shrapnel
And metallic clang

*   *   *

Men torn by shell-shards lay
Still on the ground
The living sought shelter
Not to be found

Holding their hot rifles
Flushed with the fight
Sweat-streaked survivors
Willed for the night.

That night Bert, given charge of a small platoon of men, lost most of them through sheer panic. He left the line. John had cataracts painfully forming on both eyes. He wore a perpetual frown. Giles had colic, and went around doubled up. The next day Tom Wintringham was wounded and carried away. The running battles continued. My rifle was replaced, but Nathan, our staff officer, kept me at Battalion headquarters, less than fifty yards behind the front line. Giles was there. We both acted as runners, Giles to the French sector, myself to the German anti-Nazi sector. We each knew the languages. I saw John. His eyes were getting worse. I told him to see Nathan, to get a note to the battalion doctor at our medical department, housed farther down the road. Every morning and evening we were heavily bombed by huge black planes. They were Italian, flying low in arrow formation. We could see the pilots. Our only cover was under some rocks. As the bombs fell, the very earth and rock lifted us up, then down. Then one glorious day, as we prepared to take cover, a few tiny Russian fighter planes whizzed up and buzzed around them. They turned back, slowly. One bomber came down in flames. We cheered; a Spanish company fired shots in the air and cried, 'Olé!'

John stayed at the hospital. I joined him. I vomited continually. We were both given notes recommending our repatriation. Nathan said he would let us go: 'One with an ulcer, the other almost blind, I don't see how you can be any further use to us here. Cheer up. You've both done your best, and I will take care of Giles. As for Bert Overton, I can promise nothing. He is in danger—from his own side.' When the truck came to take us away, Giles was sad. 'See you in London. Adios. Salud!' He was better now. Our old relationship was over.

Back in Albacete we saw the political commissar and offered to work in the rearguard. He gave us jobs in the Brigade news department. Later on he changed his mind. Every man was wanted at the front. Yes, he said, regardless of our disabilities. I then remembered a visit from a newspaper man who was in touch with friends in London. We were told then that on no account should we return to the front line: his contacts were working hard for a reasonable arrangement for all volunteers in our position. Did this commissar know about this? Was he acting under orders? I knew nothing, except that I was becoming almost paranoid concerning the Communist Party. I told John I still had some money. We decided to make our way home. In Valencia we were arrested. Having already given an account of what took place during the next three months, I will not deal with it all now, except the bare facts. Even this makes me feel sick, and I begin to itch with fleas and lice. It was a steady progress through jails, camps, then more jails. Our ailments became worse, especially John's. He wept with pain. And the visits by commissars with their questions. Were we fascists? Were we Trotskyists?—even worse in their minds. Who did we meet in Valencia? Had we underground contacts in Albacete? It seems unbelievable, but don't forget that this was after May 1937, when the communists, aided by the Civil Guard, mopped up all their critics and separatist, fellow anti-fascists. George Orwell was caught up in the midst of it in Catalonia. But John and I were small fry. What really bothered them was the people we knew—outside Spain. Then one day our cell door was opened, and our names were called. We were for release. It was a trick, surely. They would shoot us and then tell our friends we had been killed fighting at the front, like heroes.

However, our orders were to report to the political commissar. He told us to live in Albacete barracks and wait. I asked about Giles. He was at the front—Brunete this time. And Bert? Dead; killed in action. We waited for a month, and received some pay. Then a meeting was called. Comrade Harry Pollitt was going to speak to all British volunteers in Albacete. He gave a speech on morale, and was not entirely out of sympathy towards those of us awaiting repatriation. At the end of his talk he called me back. 'Don't be afraid, comrade,' he said. 'What with your family and your friends, you have been more trouble to me than the whole British Battalion put together.' He put his arm across my shoulders and handed me a letter. 'Here, read this and tell me what you think.' It was from Stephen. It told me that I only had to tell the bearer of the letter what I wanted, and he would arrange it. I replied that I wanted to go home. I was ill. Harry then said I would be on my way within a week. I asked about John Lepper. He said he was going to see about him also.

'You must, please,' I said. 'He is in great pain.' In Harry Pollitt's opinion,
I was told later, I was an ordinary, decent, working class chap who had got
into the hands of the kind of intellectuals the party could well do without.
Well, I can't go along with that, but perhaps, over the years, the same
could have been applied to Harry Pollitt.

I went to Madrigueras to get my clothing. It was all cleaned and
beautifully laid out, waiting for me. Father, mother and son hugged me
all at once. I gave the father my overcoat to keep him warm in the fields.
We embraced. It was goodbye. In Albacete I told John I would do all I
could to get him back, which I did. A fortnight after I returned to London
I received a letter from Harry. Why had I not been in touch with him?
After all, I was still a party member. I replied that Spain had made me
into something of a pacifist. He wrote back: 'Take your time. Have a rest
and you will soon get over it. Then, one day we will find a place in our
ranks for you again. Fraternally yours, Harry.' I think I liked him, after
all.

And now. I feel that ever since Spain I have been living with ghosts,
and as I get older they become more friendly. There are people who say
that writing a poem can help you to contain an emotional experience. I
have written a poem, but the emotion lives on. I don't think I want to lose
it. The poem is called simply 'Jarama Front'.

> I tried not to see,
> But heard his voice.
> How brown the earth
> And green the trees.
> One tree was his.
> He could not move.
> Wounded all over,
> He lay there moaning.
>
> I hardly knew:
> I tore his coat.
> It was easy—
> Shrapnel had helped.
>
> But he was dying
> And the blanket sagged.
> 'God bless you, Comrades,
> He will thank you.'
> That was all.
> No slogan,
> No clenched fist
> Except in pain.

The experiences of many people leave unseen scars, on the mind, in the heart. If this is true, my scar is Spain. Along with this condition, memories, impressions, remain. Martínez, an Anarcho-Syndicalist who lay dying in an Albacete hospital and who passed his human, mutual-aid philosophy on to me. I was his only visitor, his only mourner, walking alone behind the hearse which carried his bare coffin. Once clear of the town, the driver stopped his skinny horse, and helped me up, to ride beside him. At the burial ground I threw some wild flowers on to the coffin, before the diggers covered it with earth. Alongside the driver, we trotted back. 'A friend of yours?' he asked. 'Yes,' I said, 'a friend.' I could have added—of yours also.

The small Irish company, who held a meeting as they moved into action, elected a new leader, passed a resolution demanding their right to be kept apart from the British Battalion. Tom Wintringham, soldier and poet with infinite compassion. He blamed himself for the promotion of Bert and the tragic fiasco that followed. Giles, who years later took an overdose of pills, and was found dead in a lonely hotel room in America. John, 'seeker after truth', who died of a malignant disease in an English countryside hospital, the land he loved around him.

The solitary volunteer who walked across Spain alone. He reached Madrigueras, and asked me, 'Where's Franco?'

JASON GURNEY

'The First Day at Jarama'

from *Crusade in Spain*, 1974

There was still no firing or any other sound of activity out on the left flank, and no one appeared to know or care what the position was in that quarter. If the enemy advanced around the blind side of the Casa Blanca hill they would be able to enfilade both Harry Fry's machine-gun positions and the sunken road, which would make our whole position untenable. Wintringham told me to make my way down the sunken road to investigate the position there. I had only gone about seven hundred yards when I came on one of the most ghastly scenes I have ever seen. In a hollow by the side of the road I found a group of wounded men who had been carried back from No. 3 Company's attack on the Casa Blanca hill. They had arrived at a non-existent field dressing station from which they should have been taken back to the hospital, and now they had been forgotten. There were about fifty stretchers all of which were occupied, but many of the men had already died and most of the others would die before morning. They were chiefly artillery casualties with appalling wounds from which they could have had little hope of recovery. They were all men whom I had known well, and some of them intimately—one little Jewish kid of about eighteen whose peculiar blend of Cockney and Jewish humour had given him a capacity for clowning around and getting a laugh out of everyone, even during the most depressing period, now lay on his back with a wound that appeared to have entirely cut away the muscle structure of his stomach so that his bowels were exposed from his navel to his genitals. His intestines lay in loops of a ghastly pinkish brown, twitching slightly as the flies searched around over them. He was perfectly conscious, unable to speak, but judging from his eyes he was not in pain or even particularly distressed. One man of whom I was particularly fond was clearly dying from about nine bullet wounds through his chest. He asked me to hold his hand and we talked for a few minutes until his hand went limp in mine and I knew he was dead. I went from one to the other but was absolutely powerless to do anything other than to hold a hand or light a cigarette. Nobody cried out or screamed or made any other tragic gestures. I did what I could to comfort them and promised to try and get some ambulances. Of course I failed, which left me with a feeling of guilt which I never entirely shed. There were no ambulances to be got, but I could not free myself from the feeling that I should have done something. To this day I do not know what I could have done to help those poor wretches as they lay awaiting death in the twilight of that Spanish olive grove. They were all calling for water but I had none to give them. I was filled with such horror at their suffering and my inability to help them that I felt that I had suffered some permanent injury to my spirit from which I would never entirely recover.

JASON GURNEY

'The Second Day at Jarama'

from *Crusade in Spain*, 1974

The noise was indescribable. We were only about one hundred yards from the captured trench and the eight heavy machine-guns which it had contained were now turned on us. In addition, there must have been a couple of hundred riflemen firing high-expansion bullets. This was the first time that I had come in contact with this horrible and devastating weapon, the bullets of which exploded on impact with as much noise as a rifle being fired. Some months later I was myself wounded by one of these bullets and still bear testimony to the appalling wounds which they inflict. In size, the bullet is the same as that used in an ordinary rifle; it has no explosive charge but is, in fact, a super dum-dum. It is formed of a nickel alloy shell, in the point of which is a small slug of metal with a high coefficient of expansion, the remainder of the shell being filled with lead. The heat set up by the friction of impact causes the inner slug to expand more rapidly than the nickel jacket with the result that the whole thing explodes.

I think that at this particular moment we were all a little mad. The sheer weight of noise was tremendous and, coupled with a feeling of desperation and excitement, produced a kind of madness among us. People were running around shouting and behaving in all manner of peculiar ways. Wintringham bawled at us to fix bayonets, which was quite absurd. The original orders had been that in the line bayonets were to be kept permanently fixed since the Russian rifles were only accurate in this position. In reality the bayonets were such a bloody nuisance that almost everyone had discarded them. However, we all clustered against the bank ready to go over the top. It was rather like some totally improbable incident out of the *Boy's Own Paper*, and quite futile: a handful of men proposing to charge about two hundred yards into the face of eight Maxim guns and an unknown number of Moorish infantry.

Wintringham stood up to lead the charge, was almost immediately shot through the thigh, and collapsed into the sunken road. Aitken and about ten others jumped to their feet, scrambled over the bank of the road and charged. Very, very reluctantly I followed them.

I was running with my head down, presumably subconsciously imagining that my helmet would protect my face, and with absolutely no idea what I would do when, and if, I got to the other side. By the time that I had run about sixty yards I realized that there was no longer anyone in front or alongside me, and I dived for cover under one of the small hills built up around the foot of every olive tree. The heap of earth was only about eighteen inches wide and one foot high, but the eight-inch trunk of the tree provided cover for my head. This was the only part of my body that I was worried about at that particular moment and it felt as vulnerable as an egg shell. I had absolutely no confidence in my French tin helmet.

I was now lying in the middle of no-man's-land with rifle fire coming from both directions. I was familiar with the phrase 'to hug the ground', and I was now hugging it with a vengeance, as if I could press my way into it by pure force of will. My olive tree, and its minute hillock, gave me some protection from the front, but my backside was completely exposed to the fire coming from our own men behind me and I began to feel terrifyingly vulnerable. There was such an enormous mass of metal tearing at the air above my head that I dare not get up and try to run for the shelter of the road. I lay very close to despair. I had no thought of prayer, although I think that it might have been a very valuable consolation at such a time; nor did I think back over my past life, nor any of the other things that people are supposed to do in the face of imminent death. But I did feel very unhappy in no very specific way.

I wasn't frightened of being killed but of being mangled. The sight of a dead man did not cause me any particular distress; it was simply the end of a man which seemed to me normal and reasonable. But a living man, smashed out of shape, caused in me a reaction of the purest horror. To some extent this may have been because I was a sculptor, and the logic of the human body was for me one of its most exciting characteristics: the bone structure which maintains the basic shape; the articulation which enables the bones to operate around one another, but only in a limited and disciplined manner, making chaos impossible; the extensor and flexor muscles which act one against the other to control the movements. The perfection of the whole fascinated me, but the sight of the smashed and deformed living bodies at the end of the sunken road on the previous evening had shaken me badly. The thought of being torn and broken terrified me.

Finally my mind cleared sufficiently to arrive at conscious decision—if I stayed where I was, I was bound to be hit sooner or later, if I ran I might be able to reach the shelter of the road. I ran. I ran like hell and dived over the banking of the road and rolled to a stop on the far side of it. I have no idea how long I lay out in no-man's-land—time is not a factor in that sort of situation.

All that was now left of the Battalion was a handful of men rushing up and down the sunken road in a state of utter confusion. This was only increased when two Russian tanks appeared from the main road and started to bombard the Moors in the machine-gun trench. Their fire was erratic and there was a moment of panic when we thought that they were shooting at us. To be midway between a tank cannon and its target is a most unnerving experience when you hear it for the first time. The din of the gun firing, the roar of the projectile through the air and the explosion of the projectile on impact, all take place as one continuous sound —bang-buzz-bang. At first it is almost impossible to distinguish the noise of the gun from that of the projectile so you cannot tell from what direction the fire is coming. Only about a dozen rounds were fired, which added to the chaos but did not serve any useful purpose. It certainly failed to slow up the rate of fire pouring over our heads. The noise of a high-expansion bullet on impact is almost exactly the same as that of a rifle being fired. The bullets were bursting in the olive trees above our heads or in the ground or against whatever they struck, and the sound was completely bewildering. It seemed as if rifles were being fired from the trees over my head and out of the ground around me. There was no flash or other visible sign to tell me what was happening, and I really thought that I must be going mad.

It was the last time that I saw Rony, the cartoonist, and Hilliard, the boxing parson. They were both killed that evening. All that was left of the Battalion was about thirty men without automatic weapons, and no officers except George Aitken. One unfortunate individual who had obviously gone completely mad was rushing around enmeshed in a cocoon of insulated wire and crying, 'I have captured the Fascist communications, I have captured the Fascist communications.' Eventually he leapt up on to the parapet and was shot dead by a burst of machine-gun fire. My only feeling was one of infinite pity mixed with relief. It was horrifying, but it seemed to be the best thing, despite the fact that he had been one of my closest friends in the Battalion.

ALEC McDADE*
'There's A Valley in Spain'

(To the tune of 'Red River Valley')
Original Version of the Words

There's a valley in Spain called Jarama,
That's a place that we all know so well,
For 'tis there that we wasted our manhood
And most of our old age as well.

* Alec McDade, from Glasgow, was killed in the Battle of Brunete, 6 July 1938. At the time of his death he was assistant Company Commissar of the British Battalion of the International Brigades.

From this valley they tell us we're leaving,
But don't hasten to bid us adieu,
For e'en though we make our departure,
We'll be back in an hour or two.

Oh, we're proud of our British Battalion,
And the marathon record it's made,
Please do us this little favour,
And take this last word to Brigade:

'You will never be happy with strangers,
They would not understand you as we,
So remember the Jarama Valley
And the old men who wait patiently.'

'There's A Valley in Spain'

(Revised version of the words, modified for singing at memorial meetings and
International Brigade celebrations. The heroic nature of the revisions was thought by
many Brigaders to be a response to the undoubted and much admired bravery
of the Brigade in the Jarama fighting.)

There's a Valley in Spain called Jarama,
It's a place that we all know so well,
It is there that we gave of our Manhood,
And most of our brave comrades fell.

We are proud of the British Battalion,
And the stand for Madrid that they made,
For they fought like true Sons of the Soil,
As part of the Fifteenth Brigade.

With the rest of the International Column,
In the stand for the Freedom of Spain
We swore in that Valley of Jarama
That fascism never will reign.

Now we've left that dark valley of sorrow
And its memories we ne'er shall forget,
So before we continue this reunion
Let us stand to our glorious dead.

WOGAN PHILIPPS

'An Ambulance Man in Spain'

New Writing, New Series, Autumn 1938

We had been in repose for a month. A lovely month in the spring, in Spain, far enough back from the front for the guns only to sound a distant rumble, in glorious country, with rivers to bathe in, and flowers and warm grass to lie in. It was the first time we had had a chance to notice each other as human beings, and hear about home lives in various countries, backgrounds, loves, children. Before that, during the strenuous time of the Jarama battle, we had been just cogs in a machine, working in a frenzy, and dropping down to sleep whenever there was a chance.

But now we were returning to the war. We had been promoted from a Brigade hospital to that of a division. The army had been reorganized. The New People's Army was ready. During this last month the International Brigades had been taken out of the lines and made to train the new raw Spanish recruits. They were now Mixed Brigades, half composed of International veterans of Madrid, and half the new enthusiastic untried Spaniards. A new small front line ambulance had just arrived from England, and I had asked to be the driver of it. It bore a brass plate inscribed with the name of a midland town which had raised the money. With this ambulance I was now sent away from all my friends of the hospital to join the army and be attached to a Franco-Belge-Spanish battalion. I was given two Chinese stretcher bearers, Chang and Lou, aged 47 and 48. They were wonderful comrades; their gesticulating language made everyone laugh, and they would work for ever, helping anyone anywhere, as well as doing their own jobs. They gave friendship to an extent I have never seen before.

It was evening. The troops were entrained in a long column of lorries, singing, laughing, sharing rations. All the drivers were in their seats, and were waiting for the secret guide, the one man who knew the destination, to turn up and lead the way. We were glad our rest was over. It was much harder to keep one's morale up when doing nothing: especially in such a war as this, where everybody was there because they believed—because the cause meant more to them than life. At last we were off, with flags flying, waving and cheering to the villagers as they rushed out to greet us. The dust was appalling, and everyone became coated from head to foot. Darkness came on, and as we were allowed no lights, one strained to follow the ghostly cloud of dust ahead. Every now and then the leader stopped, and the convoy was checked up to see if anyone was missing. My ambulance came at the back. Squashed in it were the medical stores, stretchers, Chinamen, our German doctor, and a Spanish orderly. None of us could speak the other's language. The only hope was for us all to learn Spanish.

We started to climb, and the road became twisted with hair-pin bends. Up and up, on low gear for hours. Suddenly a white patch of snow at the side. Above the snow line in June! We were going up the Guadarramas. Just below the summit a figure jumped out of the doorway of a large building. It was the chief doctor of the division hospital. He pointed out the building to me and explained it was the front line hospital, to which I would rush back the wounded from the front. I caught sight of English nurses I knew, and other drivers, and we called good luck to each other. Then on we went, down into the deep valley on the other side of the mountain range, again in low gear, as the road was so twisty and steep. We were now in a thick pine forest, which made the darkness impenetrable, and one's eyes watered with the strain. At the bottom we turned into a side track, were halted, and told to disembark and sleep on the ground as best we could. It was very cold. I had lumbago, and was too excited to sleep. As dawn came I could see the men huddled in heaps beneath the trees. As the sun rose, first one and then another would wake, search in his kit-bag, and go down to the stream and wash. The never-sleeping kitchen staff were already at work over a large fire, and we were soon all having a ration of coffee. Afterwards we were collected in companies, and our officer quietly told us we were the shock troops in a big attack the next morning. It was the eagerly awaited first offensive of the new People's Army. At last they were going to be tried out. It was a new, and last, phase of the war. The Government were going to take the offensive, and roll back the Fascists from Madrid. The difficult days of defence were over. To-morrow we would be in the outskirts of Segovia. Nothing could go wrong. It had been beautifully planned, and the enemy would be completely surprised.

Then the political commissars talked and explained more to us. These commissars played a very important part in the Peoples' Army. They were political rather than military people, but they were certainly soldiers too, and took on all the duties of soldiers. They were more educated, more politically minded than the ordinary soldier could hope to be, since nearly all the lower classes in Spain were illiterate, having been denied education. They were there to explain things; what the war was about; what defeat would mean. They were to educate, keep the morale up and to see that through ignorance the troops didn't get fed up and depressed.

For it was their war; they were fighting for their interests, unlike soldiers in large imperialist wars. Again, the commissars were there to hear even the smallest complaint, discuss it, and try to put it right. Everything was to be explained. There were no orders which could not be discussed. It was a democratic army, and the commissars were the links between officers and men. Their job was to be the friends of every single soldier, and always accessible.

We sat about, under the trees, all that day, cleaning rifles, writing letters, brooding, talking to our best friends. I was so moved by the calmness of these men, far from their own country, their families, of their own free choice, because they felt they had to go and help the people of Spain in the invasion of their country. Here they were, lying on the grass beside me, talking as if it weren't they who were going to meet that first hail of machine-gun bullets as they went into the attack. What did they really feel? What could their values be? How did they regard human relationships?—those they left behind? I felt terribly in love with my home, and showed photographs of my children. They were so pleased to see them and I felt happy. I saw that they felt just the same as any of us who think ourselves more sensitive, more human. Their proportions were different because first of all they had to fight to be allowed to live as loving humans. I seemed to see real values at last and knew I would be different when I got home. I wrote to those I loved, just to talk to them because I felt so close, yet dared not tell them what I was doing, because I felt so guilty. Would anybody ever understand? I saw how cruel I was being to those who wouldn't. But many of these men around me had experienced a fascist dictatorship. Our German doctor was covered in scars.

Crying to myself, I strolled back through the trees, and suddenly realized I was amongst a crowd of camouflaged tanks. Every seeming bush was one, carefully covered with branches. The tanks had been bought and paid for, from Russia, before non-intervention. The drivers were young Spanish mechanics, who a few months before had never seen a tank. I returned, and found the last meal being served out—an extra good one, with lovely strawberries sent by a nearby village. Then, with handshakes and smiles, the troops lined up. Suddenly there was a rifle report, and a cry. Somebody's rifle had gone off by 'mistake,' wounding him in the hand. The strain had been too much for him. His hand was dressed, and I rushed him up through the forest, over the mountain, to the hospital the other side. Again I could see my friends before the morrow. They had got everything ready—theatres, wards, sterilizing rooms; and were waiting prepared for the terrific strain the next few days would bring. I left my patient and rushed back, fifteen miles without lights, to the front. I found the troops, a dark mass, moving silently down the road. No talking, no smoking. The enemy were very close, on the heights either side of the narrow valley. We moved forward, ever so slowly, with many halts. At one hand grenades were issued, at another cartridges. Another time water bottles were filled. Sometimes an officer or commissar would drop out beside the road, to shake hands with, or even kiss, the soldiers as they passed.

Zero hour was at 5 a.m. Just before dawn we reached a small sand pit at the side of the road, and in it we established the dressing station. It was 200 yards behind the line. The troops now deployed to right and left of the road, and disappeared in the darkness of the forest. I couldn't believe it; couldn't take it in. We waited, looking at our watches again and again. At a few minutes before five a tremendous drone, growing louder and louder, over the mountain. The sky became filled with aeroplanes. Yes. They were ours! It was the first time we had ever seen them. The noise was deafening and one couldn't help going wild with the thrill. Crash! went their bombs, just ahead, and the whole earth rocked. A dead silence; then the rattle of hundreds of machine-guns and the valley was mad with sound. The attack had started, and was no surprise. They had been confidently waiting, fully prepared. The valley became a death-trap.

The first casualty soon was carried in, horribly disfigured. Who was it? I never recognized him, though afterwards I discovered I knew him well. The German doctor worked swiftly and calmly. Others came pouring in. The sand pit was soon full. Moans and cries. Often a ghastly shriek. The smell made one feel sick. Flies covered everything. The first two were quickly put into my ambulance, and I drove off fast, but as gently as possible, back to the hospital.

My ambulance was very small. The heads of the wounded, as they lay on the stretchers, were level with me as I drove. I could talk to them, encourage them, or hear if they asked for anything. My ignorance was so appalling. Sometimes a man would break down completely, and scream he was dying. Another would cry for water. If it was a stomach wound he could not have any, but the denying him seemed crueller than any death. Sometimes they died on the journey. Had my ignorance let them die? Am I even now responsible for the deaths of some of my friends? I know that once an unnecessary bump over a large shell hole helped a man to death.

The road was now full of troops, guns, tanks; but at the sight of an ambulance a way was always quickly cleared, and the men would call a greeting to the wounded as they passed. As one went over the pass at the top, fascist planes were always waiting for one, and spurts of dust on the road would show where the bullets were going.

At the hospital all was calm and efficient. Stretcher bearers would unload the ambulance, and carry the wounded into the *triage* room where the doctor would classify, and sort out the most urgent cases; while the secretary would try and find out who they were, what nationality, and who to notify. Some of the mementos that came out of their pockets were extraordinary.

On my return the landscape at the front had completely changed. Clumps of trees had completely disappeared. Shells were screaming through the sand pit. Our protective bushes were blown away. Chang was hit in the chest but wouldn't stop smiling and working. (Two days later he couldn't smile any more, and had to give up.) Wounded were everywhere, and a lot of fresh ambulances had arrived. We couldn't move back from the front because that would have exposed the stretcher bearers to more risk, so we carried forward the whole dressing station to a deep sheltered ditch right in the lines. The sky was now full of enemy planes, cruising round and round, doing what they liked. Ours had had to go away to help hinder the Fascists at Bilbao.

For three days and nights it went on. The nights were worse than the days. That black journey back to the hospital as quickly as possible without lights! It seemed as if one's mind was going to snap. Tears poured down one's face as one worked. What was the point of going on? Why couldn't they stop? Anyone could see the attack was a failure. Then the commissars told me. We had drawn 200 fascist aeroplanes and a division of troops away from the Basque country. We were helping even in our failure.

That evening we were to retire. It was over. The People's Army had failed in their first offensive, but tremendous experience had been gained. I and Izzy Kupchick, a Canadian Jew driver, a mere boy of eighteen, loved by everybody to the point of being a mascot, for his gaiety, and spontaneous unselfishness, were sitting each in our own ambulance, a few yards apart, waiting. A shell pitched beside us, shattering one side of my car. I got out to examine the damage. Suddenly a blue explosion went through the whole world. My brain went loose, in pieces inside my head. At the same time something red-hot hit my arm with smashing force. I picked myself up and walked to Izzy to tell him I had been hit, and found him crouching on his knees with an agonized puzzled look on his face, holding his stomach. He said he knew he was dying, but I managed to lay him on the grass, and back his ambulance over him, to give him some protection in case another shell came. I then ran shouting for a doctor into the forest. Ours had already moved back, but I knew there must be another in some part of the line not yet retired. I at last found one, a Pole, and fought to make him understand. We got back and found Izzy still alive. He dressed him, and we got him back to the hospital. That night they told me he was dead. There could never have been such an unselfish life as his. He was absolutely on the threshold: so unspoilt: so excited, naive. Persecuted at home for being a Jew, he had joined the Communist Party, and come to Spain to help the people in their struggle against fascism.

Two days later I managed to escape from hospital, and hide in a truck which was going to the village where I knew the battalion was billeted. It was the most moving evening of my life. As we sat under the trees, an officer read us a letter of thanks from the people of Bilbao, for having done all we could to help them. Across 200 miles of intervening enemy territory that message had come. But the price had been one in three dead or wounded. These here, the remainder, would go on till perhaps not one was left. They could perhaps never go back to their countries, even if they did survive. They were labelled dangerous Reds for life.

I, privileged by birth alone, was going back to England, in a luxurious aeroplane in a few days.

TAKING SIDES

Authors Take Sides

from *Authors Take Sides on the Spanish War*, 1937

'THE QUESTION'

To the Writers and Poets of England, Scotland, Ireland and Wales

It is clear to many of us throughout the whole world that now, as certainly never before, we are determined or compelled, to take sides. The equivocal attitude, the Ivory Tower, the paradoxical, the ironic detachment, will no longer do.

We have seen murder and destruction by Fascism in Italy, in Germany —the organisation there of social injustice and cultural death—and how revived, imperial Rome, abetted by international treachery, has conquered her place in the Abyssinian sun. The dark millions in the colonies are unavenged.

To-day, the struggle is in Spain. To-morrow it may be in other countries—our own. But there are some who, despite the martyrdom of Durango and Guernica, the enduring agony of Madrid, of Bilbao, and Germany's shelling of Almeria, are still in doubt, or who aver that it is possible that Fascism may be what it proclaims it is: 'the saviour of civilisation'.

This is the question we are asking you:

Are you for, or against, the legal Government and the People of Republican Spain?

Are you for, or against, Franco and Fascism?

For it is impossible any longer to take no side.

Writers and Poets, we wish to print your answers. We wish the world to know what you, writers and poets, who are amongst the most sensitive instruments of a nation, feel.

Signed: *Paris—June* 1937

Aragon	Nancy Cunard	Pablo Neruda
W. H. Auden	Brian Howard	Ramón Sender
José Bergamin	Heinrich Mann	Stephen Spender
Jean Richard Bloch	Ivor Montagu	Tristan Tzara

'THE ANSWERS'

For the Government

W. H. Auden

I support the Valencia Government in Spain because its defeat by the forces of International Fascism would be a major disaster for Europe. It would make a European war more probable; and the spread of Fascist Ideology and practice to countries as yet comparatively free from them, which would inevitably follow upon a Fascist victory in Spain, would create an atmosphere in which the creative artist and all who care for justice, liberty and culture would find it impossible to work or even exist.

George Barker

I am for the people of Republican Spain, for the people of China, for the people of England, for the people of Germany, etc. I am against Fascism, Franco, Mussolini, Japanese Generals, Hitler, Walter Chrysler, the Archbishop of Canterbury, etc.

Samuel Beckett

¡UPTHEREPUBLIC!

Cyril Connolly

Fascism is the first process by which the cynical few exploit the idealism of the many, by violence and propaganda through the use of a dictator. Its aim is to maintain the status of the rich by using the poor to fight battles. This cannot be done until the whole nation is rendered both warlike and servile. Those who will not make soldiers are not required;those who are not required are eliminated. What we can learn from Spain is the order and extent of that elimination before the stultifying of the human race can proceed. Intellectuals come first, almost before women and children. It is impossible therefore to remain an intellectual and admire Fascism, for that is to admire the intellect's destruction, nor can one remain careless and indifferent. To ignore the present is to condone the future.

Havelock Ellis

In reply—While I recognise that there are good men on both sides, I am myself decisively on the side of the legal Government and against Franco and the Fascists.

Ford Madox Ford

I am unhesitatingly for the existing Spanish Government and against Franco's attempt—on every ground of feeling and reason. In addition, as the merest commonsense, the Government of the Spanish, as of any other nation, should be settled and defined by the inhabitants of that nation. Mr Franco seeks to establish a government resting on the arms of Moors, Germans, Italians. Its success *must* be contrary to world conscience.

Victor Gollancz

Of course I am for the legal Government and the people of Republican Spain.

Of course I am against Franco and Fascism.

Fascism is culturally and intellectually a species of dementia præcox —a refusal any longer to carry the burden of being human, and a slipping back, happy sometimes but always disgusting, into the primeval slime. The writer, poet or artist who says the whole thing is no concern of his is either a knave or a fool, or more probably both.

Geoffrey Grigson, Editor, *New Verse*

For potted shrimps in the club, for reading the *Manchester Guardian*, for holding hands in the cinema, we are paying willingly with the lies, the insolence and the cynicism hung between us and intervention in Spain.

I am equivocal enough to be *against* politically, and not *for*, to fear and distrust any mass in its own control; but for me Hitler, Mussolini and Franco are man-eating mass-giants issuing from mediocrity and obscenity. I believe it better to risk 'destroying civilisation' than to live and profit in a civilisation of Baldwinian lies by throwing them victims.

Brian Howard

A people, nearly half of whom has been denied the opportunity to learn to read, is struggling for bread, liberty and life against the most unscrupulous and reactionary plutocracy left in existence. Utterly unable to crush this people alone, their enemies have hired foreign mercenaries, whose governments self-confessedly covet Spain's raw materials, to butcher whole civilian communities. With all my anger and love, I am for the People of Republican Spain.

Aldous Huxley

My sympathies are, of course, with the Government side, especially the Anarchists; for Anarchism seems to me much more likely to lead to desirable social change than highly centralised, dictatorial Communism. As for 'taking sides'—the choice, it seems to me, is no longer between two users of violence, two systems of dictatorship. Violence and dictatorship cannot produce peace and liberty; they can only produce the results of violence and dictatorship, results with which history has made us only too sickeningly familiar.

The choice now is between militarism and pacifism. To me, the necessity of pacifism seems absolutely clear.

John Lehmann, Editor, *New Writing*

Of course I am for the legal Government and the People of Spain. No writer who is trying to create for the future, and not merely dabbling in outworn forms and sentiments, can be on any other side.

C. Day Lewis

The struggle in Spain is part of a conflict going on now all over the world. I look upon it quite simply as a battle between light and darkness, of which only a blind man could be unaware. Both as a writer and as a member of the Communist Party I am bound to help in the fight against Fascism, which means certain destruction or living death for humanity.

Hugh Macdiarmid

I am a member of the Communist Party and wholly on the side of the legal Government and the People of Republican Spain—as are the vast majority of the people of Scotland, where at successive General Elections a majority of the total poll has been cast for Socialism, and where—if we had had national independence—we too would have had a Socialist Republican Government long ago. Practically all the Scottish writers of any distinction to-day are of the same way of thinking. But for the connection with England, Fascism would never be able to raise its head in Scotland itself. If we are subjected to a Fascist terror in Scotland, the London Government will be to blame, as it is mainly to blame for the horrible tragedy inflicted on our Spanish comrades—a tragedy which must, and will, be turned yet into a glorious victory over the Principalities and Powers of Darkness, and end with the liquidation of Franco and all his fellow-murderers.

Louis MacNeice

I support the Valencia Government in Spain. Normally I would only support a cause because I hoped to get something out of it. Here the reason is stronger; if this cause is lost, nobody with civilised values may be able to get anything out of anything.

Sean O'Casey

I am, of course, for a phalanx unbreakable round those who think and work for all men, and I am with the determined faces firing at the steel-clad slug of Fascism from the smoke and flame of the barricades.

Llewelyn Powys

I am unequivocally in favour of the legal Spanish Government and opposed to Fascism and any other form of Government that seeks by means of coercion to impose its arbitrary will upon its own or other peoples.

V. S. Pritchett

I am heart and soul for the People of Spain in their brave and stoical resistance to Franco and Fascism. The lesson of Spain for the rest of western Europe, even before this struggle, lay in the innate simplicity and nobility of the uncorrupted common people. They have now burned this lesson upon the imagination of us all.

Herbert Read

In Spain, and almost only in Spain, there still lives a spirit to resist the bureaucratic tyranny of the State and the intellectual intolerance of all doctrinaires. For that reason all poets must follow the course of this struggle with open and passionate partisanship.

Edgell Rickword

Fascism has unmasked its ugly face in Spain as if to convince the waverers that it is indeed a force of destruction and human degradation. Support for the people of Spain and their legal Republican Government means the triumph of life over death. It means the doom of the gangster, the bully and the hypocrite, the birth of a free and happy world. And because Fascism is all the power of the past striving to throttle the future, no struggle ever called for greater courage and determination.

Stephen Spender

I am opposed to Franco firstly because Franco and his supporters represent the attempt of the aristocracy and clergy of Spain to prevent the history of Spain developing beyond the Middle Ages. In opposing their reaction, so far from being an extremist, I support the Protestantism of intellectuals like the great Catholic writer Bergamin against the materialism of the Catholic Church in Spain; and I support in Spain exactly such a movement of liberal and liberating nationalism as the English liberals supported in many countries still groaning under feudalism in the nineteenth century.

Secondly, I am opposed to Franco, because, supported by Hitler and Mussolini, he represents international Fascism. If Franco wins in Spain Fascism will have gained the third great victory in an international war which began in Manchuria, continued in Abyssinia, and may end in Spain. If Franco wins, the principle of democracy will have received a severe blow and the prospect of a new imperialist war, which is also a 'war of ideologies' will have been brought far nearer.

Randall Swingler

I believe that culture has always been the directive force of man's progress towards freedom: that Fascism is destructive alike to culture and to human progress; therefore that everyone who is for life and enlightenment must be wholeheartedly implicated on the side of the Spanish People's Government, who struggle to save us from Fascism and war.

Rex Warner

I am on the side of the Republican Government in Spain not only because it is a legal and democratic Government, but because it represents the forward movement of humanity and civilisation. I believe that Fascism, so far from 'saving' civilisation, attempts to arrest this forward movement and consequently must drag humanity backwards towards a kind of self-conscious barbarism.

Neutral?

T. S. Eliot

While I am naturally sympathetic, I still feel convinced that it is best that at least a few men of letters should remain isolated, and take no part in these collective activities.

Ezra Pound

Questionnaire an escape mechanism for young fools who are too cowardly to think; too lazy to investigate the nature of money, its mode of issue, the control of such issue by the Banque de France and the stank of England. You arc all had. Spain is an emotional luxury to a gang of sap-headed dilettantes.

H. G. Wells

I am not an 'anti' of any sort unless it is anti-gangster or anti-nationalist. My sympathies were all with the new liberal republic in Madrid. It has been destroyed between the Anarchist-Syndicalists on the one hand and the Franco pronunciamento on the other. The intervention of Italy and Germany is on traditional nationalist lines; it was to be expected and it has been greatly facilitated by the stupid confusion in the British mind and will.

The real enemy of mankind is not the Fascist but the Ignorant Fool.

Against the Government

Edmund Blunden

I know too little about affairs in Spain to make a confident answer. To my mind (subject to that first reservation), it was necessary that somebody like Franco should arise—and although England may not profit by his victory I think Spain will. The ideas of Germany, Italy, etc., in your document do not square with those I have formed *upon the whole* of the recent history of those countries. Memories of 1914–18 perhaps do not allow me to see some incidents you mention in the isolated and flamboyant way the manifesto has them.

Evelyn Waugh

I know Spain only as a tourist and a reader of the newspapers. I am no more impressed by the 'legality' of the Valencia Government than are English Communists by the legality of the Crown, Lords and Commons. I believe it was a bad Government, rapidly deteriorating. If I were a Spaniard I should be fighting for General Franco. As an Englishman I am not in the predicament of choosing between two evils. I am not a Fascist nor shall I become one unless it were the only alternative to Marxism. It is mischievous to suggest that such a choice is imminent.

58

CYRIL CONNOLLY

'The Cool Element of Prose'

from *Enemies of Promise*, 1938

I have also before me another document, a pamphlet published by *Left Review*, 'Authors take sides on the Spanish War'. In this one hundred and fifty writers answer the question: 'Are you for or against the legal government and the people of Republican Spain? Are you for or against Franco and Fascism?'

A hundred and fifty answers to a question that is not elastic must of necessity exhibit a certain sameness, but anybody reading through them must have been struck less by the uniformity than by the poverty of the diction, the clichés, the absence of distinction, or of any phrases which could be used as slogans, despite the sincerity of the contributors. I quote three examples, one of moth-eaten Mandarin (note the air of self-conscious loftiness which sets the author above the Spanish people, and the English reader), one of typical modern journalism, (the clichés are underlined), and one of the You-man He-man type in the new vernacular.

(1) In Politics, I care chiefly that a man's thought be not regimented or his art censored, and that he may live as long as he pleases so long as, within a rule of law he has shared in making, he offer no violence to the health and integrity of others. Neither contestant in Spain aims at this, and between them I will not choose, thinking it better to preserve the surviving liberties of England and France within the peace of Europe than to persecute in the false belief that the only alternative to a tyranny of the Right is a tyranny of the Left. (Charles Morgan.)

(2) As one who has *no political axe to grind*, is *attached to no political party* and detests all tyrannical government *whether it be of the Right or the Left*, I believe that the subjugation of the people of Republican Spain by Franco and his *foreign confederates will, if it is effected, mark the end of freedom and civilisation in Europe.* Fascism—which in practice is *merely gangsterism on a national scale*—involves the enslavement of peoples, *the destruction of culture*, and the persecution of *all real religion. And it depends for its continued existence on the perpetual* fomentation of new wars. *In the light of recent history*, and of history *now in the making*, I am astonished that *any man or woman of good will* can *remain blind to these plain facts*. (Gerald Bullett.)

(3) Don't be a lot of saps. If X and Y want to cut one another's throats over Z, why on earth must people who do not believe in the ideas propounded by either X, Y or Z have to 'choose between them'? If you want to know, I do think Fascism is

lousy. So is your Communism, only more so. But there are other ideas in the world besides either of them—thank God (whom neither of you believe in).

For the love of Mike cut loose from this fixation that the artist can no longer have the guts to be what every artist worth his salt has always been—*an individualist*. . . . (May I say how much I like your postal address?) Yours contemptuously, Sean O'Faolain.

That is the situation. Is there any hope? Is there a possibility of a new kind of prose developing out of a synthesis of Orlando and the Tough Guy?

GEORGE ORWELL

Bloody Rot

from Letter to Stephen Spender, 2 April, 1983 in *Collected Essays, Journalism and Letters*, ed. Sonia Orwell and Ian Angus, 1968

The way things are going in Spain simply desolates me. All those towns and villages I knew smashed abt, and I suppose the wretched peasants who used to be so decent to us being chased to and fro and their landlords put back onto them. I wonder if we shall ever be able to go back to Spain if Franco wins. I suppose it would mean getting a new passport anyway. I notice that you and I are both on the board of sponsors or whatever it is called of the SIA.* So also is Nancy Cunard, all rather comic because it was she who previously sent me that bloody rot which was afterwards published in book form (called *Authors Take Sides*). I sent back a very angry reply in which I'm afraid I mentioned you uncomplimentarily, not knowing you personally at that time. However I'm all for this SIA business if they are really doing anything to supply food etc., not like that damned rubbish of signing manifestos to say how wicked it all is.

MICHAEL ROBERTS

I Suspect that Kind of Symposium

from Laura Riding (ed.), *The World and Ourselves (Epilogue)*, 1938

I was in the French Alps for a month, and was followed round by circulars asking for six lines saying that Franco is a devil and Caballero is

---

* *Solidaridad Internacional Antifascista.*

a gentleman (or words to that effect). I don't think that the outside world is as simple as that. I suspect that kind of symposium: it is an easy way out for people who think that they ought to do something at this moment and ease their consciences by signing a manifesto . . . our job as writers is to clear up a few points and to state problems clearly, not to attempt the politicians' statement or formulation and vote on it.

The politician manufactures a language—a vocabulary and a rhetoric —which, if you accept it as wholly adequate, leads inevitably to the answers he wants and to the actions he wants. But the prior question is whether the language *is* adequate to the facts. And as the poet is concerned with making language do new work and finding out the implications of language, his answer is always: no. As a citizen, I'm willing to vote and maybe to fight; I'll even argue for one party rather than another, but I won't identify my special job with that party. For all parties are opposed to that job, since it undermines the basis on which they exist. The method by which they oppose analysis, reformulation, discovery of poetic truth, varies from one party to another: imprisonment, murder, stereotyped education, Sunday papers—whichever they think the more effective in the long run.

T. S. ELIOT

'Irresponsible Zealots'

from 'A Commentary', *The Criterion*, January 1937

Those who would like to believe in the progress of political institutions can take no honest satisfaction either in events in Spain or in the opinions and sympathies which these events have tended to arouse in this country. What has to be remarked is rather a deterioration of political thinking, with a pressure on everyone, which has to be stubbornly resisted, to accept one extreme philosophy or another. The situation at the moment of writing is not yet quite that of two great groups of nations, aligned against each other with a fanaticism (complicated with self-interest) that no previous combinations and coalitions in our time have shown: at present, and from our point of view, it is rather that of an international civil war of opposed ideas. The present danger for us, as individuals in this country, is that the precarious balance of ideas in our heads may be upset by one or the other extreme view, according to our individual backgrounds and temperaments. As I have suggested, the greater part of the Press not only does nothing to restrain this disintegration, but actually tends to hasten it: by simplifying the issues in very different and very imperfectly understood countries, by resolving emotional tension in the minds of their readers by directing their sympathies all one way, and consequently encouraging mental sloth.

One might think, after perusing a paper like *The New Statesman*, that the elected Government of Spain represented an enlightened and progressive Liberalism; and from reading *The Tablet* one might be persuaded that the rebels were people who, after enduring with patience more than one would expect human beings to be able to stand, had finally and reluctantly taken to arms as the only way left in which to save Christianity and civilization. Now an ideally unprejudiced person, with an intimate knowledge of Spain, its history, its racial characteristics, and its contemporary personalities, might be in a position to come to the conclusion that he should, in the longest view that could be seen, support one side rather than the other. But so long as we are not compelled in our own interest to take sides, I do not see why we should do so on insufficient knowledge: and even any eventual partisanship should be held with reservations, humility and misgiving. That balance of mind which a few highly-civilized individuals, such as Arjuna, the hero of the *Bhagavad Gita*, can maintain in action, is difficult for most of us even as observers, and, as I say, is not encouraged by the greater part of the Press.

One tendency of which we must take account is that of the winning 'idea' to deteriorate. Political fanaticism in releasing generous passions will release evil ones too. Whichever side wins will not be the better for having had to fight for its victory. The victory of the Right will be the victory of a secular Right, not of a spiritual Right, which is a very different thing; the victory of the Left will be the victory of the worst rather than of the best features; and if it ends in something called Communism, that will be a travesty of the humanitarian ideals which have led so many people in that direction. And those who have at heart the interests of Christianity in the long run—which is not quite the same thing as a nominal respect paid to an ecclesiastical hierarchy with a freedom circumscribed by the interests of a secular State—have especial reason for suspending judgment.

Some people have agitated for the raising of the embargo on the export of arms to the Spanish Government. But at this stage of the game, I suspect that those who 'support the popular demand that the ban on the export of arms to the Spanish Government be lifted' are really asking us to commit ourselves to one side in a conflict between two ideas: that of

Berlin and that of Moscow, neither of which seems to have very much to do with 'democracy'.

Irresponsible zealots who have advocated 'intervention' on one side or the other—who advocate, that is to say, the overt supply of arms—will never be deterred by considerations such as these . . .

T. S. ELIOT

Extremists of Both Extremes

from 'A Commentary', *The Criterion*, July 1937

Whatever one's opinion, at one time or another, of our Foreign Policy, it sometimes seems as if many Englishmen, as private individuals, were disposed to make any intelligent policy difficult. I wonder whether any people, except that of the United States of America, is so given to votes of moral censure upon other nations. This thought was inspired by Mr Edmund Blunden's admirable letter in *The Times* of April 24, on the subject of the bicentenary celebration of the University of Göttingen. It seems hardly credible, at the moment of writing, that the motive of the authorities of Oxford University in deciding not to send representatives to that celebration could have been to express disapproval of the German Government. But it is to be feared that their action may be so interpreted in Germany, and (pending an explanation) may be so interpreted here too. There are no doubt many individuals who, from the most generous motives, would like to see such disapproval expressed in every possible public way—without any discrimination between what is permissible to individuals and what is permissible to governments and public institutions. There are also persons who, in public positions, are inclined to behave as if they were private individuals. It may be that the effect of this 'idealism', as it is called, tends to exaggerate the silly cynicism (called 'realism') of certain foreign speakers and writers, even driving them to express their fury in billingsgate. The situation in Spain has provided the perfect opportunity for extremists of both extremes. To turn from the shrill manifestoes of the Extreme Left, and the indiscretions of the Dean of Canterbury, to the affirmations of Mr Jerrold and Mr Lunn, is only to intensify the nightmare. On the First of May *The Tablet* provided its explanation of the destruction of Guernica: the most likely culprits, according to *The Tablet*, were the Basques' own allies, their shady friends in Catalonia.

THOMAS MANN

'Epilogue to "Spain"'

(For a pamphlet publ. by the Socialist Alliance of Swiss Women, Zürich, transl. by H. T. Lowe-Porter)
from *Life and Letters Today*, Summer 1937

As little as Romain Rolland, who wrote the flaming foreword to this book, was I born a political man: that is to say, a partisan, whose will exercises restraints and limitations upon his intellect. So it was not as a partisan that I was asked to write the closing words of this appeal to humanity; and it is no interest which bids me obey the behest, but only my suffering and indignant conscience. For it is interest which—with the consciencelessness reserved, as we all know, for the 'man of action' —commits all the great rascalities in the world. As now in Spain. Then whose affair is it, if not the creative artist's—the man whose emotions are free—to assert the human conscience against the baseness of interest, at once so presumptuous and so petty; to protest against the stultifying, all-embracing confusion made in our time between politics and villainy?

There is no lower kind of scorn than that visited upon the artist who 'descends into the arena'. And the ground of that scorn is interest: interest which prefers to gain its ends in darkness and silence, unchecked by the forces of the intellect or the spirit. These, interest would confine to their proper domain of the cultural, by telling them that politics is beneath their dignity. The result is that the cultural becomes the slave of interest, its accessory and accomplice, all for the false coin of a little dignity in return. The artist must not see, that in this stately retreat to his ivory tower he is committing an act of anachronistic folly—must not see, yet to-day can hardly fail to see.

Democracy is to-day to that extent a realised and intrinsic fact, that politics is everybody's business. Nobody can deny this; it stares us in the face with an immediacy never known before. Sometimes we hear somebody say: 'I take no interest in politics.' The words strike us as absurd. Not only so, but egotistic and antisocial, a stupid self-deception, a piece of folly. But they are more: they betray an ignorance not only intellectual but ethical. For the politico-social field is an undeniable and inalienable part of the all-embracing human; it is one section of the human problem, the human *task*, which the non-political man thinks to set off, as the decisive and actual, against the political sphere. The decisive and the actual: it is indeed that; for in the guise of the political the problem of the human being, man himself, is put to us to-day with a

final, life-and-death seriousness unknown before. Then shall the artist
—he who, by nature and destiny, ever occupies humanity's furthest
outposts—shall he alone be allowed to shirk a decision?

Life-and-death seriousness. I use these words to express the conviction that a man's—and how much more an artist's—opinions are to-day
bound up with the salvation of his soul. I deliberately use a religious
terminology; so convinced am I, that an artist who, in our time avoids the
issue, shirks the human problem when politically presented, and betrays
to interest the things of the spirit, is a lost soul. He must be stunted. Not
only because he sacrifices his existence as an artist, his 'talent', and
produces nothing more which is available for life. But because even his
earlier work, not created under the pressure of such guilt, and once good,
will cease to be good and crumble to dust before humanity's eyes. That is
my conviction. I have instances in mind as I write.

I shall be asked what I mean by spirit and what by interest. Well then:
the spiritual, seen from the politico-social angle, is the longing of the
people for better, juster, happier conditions of life, more adequate to the
developed human consciousness. It is this longing, affirmed by all those
who are of good will. And interest: interest is all that which seeks to
thwart this consummation, because it would thereby be cut off from
certain advantages and privileges; seeks by every means at its command,
not scorning the basest, even the criminal. Or, well knowing that in the
long run it must fail, tries to put off as long as it can the evil day—for a
little while, for a few decades. In Spain, interest rages. Rages with a
shamelessness such as the world has seldom seen. What has been
happening there for many months is one of the most scandalous and
mortifying pages which history has to show. Does the world see it, feel it?
Only very partially. For murderous interest understands only too well
how to besot the world and throw dust in its eyes. From a lady—living, it
is true, in the most darkened quarter of the world, I mean Germany—I
have heard the words: 'Who could have thought that the Reds in Spain
would commit such atrocities, out of a blue sky?' The Reds. And out of a
blue sky.—The present book, written not by savage Bolsheviks but by
persons of Christian and middle-class views, shows how little revolutionary was the reform programme of the Spanish Popular Front, a
political alliance of republicans and socialists. It shows us to what
circumstances and conditions its legitimate and decisive triumph at the
polls was the answer. Have we then no hearts? No understanding? Shall
we let ourselves be unresistingly deprived of our last remnant of free
human judgment by interest—which unfailingly appeals to the worst
instincts, though it clothe itself in lying names such as order, culture,

God, and native land? A people held down and exploited with all the instruments of the most obsolete reaction, strives towards a brighter existence, more compatible with human dignity, a social order more creditable to the face of civilisation. Freedom and progress are there conceptions not yet vitiated by philosophical irony and scepticism. For these people they are conditions of national honour, values to be striven for to the uttermost. The government, with all the caution prescribed by the special circumstances, undertakes to remove the grossest abuses, to carry out the most imperative reforms. What happens? An insurrection of generals, occurring in the interest of the old exploiters and oppressors, concocted with the help of hopeful foreign interests, blazes up and misfires. It is already as good as beaten, when it is propped up by foreign governments inimical to freedom, in return for promises of strategic and economic advantage in case of victory. It is supported by money, men, and material, fostered and prolonged, until there seems no end to the bloodshed, the tragic, ruthless, obstinate carnage from either side. Against a people desperately fighting for its freedom and its human rights the troops of its own colony are led into battle. Its cities are demolished by foreign bombing planes, women and children are butchered; and all this is called a national movement; this villainy crying out to heaven is called God, Order, and Beauty. If the interested European Press could have its way, the capital would have fallen long since; the triumph of Order and Beauty over the Marxist rabble would long since have been consummated. But the half-demolished capital —at least at the moment of writing—is not yet conquered, and the 'Red mob', as the interested Press describes it, referring to the Spanish people, is defending its life, its higher life, with a lion-like courage which must give to think even the most besotted slave of interest, as to the moral forces here engaged.

The right of self-determination of peoples enjoys high official honour throughout the world to-day. Even our dictators and our totalitarian states lay stress upon it, finding it important to show that they have ninety to ninety-eight per cent of their people behind them. Well, so much is clear: the revolting military have not got the Spanish people behind them, and cannot pretend that they have. They must do their best with Moors and foreign troops. It may not be quite settled what the Spanish people want. But what they do not want is clear, abundantly: General Franco. Those European governments which are interested in the strangulation of freedom, have recognized as legal the rebel junta, in the midst of a furious struggle which they support even if they did not connive at its inception. At home they betray a considerable degree of sensitiveness in the matter of high treason. Here they support a man who delivers up his country to the foreigner. At home they call themselves nationalists. Here they enforce the power of a man to whom his country's independence is naught, if he can do to death freedom and the rights of humanity; who declares that rather shall two-thirds of the Spanish people die than that Marxism—that is to say a better, juster, more humane order—shall triumph. It is all too infuriating, criminal, and revolting.

This volume on Spain contains pictures of the country where interest rages. It is published by women, and pre-eminently for women; it addresses itself to the emotions of free humanity, without thereby denying its own political impetus and feeling. At a time when politics have become a matter of humanity itself, as they have to-day, it would be cowardly and hypocritical to confine oneself to the unpolitical. But in all such struggles the charitable and ameliorating task falls to woman's lot; and this book appeals to the maternal instinct to aid and to console. Likewise it is not a matter of chance that the foreword and epilogue have been written not by men of party or active politicians, but by independent men of letters.

W. B. YEATS

'Politics'

(23 May 1938), from *Collected Poems*, 1940

'In our time the destiny of man presents its meaning in political terms.'—THOMAS MANN

How can I, that girl standing there,
My attention fix
On Roman or on Russian
Or on Spanish politics?
Yet here's a travelled man that knows
What he talks about,
And there's a politician
That has read and thought,
And maybe what they say is true
Of war and war's alarms,
But O that I were young again
And held her in my arms!

GRAHAM GREENE
'Alfred Tennyson Intervenes'

from the *Spectator*, 10 December 1937

The Victorians, one is forced to conclude, were sometimes less high-minded than ourselves. The publication of the little booklet *Authors Take Sides* reminds one of an earlier group of English writers who intervened in Spain a hundred years ago. They were—questionably—more roman-tic; they were certainly less melodramatic; they were, I think, a good deal wiser. 'With all my anger and love, I am for the People of Republican Spain'—that is not the kind of remark that anyone with a sense of the ludicrous should make on this side of the Channel. Alfred Tennyson did at least cross the Pyrenees, though his motives to today's hysterical partisans may appear suspect: there is every reason to suppose that he went for the fun of the thing—fun which nearly brought Hallam and himself before a firing squad as it did the unfortunate and quite unserious-minded Boyd. He doesn't seem in later years to have wished to recall the adventure, and only a few lines in the official life of Tennyson connect him and his Cambridge club, the Apostles, with the conspiracy of General Torrijos and the Spanish exiles.

It was the fashion among the Apostles to be Radical, a fashion less political than literary and metaphysical, connected in some curious way with the reading of Charles and Arthur Tennyson's poetry, with long talks in Highgate between Coleridge and John Sterling, when the old poet did most of the talking, starting, according to Hazlitt, from no premises and coming to no conclusions, crossing and recrossing the garden path, snuffling softly of Kant and infinitudes, embroiling poor Sterling for ever in the fog of theology. When politics were touched on by the Apostles it was in an amused and rather patronising way. ''Twas a very pretty little revolution in Saxony,' wrote Hallam in 1830, 'and a respectable one at Brunswick' (the dilettante tone has charm after the sweeping statements, the safe marble gestures, the self-importance—'I stand with the People and Government of Spain'). Only in the rash Torrijos adventure did the Apostles come within measurable distance of civil war.

London in 1830 contained a small group of refugees who had been driven from Spain by the restored Bourbon, Ferdinand. Ferdinand after his long captivity in Bayonne had sworn to observe the Constitution. He broke his oath, dissolved the Cortes, and restored the Inquisition. After three years of civil war the French bayonets of the Duc d'Angoulême established him as absolute king. Foreign intervention again: it is difficult for the historian to feel moral indignation.

And so in London the Spanish liberals gathered. 'Daily in the cold spring air,' wrote Carlyle, 'under skies so unlike their own, you could see a group of fifty or a hundred stately tragic figures, in proud threadbare cloaks; perambulating, mostly with closed lips'—a grotesque vision obtrudes of those tragic figures who perambulated with open mouths —'the broad pavements of Euston Square and the regions about St Pancras new church.' Their leader was Torrijos, a soldier and diplomat, the friend of Sterling's parents, and soon therefore the friend of the literary and metaphysical Apostles. In Sterling's rooms in Regent Street the Radicals met Torrijos and talked. Sterling was 24 and Tennyson 21.

The Apostles would probably have played no active part if it had not been for Sterling's Irish cousin, Robert Boyd, a young man of a hasty and adventurous temper, who had thrown up his commission in the Army because of a fancied insult and now, with five thousand pounds in his pocket, planned to go privateering in the East. Torrijos needed capital and promised Boyd the command of a Spanish cavalry regiment on Ferdinand's defeat. Even without the promise the idea of conquering a kingdom would have been enough for Boyd, whose ambition it was to live, like Conrad's Captain Blunt, 'by his sword.' A boat was bought in the Thames and secretly armed. Boyd and the Apostles were to sail it down the river at night to Deal and there take on board Torrijos and fifty picked Spaniards. The excitement, perhaps the sudden intrusion of reality when the arms came on board, proved too much for Sterling. 'Things are going on very well, but are very, even frightfully near,' he wrote in February, 1830, and soon his health gave way and furnished him an excuse to stay behind, saved him for the Bayswater curacy, for the essays on Revelation and Sin, for death at Ventnor. But he did not avoid all danger; the Spanish Ambassador got wind of the preparations, the river police were informed, and one night they appeared over the side and seized the ship in the King's name. Sterling dropped into a wherry, a policeman brandishing a pistol and threatening to shoot, escaped to Deal and warned Torrijos. The Spaniards crossed to France, and still accompanied by Boyd and a few of the Apostles, made their way in small parties to Gibraltar.

Tennyson and Hallam were not with them—a Cambridge term intervened. But for the long vacation they had a part to play, not altogether without danger. While Torrijos waited at Gibraltar, money and dispatches had to be carried to other insurgents in the north of

Spain. So Tennyson and Hallam travelled across the Pyrenees by diligence, passing Cauteretz on the way, where Tennyson found material for a gentle poem, and reached the rebels' camp.

'A wild bustling time we had of it,' Hallam declared later. 'I played my part as conspirator in a small way and made friends with two or three gallant men who have since been trying their luck with Valdes.' One of these was the commander, Ojeda, who spoke to Tennyson of his wish '*couper la gorge à tous les curés*,' but added with his hand on his heart, '*mais vous connaissez mon coeur*.' The two came back from the 'ferment of minds and stir of events' in the steamer 'Leeds' from Bordeaux, and a young girl, who was travelling with her father and sister, paid particular attention to Hallam, 'a very interesting delicate looking young man.' He read her one of Scott's novels, and Tennyson listened in the background, wearing a large conspirator's cape and a tall hat. They did not confide their story to her.

Soon after they reached England a report came to Somersby Rectory that John Kemble—another of the Apostles—had been caught in the south and was to be tried for his life, and Tennyson in the early morning posted to Lincoln to try to find someone acquainted with the Consul at Cadiz, who might help to save his friend. But the rumour was false. It anticipated a more tragic story, for Torrijos and his band, commanded to leave Gibraltar in November, 1831, sailed in two small vessels for Malaga, were chased by guardships and ran ashore. They barricaded themselves into a farmhouse, called curiously enough Ingles, and were surrounded. It was useless to resist and they surrendered, hoping for mercy. But they received none. They were shot on the esplanade at Malaga, after being shrived by a priest. Boyd received one favour: his body was delivered to the British Consul for burial.

He was the only Englishman to die, for the Apostles, who tired of the long wait at Gibraltar, had already scattered through Spain with guide-books, examining churches and Moorish remains. Sterling, who had his cousin's death on his conscience, never quite recovered from the blow. 'I hear the sound of that musketry,' he wrote in a letter; 'it is as if the bullets were tearing my own brain.' Hallam took the adventure lightly: 'After revolutionising kingdoms, one is still less inclined than before to trouble one's head about scholarships, degrees, and such gear.' Tennyson's silence was unbroken. He may have reflected that only a Cambridge term had stood between him and the firing party on Malaga esplanade.

EVELYN WAUGH

'Fascist'

Letter in *New Statesman & Nation*, 5 March 1938

Sir,—I am moved to write to you on a subject that has long been in my mind, by an anecdote I have just heard.

A friend of mine met someone who—I am sure, both you and he himself would readily admit—represents the highest strata of 'left-wing' culture. The conversation turned on the 'Mayfair' jewel robbers and the Socialist remarked that they exhibited 'typical Fascist mentality'. This seems to me an abuse of vocabulary so mischievous and so common that it is worth discussing.

There was a time in the early twenties when the word 'Bolshie' was current. It was used indiscriminately of refractory schoolchildren, employees who asked for a rise in wages, impertinent domestic servants, those who advocated an extension of the rights of property to the poor, and anything or anyone of whom the speaker disapproved. The only result was to impede reasonable discussion and clear thought.

I believe we are in danger of a similar, stultifying use of the word 'Fascist'. There was recently a petition sent to English writers (by a committee few, if any, of whom were English professional writers), asking them to subscribe themselves, categorically, as supporters of the Republican Party in Spain, or as 'Fascists'. When rioters are imprisoned it is described as a 'Fascist sentence'; the Means Test is Fascist; colonization is Fascist; military discipline is Fascist; patriotism is Fascist; Catholicism is Fascist; Buchmanism is Fascist; the ancient Japanese cult of their Emperor is Fascist; the Galla tribes' ancient detestation of theirs is Fascist; fox-hunting is Fascist . . . Is it too late to call for order?

It is constantly said by those who observed the growth of Nazism, Fascism and other dictatorial systems (not, perhaps, excluding USSR) that they were engendered and nourished solely by Communism. I do not know how true that is, but I am inclined to believe it when I observe the pitiable stampede of the 'Left-Wing Intellectuals' in our own country. Only once was there anything like a Fascist movement in England; that was in 1926 when the middle class took over the public services; it now does not exist at all except as a form of anti-Semitism in the slums. Those of us who can afford to think without proclaiming ourselves 'intellectuals' do not want or expect a Fascist regime. But there is a highly nervous and highly vocal party who are busy creating a bogy; if they persist in throwing the epithet about it may begin to stick. They may one day find that there *is* a Fascist party which they have provoked. They will, of course, be the chief losers, but it is because I believe we shall all lose by such a development that I am addressing this through your columns.

Evelyn Waugh

ROY CAMPBELL

'Hard Lines, Azaña!'

One of 'Three Poems from Toledo' in *The British Union Quarterly*, January–April 1937

('The British intellectuals are reported to be in sympathy
with the Spanish Government.')

It's not the boys in the Alcazar
Nor Moscardó, the eagle of Castile,
That's going to bring you down (if ever)
And make you come to heel,
But these lugubrious mascots
Who never yet showed up,
Except like dogs to spy out corpses,
Off Failure's flesh to sup.
Azaña, I'm not superstitious,
I've never gambled yet,
But, if I were an augur,
This would decide my bet:
The Sodomites are on your side,
The cowards and the cranks;
The Devil's got you, tortoise-eyed,
And plus-fours zeppelin your shanks.
You'll get the ringworm soon
Around your goitred neck,
Red as the guts of nuns, the gay festoon
With which your bayonets you deck.
It's not the crushing load of guilt
That's going to get you down,
You've got the poison to the hilt

And snails have slimed your crown.
You've got the cowards on your front
But you've got these behind:
They'll bring you down, advance or shunt;
Señor Sandwich, you'll bear the brunt!
For fat though your belly, your Popular 'Front'
Is surely your Fat 'Behind'.

ERNST TOLLER

'Madrid—Washington'

Transcr. broadcast from Madrid to the USA, *New Statesman & Nation*,
8 October 1938

Crossing the Spanish frontier, and coming into the war zone, my mind
was full of memories of the Great War in which I fought as a common
German soldier. I expected to see cities as I had seen them in France: sad
deserted streets, men and women with depressed faces, weighed down
and fearful, streets haunted by the nightmare of war. I came by car from
Perpignan. In the neighbourhood of Barcelona the beaches were full of
bathing, happy people. But a few feet behind the beach I saw houses
destroyed by bombs. The car drove through the outskirts of Barcelona.
People crowded the streets and squares. Posters called from walls. Some
reminded the people to resist the rebels and foreign invaders coolly and
bravely, others invited them to theatres and concerts, films and literary
conferences. Remarkable, I thought. Every war pauses for breath,
perhaps in these few days Barcelona is going through a silent, I might
almost say a peaceful time—otherwise the city would certainly present a
more menacing appearance.

At night, eating the frugal meal in my hotel, I heard the screaming of
sirens, and almost before I had fully realised its significance, the lights
went out. Overtaken by curiosity, I went into the street. The streaming
searchlights swung across the dark sky. If I had not been aware of the
seriousness of the moment, and if I had not experienced that extraordinary sensation which makes the knees feel heavy in moments of threatening danger and at the same time sharpens the senses, making them
hear and see more clearly, I would have enjoyed the immense display of
the lights as an ethereal theatrical show, which served no further purpose
than the building up and then taking down of fiery forms; forms which

now weave themselves into a dome in which every beam is a blue-green arrow, and now part and immediately direct their meteors into the black, unbending distance.

The beams of light cross and stay still. Near me a voice cries out: 'There they are!' Yes, there they are, five aeroplanes imprisoned in the angles of light from twenty Republican searchlights, suddenly grown stiff and frozen. Slowly they fly over the city, shimmering and blinded, puny as children's toys which only in their appearance resemble the murderous weapons of grown-ups. In the sky there hangs a chain of red balls of fire. The air defences fire rockets, the slowly fading balls show them the extent of the distance. A heavy burst of explosions, the Fascists have dropped their first bombs. The Republican anti-aircraft start shooting with a whistling sound and flames forming multiple points, followed by the clear sound of bursting shrapnel. They spring upwards like fireballs and leave floating fans of cloud in the sky. The show lasts ten minutes; then all is silent and dark and over. Over? Forty houses destroyed, twenty-eight men, women and children dead, eighty-four wounded. Military aims? The houses were inhabited by harmless citizens, not manufacturers of munitions. The dead were not soldiers but harmless civilians. Death and life are at close quarters in Spain.

The next day was a Sunday. I had read in the American papers that all the churches were burnt or destroyed, and all religious services were forbidden. I went to a chapel in the Calle de Pines and I attended a crowded Mass. The organ played and a choir sang the old Christian hymns of Catalunya. No police protected the chapel. It did not need to be protected. None dreamt of disturbing the church service. No one dreamt of stopping the believer from going in.

Later I went to the Cathedral, which was only a couple of hundred steps distant; a short time before the so-called defenders of religion had bombed and destroyed the marvellous door of the West Entrance.

Only few people realise that three thousand Catholic priests live undisturbed in Barcelona; that every week two thousand Masses are read in private houses. The Republican Government is prepared to allow the reopening of the churches; the opposition comes from high functionaries of the Church, who are opposed to this not on religious, but political, grounds.

The most striking experience a foreigner has in Barcelona is that of the functioning of democracy. In Fascist States all the relations of men are ruled by fear, the fear of thinking freely, speaking freely, writing freely. Republican Spain is free from fear. You may be Catholic or Protestant, Democrat or Socialist, member of the free trade unions, or revolutionary

Syndicalist, Communist or Liberal; you are free to express your convictions. Yet none of these groups, as I discovered, is anxious to pursue now its particular aims. All co-operate in a wise narrowness, in word and deed, for one aim—for freedom and independence of Spain, for the protection and salvation of the fundamentals which alone make possible life and work worthy of humanity.

One has to repeat it and repeat it again: It is a lie that the fight is going on between Communism and Fascism. The Spanish Prime Minister, Juan Negrin, in his programmatory speech, called The Thirteen Points, declared that private property is protected in Spain. The Government is fighting rightly against exploitation of human life, and did just the same things that President Roosevelt strives to do: free the country from the power of economic Royalists. Otherwise you may do what you like. You may own a shop, a department store. You may own a textile factory or a jeweller's. Nobody will interfere with your work.

It is more admirable to see how everybody is protected when one thinks of the difficult conditions under which Spain is fighting. The legitimate Government has an international right to defend itself against a clique of rebels who called German Nazis, Italian Fascists and Mohammedan Moors to fight the war against the Spanish people for them. To say it frankly, the democracies have let down Spain.

One might expect that men who have been outlawed would lose altogether all sense of justice and sneer at an international law which they have seen revealed as phrases and hypocrisy just at the moment when it should be put into practice. Nothing of the sort. Allow me to give you an example.

I have seen with my own eyes the humane treatment of war prisoners, of Nazi pilots and Italian Fascist flyers who have killed dozens of children, dozens of women. I have seen that these prisoners got the same food as the regular soldiers of the Spanish army, far better food than the civilian population. I talked to them for hours. Everybody pretended to have come voluntarily to Franco's aid; even officers of the regular German army—presumably as deserters!

I have not time enough to tell you the details of these discussions, but one sentence I want to tell you, which a lieutenant of the German army, Lieutenant Kurt Kenner from Schwiebus, Province Brandenburg, told me: 'We in the German army,' he said, 'consider the war in Spain as a preparation for and a preventive war against France.' May this be a warning to all concerned!

I referred to the food situation of the civil population. Their sacrifices are as heroic as the fight of the soldiers. They are living under the minimum of existence which a man needs. Meat and milk and eggs, fruit and fresh vegetables are unknown to them for weeks on end.

But do not believe that this lack of food will break their resistance. No power in the world will break this will to win. Let me tell you the words of a young woman whom I met, a worker in a munition factory. She said to me: 'My stomach is sore with hunger, but it does not matter. One day we shall triumph. There will be time enough to fill the stomach.'

I ask you, my friends in America, living witnesses of a war which is fought not only for Spain, but for all democracy: Have we the right to be deaf and blind? Have we not the responsibility which obliges us to help them? Private committees in all democratic countries are doing marvellous work. But the time has come when something more extensive has to be done. When famine reigned in Russia in 1921, a great man, Fritjof Nansen, organised an international work of assistance. When the German people suffered after the Great War, it was the American administration which spent millions of dollars and authorised Mr Hoover to send food to Germany.

The United States is to-day led by a man whom the whole world respects as one of the greatest democrats of our time, Franklin Roosevelt. May I be allowed from this broadcasting station in Madrid, a few hundred feet from the front-line trenches, hearing as I speak the roar of bursting grenades and shells, which will kill now sleeping civilians, may I be allowed to appeal to you, Mr President, with deep deference and profound respect, to take the initiative for a national or international government action to help the civil population of Spain?

What right have I to appeal to you? The right of a human being who has seen the misery of war, who has watched in three weeks seventeen bombings, who has seen in ruined houses and in the morgue the bodies of murdered children who a few hours before were playing and laughing and hoping that the future would bring them that which all of us have a right to expect: 'Life, Liberty and the Pursuit of Happiness.'

ERNST TOLLER

[Mr Toller's appeal has been followed up by a campaign in America and Europe to obtain food for Spain. It is suggested that governments should be asked to donate and distribute supplies in the manner that world war relief was administered by ex-President Herbert Hoover. The appeal would cover the needs of civilians on both sides of the battle lines. Distribution would be made either by representatives of neutral Governments or by Quaker organisations in co-operation with the Spanish Committees.—Ed. *N.S. & N.*]

W. E. JOHNS

Seeing Spain Slaughtered

from 'The Editor's Cockpit', *Popular Flying*, March 1939

I had hoped this month to be able to give you some reliable information as to what has been done, and what we are doing, to prevent a repetition of the shaking up the Dictators gave us last September; but I am afraid that it can't be done. One hears so many tales, and the air is more pregnant with rumour than ever it was during the war. That some of these rumours are said to be started deliberately in official quarters only makes matters more confusing. One day I hear glowing reports of rising production figures, and the next, tales of such ghastly inefficiency that I wonder seriously if a democratic government can long survive in the face of totalitarian thoroughness.

I use the word democratic with hesitation, for I have an increasing suspicion that our so-called democracy is nothing like as democratic as it pretends to be. If it was—to take only one example—could it stand by unmoved and watch the cold-blooded murder of its friend in democracy —Spain? For do not be misled. The Spanish Government—by which I mean Republican Spain—is as democratic as a government can be. It was elected by the vote of the people. That it was a Left Wing government makes not the slightest difference. It was the will of the people, and the soul of democracy lies in the simple fact that the people are always right. But our government, being Right Wing, does not hold that view. So it prefers to see Spain slaughtered by its own sworn enemies rather than lift a finger to save it. There you have the truth of the affair.

This is not a matter of politics. I have no politics myself because I believe that party politics belong to the past. It is a matter of right and wrong. I am concerned only with our own preservation, and in the end only truth and justice can survive. If that is not so then our entire scheme of things, including religion, is awry.

Of all the foul and craven hypocrisy of which those in power in Britain have been guilty during the last decade—and nowhere in history will you find such a sequence of faint-hearted perfidiousness—this Spanish business is the worst. Regarding it to-day I can find only one crumb of comfort. We can sink no lower. We have touched the very bottom of the slough of baseness into which the short-sightedness and personal ambitions of our leaders have thrown us. For evermore, every Spaniard who survives the massacre, be he Franconian or Republican, will spit at the very name of England. And well he might. I could myself spit at this farce, this lie called non-intervention. What infamy! What does our Government of governesses think we are? A nation of fools? If this is the wages of democracy then let us for God's sake change our tune and be Fascist—Bolshevist—anything as long as we can be men again, instead of the mob of bleating sheep that the Government would have us be. What a different story it will be when we are getting what Barcelona is getting now.

Nothing we may do in the future will atone for the wrongs we have done since a parcel of imbeciles, or knaves (I don't know which), drew the Lion's teeth. When all the mediocrity and minor issues of this era have dropped away, and the events of to-day have become history, rising high out of the slime will be the brazen pyramids of Perfidious Albion. And their colour will be yellow. Have no doubt of that.

But forgive this long digression. As my pen formed the word Spain it became suddenly overheated and ran away with me. I trust that at least some of you will understand. Or shall I explain? You see, a man I knew had just thrown away his life in Spain, fighting for that most hopeless of all causes—Freedom. It was not his quarrel. He had nothing to gain and everything to lose by going. Yet he went. This was courage such as I do not possess.

What is there so irresistible to some men about this simple word that is at once both a prayer and a war-cry? Freedom! More people than are alive on earth to-day have died with it on their lips. Countless parents have been bereaved, countless wives widowed, and countless children orphaned, that somebody, somewhere, may be free. Who? They seldom stop to ask themselves that question, or they would see what one day all the people of the world will see—that the word is but the goad of the unscrupulous who use it to serve their purpose and ambitions. When that time comes, and not before, will suffering mankind achieve some kind of freedom; to live and die as Nature intended men should live and die. Pah! Let us not talk about it.

STEPHEN SPENDER

Poems for Spain

Introduction to *Poems for Spain*, ed. Stephen Spender & John Lehmann, 1939

This collection of poems about the Spanish War, written and translated by English writers, is a document of our times.

We do not claim that these are the best poems written in English during the past two and a half years; but we do claim that any anthology selected purely for merit would be bound to overlap with the poems printed here.

The fact that these poems should have been written at all has a literary significance parallel to the existence of the International Brigade. For some of these poems, and many more which we have not been able to publish, were written by men for whom poetry scarcely existed before the Spanish War. Some of these writers, first awakened to poetry by Spain, died before they had the opportunity to cultivate their talent.

Poets and poetry have played a considerable part in the Spanish War, because to many people the struggle of the Republicans has seemed a struggle for the conditions without which the writing and reading of poetry are almost impossible in modern society:

> To-morrow for the young poets exploding like bombs,
> The walks by the lake, the weeks of perfect communion . . .
> But to-day the struggle.

Primarily, this struggle consists in taking action to obtain freedom, education, leisure. Whilst the struggle is going on, there is little time for the maturing of poetry in minds which are violent and unsettled. But nevertheless, the poets do 'explode like bombs,' and the struggle does provide inspiration. To quote Auden again:

> Madrid is the heart. Our moments of tenderness blossom
> As the ambulance and the sandbag;
> Our hours of friendship into a people's army.

Moreover, where the issues are so clear and direct in a world which has accustomed us to confusion and obscurity, action itself may seem to be a kind of poetry to those who take part in it. Therefore these poems often seem like hasty transcriptions into words of an experience expressed not in words at all, but in deeds. 'All a poet can do to-day is to warn,' the greatest of the English war poets, Wilfrid Owen, wrote in 1918. That is true always of poetry written in the midst of a great social upheaval; but the poets of the International Brigade have a different warning to give from that of the best poets of the Great War. It is a warning that it is necessary for civilization to defend and renew itself. As Hernandez writes:

> Singing I defend myself
> and I defend my people when the barbarians of crime
> imprint on my people their hooves
> of powder and desolation.

No one can read the poems of Alberti, Cornford, Hernandez, Wintringham, without realizing that these poets and fighters are fighting not out of love for war, but because they are defending a life and culture which they see threatened. Unless they both fight and write, they seem to say, there will be a future in which they are spiritually dead. Again, Hernandez:

> A future of dust advances,
> a fate advances
> in which nothing will remain;
> nor stone on stone nor bone on bone.

They have chosen death rather than that 'future of dust'.

To these writers, the Spanish War is, in the words which Keats used of Peterloo: 'No contest between Whig and Tory—but between Right and Wrong.'

The long, crushing, and confused process of defeat, which the democratic principle has been undergoing, has been challenged in Spain, and this challenge has aroused hope all over the world. That hope has expressed itself not only in English poetry, but in poems of many languages, particularly German, French and Italian. In a world where poetry seems to have been abandoned, become the exalted medium of a few specialists, or the superstition of backward peoples, this awakening of a sense of the richness of a to-morrow *with* poetry, is as remarkable as the struggle for liberty itself, and is more remarkable than the actual achievement. The conditions for a great popular poetry are not yet obtained; what we note is the desire for such a poetry.

Spain does not only symbolize what André Malraux has so magnificently interpreted in all its implications in his novel *The Hope of A People*—hope—it also symbolizes tragedy. At Guernica, at Irun, wherever the Republic has sustained defeat, its cause represents pure tragedy, because these defeats are the real and entire destruction of a life and a principle by the death-bearing force that opposes them. In the rest of Europe one sees principles confused, betrayed, compromised: but in

Spain the idea clothed in flesh and blood is continually being destroyed, and therefore as continually and as purely reborn in the mind of a world which remains a spectator.

Whenever History provides such a heroic and tragic spectacle, it has been the subject of poetry. The poets of the English Liberal tradition responded to Spain crushed by Napoleon as they do to contemporary Spain crushed by Fascism. Here is Wordsworth's sonnet entitled 'Indignation of a High-minded Spaniard':

> We can endure that He should waste our lands,
> Despoil our temples, and by sword and flame
> Return us to the dust from which we came;
> Such food a Tyrant's appetite demands:
> And we can brook the thought that by his hands
> Spain may be overpowered, and he possess,
> For his delight, a solemn wilderness,
> Where all the brave lie dead. But, when of bands,
> Which he will break for us, he dares to speak,
> Of benefits, and of a future day
> When our enlightened minds shall bless his sway;
> *Then*, the strained heart of fortitude proves weak;
> Our groans, our blushes, our pale cheeks declare
> That he has power to inflict what we lack strength to bear.

The ideas that inspire such poetry are fundamental, political and moral ideas of liberty, justice, freedom, etc. Usually policy, although it is continually invoking these ideas—which are only kept alive and separate from their prostitution to public interests by the poets—is entirely removed from them. But occasionally, in a revolution, a national resurgence, a war against an aggressor, there is a revival of the fundamental ideas and there is actually an identity of the ideas of public policy and poetry. This is the sense in which poetry is political; it is always concerned with the fundamental ideas, either because they are being realized in action, or, satirically, to show that they are totally removed from public policy. In the one case, we get a poem like Auden's 'Spain' discovering the poetry in the Spanish Republican Cause; in the other case, satire, like Edgell Rickword's on Non-Intervention, in which the fundamental ideas are turned against the politicians, in order to expose an imposture and a sham. Edgell Rickword is here concerned with politics in a far profounder sense than the members of the Non-Intervention Committee, who are concerned with faking politics in order to cover up a deal.

The action of the Republicans is therefore the subject of poetry because the Spanish Republican Leaders act with an awareness of men's psychological needs, an understanding of the fundamental nature of political ideas, which is a subject worthy of poetry. They realize in their actions a thought which Cecil Day Lewis expresses in his poem 'The Nabara', which, unfortunately, we could not arrange to include:

> Freedom was more than a word, more than the base coinage
> Of politicians who hiding behind the skirts of peace
> They had defiled, gave up that country to rack and carnage;
> For whom, indelibly stamped with history's contempt,
> Remains but to haunt the blackened shell of their policies.

Auden's 'Spain' is in the tradition of Wordsworth's Sonnets on Spain. It translates a political action into terms of the imagination and thus tests the implications of a particular, contemporary situation by the whole tradition of values which exists in poetry. If there were, in a good sense, academic poetry, this poem with its finely conscious summary of the significance of the Spanish war to spectators *outside* Spain, might be called academic. In order to achieve his effect, it stands at a certain distance from the actualities of the war; Auden has, as it happens, been to Spain, but this is irrelevant to his poem in a way in which it is not irrelevant to the poems of Cornford and Wintringham.

For the essential quality of other poems here is that they are written from *inside* Spain; they have the merits and defects of being extremely close to experience. Of the fighters here, John Cornford was killed, the day after his 21st birthday. Charles Donnelly was also killed; Tom Wintringham, who was Political Commissar in the Brigade, was wounded at Jarama. In spite of his youth and his preoccupation with the life of political action, Cornford's few poems have remarkable and insistent qualities which may indicate one of the directions in which an orthodox communist poetry might develop. His problem is to attain just this orthodoxy, to express in poetry the unity of thought and action, to translate necessity into terms of the poetic imagination. Most contemporary literature seems to be written from the sensibility, Cornford's poems seem to be written by the will:

> No abstraction of the brain
> Will counteract the animal pain.
> The living thought must put on flesh and blood.
> Action intervenes, revealing
> New ways of love, new ways of feeling,
> Gives nerve and bone and muscle to the word.

The problem of achieving orthodoxy also preoccupied mystics; it is expressed at its finest and rarest in the poems of St John of the Cross. This is to suggest no comparison between the poems of the Spanish saint and Cornford, but merely that the real originality of Cornford's work lies in its seeming to be at the beginning of a road which leads to a far greater purification of expression than, at so early a stage, he was able to attain. In the poems of Tom Wintringham, Margot Heinemann, H. B. Mallalieu, the same necessity is felt, but yet, as these lines of Mallalieu's witness, there is less intensity, less vision:

> Let sanity have strength and men unite
> Who in their individual hearts are glad
> That what remains of peace may yet prove strong.
> We have the will, then let us show the might,
> Who have forborne and pitied far too long.

Wintringham's poems are not just weaker expressions of Cornford's mood, they are direct transcriptions of the actual experiences of the war. What Cornford calls the 'animal pain,' which cannot be countered with an abstraction, Wintringham re-creates for us:

> Minutes are told by the jerked wound,
> By the pain's throb, fear of pain, sin
> Of giving in,
> And the unending hardness of the pillow.

The anonymous author of 'Eyes,' T. A. R. Hyndman, J. Lepper also convey their immediate experiences. Charles Donnelly achieves a greater detachment in 'The Tolerance of Crows':

> And with flesh falls apart the mind
> That trails thought from the mind that cuts
> Thought clearly for a waiting purpose.

The poems of Sylvia Townsend Warner, and Stephen Spender give us another immediate impression of Spain; that of members of some of the many delegations who have visited the country since the War. Whilst Louis MacNeice's long section from a longer poem is the confession of a tourist who visited Spain shortly before the war, seeing what a tourist sees, and who since then has discovered that Spain has a quite different significance for him.

The Spanish poets, with few exceptions, have supported the Republic, because they defend the spoken Castilian and Catalan and Basque word against the unified centralized speech or against the foreign tongue; they defend their own lives whose fate under Fascism is foretold in the murder of Garcia Lorca; they defend a government which makes the exercise of their tradition of a popular romantic Spanish poetry possible; they are prepared, for the time being, to merge the life of literature in the life of action in order that, afterwards, they may continue to write poetry.

WRITERS' CONGRESS

STEPHEN SPENDER

'Spain Invites the World's Writers'

(Notes on the International Congress, Summer 1937)
from *New Writing*, Autumn 1937

From the moment of our arrival in Spain, our congress was over-shadowed by the wonderful country, the Spanish people and the civil war. Port Bou itself makes the strangest impression—a town in which the people are particularly friendly, in which a third of the population seems to be occupied in military training in the hills, a third bathing and sun-bathing in the harbour, while the rest sit at cafés or stand about, impressing us with that peculiar feeling of a war, that the people are not so much living in the town as haunting it; they are spirits obsessed by their idea, easily transferable to some other scene of war; and their relation to their homes, their material surroundings, is very slight. I have been at Port Bou three or four times during the past few months, so this was not new to me, but I was very conscious of its effect on the South American delegates. We were shown parts of the town which have been destroyed in the course of several unsuccessful attempts to bomb the station. The South Americans were upset, and their usual gaiety seemed rebuffed. They noticed with a certain anguish the thing that is *amusing* about bombardments: the single piece of furniture left quite undisturbed at the edge of a room which has been cut down, as though by a knife. But all this time we were preoccupied by two other things which are Spanish; the heat, and the monumental delay in the preparations for our midday meal.

After that excellent meal, we set out in a fleet of cars along the beautiful mountainous coastal road to Valencia. The English delegation were given a Rolls Royce and a chauffeur whose one idea of driving was to 'show her paces.' The wheels screamed round corners, he never 'changed down' up hills. For the purposes of the war, one of the most serious defects of the Spanish character is this reckless mishandling of machinery. In the early months of the war the banks of the Valencia —Madrid road were littered with wrecked motor-cars. Even now in the course of our journeys, we saw a great many wrecks on the sides of roads, and so much dangerous driving that I wondered there were not many more.

By the time we reached Gerona I was on back-slapping, embracing terms with most of the Spanish-American delegates—magnificent, bronzed, emotional speakers, most of them. André Malraux seemed slightly disappointed with the Mexican delegates: he said that our massively built, jet-eyed, warm colleagues—impressive for their immediate responsiveness and their directness of manner—were mere university professors compared with what Mexico could provide. Mexican poets should be utterly mad; they should be dressed like cowboys, carry hide whips and fire off revolvers from each hand.

We reached Barcelona at eight or nine in the evening. We were received by the Minister of Propaganda who asked us whether we wished to stay the night in Barcelona. Sylvia Townsend Warner, who was dead tired, amused us all by saying, on behalf of the English, 'Of course we are quite willing to go on, but I think that out of consideration for this Mexican comrade,' dragging one of the Mexicans forward, 'who has been travelling for ten days, we *ought* perhaps to stay the night.'

We were entertained by the Catalan Government at the Majestic, the best hotel in Barcelona. Next morning, we got up at six and waited for the usual two or three hours, before starting for Valencia. We were no longer in the Rolls Royce, as that had belonged to the Catalans, and the new fleet of cars was from Valencia. I travelled with Malraux and Aveline. During the Congress, Malraux, with his youthful appearance, his close-set greenish eyes, pale looming face, with one lock of hair overhanging his forehead, his hands in the pockets of his rough tweed suit, his rather slouching walk, and at intervals his long nervous sniff, had the air of being a senior, if not altogether respectable boy. But for me he was and is a hero, and I think of him with emotion. We talked a good deal during the journey to Valencia. I believe that for Malraux the creation of his own legend—his political activities, the 'Malraux squadron'—fulfils a spiritual need which is essential for him as an artist. The writer must create from a centre which is his environment: and it sometimes happens (it has happened repeatedly with bourgeois writers during this generation —and that indeed is the root of the interest of so many contemporary writers in politics) that the writer does not fit into his environment. He is then driven to discover some other environment, or, if he is intensely individualist, to create his environment: first to create his environment, and then to create literature from the centre of his environment, from the centre of his own legend. That is the task of a T. E. Lawrence or an André Malraux. For the environment of André Malraux is the life of action. 'If you ask me what it is necessary to do, *il faut agir*—it is necessary to act.'

I remember one conversation in which we discussed politics and poetry, when he emphasized the influence of environment on the poet's vocabulary. Set the poet in simple surroundings of the earth, the ox, the woman and the mountain, and the imagery suggested by this environment will recur in his poetry. To the modern poet who does not accept the bourgeois environment and the bourgeois ideology, a problem exists which is not merely one of style but a problem of will. He must deliberately change his environment.

When we reached Valencia, on the 5th, we were immediately taken to a session of the Congress, where we met Ralph Bates, whom we elected leader of the English delegation for as long as we were in Spain. The session was held in a council chamber of the bombed town hall. All except this wing of the building had been gutted out, and the marble stairs leading to our meeting place had been filled with concrete where the marble was destroyed, like the fillings of teeth. In the Congress it was exceedingly hot, and made still hotter by the blaze of lights for the cinematographer. Ralph Bates spoke in Castilian, welcoming us. He was in a very dynamic mood and hammered a lot with his fist. He had been inspired by a speech made by Del Vayo that morning, which we missed. Del Vayo was there with his broad, red intelligent face, amiable and gleaming as always. Alexei Tolstoi made a speech attacking Trotsky. Tolstoi is a robust clever immensely prosperous man who yet does not seem to belong to the new order. Whenever I saw him he was perspiring profusely, and perhaps for that reason, I have an image of him in flannels and a silk shirt, handkerchief in hand, panting strenuously at the end of a successful race to keep up with the time. José Bergamín made one of his paradoxical, careful and sincere speeches; as president of the Congress he was its most popular member. With his slight, beautiful face, one always listens to him because he never intrudes, one always watches him because he seems almost invisible.

That evening I saw a performance of a play by Lorca and got to bed, as usual, very late. We were woken up at 4 a.m. by the air-raid alarms, and the pale morning sky was shot across with the red stains of anti-aircraft shrapnel, the guns making a rather hollow pleasant popping noise like the drawing of corks. Frank Tinsley, Reuter's correspondent, who had very kindly put me up in his room of the Hotel Victoria said that we ought to get dressed and go downstairs. There I met Fernsworth, *The Times* correspondent, who is afraid neither of bombs nor shrapnel, and invited me to walk down to the hospital opposite the British Embassy with him to see if we could gain any news of the seriousness of the raid. We went, but there was no news. The only danger we ran was from the anti-aircraft shrapnel, which has to come down somewhere.

At ten o'clock our caravan of cars left Valencia for Madrid. By this time most of us were very exhausted. In Spain I have found myself getting so exhausted that my tiredness has taken an entirely different form from the routine tiredness I often feel at home. One can, I think, become so fatigued that one is actually more receptive than normally—because fatigue breaks one's ordinary habits of resistance down. For example, I am shockingly bad at listening to public speeches. But, in Spain, at the Congress, I have at times had the experience, when excessively tired, of understanding every word that was said, even of difficult speeches in French, German and Spanish: where ordinarily the fact that the speech was in a foreign language would have persuaded me that I could not understand it, and thus set up my machinery of resistance.

I mention this because anyone who has been in a war—or even at the edge of it—will realize how important an element fatigue is in war psychology.

On our way to Madrid we stopped for lunch at a village called Minganilla—memorable to every delegate of the Congress. It was a very hot, dazzling day, I remember walking up a straggling, dusty village street, with charming children and peasant women picturesquely dressed, whom Alexei Tolstoi photographed, with their donkeys. We drank lemonade in a guest-house, whilst we waited for our meal to be prepared. After two hours—or so it seemed—of waiting and talking we were told that lunch was ready and we adjourned to the long, low, first-storey room of the Fonda, where we sat down at long tables, to eat omelettes and flat, white hunks of Spanish bread, followed by slabs of raw bacon. Whilst we were eating we were interrupted by the singing of all the children of the village outside our windows. First they sang the International, then they sang other songs, of the Spanish Republic. We got up and stood at the windows to thank and applaud them. When we had finished eating we went down the stone steps of the Fonda where the children had cleared a little space in their crowd in the square and they were dancing a dance which consisted of running up and down from one end of this oblong space to the other. There were no men in the village—they were all either in the fields or fighting—and the women stood watching their children dance, suddenly weeping. When we went into the square to get back into our cars, the women began talking to us about the war and they asked that one of us should speak from the balcony of the Fonda in order to show that we understood their fate (these were their words). One of the Mexicans spoke, very effectively. After that one of the women took Pablo Neruda and me back to her house, which was beautifully clean, and showed us photographs of her two sons at the front, and, in spite of our earnest protestations, insisted on our taking about half of all the sausages she had, because we would be hungry on the rest of the journey. We were all of us more moved by our few hours in Minganilla than by any other single incident of our stay in Spain.

A happy evening after dinner in the Hotel Victoria at Madrid, with the Spanish singing Flamenco songs, clapping their hands rhythmically. They sang the traditional tunes for which the modern poets have written new words about the Civil War. Rafael Alberti sang a ballad which he had written about Franco. Later the growing din was interrupted by Alberti, a massive, leonine figure, dressed in blue dungarees, with fine hair and magnificent sculptural features, leaping on to a chair and shouting with passionate fury to everyone to be quiet. Then he told us that a bombardment had started. Frank Pitcairn, Rickword, René Blech and I walked to the Puerta del Sol and watched the upper storeys of the Ministry of the Interior blazing, where they had been struck by an incendiary shell. René Blech walked out into the centre of the square looked up, came back and shrugged his shoulders with the one word '*ignoble*'. Then we returned to the hotel.

The impression made by Madrid to-day is sublime; the great, tall ugly town, whole quarters of which are silenced and destroyed, yet through which the stream of life still flows quite normally; Madrid with its blue summer sky torn open by the sound of aeroplanes machine-gunning, as they battle above the streets whilst the people stand in their doors, at windows and in the open street, watching; Madrid drummed all day by the roar of artillery from the city fronts, and sullenly illuminated at night by the red glow where incendiary shells have struck; above all, the city defended by the people who have already begun to live there the life of communal ownership which will be their future if they win the war. In this environment the endless stream of our oratory continued to flow, rather ineffectively.

What we said in public was of little interest, besides which it has been published elsewhere, and for that reason I have thought it worth while to record some of the things which were said in private and which were, in fact, attempts to discuss problems which the Congress should have discussed. There was André Chamson, pale and furious with the Congress because we had stayed longer than three hours in Madrid, and because, having stayed there, all the delegates didn't feel as he did about it. *'Le devoir d'un écrivain est d'être tourmenté'*—and none of us was tormented. *'Moi, moi je suis responsable.'* One of us would get killed by a Franco 'obus' and then the World Press would shriek that the Reds had assassinated him—and Chamson, as secretary of the French Association, would bear the responsibility. Every morning I would go up to Chamson to inquire how he was and he would reply, *'Mal, mal, MAL!'* He would go on to say that the intellectual level of our Congress was appallingly low, that we were light-hearted, irresponsible, we did not *feel*. I quote all this, not out of malice, but because I think that in a way he was right. Along paths which I can scarcely follow, Chamson had arrived at a truth which few of the Congress—fêted, banqueted, received enthusiastically, the women bridling with excitement at Ralph Bates's or Ludwig Renn's uniform—had even glimpsed, that the war is terrible, that the mind of Madrid, if it is sublime, like Shakespeare's, is also terrible, like Shakespeare's. I myself had learnt this through painful experiences some months before, not at the Congress. I applaud Chamson.

From reading the Romances of the Civil War by Spanish poets, one might conclude that the whole of Spanish poetry on the Government side has adopted an uncritical, heroic attitude towards the war. Yet this is not so. I myself, because I am not a writer of heroics, have felt rather isolated for the cause and the people I greatly care for, because I could not share this uncritical attitude, but when I spoke to Alberti, Altolaguirre and Bergamín, I found that they felt about the propagandist heroics of the war much as I did myself. Alberti, a brilliant, arrogant, passionate individualist, is himself rather isolated, I feel. He is in a peculiar position as the recognized successor to Lorca, who yet is not a great influence on other contemporary Spanish poets.

On July 13th, we sat once more in the little port of Cerbère, very tired after a banquet in Barcelona and a terrific day of sight-seeing. A few of us had crossed the frontier before the other delegates, and I found myself next to Bergamín. We began talking about the poetry of the Spanish war, about Gide, about some personal tragedies occasioned by the war, about Bergamín's own family, about the assassination of Ramòn Sender's wife by the fascists. Bergamín has a paradoxical involved mind which at times surprises one by its whimsicality not unlike E. M. Forster's, but, also like E. M. Forster's, surprises one even more by its combination of paradox with penetrating honesty and a concrete unevasive grasp of every problem. Bergamín knows what the tragedy and horror of war are: he knows also the lies which war produces, and yet his mind seems to penetrate through all these obstructions to a position where he is absolutely secure, where he accepts the tragedy and horror, relates the lies to the forces which render them inevitable. In a word, he was the only member of our Congress who was entitled to rebuke Gide, because he does not resent that which is honest in Gide (as far too many of his detractors seem to do), but because he, Bergamín, has a mind of even greater honesty, a mind which sees not merely the truth of isolated facts which Gide observed in the USSR, but the far more important truth of the *effect* which Gide's book is going to have.

During this conversation, one question troubled me—Bergamín's Catholicism. At last I dared to ask him: 'Are you still a Catholic?' He held up his hand, placing together the index finger and the thumb, thus forming a small circle, and said in his thin, nasal French: 'If you ask me do I believe in the articles of Faith, I say, yes, yes, yes, I accept all of that. But if you ask me do I believe that the Church has the right to interfere in the political life of the people and to represent the interests of one possessing class, I say no, not at all. Indeed, I go further than that. I say the Church should have no influence in public affairs at all. I even say that there should be no public ceremonies and demonstrations which the Church is able to use for religious propaganda, there should be no system of religious education, the end of which is to make men and women good members of the Church. Religion is a question for the private conscience of the individual and for that only. Now, I am writing a book in which I state my own position, and I cannot doubt but that this book may be placed on the Index. Good. In that case, I confidently make my appeal not to the Pope, but to an authority greater than the Pope's on the day of Judgement. In doing this, I maintain that I stand within the great tradition of Spanish Catholicism. I am fighting for the spiritual life and the spiritual freedom of Catholic Spain. But, unfortunately, the Church has used its power to support propertied interests, to represent materialism and to oppose the spiritual growth of our people.'

It has been said that a revolution corresponding at once to the French and the Russian revolutions is taking place in Spain. But there is yet another great change taking place: it is Spanish Protestantism and the Spanish Reformation.

SYLVIA TOWNSEND WARNER
'What the Soldier Said'

from *Time & Tide*, 14 August 1937

'In the name of the soldiers of the Sixth Army Corps, I am come to say a few words to you. We are defending the legitimate cause of the Republic, and the cause of justice. We will defend them with courage and with all the strength that is in us. Now we, the Sixth Army Corps, say this to you. We fight in defence of justice and culture. We will fetch peace and culture at the point of the bayonet for the sake of our own happiness and that of our children. That's all. Greeting, comrades.'

It was July, 1937. The International Association of Writers in Defence of Culture was holding its second congress. War had not, as we feared it might, deflected our intention of holding that Congress in Spain. The Spanish Government had confirmed the original invitation of the Spanish members of the Association. War had not affected, either, the arrangements for that congress. We held our sessions in Madrid; it was in Madrid that the delegate soldier from the Sixth Army Corps made us his speech. His was not the only military voice to be raised at our congress. Many of the writers in defence of culture who took part in our sessions came to us on special leave, fighters in the defence of culture as well as writers: Ludwig Renn, Jef Last, Ralph Bates, were among these. And through all the various languages of the delegates from twenty-six countries sounded the international language of cannon; for we sat discussing questions of culture and humanism within earshot of the battle.

'What the soldier said is not evidence.' This dictum is by now almost an axiom of British thinking. Even in the improbable event of a private soldier of the British Army addressing a congress of writers, it seems unlikely that his speech would be received as evidence. His interest in culture must be felt as one of two things: a private idiosyncrasy of extraordinary force, or an indication that the War Office had issued orders that at such and such a moment interest in culture should be manifested.

The hypothetical soldier in the British Army should, ideally, be better equipped for interest in culture than the Spanish soldier who addressed us. He would have learned, at any rate, how to read and write, whereas it is quite possible that our Spanish soldier had learned neither of these arts, or was but just now learning them, in the schools staffed by the

Cultural Militia of Spain—an organization of the lettered classes whose duty it is to teach the fighting men, in the barracks, and in the actual trenches.

But we could feel no doubt but that what the Spanish soldier said was evidence. His speech, as you see, expressed no subtlcty of thoughts, no yearning for culture; it expressed a more solid appreciation than yearning, an intention to have and to hold. And what the soldier said to us was borne out by a hundred speeches we heard in Spain.

One of the long discontents of Spain has been its illiteracy. The Spaniard has a natural appreciation of culture; this shows itself in a hundred manifestations, in the decoration of a wayside inn, in the turning of a phrase, the lingual consciousness of those who use dialect (a cook in Barcelona said to me, 'This is our Catalan word. In Castile you must say *manzana*'), in the common people's appreciation, passionate and passionately critical, of points of style in such things as the singer's coloratura or the gestures of the bullring. Even such affairs as the arrangements of wares on market stalls are stylized: a novel juxtaposition of fruits will call out interested comment and discussion.

But these people who have preserved a traditional culture and preserved it alive and kicking, have been in great number denied any education. In the streets one hears the clacking of typewriters, and the clacking comes from the public letter-writers' booths, where men and women whose faces bear the unmistakable imprint of intellect and thought wait in a queue to dictate the letters they are not able to write for themselves.

The Government of 1936 came into office pledged to carry out a programme of education. In spite of the war, this programme is being steadily carried out. New schools have been built and are a-building, every month the Cultural Militia render their figures of the numbers of soldiers who have passed from being analphabetics to being literates (the figure for May 1937, was over 4,000). Other war-time Governments might have hesitated to offer hospitality to eighty literary delegates, people who would consume food and petrol and accommodation and care. Going from Barcelona to Valencia, from Valencia to Madrid, we had no doubt that this hospitality of the Government of Spain was the hospitality of the people of Spain also. Hotel-workers, shopkeepers, people in villages, harvesters in the fields, welcomed us, not as curiosities, not even as possible propagandists, but as representatives of something they valued and understood. To us, the British delegates, this unfeigned and natural welcome was a particularly interesting experience. We learned to hear ourselves spoken of as *los intelectuales* without dreading words usually so dubious in good intent, without feeling the usual embarrassment and defiant shrinking. We were released from the old fear that by giving one's support as a representative of culture to a cause one had at heart one might be doing that cause more harm than good.

The experience was the more impressive in contrast to a recent experience in our own country.

For we had applied for permits to travel to Spain as delegates to the second congress of our Association, and had been refused them. With patience and firm serenity an official of the Foreign Office had assured us that there was no political bias underlying this refusal; it was merely that as representatives of culture we were not included in the Foreign Office's *Weltanschauung*, cultural reasons are not among those reasons recognized as valid reasons for wishing to travel to Spain. If you go (so he explained) as an accredited journalist, yes. If you go on a humanitarian errand, yes. If you go as a man of business, YES! But if you go for purposes of culture, no.

JEF LAST

Noble Pages in History's Book

from *The Spanish Tragedy*, 1939, transl. David Hadett

The bomb-shattered hall of the town council of Valencia. The meeting was opened by Negrin, the Prime Minister, who withdrew immediately afterwards, and grey-haired Anderson-Nexö took the chair. In letters of gold the names of our honoured dead stood out in the hall: Garcia Lorca, Valle Inclan, Ralph Fox, General Luckasz . . .

Our comrades Prados and Regler were lying gravely wounded in hospital. Many of those present were front-line soldiers—Malraux, Renn, Bates, Uhse, Kantorovich, Alberti, Paraguas, Duran. Cordoba Uturburi had been travelling from front to front, inspiring the soldiers to courage; in the thick of the war Josephine Herbst and John dos Passos had visited Madrid in danger; Koestler had been arrested at Malaga.

And now they were here, while only that morning the sirens gave warning of yet another air raid: Dr Brouwer, Jean Richard Bloch, Leon Felipe, Champsom, Ehrenburg, Kisch, Nordahl Grieg, Anna Seghers, Huidobro; writers from Spain, China, Chile, Iceland, France, Germany,

England, Holland. In the background, sitting beside the austere Marchwitza, I caught sight of the smiling faces of Karl Bredel and Erich Weinert, who had come to join the International Brigade when the congress was over.

Whoever considers this list of names will realize that not a single bourgeois journalist would be likely to report upon this congress for his newspaper. But it is not difficult to imagine the cry of jubilation that would go up if a single scientist of the calibre of Hodan, a single humanist of Bergamín's distinction, could be reported on the side of Franco! Indeed, it may be asked how there could be such names in the ranks of those who stupidly shot down even the tender García Lorca, and who flash out their Browning when the word culture is so much as mentioned.

Literature is not to be made with lies, and no Fascist writer would venture to tell the truth on the subject of the prisoners of Malaga or the voluntary character of the Italian troops. It is no accident that the writers' congress for the defence of civilization should be held this year in Madrid . . .

Before dealing with the congress itself, I should like to touch upon a painful subject. Without exception all the writers who have come here are brave men and women. They have had a surfeit of the false coinage that distinguishes words from deeds and they have stepped out of their ivory towers to hold the fort for civilization, and if necessary at the cost of their own lives. And yet . . .

It is good that the congress should have indicted the murder of Mühsam, the incarceration of Ossietzky, and espoused the cause of all the great writers who have been exiled from the Fascist countries or have lost their civic rights. But in the course of the proceedings other names were not so much as mentioned; such names as Ottwald, Günther, Tarassov, Rodianov, Rom, Mandelstam, Tretiakov, Bezunienski, Jossiensky, Gronski, Kliuiev? Why?

Why this conspiracy of silence around the cultural reaction in Russia, about which we are all agreed in private? When we heard in Madrid that yet another school had been bombed, Kisch remarked: 'When you hear of such horrors, when you realize what our enemies are, then your courage returns and again you feel inclined to defend everything that has been done on our side, *even the trials!*'

But does this argument really clinch the matter?

It might be alleged that conditions in Russia were here irrelevant, that what mattered was the defence of Spain, and that everything that was liable to impair this defence had to be avoided. This was Bergamín's point of view. At the same time it must be recorded that already at

Valencia, the Russian delegation, which again included the ominous Bola, began by upsetting even the Spaniards by their entirely gratuitous attack upon the Trotskyists. From that moment it was clearly the main object of the Russian delegation to get some sort of motion carried against André Gide. Naturally I came to find myself in the very centre of these intrigues. From all sides (except the Spanish) I was approached, pulled about, and badgered. In these circumstances, it was difficult for me to express my full meaning although I already had done so in January in an article for the *De Kroniek voor Kunst en Kultuur*, which, through no fault of my own, though fortunately for me, was not printed. However, the speech I made was clear enough for any understanding person, and consequently was not published in the congress report of *Das Wort*, and only in a garbled form in *Commune*. Its full text appeared only in *La Hora de España*.

Subsequently the Russians endeavoured to have the motion introduced by the Argentine delegation. Supported by two eminent French writers, I protested against this attempt on the simple ground that the books of André Gide had not yet been translated in Spanish and could not be obtained anywhere in Madrid. It seemed to me a foolish procedure to expect this congress to sit in judgment over books with which the majority of its members were unacquainted. The Committee were of the same opinion, and the Russians had to be content with a personal declaration from Bergamin which was not further discussed.

I can only say again with all the emphasis at my command that my defence of André Gide's criticism of Russia—which was morally brave and objectively necessary—did not imply that I agree with every aspect of his book. Furthermore I considered the publication of *Retour de l'URSS* at the time when it occurred as inopportune, and the book itself as dangerously one-sided. Whoever denies or minimizes the positive results of the Russian revolution—which can never be entirely undone, even by Stalin—throws away the good with the bad and risks infecting the working class with the mood of Madam Angot: 'Ca ne valait pas la peine, vraiment, de changer de gouvernement.'

It should never be forgotten that in Russia, for the first time in history, an interest in art and literature had been aroused among a whole people. I have seldom been so impressed as by the 1934 Congress of Soviet Writers in Moscow. From a human standpoint the speeches of Red soldiers and underground workers, of peasant women from the Kolkhosi farms and representatives of the youth movement, were often almost as important as the elaborate revolutionary reports of Bukharin and Radek. It was also the first occasion when an almost passionate interest was evinced by both writers and general public in their contacts with one another.

What took place in Russia then is now being repeated in Spain. There is the same sudden craving for reading, which has made the selling of second-hand books in the streets of Madrid the most lucrative of all trades. Here too, circulating libraries are being installed in every town, in every village with a garrison, and in every trench. Here too, throughout the press, interest in the congress is so great as to overshadow even the military operations on the various fronts. Here too, the writers are not just among themselves: factory girls, boys of the Alerta, university students, and militiamen take part in the discussions. Soldiers were showing us the banners captured at Brunete, at the same time as the stolen feminine trinkets that had been found on a Fascist officer. The words of their leader, 'We are writing history with these bayonets,' was no empty phrase.

The writers' congress in Madrid was, also from the technical point of view, better organized than any I ever attended. A staff of young enthusiastic artists performed miracles, the full significance of which can only be understood by somebody who has lived in Spain during the war. The waiters' trade union and the town council of Madrid made it a point of honour to make such arrangements as to prevent their foreign guests from noticing any difference in the standard of living between Paris and Madrid. The translations were done with unexampled care. When I expressed my admiration for the fact that already the following morning the reports were at the disposal of members and duplicated in four languages, one of the young student in the office simply replied: 'That's only because we've worked through the night.' It was also an impressive performance on the part of our hosts that they were able to maintain an atmosphere of true culture in the very thick of the bombardments. The somewhat self-conscious advertising air of Russian congresses was tempered here by good taste rooted in centuries of tradition. The floral decorations of the hall were exquisite in every detail, and nobody is likely to forget the magnificently lyrical and stylized performance of Garcia Lorca's play, *Maria Pineda*, the concert where young composers conducted their own works, and the grand performance of the front marionette theatre at the Alianza. Dignity and grace presided over all.

Speech delivered in Madrid at the International Congress of Writers for the defence of civilization against war and Fascism.

Comrades,

There was a time when I hated Fascism with what I might describe as an intellectual hatred. All I knew of its teaching and its deeds, all I had read in books, and been told by comrades, struck me as not only repulsive but also as the very negation of our conceptions of civilization and life. I felt that it was better to die than to have to live under such a system, better to leave wife and children behind and come to Spain than to have to witness the poisoning of my children's minds which would inevitably result from the triumph of Fascism in Europe.

This hatred, comrades, which was an artist's hatred of ugliness, an intellectual's hatred of stupidity and lies, a human being's hatred of bestial cruelty—this hatred was already deep-rooted, but I must admit that now, after nine months of struggle in Spain, its character has changed entirely.

It is no longer intellectual; it has gone over into my blood. It is an integral part of my being just as it has taken root in the very vitals of my noble companions, with whom I am fortunate enough to be allowed to struggle, shoulder to shoulder, in the same trench.

It is one thing to listen to what others have to say and to look at photographs. It is another thing to touch with one's own hands the mutilated body of a woman one has revered, to dig up the dismembered fragments of children who once played at your side, or to return to find in ruins the humble house where you were once a guest.

The totalitarian war, which is being waged against us, not only exceeds in cruelty, brutality, and cowardice everything the world has ever seen, but it also leaves far behind the most perverted and cruel fantasies of mankind. After all we have seen, we can no longer be impressed by the imaginative powers of an Octave Mirbeau, an Edgar A. Poe. A Dutch proverb says that one gets used to everything, even to hanging, and it is a fact that the Spanish people, and more particularly the people of Madrid, have grown accustomed to living in heroism, whereas other nations, alas! are more and more developing the habit of living in cowardice. Your coming here has been a symbolical act, a proof of courage, an expression of faith in our victory, a gesture of alliance with the proletariat under arms. But it seems to me that your coming here is also important from another point of view.

If our struggle had only been a negative struggle against a certain thing; if it had not also been—as our soldiers see it—a positive struggle for increasing the sum of love and righteousness in the world, for more freedom and more civilization, then this struggle would have been lost in advance.

What unites us here to-night is the struggle for civilization.

The one-time illiterate soldier in my company, who in his first letter to his wife, wrote: 'I feel happier every day that I came here because in the trenches I have learnt everything I was unable to learn in the village,'; the soldiers who post up mis-spelt notices in the buildings of the University City, saying, 'Comrades, do not touch these instruments, they serve the cause of science'; the militiamen who at the risk of their own lives have saved works of art from the burning palace of the Duke of Alba—all these are defending the civilization that we are defending, a civilization they revere without ever having tasted of its fruits.

In his book on Don Quixote and Sancho, Miguel de Unamumo says that of the two figures Sancho Panza was the true idealist because he believed in Don Quixote. Certainly, one cannot read the masterpiece of Cervantes without noting on every page the reverence aroused in the plain man of the people by his master according to the spirit. Sometimes his veneration induces him to follow the intellectual even when with his sober peasant horse sense he realizes the foolishness of Don Quixote's words.

Far be it from me to set up a comparison between the proudly conscious and heroic Spanish people of these days and the Sancho Panza who, without defending himself, took all the blows, merely in the hope of acquiring his famous island. Such a comparison would be more apposite in the case of the Catholic peasant of the old days who was given the consolations of a hereafter. I venture to maintain, however, that in the integrity, courage, and righteousness of Governor Sancho all the essential characteristics of our brave soldiers are already to be found. Cervantes knew that when the proletariat assume the burdens of re- sponsibility upon their own shoulders, they grow in stature and can rule more effectively than any duke.

Other writers have compared Don Quixote to the intellectual of the present day. Such a comparison lays an enormous responsibility upon us. If it be true that writers, according to Stalin's famous words, are the engineers of the soul, then we must exact from ourselves a quality of mathematical precision if we are to live up to this definition.

'Vigilance, vigilance, and still more vigilance,' is another of our great leader Stalin's watchwords. Sometimes a doctor who is combating an epidemic is the first to become infected with the bacilli of the disease. Let us guard against all contamination. We have had enough of what a French writer has called 'la trahison des clercs'; enough of mechanical proceedings and of the complacency of labels. Our purpose must never be merely to follow in the footsteps of journalists and orators. We have our own clearly defined duty: to deepen the significance of the Homeric struggle in which to our honour and joy we are allowed to take part. Let it not be said of us that moral courage is more difficult of attainment than the physical courage of the soldiers in the trenches.

It should never be forgotten that the basis of all civilization is criticism, including that self-criticism which Lenin never ceased to enjoin upon us. Where criticism is lacking, injustices grow and begin to fester like unattended wounds. They require to be lanced in order to be cured. Whoever maintains silence lest the enemy should turn his criticism into a weapon against us will sooner or later suffer the bitter experience of seeing abuses steadily growing by his very silence until these abuses speak louder than the word of any critic. The patient's life is threatened by the disease, not by the diagnosis of the doctor.

But I was speaking of deepening the significance of the struggle.

With all my heart I welcome the popular front that unites us in our struggle for democracy. I see in this popular front not only the guarantee of victory but the realization of one of the first wishes of the proletariat, and the first step on the road leading to the fulfilment of Marx's watchword: 'Proletarians of all nations, unite.'

There are times, however, when I feel that this popular front still assumes a too purely opportunist character. We must not leave matters as they are. Closer bonds than temporary expediency unite us to friends such as our chairman José Bergamin and to the heroic Catholic defenders of the Basque country. Marx's reference to religion as the opium of the people will not do; it does not explain the genuine sympathy with which an ever-increasing portion of the Catholic youth come out to meet us. It is the intelligentsia's duty to probe into the factors that unite us; not by congresses, but by going back to St Francis of Assisi, to the Fathers of the Church, and to the religious socialists of the Middle Ages who were persecuted in the name of the same creed against which Hitler at this moment is taking up arms.

And there is another factor we must realize: the struggle of the proletariat is a struggle for the happier existence of future generations. The intellectuals must fight for the same purpose. Merciless war must be declared against all that remains of a bourgeois, capitalistic, or ascetic ethics, which is standing in the way of this happiness. The proletariat have the right to expect from us the foundations of a new ethics and a new art, in conformity with their requirements. Once liberated the eagle never returns to its cage. The modern Don Quixote must not be allowed to rest content in exploiting Sancho Panza for his own purely personal glory. He must unite with the very soul of the people for the satisfaction of requirements that have been sanctified by so much human blood.

The struggle of the Spanish people is the struggle of the world proletariat for freedom, justice, and civilization. There have been moments when it has seemed to me a desperate venture. But in such moments I recall to my mind that other struggle which was waged by my own people against the proudest monarchy in the world, allied to an omnipotent church. I recall the year 1572 when the burden of the struggle was borne by only two of the seven provinces, when the regular army was destroyed, and when only the people in arms were defending what still remained of the free cities. All of you know the issue of this struggle. A few years later the liberated Netherlands entered upon their golden age; in the arts and the sciences all the autocratically governed countries were outstripped. The struggle of our Beggars, the French Revolution, the glorious revolution in Russia are only episodes in the evolution of mankind. No stream ever returns to its source. The stream of human evolution has its source in the murky, blood-stained, fanatical past which the Fascists of to-day would like to re-instate. Evolution flows towards the untrammelled sea where 'the International will be the human race.' All honour to the Spanish people for being the first to break the dykes with which it was endeavoured to hold up this stream and for saving Europe from being transformed into a swamp in which every shoot of human civilization must needs be stifled. Honour and victory to my comrades in the trenches, who with their blood are writing nobler pages in the book of history than any that we shall ever write.

V. S. PRITCHETT

Last's Disillusionment

from a review of *The Spanish Tragedy*, *New Statesman & Nation*, 11 November 1939

I wonder what the Gibraltar set now think about our success in teaching Russia the moral marvels of non-intervention; and I wonder also if the Left are yet willing to consider more coolly what Russian intervention in Spain really was. Mr Jef Last, a Dutch Communist who fought in the International Brigade from October, 1936, until the end of 1937, faces this question in the foreword and epilogue to his letters from the trenches of Madrid. The only sense in which this is an unsatisfactory book is that it was written before the Republican defeat; certain passages are thereby dated. For the Russians Spain was but a counter in the game of power

politics; and things like Last's disillusionment about the Russian contribution in Spain, would certainly have grown greater if he had waited. A
friend of Gide's who thought Gide's protest true but inopportune, he is
one of those Communists who have turned against Stalinism since the
purges. And for him the lesson of the Spanish war is that the working
class has put too much faith in organisation and has neglected morality
and the value of individual action. The Dutch never lose their Protestant
roots; they saved Last from the violent bitterness and cynicism which is
characteristic of so many Communist apostates. He keeps his head about
the wretched POUM and the Anarchists, and even about the Communists and in his book one is coming round to a more considered view
of the war.

I-WITNESSES

JAY ALLEN
'Blood Flows in Badajoz'

from *Chicago Tribune*, 30 August 1936; reprinted in Marcel Acier (ed.),
From Spanish Trenches: Recent Letters from Spain, 1939

Elvas, Portugal, August 25, 1936

This is the most painful story it has ever been my lot to handle: I write it at four o'clock in the morning, sick at heart and in body, in the stinking patio of the Pension Central, in one of the tortuous white streets of this steep fortress town. I could never find the Pension Central again, and I shall never want to.

I have come from Badajoz, several miles away in Spain. I have been up on the roof to look back. There was a fire. They are burning bodies. Four thousand men and women have died at Badajoz since General Francisco Franco's Rebel Foreign Legionnaires and Moors climbed over the bodies of their own dead through its many times blood-drenched walls.

I tried to sleep. But you can't sleep on a soiled lumpy bed in a room at the temperature of a Turkish bath, with mosquitoes and bed bugs tormenting you, and with memories of what you have seen tormenting you, with the smell of blood in your very hair, and with a woman sobbing in the room next door.

'What's wrong?' I asked the sleeping yokel who prowls around the place at night as a guard.

'She's Spanish. She came thinking her husband had escaped from Badajoz.'

'Well, didn't he?'

'Yes,' he said, and he looked at me, not sure whether to go on. 'Yes, and they sent him back. He was shot this morning.'

'But who sent him back?'

I knew, but asked nevertheless.

'Our international police.'

I have seen shame and indignation in human eyes before, but not like this. And suddenly this sleepy, sweaty being, whose very presence had been an added misery, took on the dignity and nobility that a fine dog has and human beings most often have not.

I gave it up. I came down into the filthy patio, with its chickens, rabbits, and pigs, to write this and get it over with.

To begin at the beginning, I had heard dark rumors in Lisbon. Everybody there spies on everybody else. When I left my hotel at 4:00 p.m. August 23, I said I was going to Estoril to try my luck at roulette. Several people noted that down, and I hope they enjoyed their evening at Estoril.

I went to the Plaza de Rocio instead. I took the first taxi. I drove around and around and finally picked up a Portuguese friend who knows his business.

We went to the ferry that crosses the Tagus. Once on the other side we told the chauffeur, 'Elvas.' He looked mildly surprised. Elvas was 250 kilometers (about 150 miles) away. We streaked through an engaging country of sandy hills, cork oaks, peasants with side-burns, and women with little bowler hats. It was 8:30 o'clock when we pulled up the hill into Elvas, 'the lock nobody ever opened.' But Elvas knows humiliation now.

It had been nine days since Badajoz fell on August 14th. The Rebel armies had gone on—to a nasty defeat at Medellin, if my information was correct, as it sometimes is—and newspapermen, hand-fed and closely watched, had gone on in their wake.

Nine days is a long time in newspaper work; Badajoz is practically ancient history, but Badajoz is one of those damned spots the truth about which will not be out so soon. And so I did not mind being nine days late, if my newspaper didn't.

I know Badajoz. I had been there four times in the last year to do research on a book I am working on and to try to study the operations of the agrarian reform that might have saved the Spanish Republic—a republic that, whatever it is, gave Spain schools and hope, neither of which it had known for centuries.

We began to hear the truth before we were out of the car. Two Portuguese drummers standing at the door of the hotel knew my friend. Portugal, as usual, is on the eve of a revolution. The people seemed to know who 'the others' are. That is why I took my friend along.

They whispered. This was the upshot—thousands of Republican, Socialist, and Communist militiamen and militiawomen were butchered after the fall of Badajoz for the crime of defending their Republic against the onslaught of the Generals and the landowners.

Between fifty and one hundred have been shot every day since. The Moors and Foreign Legionnaires are looting. But blackest of all: The Portuguese 'International Police,' in defiance of international usage, are turning back scores and hundreds of Republican refugees to certain death by Rebel firing squads.

This very day (August 23) a car flying the red and yellow banner of the Rebels arrived here. In it were three Phalanxists (Fascists). They were accompanied by a Portuguese lieutenant. They tore through the narrow streets to the hospital where Señor Granado, Republican Civil Governor of Badajoz, was lying. Señor Granado, with his military commander, Col. Puigdengola, ran out on the Loyalist militia two days before the fall of Badajoz.

The Fascists ran up the stairs, strode down a corridor with guns drawn, and into the governor's room. The governor was out of his mind with the horror of the thing. The director of the hospital, Dr Pabgeno, threw himself over his helpless patient and howled for help. So he saved a life.

We drove to Campo Maior, which is only seven kilometers (about four miles) from Badajoz on the Portuguese side. A talkative frontier police-man said: 'Of course, we are handing them back. They are dangerous for us. We can't have Reds in Portugal at such a moment.'

'What about the right of asylum?'

'Oh,' he said, 'Badajoz asks extradition.'

'There is no such thing as extradition for a political offense.'

'It's being done all up and down the frontier on orders of Lisbon,' he said belligerently.

We cleared out. We drove back to Elvas. I met friends who are as much Portuguese and vice versa.

'Do you want to go to Badajoz?' they asked.

'No,' I said, 'because the Portuguese say their frontier is closed and I would be hung up.'

But they offered to take me through and back again without compli-cations. So we started. Suddenly we drove out of the lane on to a bridge that leads across the Guadiana River into the town of Badajoz. Now we were in Spain. My friends were known. The extra person in the car (myself) passed unnoticed. We were not stopped.

We drove straight to the Plaza. Here yesterday there was a ceremonial, symbolical shooting. Seven leading Republicans of the Popular Front (Loyalists), shot with a band and everything before three thousand people. To prove that Rebel generals didn't shoot only workers and peasants. There is no favoritism to be shown between the Popular Fronters.

Every other shop seemed to have been wrecked. The conquerors looted as they went. All this week in Badajoz, Portuguese have been buying watches and jewelry for practically nothing. Most shops belong to the Rightists. It is the war tax they pay for salvation, a Rebel officer told me grimly. We passed a big dry goods shop that seems to have been through an earthquake. 'La Campaña,' my friends said. 'It belonged to Don Mariano, a leading Azañista (follower of Manuel Azaña, President of Spain). It was sacked yesterday after Mariano was shot.'

We drove by the office of the Agrarian Reform, where in June I saw the Chief Engineer, Jorge Montojo, distributing land, incurring naturally the hatred of the landowners and, because he was a technician following strictly bourgeois canons of law, the enmity of the Socialists, too. He had taken arms in defense of the Republic, and so—

Suddenly we saw two Phalanxists halt a strapping fellow in a workman's blouse and hold him while a third pulled back his shirt, baring his right shoulder. The black and blue marks of a rifle butt could be seen. Even after a week they showed. The report was unfavorable. To the bull ring with him.

We drove out along the walls to the ring in question. Its sandstone walls looked over the fertile valley of Guadiana. It is a fine ring of white plaster and red brick. I saw Juan Belmonte (bullfight idol) here once on the eve of the fight, on a night like this, when he came down to watch the bulls brought in. This night the fodder for tomorrow's show was being brought in, too. Files of men, arms in the air.

They were young, mostly peasants in blue blouses, mechanics in jumpers. 'The Reds.' They are still being rounded up. At four o'clock in the morning they are turned out into the ring through the gate by which the initial parade of the bullfight enters. There machine guns await them.

After the first night the blood was supposed to be palm deep on the far side of the lane. I don't doubt it. Eighteen hundred men—there were women, too—were mowed down there in some twelve hours. There is more blood than you would think in eighteen hundred bodies.

In a bullfight when the beast or some unlucky horse bleeds copiously, 'wise monkeys' come along and scatter fresh sand. Yet on hot afternoons you smell blood. It is all very invigorating. It was a hot night. There was a smell. I can't describe it and won't describe it. The 'wise monkeys' will have a lot of work to do to make this ring presentable for a ceremonial slaughter bullfight. As for me, no more bullfights—ever.

We passed a corner.

'Until yesterday there was a pool blackened with blood here,' said my friends. 'All the loyal military were shot here and their bodies left for days as an example.'

They were told to come out, so they rushed out of the house to greet the conquerors and were shot down and their houses looted. The Moors played no favorites.

Back at the Plaza. During the executions here Mario Pires went off his head. [Mario Pires is a Portuguese newspaper correspondent who had been entirely favorable to the Franco rebellion before his visit to Badajoz.]* He had tried to save a pretty fifteen year old girl caught with a rifle in her hands. The Moor was adamant. Mario saw her shot. Now he is under medical care at Lisbon.

I know there are horrors on the other side aplenty. Almendra Lejo, Rightist, was crucified, drenched with gasoline, and burned alive. I know people who saw charred bodies. I know that. I know hundreds and even thousands of innocent persons died at the hands of revengeful masses. But I know who it was who rose to 'save Spain' and so aroused the masses to a defense that is as savage as it is valiant.

'But they didn't burn the jail.' I had read in the Lisbon and Seville papers that they had. 'No, the brothers Pla prevented it.'

I knew Luis and Carlos Pla, rich young men of good family, who had the best garage in southwestern Spain. They were Socialists because they said the Socialist Party was the only instrument which could break the power of Spain's feudal masters.

They harangued the crowd that wanted to burn the three hundred Rightists in the jail just before the Moors entered, saying they were going to die in defense of our Republic, but they were not assassins. They themselves opened the doors to let these people escape.

'What happened to the Plas?'

'Shot.'

'Why?'

No answer.

There is no answer. All these people could have been allowed to escape to Portugal three miles away, but they weren't.

On the moon drenched streets there was a smell of jasmin, but I had another smell in my nostrils. Sweet, too horribly sweet. So back to Elvas.

There in the white Plaza by a fountain, a youth leaning against the wall

---

* Comment within brackets here is the original editor's.

with his feet crossed was playing his guitar and a soft tenor sang a melting Portuguese love song.

At Badajoz in June boys still sang beneath balconies. It will be a long time before they do again.

Suddenly through the square shot a car with a red and yellow flag. We halted. Our drummers came to meet us.

'They are searching the hotel.'

'For whom?'

'Don't know.'

We shall go away, as soon as it is light. People who ask questions are not popular near this frontier, if it can be called a frontier.

RALPH BATES

'Compañero Sagasta Burns a Church'*

from *Left Review*, 13 October 1936

I was in a small Pyrenean village, Espot, in the Lérida province, when the militia came up. They were all of them members of the FAI, the anarchist organisation, fine fellows (and the standard of impossible bravery for the future must be 'brave as a Spanish worker') and very much aware of their moral superiority. They came overnight in a confiscated motor and billeted themselves on the hotel where I was staying. Within five minutes the words 'They're going to burn the saints to-morrow' were on everyone's lips. By morning they had become '*We're* going to burn the saints.' And note, in Spain one does not say the 'images or statues of the saints,' but saints (*los santos*, or in Catalunya *'els sants*).

It was a grand bonfire. A little technical commission (to which I was elected) stood at one side of the door, passing judgment on the saints as they were carried out. Compañero Sagasta relies on my judgment.

* In sending us this contribution from the scene of the Spanish War, Ralph Bates writes: 'In Madrid, where the Marxist movement is the predominant influence among the workers, out of all the hundreds of churches only one was burnt. In Barcelona, and Catalonia in general, the Iberian Anarchist Federation is the most powerful force.' Ralph Bates neither wishes to condone nor to condemn the forms which anti-clericalism has taken. He wishes only to explain the feelings of the Spanish workers, and to pay tribute to the heroism which they have shown in the actual tasks of repelling the insurgent soldiery, a task in which Liberals, Marxists, and Anarchists have formed a common front.

'This one, compañero?'

'Revolting, burn him.'

'Very good, compañero.'

Poum! The bearers run to the fire and St Peter throws up a billow of sparks.

'This one, compañero?'

'Absolutely nauseating, pitch her on the fire.' (Why do female saints appear to suffer from permanent disorders of the kind proper to their sex?)

'This one?'

'H'm, looks rather old, the carving's direct; probably deserves a second thought.'

'Very good.' The saint is dumped on his back among the silver plate candelabra, the books with parchment backs, which may make binding for school books, the electric bulbs, the linen, good for bandages, and, in short, anything that possibly has artistic or secular value.

This not-gaudy candelabra, for instance: when it came out I yelled, 'Eh, bring that here.'

'It's only iron.'

'Only iron! Christ Jesus, it's pure Catalan work of the fifteenth century; look, no rivets, no clips, everything is welded and drawn under the hammer.'

The iconoclasts reverently place the candelabra to one side, reverently I say, for a compañero has said this is art, and feeling out of it, they rush into the church for another trophy.

'Now then, what do you say to this one?' they say, dragging out a polychrome of the Holy Family. I think Mr Belloc would have burnt that polychrome.

Going to the hotel for a drink, I asked an old man, knowing him to be a leading Catholic, what he thought of the burning. Restraining his words, no doubt, because the FAI were not far off, he answered, 'Oh, one dances the way the music plays, señor.'

'But tell me, if you are stricken with horror and grief and your soul is a flood of tears, does nothing at all show in your face? Do you roll a cigarette and borrow a light from Compañero Sagasta, church-burner?'

In the hotel vestibule Compañero Sagasta himself was saying to the proprietor, 'Señor, you are sure you have no saints in your house? If you do not bring them out I shall fine you 100 pesetas.'

'No, señor, we have no saints.'

'Bueno, I ought to say if you bring one out now I shall have to fine you 200 pesetas.'

'Señor, there is not one single head of a saint in this hotel.'

The anarchist smiles and rests his hands on the musket mouth. 'I'm very glad, señor, because after this I should have to fine you 500 pesetas.'

The proprietor thinks visibly, throws up his arm in simulated annoyance, and goes off into his private quarters. He returns dragging a wooden Virgin as a child drags a rag doll. 'I had forgotten this, it belongs to the old lady.'

The anarchist does not even smile. 'Five hundred pesetas, please, señor.'

'Five hundred!' the proprietor whispers and hurries to the fire and burns his Virgin. The fine is 500 pesetas, none the less.

I went back to the church, where, in the shadows in the heights of the sanctuary, black figures crawled about the summit of the reredos (a roundabout façade of gilt and paste). It took an hour to lever it away from the walls, then with a fierce shout everyone dashed out of the church. The F A I took refuge in the baptistery where I was smoking. A grinding smash and a column of brown dust shot out over the bonfire, across a field of potatoes, down to the Escrita torrent, colouring the white foam among the stones.

'One might say the Church is holy, but one could not say she is clean,' the anarchist leader remarked, peeping out through the door chink.

Rain spoiled the bonfire in the end, but all the peasants, cowherds, shepherds, lake fishermen and militia men sit along the wall and watch it, for hours. Sometimes a man jumps up and kicks a wooden head back into the embers; by and by they are talking of the sheep of Aragon, the traditional wandering flocks which pasture here in summer. That night on the committee table in the village hall my hands toyed with a burnt parchment roll. I opened it, it was a marriage deed of 1760, in crabbed but stately Latin, bartering a bride.

You have to get right into the imagination of Spain to feel it the way I do, or a Spaniard does. Two days before this burning in Espot I was in the Enchanted Mountains, some eight miles above the village, camping on a bluff above the Lake of St Maurici; two cowherds were the only Spanish companions I had, illiterate men, therefore having unadulterated imaginations, authentic Spaniards.

'What is happening below on the plains?' I asked them.

'Oh, it is an affair of captains and princes,' one cowherd said.

'And the bishops.'

'Ah, the bishops are a hard folk, and valiant.'

In that scrap of conversation you have the whole of old Spain. 'Captains and princes.' He knew, of course, that Spain was a republic, but the ancient formula still served to describe this confused battle of classes. And the bishops he was describing were not, I think, the discreet and apologetic gentlemen one meets in England. You've got to get a legendary feeling into your imagination to grasp the quality of these events. In a sense, simply because it is a history of stark passion, it is above passion, or the passions are taken for granted and so not greeted with amazement, that contemporary and childish exacerbation of natural curiosity. There is a sense of Fate, or, better put, of the Inevitable about Spain at all times, and it is that which makes this war so grim, it is something which reason cannot modify, nor sentiment ameliorate. Would you sigh for an aspidistra when the pine forest is ablaze?

I watch these men at night, sitting, weary with vigilance, around a wood fire behind their barricade, and I feel subtly that at the very bottom of Anarchism is the belief that Anarchism is impossible, that it is noble, just and beautiful, but unrealisable. That is the Fate tradition again. I think it is the profound sense of tragedy which Anarchism possesses that makes its followers so utterly desperate in their courage. Those image burners, one or two of them had slashed faces, stitched weals of former battles, perhaps tortures. They are probably dead by now, for thousands of their faith have been killed on the Aragon front.

And when, on that Sunday morning, the Barcelona rebels marched out of their barracks against a sleeping population, they were met by hordes of workers, the *mob*, half-dressed, unarmed or badly armed, called out of their houses by some strange insurrectional telepathy. The military opened fire with rifles, machine-guns and artillery, and that *mob* charged them with knives, sticks, stones, little automatic pistols, and here and there a rifle. Or charged them with nothing at all but fists and teeth and wiped them out . . .

Make this drama for yourself. The Paseo de Colón is a long avenue of date palms, on one side of which are the dock warehouses and the railways serving them. On the other, shops, ship chandling and broker-age firms, public offices, the post office and the military headquarters. In front of the headquarters and firing down the long avenue is a garrison of about five hundred fully armed soldiers; about twelve machine-guns, three or four pieces of artillery (the figure is disputed) of between three- and four-inch calibre. The charge begins well down the avenue, the workers are creeping along inside the walls that shut off the railway from the avenue, firing through the railings. A few run along the warehouse roofs, one falls shot dead on to a wagon of tallow barrels. Suddenly the workers burst through a drive-in and emerge among the palms. All the machine-guns, rifles *and artillery* open fire, at once. The crowd goes roaring up the avenue, hundreds falling, the shells tearing lanes through them, bullets slashing the trunks of palms, smashing windows and chipping stone as the machine-guns spray.

They reach the military lines and unarmed men leap on the gunners, wrestle with them, strangle them, drag them to the ground and stab them with knives. Men dive at the machine-guns like football players and upset them with their hands, kicking, cursing, and tearing with nails, hammering out the brains of soldiers with lumps of paving stone. The soldiers break, but before they can withdraw, groups of workers drag the artillery round and at ten yards' range a shell smashes the headquarters gate. Others, not knowing how to aim, send their shells flying high into the façade, smashing a pillar, blowing in a cornice. The *mob* pours into the barracks with captured arms, and one docker and his mate, carrying a machine-gun, stagger up the stairs, firing from the chest. In another wing armed soldiers are trapped in a room and four anarchists blaze at them from open doors; the two survivors race along the corridor and open fire with a machine-gun across the quadrangle.

Suddenly, silence. Within a minute the *mob* is rushing the abandoned artillery to the central square, the Plaza de Cataluña, where the military have fortified themselves in the Columbus Hotel; men, and women, at last with us, are already streaming out of the side streets; a youth is pressed against the belly of a nude statue, his forearm is on its breast, he fires with a tiny pistol; another is stretched beside the fountain basin with a cheap revolver. The moment the workers arrive they rush the hotel; again the same drama is played, scores fall; but now they have arms, and *bombs*. The door collapses and the bedrooms, saloons and corridors are choked with frenzied men, swinging at Fascists with chairs, bars of iron, knives and rifle butts. Fascists are flung bodily out of windows, or down the lift shafts, or driven into a lavatory; a bomb is pitched in after them.

Again quiet, and the crowd streams off to another barracks. By two of the afternoon, with perhaps twelve hundred killed and wounded, the city is quiet, in the hands of the workers. By three o'clock a score of black smoke columns would tell which side has won, if one did not know. Only the churches of architectural value remain in Barcelona; certainly Sta. Maria del Pino is damaged beyond repair (I should think), but bullets came out of that church. The Augustinian convent, too, and four monks dead, but that had to be taken at the charge, against the rifle fire of its military guests. The classical refrain in Barcelona, anyway, is 'The pity is not that there should be a convent, or four monks less, but that there were once so many.'

It is the legendary heroic quality of this struggle that I am trying to make clear, not its violence. Its suddenness, sharpness and decisiveness (for Barcelona is tranquil enough now) is alien to your Saxon minds. But here in Cataluña we expect these things; one boasts a little, one insults the defeated enemy with classical rhetoric, one celebrates quietly in the streets; but, of course, there *was* nothing else to do but to get out of bed, drag on your trousers, tell the wife to fill up the spare cartridge magazine and rush out, in all probability to die; or if to kill, then fiendishly, without quarter. And the following night, to dance a grave, a stately dance beneath the plane trees behind your barricade.

Why, then, does the burning of a few churches seem strange, or, perhaps a staggering question, why does it seem irreligious? I have said in *The Olive Field* that the psychology of anarchism is religious. Its tragic courage, its total selflessness, its sense of drama, its worship of Action, its fanatical belief in the Myth (for that is even the term such theorists as Sorel employ), its *burning*, I say burning mystical love for its leaders, its unquestioning obedience, its subtle and amazing intuition, all this, it is evident, discloses anarchism to be a religion. Does one live like that for a wage increase? Does a man leap at discharging cannon for improved lavatory facilities?

The spirituality of the average priest, it seems to Compañero Sagasta, is a vulgar materialism beside his white mysticism; it seems less still beside the love of his followers.

But there are other aspects of church-burning, it will be said. There are, but I shall only write about the aspects a Spaniard will observe.

The church I described in *Lean Men*, that church which by some celestial economy has been dedicated to two saints, St Pastor and St Just, is one of the oldest churches in Barcelona. In front of it is a cobbled square, a massive stone fountain in one corner draped with creeper and ferns, two stone bollards protecting it from the approach of horses. Around St Pastor and St Just the streets are narrow; tall houses shut out the light and one could leap from balcony to balcony across the streets. It is a beautiful place, and easy to attack.

In its beauty, you say, it would seem to be a church made for burning; yet it stands intact. From its roof the enemy can command no streets with his troops, they are too narrow; the houses are tall enough to give us the same advantage as he himself possesses. St Just, therefore, has *never* been the centre of fighting; there is no tradition of struggle at this spot, as feet do not turn themselves that way by instinct when rifle fire is heard.

And again, anarchism makes great play with the word 'culture'—no, get inside anarchism! We live miserably on thirty-five pesetas a week, find no woman to love us the way a man should be loved, with body and mind—they are dominated by the Church so that we are driven to the brothel; or we marry in despair, we live in filth, we starve, we are despised, our masters are contemptuous. Then comes the spiritualising doctrine, the fatal dream; through struggle and culture, if only it were possible, we could be free. We crowd the Montjuich concert hall to hear Casals and his orchestra because the first revolution has given us cheap music. Perhaps we can go on! We buy little pamphlets, second-hand books, we hear lectures on Art. Architecture is one of the Arts, and St Just is a fine church; so that, if some reckless barbarian, profiting by a back alley, sets fire to the vestry door, we call to our compañeros and extinguish the fire. There is the back door of St Just to prove it!

There is the cathedral, its 60,000,000 pesetas of Christ's penniless apostles hidden within it. (Since found, September 2nd.) The Church protects and fosters art; go into the nearest Catholic church and write to me as truthfully as I have written to you. Or come here and climb to our museum on Montjuich and see in what state the Church has kept its lovely primitive paintings, or its frontals, its things of ritual. Or march to Toldeo on foot, across that blinding plain as I have done, to see the Grecos, and perceive how this Church has preserved art. There goes a lorry, Conpañero Sagasta on guard over filthy, dusty treasure from the lightless cathedral, *en route* to the museums.

And note with what courtesy the churches have been burnt! One would have thought that the flanking houses would have been destroyed also (for many of them form part of a street, having no isolating space round them). That is not the case. Compañero Sagasta knocks at the doors of the neighbouring houses and the concierge comes out, without fear. 'A good evening to you, compañero.'

'Have the goodness to request your folk to come out, we're going to burn the church. And may you have good evenings.'

'Very well, give us ten minutes, compañero.' Perhaps Compañero Sagasta sends for a fire brigade and tells them to stand by; then, finally, the petrol cans are poured on the piled-up benches, chairs, saints and vestments. By and by the roof falls in and the flames die down. At last the two hundred compañeros who have been protecting the houses go home, or look for another church, or man the barricades. To-morrow they will go off to Saragossa, to hold hot rifles in quivering fields. There is no frenzy, no ill-temper, there are no speeches, no yelling hordes; with great care not to frighten Señora Fuster, or damage her house, Compañero Sagasta courteously burns down a church, with the same courtesy the Americans use in lynching a black temple of the Holy Ghost.

But *why* this antagonism in the first place? I am barely patient enough to answer you. Here, the first two books on my shelves, '1680, the Authentic Relation of the Auto de Fé celebrated in the plaza ... at Madrid. Nihil Obstat Imprimatur.' And here the New Catechism, dated 1914, in its 14th edition, published here in Barcelona by a man I knew, a book which was in every church.

QUESTION: *What sin is committed by those who vote liberal?*
ANSWER: *Usually, mortal sin.*

There on that cinder heap is a charred picture of the hell to which mortal sin condemns you, or your frightened wife. The street is brighter, purer, it seems to Compañero Sagasta and to me, when the church is burnt down. Perhaps now we may argue reasonably with our women.

Enough of that, all men know it. The Archbishop of Burgos, is he not on the Fascist committee in Portugal? Safe, while the dregs of Moham-medanism defend Christ's Immaculate Bride with rape and death and lead and fire. Before me is a photograph of six men crucified like Christ the Lord, and burnt with fires at their feet. Perhaps Compañero Sagasta is among them.

If we find 12,000,000 pesetas in Malaga Cathedral, if we relieve the Bishop of Jaen's escaping sister of 1,500,000 pesetas, if we discover 10,000,000 pesetas in Vich (although of the hundreds we killed, just one priest), if we unearth 60,000,000 in Barcelona sacristy, if we acquire 8,000,000 pesetas from the Jesuits, if we rob His Church, who had nowhere to lay His head, of silver and gold, if we give our bread, and our children's bread, English compañeros, will you *sell* us rifles? Italian aircraft, from Peter's Rome, roar overhead.

W. H. AUDEN

'Impressions of Valencia'

from *New Statesman & Nation*, 30 January 1937

The pigeons fly about the square in brilliant sunshine, warm as a fine English May. In the centre of the square, surrounded all day long by crowds and surmounted by a rifle and fixed bayonet, 15ft high, is an enormous map of the Civil War, rather prettily illustrated after the manner of railway posters urging one to visit Lovely Lakeland or Sunny Devon. Badajoz is depicted by a firing-party; a hanged man represents Huelva; a doll's train and lorry are heading for Madrid; at Seville Quiepo el Llano [sic] is frozen in an eternal broadcast. The General seems to be the Little Willie of the war; in a neighbouring shop window a strip of comic woodcuts shows his rake's progress from a perverse childhood to a miserable and well-merited end.

Altogether it is a great time for the poster artist and there are some very good ones. Cramped in a little grey boat the Burgos Junta, dapper Franco and his bald German adviser, a cardinal and two ferocious Moors are busy hanging Spain; a green Fascist centipede is caught in the fanged trap of Madrid; in photomontage a bombed baby lies couchant upon a field of aeroplanes.

Today a paragraph in the daily papers announces that since there have been incidents at the entrances to cabarets, these will in future be closed at nine p.m. Long streamers on the public buildings appeal for unity, determination and discipline. Three children, with large brown eyes like some kind of very rich sweet, are playing trains round the fountain. On one of the Ministries a huge black arrow draws attention to the fact that the front at Teruel is only 150 km away. This is the Spain for which charming young English aviators have assured us that the best would be a military dictatorship backed by a foreign Power.

Since the Government moved here the hotels are crammed to bursting with officials, soldiers and journalists. There are porters at the station and a few horse-cabs, but no taxis, in order to save petrol. Food is plentiful, indeed an hotel lunch is heavier than one could wish. There is a bull-fight in aid of the hospitals; there is a variety show where an emaciated-looking tap-dancer does an extremely sinister dance of the machine-guns. The foreign correspondents come in for their dinner, conspicuous as actresses.

And everywhere there are the people. They are here in corduroy breeches with pistols on their hip, in uniform, in civilian suits and berets. They are here, sleeping in the hotels, eating in the restaurants, in the cafés drinking and having their shoes cleaned. They are here, driving fast cars on business, running the trains and the trams, keeping the streets clean, doing all those things that the gentry cannot believe will be properly done unless they are there to keep an eye on them. This is the bloodthirsty and unshaven Anarchy of the bourgeois cartoon, the end of civilization from which Hitler has sworn to deliver Europe.

For a revolution is really taking place, not an odd shuffle or two in cabinet appointments. In the last six months these people have been learning what it is to inherit their own country, and once a man has tasted freedom he will not lightly give it up; freedom to choose for himself and to organize his life, freedom not to depend for good fortune on a clever and outrageous piece of overcharging or a windfall of drunken charity. That is why, only eight hours away at the gates of Madrid where this wish to live has no possible alternative expression than the power to kill, General Franco has already lost two professional armies and is in the process of losing a third.

T. C. WORSLEY

'The Flight from Malaga'

from *Left Review*, 3 April 1937

The road between Almeria and Motril winds slowly for 100 kilometres between the sea and the blue hills. At any other time it is probably as beautiful as any other road in Spain. But between February 10th and 14th there was passing along it one of the most pitiful and tragic processions in the history of Europe. From the town and province of Malaga some 100,000 people were fleeing from the Fascist terror. Many of the women knew already that they were widows and the children that they were fatherless, many more that they would soon learn it.

The seemingly endless procession shuffled along the road, shuffling because the shoes in which they started out, carpet-slippers or thin rubber—all they had—are now in ribbons, or are long since gone. Their feet, bare, blistered, bleeding or top-heavily swathed in rags, shuffle down the road. Five, six or seven days they have been walking without food, and scarcely daring to stop for the shortest rest; they move forward with short shuffling steps.

Every age and every kind is here. A few lucky ones with donkeys, mules or horses, but most on foot. Old women with faces creased as printers' blocks, mothers with children at their breasts, an old man with over-tortured feet crawls on his hands and knees, children of five or six struggle with some precious household possessions which, sooner or later, must for sheer tiredness be abandoned. The road is littered with these abandoned possessions, pots, mattresses, sacks of wool; and here a mule is dying from exhaustion between the shafts of a cart.

Too tired to speak, there arises from this procession a continuous plaintive moan, like a Greek chorus—'Aiee! Aiee!'—uninterrupted for four days and nights. Night time is worse, the evening mist descends and soaks their clothes; after the warm day, the night is bitter, and 'Frio!'

(cold, cold) is mingled with the 'Aiee!' Fires are started by the roadside and flare up, throwing the whole into fantastic silhouette. But no one dares to stay long. The Fascists are coming, though only rumour knows when. So the children are roused from their half-hour's sleep, in spite of hunger, cold and exhaustion. Now a new terror arises, for in the darkness and confusion children are lost, and frightened cries of 'Maria,' 'Antonia,' cut across the uninterrupted moan. As one stands on the roadside watching, figures come up to one and, too weak or hoarse to speak, whisper—some pleading. Because one is not fleeing with them, one must in some way be able to help. They mutter their individual sorrow and pass on, to swell the collective agony, almost unendurable to watch without being able to relieve.

It seemed incredible that this tragic and terrible sight should really be in the twentieth century. It belonged to some barbaric past; perhaps a scene transcribed from the Old Testament. There were many groups, mother and child riding on a donkey and father walking behind, which dimly reminded one of Italian paintings of the flight of Mary and Joseph. But this was pitiful reality.

In our ambulance we managed to rescue a number of the worst cases from near Motril. But there were always four as desperate people left behind for every one we took; and each last seemed to me more awful than the last. A pregnant woman with a broken leg, a child dying from exhaustion, a woman with a three-day child, a boy unconscious, knees doubled to his chin in pain, babies with running sores, all exhausted, all foodless.

Almeria was the destination of this procession. There they hoped for food and shelter. Mercifully, most of them, in spite of the strained resources of the town, got a little food and milk. But Almeria is a small town, and there was nowhere to house 100,000 people. They camped as best they could in the streets and squares until arrangements could be made to evacuate them. As for safety, on the Friday at 7.30 in the evening, with the centre of the town packed to density and the stream still flowing in, Almeria was suddenly plunged into darkness and the streams of the sirens were answered by cries of panic. Before such safety as the town offered could be reached, a Junker plane dropped eight bombs. The crash of the explosions, screams of dying and wounded, the chaos of the stampeding mass were horrible beyond imagination and description. We picked up the bodies of nine children flattened against a wall in the main street. And then the representatives of the religion of universal love roared away, leaving more than thirty dead, and still more wounded.

Three of the many acts of heroism and self-sacrifice we saw: the lame old man who gave up his place in our ambulance for a sick child; the boy of eight who had walked the whole 200 kilometres on his own; another who refused the offer of a lift because that entailed leaving his mother. The full story of that week of horror will never be told; but, apart from the agony, the impressive thing is that 100,000 people preferred to endure it rather than to submit to living under the Fascist terror.

The bourgeoisie who lightly dismiss the Spanish struggle as a fight between two factions, and who comfortably assure themselves that the real Spanish people want neither of the two, could learn, if they wanted to learn, from this. For here were the real Spanish people, the peasants and the workers and their wives and children, preferring even this desperate flight to awaiting the arrival of the Fascists.

Even to the Fascists it was a surprise. For we heard that on that terrible stretch of road between Malaga and Motril which they had shelled, and over which flew aeroplanes, they did not at first fire on the people. They wanted to scare them back, since otherwise there would be none left whose labours they could exploit. Only when they saw this was impossible did the planes dive down, machine-gunning the refugees.

So Malaga fell, and the people fled. But that is not, as the English capitalist Press exultingly proclaims, the end of the war. On the contrary. The first shock of horror has been succeeded by a storm of anger which has swept the Spanish people, as it should have swept Europe. And that anger in turn has been translated into action; for in the month which has elapsed since I was last in Barcelona, the town has changed: there is a new spirit in the air. The new offensive which is to be the Spanish people's answer to Malaga will be such that even that agony of suffering will not have been in vain.

JOHN DOS PASSOS
'Madrid Under Siege'

from *Journeys Between Wars*, 1938

Room and Bath at the Hotel Florida

I wake up suddenly with my throat stiff. It's not quite day. I am lying in a comfortable bed in a clean well-arranged hotel room staring at the light indigo oblong of the window opposite. I sit up in bed. Again there's the hasty loudening shriek, the cracking roar, the rattle of tiles and a tinkling shatter of glass and granite fragments. Must have been near because the hotel shook. My room is eight or nine stories up. The hotel is on a hill. From the window I can look out at all the old part of Madrid over the crowded tiled roofs, soot-color flecked with pale yellow and red under the metal-blue before dawn gloaming. The packed city stretches out sharp and still as far as I can see, narrow roofs, smokeless chimney-pots, buff-colored towers with cupolas and the pointed slate spires of seventeenth-century Castile. Everything is cut out of metal in the steely brightening air. Again the shriek, the roar, rattle, tinkle of a shell bursting somewhere. Then silence again, cut only by the thin yelps of a hurt dog, and very slowly from one of the roofs below, a smudge of dirty yellow smoke forms, rises, thickens and spreads out in the still air under the low indigo sky. The yelping goes weakly on and on, then stops.

It's too early to get up. I try going to bed again, fall asleep to wake almost immediately with the same tight throat, the same heavy feeling in my chest. The shells keep coming in. They are small but they are damn close . . .

Metropolitan Stroll

The mid-morning sunlight was hot on the Gran Via in spite of the frigid dry wind of Castilian springtime. Stepping out of doors into the bustling jangle of the city I couldn't help thinking of other Madrids I'd known, twenty years ago, eighteen years ago, four years ago. The streetcars are the same, the long-nosed sallow madrileño faces are the same, with the same mixture of brown bullet-headed countrymen, the women in the dark-colored shawls don't look very different. Of course you don't see the Best People any more. They are in Portugal and Seville or in their graves. Never did see the Best People at this time of the morning. The shellholes and the scars made by flying fragments and shrapnel have not changed the general look of the street, nor have the political posters pasted up on every bare piece of wall, or the fact that people are so scrappily dressed and that there's a predominance of uniforms in khaki and blue denim. It's the usualness of it that gives it this feeling of nightmare. I happen to look up at the hotel my wife and I stayed in the last time we were here. The entrance on the street looks normal and so does the department store next door, but the top floor with the balconies where our room was is shot as full of holes as a Swiss cheese.

Nobody hurries so fast along the street, and hardly anybody passes along the Gran Via these days without speeding his pace a little because it's the street where most shells fall, without pausing to glance up at the tall New Yorkish telephone building to look for new shellholes. It's funny

how the least Spanish building in Madrid, the proud New York baroque
tower of Wall Street's International Tel and Tel, the symbol of the
colonizing power of the dollar, has become in the minds of the madrileños the symbol of the defense of the city. Five months of intermittent
shellfire have done remarkably little damage. There are a few holes and
dents but nothing that couldn't be repaired in two weeks' work. On the
side the shelling comes from the windows of several storeys have been
bricked up. The historically exact ornamentation has hardly been
chipped.

Inside you feel remarkably safe. The whole apparatus of the telephone
service still goes on in the darkened offices. The elevators run. It feels
like Sunday in a New York downtown building. In the big quiet office you
find the press censors, a cadaverous Spaniard and a plump little pleasant
voiced Austrian woman. They say they are going to move their office to
another building. It's too much to ask the newspapermen on the regular
services to duck through a barrage every time they have to file a story, and
the censors are beginning to feel that Franco's gunners are out after them
personally. Only yesterday the Austrian woman came back to find that a
shell fragment had set her room on fire and burned up all her shoes, and
the censor had seen a woman made mincemeat of beside him when he
stepped out to get a bite of lunch. It's not surprising that the censor is a
nervous man; he looks underslept and underfed. He talks as if he
understood without taking too much personal pleasure in it the importance of his position of guardian of those telephones that are the link with
countries technically at peace, where the war is still carried on with gold
credits on bankledgers and munitions contracts and conversations on red
plush sofas in diplomatic ante-rooms instead of with six-inch shells and
firing squads. He doesn't give the impression of being complacent about
his job. But it's hard for one who is more or less of a free agent from a
country at peace to talk about many things with men who are chained to
the galley benches of war.

It's a relief to get away from the switchboards of power and walk out in
the sunny streets again. If you follow the Gran Via beyond the Plaza de
Callao down the hill towards the North Station, stopping for a second in
an excellent bookshop that's still open for business, you run into your
first defense barricade. It is solidly built of cemented pavingstones laid in
regular courses high as your head. That's where men will make a last
stand and die if the Fascists break through.

I walk on down the street. This used to be the pleasantest and quickest
way to walk out into the country, down into the shady avenue along the
Manzanares where the little fat church is with Goya's frescoes in it, and

out through the iron gate into the old royal domain of El Pardo. Now it's the quickest way to the front.

At the next barricade there's a small beady-eyed sentry who smilingly asks to see my pass. He's a Cuban. As Americans we talk. Somehow there's a bond between us as coming from the western world.

There are trenches made with sandbags in the big recently finished Plaza de España. The huge straggling bronze statues of Don Quixote and Sancho Panza look out oddly towards the enemy position in Carabanchel. At a barracks building on the corner a bunch from the International Brigade is waiting for chow. French faces, Belgian faces, North-of-Italy faces; German exiles, bearded men blackened by the sun, young boys; a feeling of energy and desperation comes from them. The dictators have stolen their world from them; they have lost their homes, their families, their hopes of a living or a career; they are fighting back.

Up another little hill is the burned shell of the Montana Barracks where the people of Madrid crushed the military revolt last July. Then we're looking down the broad rimedge street of the Paseo de Rosales. It used to be one of the pleasantest places in Madrid to live because the four- and five-storey apartment houses overlooked the valley of the Manzanares and the green trees of the old royal parks and domains. Now it's no-man's land. The lines cross the valley below, but if you step out on the paseo you're in the full view of the enemy on the hills opposite, and the Moors are uncommonly good riflemen.

With considerable speed the sightseers scuttle into a house on the corner. There's the narrow hall and the row of bells and the rather grimy dark stairs of the regular Madrid apartment house, but instead of the apartment of Señor Fulano de Tal on the third floor you open a ground-glass door and find . . . the front. The rest of the house has been blown away. The ground-glass door opens on air, at your feet a well opens full of broken masonry and smashed furniture, then the empty avenue and beyond, across the Manzanares, a magnificent view of the enemy. On the top floor there's a room on that side still intact; looking carefully through the half-shattered shutters we can make out trenches and outposts at the top of the hill, a new government trench halfway up the hill and, closing the picture, as always, the great snowy cloud-topped barrier of the Guadarramas. The lines are quiet; not a sound. Through the glasses we can see some militiamen strolling around behind a clump of trees. After all it's lunchtime. They can't be expected to start a battle for the benefit of a couple of sightseers.

Walking back to the hotel through the empty streets of the wrecked quarter back of the paseo we get a chance to see all the quaint possibilities of shellfire and airbombing among dwelling houses. The doll's house effect is the commonest, the front or a side of a house sliced off and touchedly revealing parlors, bedrooms, kitchens, diningrooms, twisted iron beds dangling, elaborate chandeliers hanging over void, a piano suspended in the air, a sideboard with dishes still on it, a mirror with a gilt stucco frame glittering high up in a mass of wreckage where everything else has been obliterated.

Afternoon Call

After lunch I walk out into the northern part of the city to see the mother of an old friend of mine. It's the same apartment where I have been to visit them in various past trips. The same old maid in black with a starched apron opens the door into the dim white rooms with the old oak and walnut furniture that remind me a little of Philip II's rooms in the Escorial. My friend's mother is much older than when I saw her last, but her eyes under the handsomely arched still dark eyebrows are as fine as ever, they have the same black flash when she talks. With her is an older sister from Andalusia, a very old white-haired woman, old beyond conversation. They have been in Madrid ever since the movement, as they call it, started. Her son has tried to get her to go to Valencia where he has duties but she doesn't like to leave her apartment and she wouldn't like the Fascists to think they'd scared her into running away. Of course getting food is a nuisance but they are old now and don't need much, she says. She could even invite me to lunch if I'd come some day and wouldn't expect to get too much to eat. She tells me which paper she likes, then we fall to talking about the old days when they lived at El Pardo and her husband the doctor was alive. I used to walk out to see them through the beautiful park of liveoaks that always made me feel as if I were walking through the backgrounds of Velasquez's paintings, still full in those days of the Bourbons of mantraps and royal gamekeepers in Goya costumes. Over the big white cups of hot tea and the almond paste cakes we used to talk about walks in the Sierra and skiing and visits to forgotten dried-up Castilian villages and the pleasure of looking at the construction of old buildings and pictures and the poems of Antonio Machado.

Street Life

As I stepped out into the empty street I heard shelling in the distance again. As a precaution I walked over to the metro station and took the crowded train down to the Gran Via. When I got out of the elevator at the station I found that there weren't so many people as usual walking down towards the Calle de Alcalá. There was a slight tendency to stand in doorways. I was thinking how intact this part of the town was when, opposite Molinero's, the pastry shop where we used to go in the intermission of the symphony concerts at the Price Circus and stuff with almond paste and eggyolk and whipped-cream pastry in the old days, I found myself stepping off the curb into a pool of blood. Water had been sloshed over it but it remained in red puddles among the cobbles. So much blood must have come from a mule, or several people hit at one time. I walked around it.

But what everybody was looking at was the division El Campesino in new khaki uniforms parading with flags and Italian guns and trucks captured at Brihuega. The bugles blew and the drums rattled and the flags rippled in the afternoon sunlight and the young men and boys in khaki looked healthy and confident walking by tanned from life at the front and with color stung into their faces by the lashing wind off the sierras. I followed them into the Puerta del Sol that, in spite of the two blocks gutted by incendiary bombs, looked remarkably normal in the later afternoon bustle, full of shoe-shine boys and news-vendors and people selling shoelaces and briquets and paper-covered books.

In the island in the middle where the metro station is an elderly man shined my shoes.

A couple of shells came in behind me far up a street. The dry whacking shocks were followed by yellow smoke and the smell of granite dust that drifted slowly past in the wind. There were no more. Perhaps a few more people decided to take the metro instead of a streetcar. An ambulance passed. The old man went on meticulously shining my shoes.

I began to feel that General Franco's gunner, smoking a cigarette as he looked at the silhouette of the city from the hill at Carabanchel, was taking aim at me personally. At last the old man was satisfied with his work, and sat down on his box again to wait for another customer while I walked across the halfmoon-shaped square through the thinning crowd, to the old Café de Lisboa. Going in through the engraved glass swinging doors and sitting down on the faded chartreuse-colored plush and settling down to read the papers over a glass of vermouth was stepping back twenty-one years to the winter when I used to come out from my cold room at the top of a house on the other corner of the Puerta del Sol and warm up with coffee there during the morning. When I come out of the café at closing time and head for the Hotel Florida it's already almost dark. For some reason the city seems safer at night.

The Nights Are Long

The correspondents take their meals in the basement of the Hotel Gran Via almost opposite the Telephone Building. You go in through the unlit lobby and through a sort of pantry and down some back stairs past the kitchen into a cave-like place that still has an air of pink lights and nightclub jippery about it. There at a long table sit the professional foreign correspondents and the young saviours and the members of foreign radical delegations. At the small tables in the alcoves there tend to be militiamen and internationals on sprees and a sprinkling of young ladies of the between-the-sheets brigade. This particular night there's at a special table a group of visiting parliamentary bigwigs, including a countess. It's been a big day for them, because General Franco's gunners have bagged more civilians than usual. Right outside of the hotel, in fact under the eye of the countess, two peaceful madrileños were reduced to a sudden bloody mess. A splatter of brains had to be wiped off the glassless revolving doors of the hotel. But stuffed with horrors as they were, the visiting bigwigs had eaten supper. In fact they'd eaten up everything there was, so that when the American correspondents began to trickle in with nothing in their stomachs but whiskey and were fed each a sliver of rancid ham, there was a sudden explosion of the spirit of Seventy-Six. Why should a goddam countess eat three courses when a hardworking American newspaperman has to go hungry. A slightly punchdrunk little ex-bantamweight prizefighter, who was often in the joint wearing a militiaman's uniform and who had tended in the past to be chummy with the gringo contingent who were generous with their liquor, became our champion and muttered dark threats about closing the place up and having the cooks and waiters sent to the front, lousy profiteers hiding under the skirts of the CNT who were all sons of loose women and saboteurs of the war and worse than Fascists, *mierda*. In the end the management produced a couple of long-dead whitings and a plate of spinach which they'd probably been planning to eat themselves, and the fires of revolt died down.

Still in Madrid the easiest and most sustaining thing to get, though it's high in price, is whiskey; so it's on that great national food-drink that the boys at the other end of the wires tend to subsist. One of the boys who'd been there longest leaned across the table and said plaintively, 'Now you won't go home and write about the drunken correspondents, will you?'

Outside the black stone city was grimly flooded with moonlight that cut each street into two oblique sections. Down the Gran Via I could see the flashlight of a patrol and hear them demanding in low voices the password for the night of whoever they met on the sidewalk. From the west came a scattered hollow popping lightly perforating the horizon of quiet. Somewhere not very far away men with every nerve tense were crawling along the dark sides of walls, keeping their heads down in trenches, yanking their right arms back to sling a handgrenade at some creeping shadow opposite. And in all the black houses the children we'd seen playing in the streets were asleep, and the grownups were lying there thinking of lost friends and family and ruins and people they'd loved and hating the enemy and hunger and how to get a little more food tomorrow, feeling in the numbness of their blood, in spite of whatever scorn in the face of death, the low unending smoulder of apprehension of a city under siege. And I couldn't help feeling a certain awe, as I took off my clothes in my quiet clean room with electric light and running water and a bathtub and lay down on the bed to read a book, but instead stared at the ceiling and thought of the pleasant-faced middle-aged chambermaid who'd cleaned it that morning and made the bed and put everything in order and who'd been coming regularly every day, doing the job ever since the siege began just as she'd done it in the days of Don Alfonso, and wondered where she slept and what about her family and her kids and her man, and how perhaps tomorrow coming to work there'd be that hasty loudening shriek and the street full of dust and splintered stone and instead of coming to work the woman would be just a mashed-out mess' of blood and guts to be scooped into a new pine coffin and hurried away. And they'd slosh some water over the cobbles and the death of Madrid would go on.

Madrid, April, 1937

ANTOINE DE SAINT-EXUPÉRY
Secretly Infected Men

from *Wind, Sand and Stars*, transl. Lewis Galantière, 1939

Human drama does not show itself on the surface of life. It is not played out in the visible world, but in the hearts of men. Even in happy Perpignan a victim of cancer walled up behind his hospital window goes round and round in a circle striving helplessly to escape the pain that hovers over him like a relentless kite. One man in misery can disrupt the peace of a city. It is another of the miraculous things about mankind that there is no pain nor passion that does not radiate to the ends of the earth.

Let a man in a garret but burn with enough intensity and he will set fire to the world.

Gerona went by, Barcelona loomed into view, and I let myself glide gently down from the perch of my observatory. Even here I observed nothing out of the way, unless it was that the avenues were deserted. Again there were devastated churches which, from above, looked untouched. Faintly visible was something that I guessed to be smoke. Was that one of the signs I was seeking? Was this a scrap of evidence of that nearly soundless anger whose all-destroying wrath was so hard to measure? A whole civilization was contained in that faint golden puff so lightly dispersed by a breath of wind.

I am quite convinced of the sincerity of people who say: 'Terror in Barcelona? Nonsense. That great city in ashes? A mere twenty houses wrecked. Streets heaped with the dead? A few hundred killed out of a population of a million. Where did you see a firing line running with blood and deafening with the roar of guns?'

I agree that I saw no firing line. I saw groups of tranquil men and women strolling on the Ramblas. When, on occasion, I ran against a barricade of militiamen in arms, a smile was often enough to open the way before me. I did not come at once upon the firing line. In a civil war the firing line is invisible; it passes through the hearts of men. And yet, on my very first night in Barcelona I skirted it.

I was sitting on the pavement of a café, sipping my drink surrounded by light-hearted men and women, when suddenly four armed men stopped where I sat, stared at a man at the next table, and without a word pointed their guns at his stomach. Streaming with sweat the man stood up and raised leaden arms above his head. One of the militiamen ran his hands over his clothes and his eyes over some papers he found in the man's pockets, and ordered him to come along.

The man left his half-emptied glass, the last glass of his life, and started down the road. Surrounded by the squad, his hands stuck up like the hands of a man going down for the last time.

'Fascist!' A woman behind me said it with contempt. She was the only witness who dared betray that anything out of the ordinary had taken place. Untouched, the man's glass stood on the table, a mute witness to a mad confidence in chance, in forgiveness, in life. I sat watching the disappearance in a ring of rifles of a man who, five minutes before, within two feet of me, had crossed the invisible firing line.

.   .   .   .   .   .

My guides were anarchists. They led me to the railway station where troops were being entrained. Far from the platforms built for tender farewells, we were walking in a desert of signal towers and switching points, stumbling in the rain through a labyrinthine yard filled with blackened goods wagons where tarpaulins the colour of lard were spread over carloads of stiffened forms. This world had lost its human quality, had become a world of iron, and therefore uninhabitable. A ship remains a living thing only so long as man with his brushes and oils swabs an artificial layer of light over it. Leave them to themselves a couple of weeks and the life dies out of your ship, your factory, your railway; death covers their faces. After six thousand years the stones of a temple still vibrate with the passage of man; but a little rust, a night of rain, and this railway yard is eaten away to its very skeleton.

Here are our men. Cannon and machine-guns are being loaded on board with the straining muscles and the hoarse gaspings that are always drawn from men by these monstrous insects, these fleshless insects, these lumps of carapace and vertebra. What is startling here is the silence. Not a note of song, not a single shout. Only, now and then, when a gun-carriage lands, the hollow thump of a steel plate. Of human voices no sound.

No uniforms, either. These men are going off to be killed in their working garb. Wearing their dark clothes stiff with mud, the column heaving and sweating at their work look like the denizens of a night shelter. They fill me with the same uneasiness I felt when the yellow fever broke out among us at Dakar, ten years ago.

The chief of the detachment had been speaking to me in a whisper. I caught the end of his speech:

'. . . and we move up to Saragossa.'

Why the devil did he have to whisper? The atmosphere of this yard made me think of a hospital. But of course! That was it. A civil war is not a war, it is a disease. These men were not going up to the front in the exultation of certain victory; they were struggling blindly against infection.

And the same thing was going on in the enemy camp. The purpose of this struggle was not to rid the country of an invading foreigner but to eradicate a plague. A new faith is like a plague. It attacks from within. It propagates in the invisible. Walking in the streets, who ever belongs to a Party feels himself surrounded by secretly infected men.

This must have been why these troops were going off in silence with their instruments of asphyxiation. There was not the slightest resemblance between them and regiments that go into battle against foreign armies and are set out on the chessboard of the fields and moved about by strategists. These men had gathered together haphazardly in a city filled with chaos.

There was not much to choose between Barcelona and its enemy, Saragossa: both were composed of the same swarm of communists, anarchists, and fascists. The very men who collected on the same side were perhaps more different from one another than from their enemies. In civil war the enemy is inward; one as good as fights against oneself.

What else can explain the particular horror of this war in which firing squads count for more than soldiers of the line? Death in this war is a sort of quarantine. Purges take place of germ-carriers. The anarchists go from house to house and load the plague-stricken into their tumbrils, while on the other side of the barricade Franco is able to utter that horrible boast: 'There are no more communists among us.'

The conscripts are weeded out by a kind of medical board; the officer in charge is a sort of army doctor. Men present themselves for service with pride shining in their eyes and the belief in their hearts that they have a part to play in society.

'Exempt from service for life!' is the decision.

Fields have been turned into charnel-houses and the dead are burned in lime or petroleum. Respect for the dignity of man has been trampled under foot. Since on both sides the political parties spy upon the stirrings of man's conscience as upon the workings of a disease, why should the urn of his flesh be respected? This body that clothes the spirit, that moves with grace and boldness, that knows love, that is apt for self-sacrifice —no one now so much as thinks of giving it decent burial.

I thought of our respect for the dead. I thought of the white sanatorium where the light of a man's life goes quietly out in the presence of those who love him and who garner as if it were an inestimable treasure his last words, his ultimate smile. How right they are! Seeing that this same whole is never again to take shape in the world. Never again will be heard exactly that note of laughter, that intonation of voice, that quality of repartee. Each individual is a miracle. No wonder we go on speaking of the dead for twenty years.

Here, in Spain, a man is simply stood up against a wall and he gives up his entrails to the stones of the courtyard. You have been captured. You are shot. Reason: your ideas were not our ideas.

This entrainment in the rain is the only thing that rings true about their war. These men stand round and stare at me, and I read in their eyes a mournful sobriety. They know the fate that awaits them if they are captured. I begin to shiver with the cold and observe of a sudden that no woman has been allowed to see them off.

The absence of women seems to me right. There is no place here for mothers who bring children into the world in ignorance of the faith that will some day flare up in their sons, in ignorance of the ideologist who, according to his lights, will prop up their sons against a wall when they have come to their twenty years of life.

G. L. STEER

'Guernica'

from *The London Mercury*, August 1937, reprinted in *The Tree of Gernika: A Field Study of Modern War*, 1938

They told us at the General Staff that afternoon of the bombardment of Markina, Bolibar, and Arbacegui-Guerricaiz. All the villages had been smashed up on the way back to Gernika.*

The destruction at Arbacegui barred our way. There were four dead near the church. Two cottages sprawled in smoking pieces across the road, and we climbed over them and down the fields to see the biggest bomb-holes we had ever seen, warm and stinking of metal still. They were over twenty feet deep and forty feet wide. They were mooncraters. We looked in wonder at them. Suddenly on the hillside behind us the bell of the little church began to tinkle. We saw the two old priests and a few villagers stumble across debris and torn green grass into the tower door. Then silence in the village; nothing to see but the smoking houses and walls smirched grey with fire.

Over the ridge to the north-west, from the direction of Gernika, came six fighting planes in echelon. They were flying very fast, level and straight, and their engines made a noise which meant immediate war. In a few seconds they were on the village. They were so low that one could see with the naked eye the pilots and every detail of the planes down to the split wheels and characteristic pin-nose of the German army fighter, Heinkel 51. These were the same planes that Kienzle and Schulze-Blanck said that they had flown from Vitoria—six Heinkel 51's in battle formation.

Christopher Corman and I thought that the bomb-hole was the best place. We reached the bottom in two jumps. It looked less safe from

* This is the Basque spelling of 'Guernica.'

down below, for the sides were unusually wide and one could see too much sky. But it was a hole, and we lay on the shady side face down in tumbled clay and jagged bomb splinters.

There can have been no movement visible in the village, and there was no traffic moving or stationary upon the road, except our car. But they dropped a few light bombs and machine gunned the place until they must have shot all the dust off the roofs that still stood.

Then they circled and spotted us. For between fifteen and twenty minutes they dived over our hole at full throttle, loosing off their double guns at us from anything down to two hundred feet. The only thing was to pretend to be dead already, and sometimes we wondered whether we were. Old Corman was spinning a long story about the ineffectiveness of aerial machine-gunning on entrenched positions, but somehow to-day he sounded much less impressive, and I asked him to be silent and to wait and see. It struck me, too, as very undignified for an Englishman to eat earth before the German aviation: but I was bothered if I could think of any safe alternative. It was difficult to think at all. As soon as that very material process known as the collection of one's thoughts was nearly complete another bloody little fighter was roaring down at us, and we were spreadeagled and passive again.

Of course, it's all noise. The shooting was wild, and after a quarter of an hour of it we could not find a bullet in the bomb-hole. And when they had gone we recollected how often the pilots had kept on gunning when the planes were soaring upwards fit to hit the stars. Terror, noise were their weapons, not death.

I had been machine-gunned a few times before and was machine-gunned many times afterwards, but I never figured in so pretty a target. It impressed me. My experience must be much the same as that of any young recruit. Continual strafing from the air does not frighten; it paralyses. We pulled ourselves out of the hole very slowly. We didn't look about us much. We were thinking all the time of the experience which we had suffered, and not a thought did we give to the future or the present. We were raw material for any surprise.

None of the villagers were hurt, but they stayed huddled in the blackness of the church tower, I suppose till nightfall. Their terror was real, not half exorcised like ours. We turned our car in front of the burning barricade. It, too, was untouched. The chauffeur was told to go straight back to Bilbao.

As we made homewards we had to stop twice and wait for enemy aeroplanes to pass. Their type was the light bomber Heinkel 111, and we saw several fly across to our right towards the Gernika inlet. The same alarm chained the peasantry to their holes and hedges; the fields were tragically deserted and bare. As we passed the level-crossing we heard bombing to the north, where the inlet settles down into green valley. We saw nothing, for there were hills between. The bombs must have been dropped by the planes which passed us. We had experienced quite enough that day, and we went on without stopping to Bilbao to write our stories.

It was about four-thirty by the clock of our car on Monday, April 26th.

*   *   *

Monday was the weekly market day of Gernika, when the town existed. At about four-thirty the market, in summer, was at its fullest. The civil war had not made great difference to the Gernika farmers who brought in their animals and produce for sale from the rich valley. Rather there was better business. In Gernika, where the population was usually seven thousand, there were now an additional three thousand refugees and two Basque battalions, who had plenty of pesetas to spend. A few of the factious rich had been jailed or run away, but only a few. Their fine stone houses with the floreate blazons engraved hugely over wide doors were shut: but they never had used the market much, and most of them visited peacetime Gernika little.

Gernika remained a modest Vizcayan country town. The population behaved itself, the priests walked about in the cloth, mass was held in the churches all day and every day. The two Basque Nationalist battalions quartered to the north of the town, where a water-green avenue of plane-trees rippled out towards Bermeo, were popular with the people, and in Gernika itself there was the usual post of Basque motorized police. There were no troops retreating through the town. The armies were beyond Markina, miles to the east, and at Oitz, miles to the south. Gernika lay well behind the front, on part of its communications with Bilbao: to destory it would cut off the retreating armies from the General Staff and their base.

After four there were farm carts coming into Gernika, rolling on solid wooden wheels and drawn by oxen whose heads were shaded under fleeces of sheep. Basque peasants in their long puckered market smocks walked backwards in front of them, mesmerizing the oxen to Gernika with their slim wands, with which they kept touching the horns and yoke gently. They talked to the oxen. Others were driving sheep to market. There was an assembly of animals near the parish church, a stately structure cavernous and dark within, standing upon a flight of thin steps like leaves piled one upon the other.

It is improbable that anyone was thinking about the war, when at four-thirty the church bell rang out loud. All over Spain a peal on a single bell is an air-raid warning. The population took cover, and the sheep in the square were left to their own devices.

There were numerous air-raid shelters in Gernika, constructed after the terrible raid on Durango on March 31st. Any cellar was covered with sandbags, and the entrance protected in the same way: a cardboard at the door painted ornamentally REFUGIO showed where the people had to dive. Though there had been few raid warnings at Gernika since the war began, the whole Basque population by now took their church bells seriously.

In a few minutes a Heinkel 111 came over and dropped six medium bombs, probably fifty-pounders, near the station, with a shower of grenades. A director of the railway company who was in the office rang up Bilbao to inform them that an aeroplane was bombing Gernika.

A few minutes later another Heinkel 111 appeared, to bomb the same area, but nearer the centre. The telephone with Bilbao was now cut. The plane from its slant and speedy sides machine-gunned the town at random, then veered homeward.

The parish priest, Aronategui, left his church with the sacraments, for dying people were reported near the railway station. He went calmly through the deserted streets with the bread. No fires had yet started.

Fifteen minutes passed, and the people were coming out of their shelters. A heavy drumming of engines was heard to the east. It was what we called in lighter moments the tranvias—the trams—the Junker 52's, who were so clumsy that they seemed to clang rather than to fly. These were the heaviest bombers that Germany had sent to Spain.

Over the town, whose streets were once more empty trenches, they dispersed their load a ton at a time. They turned woodenly over Gernika, the bombs fell mechanically in line as they turned. Then came the crack of the explosions; smoke stood up over Gernika like wool on a negro's head. Everywhere it sprouted, as more heavy bombers came.

Besides many fifty- and hundred-pound bombs, they dropped great torpedoes weighing a thousand. Gernika is a compact little town, and most of these hit buildings, tearing them to pieces vertically from top to bottom and below the bottom. They penetrated refuges. The spirit of the people had been good, but now they panicked.

An escort of Heinkel 51's, the same perhaps that had molested us that afternoon, were waiting for this moment. Till now they had been machine-gunning the roads round Gernika, scattering, killing or wounding sheep and shepherds. As the terrified population streamed out of the town they dived low to drill them with their guns. Women were killed here whose bodies I afterwards saw. It was the same technique as that used at Durango on March 31st, nearly a month back.

The little fighting planes came down in a line, like flashing dancing waves on shingle. They burst in spray on the countryside as they merrily dived. Twenty machine-guns working together in line, and the roar of breakers behind them from ten engines. Always they flew nose towards Gernika. For the pilots it must have been like surfing. The terrified people lay face down in ditches, pressed their backs against tree trunks, coiled themselves in holes, shut their eyes and ran across sweet green open meadow. Many were foolish, and fled back before the aerial tide into the village. It was then that the heavy bombing of Gernika began.

It was then that Gernika was smudged out of that rich landscape, the province of Vizcaya, with a heavy fist.

It was about five-fifteen. For two hours and a half flights of between three and twelve aeroplanes, types Heinkel 111 and Junker 52, bombed Gernika without mercy and with system. They chose their sectors in the town in orderly fashion, with the opening points east of the Casa de Juntas and north of the Arms Factory. Early bombs fell like a circle of stars round the hospital on the road to Bermeo: all the windows were blown in by the divine efflatus, the wounded militiamen were thrown out of their beds, the inner fabric of the building shook and broke.

On the shattered houses, whose carpets and curtains, splintered beams and floors and furniture were knocked into angles and ready for the burning, the planes threw silver flakes. Tubes of two pounds, long as your forearm, glistening silver from their aluminium and elektron casing: inside them, as in the beginning of the world in Prometheus' reed, slept fire. Fire in a silver powder, sixty-five grammes in weight, ready to slip through six holes at the base of the glittering tube. So as the houses were broken to pieces over the people sheathed fire descended from heaven to burn them up.

Every twenty minutes fresh raiders came. And between the explosions and the spurts of flame as the burning metal seeped into curtains and beams, doors and carpets, while a grey pall stood over Gernika supported from below by white pillars where fires were starting, in the pauses of modern battle the population ran about the streets to clear away the doors of smothered refuges, to pull children and other small worthless belongings from houses afire.

There was much groaning in Gernika, much breathless work to dig out wounded people before the next planes came. Twenty minutes was the interval between fire, and the priests spoke to the people to keep them calm. By now something like a spirit of passive resistance had been built up in them. Gernika's face was turning to ashes, everybody's face in Gernika was ash-grey, but terror had reached a condition of submissive stubbornness not seen before in Vizcaya.

In the intervals people moved out of the town, but the fear of the fighting plane and separation from their families persuaded many to remain in Gernika. And then the planes returned with their tinsel tubes to shower over Gernika and another part was destroyed, and more were buried in the refugios.

I do not know whether you have ever sat in a railway station having lost one train and waiting for another which will come in two and a half hours' time. A country railway station, where you can buy nothing to read or smoke or eat: and the hours take days to pass if you cannot go to sleep. Now in Gernika it was wellnigh impossible to go to sleep, except in an obligatory sleep which had no morrow in Gernika, or Vizcaya, or this world. And since there was nothing to eat or smoke, and fumes prevented one from reading, no other diversion remained but to allow terror to expand those hours past days into months and years. Years half spent in dugouts that might crash at any moment, and half spent in streets of an unrecognizable town looking for people who may now be unrecognizable.

And so you see that to be in Gernika when it was destroyed was, in a limited sense, like waiting for a train in a country station. Time in both cases passed slowly.

Soon there was little of the town to move about in. The Church of San Juan was burning fiercely, with a huge bomb-hole through its roof and its altar and pulpit rippling fire. Even a few isolated buildings were touched: at the old Parish Church of Andra Mari, in the corner of the square where the sheep had been gathered, the chapel behind the altar was aflame.

As the people not trapped in the refuges moved northwards before the general fire the planes that raided Gernika came very low. It must have been difficult for them to sight their target in the smoke and grit which rose from the spreading campfire below them. They flew at six hundred feet, slowly and steadily shedding their tubes of silver, which settled upon those houses that still stood in pools of intolerable heat; then slipped and dribbled from floor to floor. Gernika was compact as peat to serve as fuel for the German planes. Nobody now bothered to save relatives or possessions: between bombardments they walked out of Gernika in front of the stifling smoke and sat in bewildered hundreds on the roads to Bermeo and Mugika. Mercifully, the fighters had gone. They no longer glanced down to mutilate the population in movement and chase them across the open fields. The people were worn out by noise, heat, and terror; they lay about like dirty bundles of washing, mindless, sprawling, and immobile. There was nothing to save in Gernika but the few old mattresses and pillows, kitchen tables and chairs which they had dragged out of the fire. By seven-thirty that evening fire was eating away the whole of crowded little Gernika but the Casa de Juntas and the houses of the Fascist families. These, being wealthier than the others, lived in stone mansions apart from the rest of the people: their properties did not catch the infection of the running fire, even when under pressure of the wind it stretched its savage arms to stroke them.

At seven-forty-five the last plane went away. One could hear now, through ears half-numbed by the engines of the heavy bombers and explosion of the heavy bombs, the nervous crackle of arson all over the town and the totter and trembling collapse of roofs and walls. Gernika was finished, and as night fell and the motorized police stumbled along the road to ring up Bilbao to say that all was over, the total furnace that was Gernika began to play tricks of crimson colour with the night clouds. Very gently and softly they throbbed reflections of her death movement. They lay over her like a crimson-cushioned ceiling, like the hangings of a dying monarch, billowy and rich, stirring to the Gernika light.

Around the corpse of the Basques' oldest village caserios aflame in the hills made candles. The aviation had spent the residue of its fire upon them and had struck many.

Beginning to talk and to try to understand their experience, the Basques asked each other how many planes had attacked their town. Some said 80, others 100, others 200, others more. They could not tell: but those who were outside Gernika the whole afternoon say that between 40 and 50 German planes attacked her, including 10 fighters. The bombers reappeared again and again with fresh loads.

To the people within Gernika it was not a question of figures, but of inquantitative and immeasurable terror. All they could hear was the drumbeat of the engines and the split of the explosions again and again until they sounded dull enough. They could see no more but the trembling doors of their refuges and their own helpless faces, and sometimes if they were in the streets the points of fire where the silver tubes struck: these fell many at a time, for they were dropped twenty-four together on a single spinning rod. Sometimes, too, before they bolted below they saw through the smoke the stiff, stubborn wings of the planes which molested them and heard the wingless flight of the metal that spurted blindly all over the town, crushing walls and roof tiles and stripping trees of their leaves and branches.

When they crept back to the town between the soft breeze of the flames now blowing on every house they saw what I saw later that night.

* * *

At Bilbao we sent our day's story off: it dealt with the bombardments all along the communications that day, from Markina to Arbacegui-Guerricaiz. Some time about seven Arbex told me that Gernika was being bombed: he said that they had had news earlier of it, but there were no details. He did not seem to give the bombardment much importance. I did not mention it in my story that night.

We were having dinner at eight-thirty in the Torrontegui that evening: quite a number of us. Captain Roberts of the *Seven Seas Spray* and his daughter Fifi, Arbex, Christopher Holme, and some other journalists sat down with me in the wide sombre dining-room, peopled by the near-ghosts of women and old men of the Right, who talked in a whisper and glided rather than walked. The dinner was going fairly well, when at ten o'clock Antonio Irala rang up.

'Gernika is in flames,' he said.

We got cars, threw our napkins on the floor, and drove out into the dark towards Gernika. I recollect the mood in which I went to that fire: the same mood as that with which many people in England heard the news of it. Irala must be exaggerating, I felt. The whole town cannot be burning.

We followed Arbex's car through the countryside along the road which we had followed that morning. Arbex drove like a lunatic, with a cigarette-holder sticking out of his open glass. It glowed ahead of us, until we lost it against a brighter sky.

* * *

Fifteen miles south of Gernika the sky began to impress us. It was not the flat dead sky of night: it seemed to move and carry trembling veins of blood: a bloom of life gave it body, flushed its smooth round skin.

Nearer it became a gorgeous pink. The sort of pink that Parisians have dreamed of for centuries. And it seemed enormously fat: it was beginning to disgust us.

It still had no source. Gernika was hidden behind the hills through which we careered. But we could see now that the fatness was great bellying clouds of smoke and the pinkness the reflection of some great fire upon them. The skies in their vague, all-embracing way were mirroring Gernika, and pulsed more slowly to the destruction that danced a war dance over the home of seven thousand human beings.

Out of the hills we saw Gernika itself. A Meccano framework. At every window piercing eyes of fire: where every roof had stood wild trailing locks of fire. The Meccano framework was trembling, and a wild red disorder was taking the place of its rigid geometry. We drove down the street which led into Gernika from the south carefully, for it was a street no longer. Black or burning beams and tattered telephone wires rolled drunkenly, merrily across it, and the houses on either side streamed fire as vapour rises effortless from Niagara. Four dead sheep lay to our right in a trickle of blood, and as we approached the central place over huge bomb-holes and volcanoed fresh earth before the Casa de Juntas, we saw a dazed score of militiamen, Batallion Saseta, standing by the roadside, half waiting for, half incapable of understanding, their orders. The fire of the houses lit up their spent, open faces.

In the plaza, in the dark shadow of the Casa de Juntas which made the only shade in Gernika that night, people sat upon broken chairs, lay on rough tables or mattresses wet with water. Mostly women: some hundreds of them were littered around in the open space, and as we passed they groped about, fiddled with dirty pillows, tried to sleep, tried feebly to talk. We talked to them: they told me all that had happened, this stricken people were my authority for all that I have written. Two priests were with them: Aronategui was not to be found, and they supposed him dead. They conversed in tired gestures and words unnaturally short for Spain, and they made the funny noises of bombers poising, fighters machine-gunning, bombs bursting, houses falling, the tubes of fire spurting and spilling over their town. Such was the weary, sore-eyed testimony of the people of Gernika, and it was only later that people who were never in Gernika thought of other stories to tell.

Some of the witnesses were quite dumb. They were digging them out of ruined houses, families at a time, dead and blue-black with bruising: others were brought in from just outside Gernika with machine-gun bullets in their bodies. One a lovely girl. The militia cried as they laid her out on the ground in the broken hospital: they could give no reason for their tears, they just cried.

A fire brigade with a feeble piddle was playing on the chapel of Andra Mari. I went up into the shades of the Casa de Juntas. The gardens were torn about, windows were broken, but behind the Casa stood the oak of Basque civil liberty. Untouched. The black old trunk, under which when it flowered the Catholic kings promised to respect Basque democracy, stood there in its mummified death, untouched between thick white pillars. The seats engraved with the arms of Vizcaya, tree and lurking wolves, where the Señor of Vizcaya took the oath of suzerainty and respect, untouched. The newsprung oak from the loins of the older, untouched and green. A few rose petals lay on the stones around, pink confetti blown there in the twilight by the bombardment of Gernika.

In the centre of the town the smaller tongues of fire were tuning into a single roar. The motorized police, with Monzon, Minister of the Interior, stood helpless beyond the plaza, where streets tightened and intertwined to make the heart of our conflagration. We tried to enter, but the streets were a royal carpet of live coals, blocks of wreckage slithered and crashed from the houses, and from their sides that were still erect the polished heat struck at our cheeks and eyes. There were people, they said, to be saved there: there were the frameworks of dozens of cars. But nothing could be done, and we put our hands in our pockets and wondered why on earth the world was so mad and warfare become so easy.

We talked with the people round the great furnace for two hours. I smoked a number of cigarettes to settle my mood, drove back to Bilbao, and slept on my story.

Government lorries and ox-carts carried away the refugees. Our headlights illumined the slack shoulders and loose blankets of hundreds who walked slowly towards Bilbao and Munguia.

Between cigarettes I played with three silver tubes picked up that evening in Gernika. The argent thermite distilled itself slowly from their bases; they came from the German RhS factory in 1936, said their stamp. And over the legend stood a symbol in miniature, the Imperial eagle with scarecrow wings spread.

ARTHUR KOESTLER
'Dialogue with Death'

from *Spanish Testament*, 1937

Thursday, March 11th

When the prisoners are led out into the patio and when they come back, they march four abreast along the corridor past my cell. They walk slowly, with shuffling steps; most of them wear felt slippers or bast sandals; I stand at my spy-hole and follow the procession with my eyes, as one face after another comes within my field of vision. All have a habit of reading out the name-cards on the cell doors as they pass. Often I hear my name spelled out in undertones fifteen or twenty times in succession:

'Ar-tu-ro-ko-est-ler'. Sometimes one of them will read the rest, too:
'*In-co-mu-ni-ca-do. O-jo*'. '*O-jo*' means: 'keep an eye on him'. Sometimes, when I am absorbed in reading or lost in a reverie, the sudden
murmuring of my name seems to come from a chorus of ghosts.

To-day midday, as they came in for siesta, someone threw a piece of
paper into my cell as if in fun . . .

London, Autumn, 1937

It was a piece of brown cigarette paper screwed up into a ball.
Unfolding it, I read the following lines:

'Comrade, we know that you are here and that you are a friend of the Spanish
Republic. You have been condemned to death; but they will not shoot you. They
are much too afraid of the new King of England. They will only kill us—the poor
and humble (los pobres y humildes).

'Yesterday again they shot seventeen in the cemetery. In our cell, where there
were once 100 there are now only 73. Dear comrade foreigner, we three are also
condemned to death, and they will shoot us to-night or to-morrow. But you may
survive and if you ever come out you must tell the world all about those who kill us
because we want liberty and no Hitler.

'The victorious troops of our Government have conquered Toledo and have
also got Oviedo, Vitoria and Badajoz. And soon they will be here, and will carry us
victoriously through the streets. Further letters will follow this one. Courage. We
love you.

'THREE REPUBLICAN MILITIAMEN.'

No further letters followed. I learned later that two of the men were
shot that very night, and the third, whose sentence was commuted, was
sentenced to thirty years penal servitude—the Spanish equivalent to a
life term.

I had to learn that letter by heart. It has literally become a part of my
body, for half an hour after I received it my cell was visited by the guard of
inspection. I had no time to tear up the note, and so was obliged to
swallow it.

·   ·   ·   ·   ·

I had spent the first two months in the Seville prison in complete
isolation. Only now, when I came into contact with the other prisoners,
did I learn what was going on around me.

I learned that in the week after my transfer to the prison thirty-seven
men from the big patio had been executed.

In the last week of February no executions had taken place, in March
forty-five—almost all the victims prisoners of war from the various
fronts. In every case the procedure had been exactly the same as in that of

Nicolás. True, not a single man had been shot without trial. But these trials were far more disgraceful than the unceremonious slaughter of prisoners in the front lines immediately after a battle.

In the case of every single prisoner of war, without exception, the charge was one of 'rebelión militar'. Those who were defending the legal Government against open rebellion, were condemned for taking part in a rebellion—by an authority that claimed to be a court of law and to pronounce judgment in the name of justice.

The course taken by this grim comedy was always the same. The proceedings lasted two or three minutes. The so-called Prosecutor demanded the death sentence; always and without exception. The so-called Defending Officer—always and without exception—asked for a life sentence in view of mitigating circumstances. Then the prisoner was marched off. He was never informed of his sentence. Sentence was passed the moment he was out of the door; it was one of death; always and without exception.

The record of the sentence was passed on to the Commander-in-Chief of the Southern Forces, General Queipo de Llano. The sentences were carried out by Queipo in the order listed. Twenty to twenty-five per cent of the prisoners—according to Queipo's mood or the situation at the front—were reprieved. The rest were shot.

From the moment he left the court martial the accused was left in uncertainty as to his fate. Were his sentence commuted to thirty years' imprisonment he was informed by letter—a week or a month or six months later. Were the death sentence confirmed, he learned of it only at the moment of execution.

In the interval he was left to play football and leapfrog in the patio, and count his buttons every morning to see whether he was going to be shot that night.

There were men in the patio who had been waiting for four months to be shot. The record was held by a Captain of the Militia—four and a half months. He was executed a few days before my release.

Nicolás had been lucky; he had had to wait only four days.

During March forty-five men were shot.

During the first thirteen days of April there were no executions.

During the night of April 13th to 14th seventeen men were shot, in celebration of the anniversary of the proclamation of the Republic. Nicolás was among them.

Two nights later, the night of Thursday, eight were shot. This was the first time I heard anything.

The proceedings were very subdued; perhaps that explains why I hadn't heard them before. But now I was on the watch.

I knew that the critical time was between midnight and two o'clock in the morning. For some days I stood from midnight until two o'clock with my ear pressed to the door of my cell.

During the first night of my vigil, the night of Wednesday, nothing happened.

During the second night . . .

A feeling of nausea still comes over me when I remember that night.

I had gone to sleep, and I woke up shortly before midnight.

In the black silence of the prison, charged with the nightmarish dreams of thirteen hundred sleeping men, I heard the murmured prayer of the priest and the ringing of the sanctus bell.

Then a cell door, the third to the left of mine, was opened, and a name was called out. '*Qué?*' (What?) asked a sleepy voice, and the priest's voice grew clearer and the bell rang louder.

And now the drowsy man in his cell understood. At first he only groaned; then in a dull voice, he moaned for help: '*Socorro, socorro.*'

'*Hombre*, there's no help for you,' said the warder who accompanied the priest.

He said this neither in a hostile nor in a friendly tone, but simply as though stating a fact. For a moment the man who was about to die was silent; the warder's quiet, sober manner puzzled him. And then he began to laugh.

It was not the loud, shrill laughter of an actor feigning madness; the man kept patting his knees with his hands, and his laughter was, rather, quiet and subdued, full of little gasps and hiccoughs.

'You are only pretending,' he said to the priest. 'I knew at once that you were only pretending.'

'*Hombre*, this is no pretence,' said the warder in the same dry tone as before.

They marched him off.

I heard him shouting outside. But the sound of the shots came only a few minutes later.

In the meantime the priest and the warder had opened the door of the next cell; it was No. 42, the second to my left. Again, '*Qué?*' And again the prayer and the bell. This one sobbed and whimpered like a child. Then he cried out for his mother: '*Madre, madre!*'

And again: '*Madre, madre!*'

And again: '*Madre, madre!*'

'*Hombre*, why didn't you think of her before?' said the warder.

They went on to the next cell. When my neighbour was called, he said nothing. Most probably he was already awake, and, like me, prepared. But when the priest had ended his prayer, he asked, as if of himself: 'Why must I die?' The priest answered in five words, uttered in a solemn voice but rather hurriedly:

'Faith, man. Death means release.'

They marched him off.

They came to my cell and the priest fumbled at the bolt. I could see him through the key-hole. He was a little, black, greasy man.

'No, not this one,' said the warder. They went on to the next cell. He, too, was prepared. He asked no questions. While the priest prayed, he began in a low voice to sing the 'Marseillaise'. But after a few bars his voice broke, and he too sobbed.

They marched him off . . .

     .   .   .   .   .

And now I realized why the merchant from Gibraltar had said that he and his friends would shortly be moving in to No. 39.

I frequently awoke during this night feeling my bed shaking, as though in an earthquake. Then I realized that it was my own body that was trembling from head to foot. The moment I awoke my body grew still; the moment I fell asleep the nervous trembling began again. I thought at first that it was a permanent affliction like shell shock: but I only had two further attacks in the next few days; then it passed off.

Carlos was in a far worse plight. He had heard all that I had heard. During the night of Friday, nine were shot; during Saturday night, thirteen. We heard everything, four nights running. On Monday morning I was called to Carlos's cell; he was lying on the ground by the door, foam on his lips, both legs stiff and paralysed.

In the space of five days they had shot forty-seven men. Even for this prison it was a record. The faces in the patio were grey; during a game of football two men had a set to and pulled each other's hair out in handfuls. In the morning the warders who had been on night duty crept along the corridors, pale, scared, and troubled. Even Angelito, who had to open the doors of the condemned cells night after night, arrived one morning red-eyed. 'If this goes on,' he said, 'they'll finish us all off.'

Our two Republicans in the siesta patio carried it off best. Once, on Sunday, when we looked up at the window of one of the mass cells, from which one of their friends used to wave through the iron bars at three each afternoon, his cell companions signalled back that his turn had come the night before. Whereupon Byron had to vomit; then he lit a cigarette and uttered an obscenity.

When we were marched back to our cells, we did not dare, out of superstition, to say '*hasta mañana*' (until to-morrow). We murmured '*hasta . . .*' and were ashamed of being so superstitious.

One evening Don Antonio came back into my cell after serving out the food. 'Why are you eating so little?' he asked. I said I had no appetite. 'Are you afraid?' he asked. I reflected for a while and then said 'Yes'. He did not reply, but shrugging his shoulders, offered me a cigarette and pulled the door carefully to, without slamming it.

Carlos told me that two had been taken from Johnnie's cell the night before. Johnnie had told him that they had both wept and he had cracked jokes about the cowardice of the Reds. Carlos had asked Johnnie whether he himself was not afraid. Johnnie said that he wasn't a lousy Red. One of the executed Reds had lent him two pesetas the day before; at least he wouldn't have to return the money now.

I asked Carlos whether he proposed to go on being friends with Johnnie. He said he would like to strangle him with his bare hands.

We had become very free with such expressions. Death stalked the prison; we felt the beating of his wings, he buzzed round our faces like a tiresome fly. Wherever we went, wherever we stood, we could not get rid of that buzzing.

During the night of Saturday I again heard laughter—like that that had come from No. 43.

It was pretty infectious, and I wonder things went off so smoothly.

.   .   .   .   .

On the night of Tuesday seventeen were shot.
On Thursday night eight.
On Friday night nine.
On Saturday night thirteen.

I tore strips off my shirt and stuffed my ears with them so as not to hear anything during the night. It was no good. I cut my gums with a splinter of glass, and said they were bleeding, so as to obtain some iodised cotton wool. I stuffed the cotton wool in my ears. This was no good, either.

Our hearing became preternaturally sharp. We heard everything. On the nights of the executions we heard the telephone ring at ten o'clock. We heard the warder on duty answer it. We heard him repeating at short intervals: 'ditto . . . ditto . . . ditto . . .' We knew it was someone at military headquarters reading out the list of those to be shot during the night. We knew that the warder wrote down a name before every 'ditto'. But we did not know what names they were and we did not know whether ours was among them.

The telephone always rang at ten. Then until midnight or one o'clock there was time to lie on one's bed and wait. Each night we weighed our lives in the balance and each night found them wanting.

Then at twelve or one we heard the shrill sound of the night bell. It was the priest and the firing squad. They always arrived together.

Then began the opening of doors, the ringing of the sanctus bell, the praying of the priest, the cries for help and the shouts of 'Mother'.

The steps came nearer down the corridor, receded, came nearer, receded. Now they were at the next cell; now they were in the other wing; now they were coming back. Clearest of all was always the priest's voice. 'Lord, have mercy on this man, Lord, forgive him his sins, Amen.' We lay on our beds and our teeth chattered.

On Tuesday night seventeen were shot.

On Thursday night eight were shot.

On Friday night nine were shot.

On Saturday night thirteen were shot.

Six days shalt thou labour, saith the Lord, and on the seventh day, the Sabbath, thou shalt do no manner of work.

On Sunday night three were shot.

GEORGES BERNANOS

Straight to the Cemetery

from *A Diary of My Times*, 1938
(*Les Grands Cimetières Sous La Lune*, Paris, 1938, transl. Pamela Morris)

Then appeared the General Count Rossi.

Of course the new-comer was neither a general nor a count, but an Italian official belonging to the Black Shirts. One morning we saw him disembark his scarlet racing-car. First he called on the military governor appointed by General Godet. The governor and his officials received him politely. Emphasizing his remarks with thumps upon the table, he announced himself as the herald of true Fascism. A few days later the general and his staff took up their abode in the prison of San Carlos, and Count Rossi was in control of the *Phalange*.

In black robes, with a huge white cross on his chest, he tore round the villages, driving his racing-car himself; other cars, crammed with men armed to the teeth, strove to keep up with him in a cloud of dust. Every morning the papers told of these oratorical excursions. Accompanied by the alcalde and the priest, in a strange mixed jargon of Spanish, Italian and Majorcan dialect, he announced the 'Crusade'.

In all fairness let it be said that the Italian government possessed in Palma some less glaring agents than this gigantic brute, who asserted one day at the table of a distinguished lady of Palma—whilst wiping his fingers on the tablecloth—that he required at least 'one woman per day'.

But the particular mission entrusted him was marvellously suited to his gifts: the organizing of Terrorism.

From that time, every night, gangs of his own recruiting commenced operations in the villages and in the very suburbs of Palma. Where these gentlemen were most effective, there was barely any outward change. Always the same gentle knock at the door of a comfortable flat or a workman's cottage, the same crunching of steps in the darkness of the garden, or the same whispering of death on the landing, to which the victim listens from the other side of the wall, his ear to the keyhole, and anguish pinching his heart. 'Follow us.' The same words to the distracted woman; trembling hands struggling into well-worn clothes that a few minutes earlier had been discarded for the night, and the purr of the engine out there in the road. 'Don't wake the kids—what's the use? You're taking me to prison aren't you, señor?'

'*Perfectamente*,' answers the killer, who sometimes is under twenty.

You climb into the lorry where you find two or three other fellows you know, sombre and resigned as yourself, with uncertain eyes . . . *Hombre!* A screech of brakes and the lorry sets off. A few moments of hope whilst it still keeps to the main road. But now it is slowing down, turning, goes jolting along a hollow earthen pathway.

'Get down!'

You get down, you line up, you press your lips to a medal—or merely to your own thumb nail.

Bang! Bang! Bang!

The bodies are piled against a bank, where the grave-digger will find them next day, their heads burst open, and their necks resting on a hideous cushion of black coagulated blood. I say the grave-digger, because all this has been carefully arranged to take place not far from a cemetery. The alcalde will record in his register: 'So-and-So, So-and-So, So-and-So, died of congestion of the brain.'

The first phase of the purge lasted four months, in the course of which this foreigner, who was mainly responsible for the slaughter, made a point of being well to the fore in all religious manifestations. He was usually supported by a chaplain picked up on the spot, in army-breeches and top-boots, a white cross on his chest and pistols stuck in his belt. (That particular priest has since been shot by his own side.)

None would have dared question the discretionary powers of the Italian general. I remember one unhappy priest who humbly begged of him to spare the lives of three young women of Mexican origin, whom he deemed to be without malice, after hearing their confession.

'Right,' said the count. 'I'll sleep on it.' The following morning he had his men shoot them down.

Thus, until December, the hollow pathways of the Island, round the cemeteries, regularly received their deathly harvest of 'wrong thinkers'. Workmen, peasants, and middle classes too—chemists, lawyers. One day as I was asking a doctor friend of mine for a negative taken some time previously by his colleague, a radiologist—the only one in Palma—he smiled and said: 'I wonder what's happened to the apparatus? . . . Poor old X . . . he was taken for a ride the other evening.'

These facts are common knowledge.

When the purging of the homes was nearly over, there were the prisons to deal with. You can imagine how crammed full they were! And the concentration camps! And the disarmed ships! Sinister hulks guarded night and day, with the grim ray of a searchlight—by way of extra precaution—sweeping backwards and forwards across them all night. Alas, I could see it from my bed.

The second phase was the purging of these prisons.

A large number of suspects, both men and women, escaped martial law for lack of any shred of evidence against them on which a court-martial could convict. So they began setting them free in groups, according to their birth-place.

But half-way, the car-load would be emptied into a ditch.

I know . . . you don't wish me to go on. How many dead? Fifty? A hundred? Five hundred? The figure I shall tell you was given to me by one of the heads of the Palma Crusade. (The evaluation of the people is a very different one: never mind that.) Early in March 1937, after seven months' civil war, there were three thousand assassinations of this kind. Seven months are two hundred and ten days, which means an average of fifteen executions a day. Let me remind you that this tiny island can easily be crossed in two hours, from one end to the other. So that any inquisitive person with a car, if he took the trouble, could successfully wager that he would witness the blowing-out of fifteen wrong-thinking brains per day. These figures are not unknown to his Lordship the Archbishop of Majorca.

You may hate to read of this. Believe me, I hate to write of it. Above all,

I hated the sound and sight of it. We stuck it out, my wife and I, not through bravado, not even hoping to be of much use—there was so little we could do, after all—but rather out of a deep sense of solidarity towards a group of decent people, of which there were more each day, who had known our hopes and illusions, stubbornly held their ground against overwhelming evidence, and now finally shared in our sorrow. They were not free, as we were. I remember those young Phalangistas, those old priests—one of them for having spoken his mind too freely was made to swallow, on pain of death, a litre of castor-oil. Had I lived there among the Left, it is possible that their methods of protest might have awakened in me certain partisan reflexes which one is not always able to control. But disillusion, distress, pity and shame, bind one far more closely than revolt or hate. You arise wearily from your bed, you are on your way, and there, in the street, at a café table, on the church steps, is one whom you thought was on the side of the killers, and he suddenly cries out to you, with eyes full of tears:

'I've had enough! I can't go on! Look—look what they've done now!'

.   .   .   .   .

The military authorities now became uneasy at the growing disgust surrounding them, which the animosity of the *Phalange*—all arms and leaders had suddenly been confiscated from them—was likely to render dangerous, so they adopted a third method of purging, the most discreet of all. Here it is, in all its simplicity:

Prisoners deemed undesirable received one morning notice of their discharge, together with a certificate of wrongful arrest. They signed the gaol book, gave a receipt for objects confiscated, tied up their bundle of belongings, in short went through every formality, one by one, required to free the prison administration from any further liability. At two o'clock in the morning they were set free, in couples. That is to say they found themselves outside the doors in a deserted road, facing a lorry and surrounded by men covering them with revolvers.

'Silence. We're taking you home.'

They were taken straight to the cemetery.

The person whom good manners suggest that I should refer to as His Lordship the Archbishop of Majorca, signed the collective letter of the Spanish Episcopate. I only hope the pen shook in his senile hand. He cannot have been unaware of these murders. I will tell him so to his face, when and where he pleases. And I will bring him this further testimony: One of the canons of his cathedral whom he knows well, a famous preacher, a doctor of divinity, had always seemed to approve the military authorities without any restriction. This prejudice troubled one of his lady parishioners, though she never dared mention the matter. But when she heard of the facts referred to above, she felt the time had come to speak out.

The creature listened without showing the slightest surprise.

'But surely you *can't* agree with—'

'I neither agree nor disagree,' came the sinister answer. 'Your Grace has unfortunately no idea of the difficulties of our ministry, in this island. At the last general meeting of parish priests, over which his Lordship presided, we had proof that last year only fourteen per cent of Majorcans made their Easter. So grave a situation justifies exceptional measures.'

. . . . . .

Civil war is wished for by a few, but to start with, it is the release of a psychological complex: 'Let's finish things once for all!' The enemy is not, in this case, a man to be converted, but suppressed, since the social order finally admits being unable to keep him within its bounds. He is outside the law, the law protects him no longer. He has nothing to expect further, but pity. But in civil war any act of pity would be a shocking example to the troops! You don't mean to tell me that General Franco's soldiers would have tolerated seeing Spaniards run through by lousy Moors—Spaniards who were asking for mercy in their own language —if they hadn't believed, on the word of honour of their leaders, that these fellow-countrymen of theirs were outside the pale? There is no pity in civil war, there is no longer any justice.

The Reds in Palma belonged, for the most part, only to the moderate parties of the Left, and had no share in the assassinations in Madrid or Barcelona; they were shot down like dogs just the same. You don't set out for civil war with lawyers, judges and Criminal Codes in the ammunition-lorries! I've no liking for this kind of enterprise, but there's a chance that they'll thrust me into it one day. It seems to me that then I shall try to look my job in the face before I roll my sleeves up. I blame your men in command for behaving about injustice precisely as they behave about a brothel: slinking along by the walls, and itching to preach morality once they have had what they want—morality in fatherly fashion to the poor child with only a pair of stockings on, who listens and yawns, sitting on the edge of her bed. Isn't the law as to suspected persons, for instance, printed in unmistakable type in any and every charter of civil war? What is the use of pretending not to see it? 'Halt, or I fire!' You will admit that the most eminent lawyer won't be able to talk round such a maxim as that. Does it matter if the man who didn't halt was wounded or dying? Not a single one of the sick or wounded who were taken prisoner during the military operations in August and September 1936, against the Catalonians in Majorca, was spared by the Nationals. Why should they have been, I ask you? They were beyond the law, and they found themselves beyond humanity too, among ferocious animals—*feras*—beasts!

Wasn't that enough for you? Are you going to make these wretched men your reprobates as well? Up to now, the Church has tolerated their suppression. Is it fitting henceforward to give this suppression the character of being a praiseworthy act, justified by motives that are above the ordinary? I know nothing about it: I should like someone to make it plain to me. It is difficult to deal with the soldiers of the Army of Evil as if they were any sort of belligerents. Wouldn't they, by reason of this fact, come under ecclesiastical jurisdiction? Their sin is the very one that was punished with the utmost severity by the tribunals of the Holy Office, and history teaches us that these tribunals spared neither women nor children. What ought we to do about women and children? I ask myself why anyone should find ridiculous the question I put here. It is useless to hold the Church or the Catholic kings responsible for the Inquisition —moral principles brought it about. After all, when those faggots were lighted throughout Spain, the country included many more eminent theologians than it does to-day, and since the Gospel had already been preached there for fifteen hundred years, there is reason to believe that we have not learnt very much since. Customs evolve more slowly than morals, or rather morals don't evolve, they appear to be subject to abrupt and radical changes which distinguish the rise and fall in periods of history, as they do in the animal or vegetable kingdom. The world is ripe for every kind of cruelty, as it is for every kind of fanaticism or superstition. All that is necessary is that certain of its customs must be honoured, as, for instance, that one should abstain from violating its strange feeling about kindness to animals, one of the few advantages, perhaps, of Western sensibility to-day. I believe the Germans would very soon get used to burning their Jews in public, and the followers of Stalin their Trotskyists.

I have seen—I've seen with my own eyes, I tell you—a small Christian people, with peaceable traditions, extremely, almost absurdly friendly —I've seen them suddenly turned to stone, seen their faces hardening, even their children's faces. So it is no good to claim that we can keep a hold on certain emotions once they are let loose. Shall we make use of them whatever they are like? Shall we run this risk? Shall we drown in blood, as did the contemporaries of Philip the Second, these great heresies hardly above the surface as yet, but to be heard even now rumbling underground? For months, in Majorca, killer-gangs, swiftly transported from village to village in lorries requisitioned for the purpose, shot down in cold blood for everybody to see, thousands of persons who were held to be suspect, but against whom the military tribunal itself could not produce the faintest legal allegation. The Bishop of Palma was informed of this fact, like everybody else. Nevertheless he showed himself to be on the side of the executioners whenever he could —though it was notorious that some of them had the blood of a hundred men on their hands. Will this be the Church's attitude to-morrow?

.   .   .   .   .

Civil wars, to their eternal shame, are basically manoeuvred by police agents. They are inspired and controlled by the police. If I had presumed to put up any opposition to the summary executions in Spain, I should have been shot myself. You don't wage civil war in kid gloves. Terrorism is the order of the day, and you know it. The Spanish bishops know it so well that they have been obliged to refer to 'regrettable excesses' and 'inevitable abuses', in accents that have nothing soldierly about them. I am sorry to have to confess that these conventional forms of general absolution count for nothing with me. Their Excellencies' mistake is always the same. They seem to think that war is like Shrove Tuesday, that it's a jolly respite, as it were, from social morality, and that men can give themselves up to being cruel just as gay sparks at Carnival-time indulge in bottom-pinching! Once the illuminations go out, we must welcome the dear lad home with a smile that's both knowing and fatherly. 'Don't worry, my dear boy. We can none of us resist a little fun sometimes. Think no more about it.'

But, Your Excellencies, this is something more than a little fun!

.   .   .   .   .

I am not aware of what the Crusaders of the Peninsula did or did not do. I only know that the Crusaders of Majorca put to death, in a single night, all the prisoners who were huddled in the Catalonian trenches. They took the whole herd down to the shore and shot them, one beast at a time—they were quite leisurely about it. Oh no, your Excellencies, I don't at all wish to bring your Venerable Brother, the Lord High Archbishop of Palma, into it! He arranged to be represented at the ceremony, as was his wont, by a certain number of his priests, who, under military inspection, offered their ministrations to these hapless human beings. You can picture the scene, can't you? 'Come on, father, isn't that one ready?'—'Just a moment, captain, I'm handing him over to you at once.' Their Excellencies may say that they have obtained satisfactory results in crises like these, but I'm afraid I'm not interested. With a little more time on their hands, and if they had taken the trouble, for instance, to make the patients sit over a cauldron of boiling water, these Church-men would no doubt have had still greater success. They might even have made them intone vespers, why not? It's all one to me . . . When the job was finished, the Crusaders piled their cattle in two heaps—those who'd been given absolution and those who hadn't—then sprinkled petrol over them, which they call gasolene over there. It is quite likely that this Purification by Fire may then have taken on, by reason of the presence of the priests officiating, a liturgical significance. Unfortunately I only saw these blackened, shiny creatures two days after that, contorted by the flames, some of them counterfeiting obscene poses in death, which must have been very distressing for the ladies of Palma and for their eminent confessors.

A reeking tar oozed out of them, and smoked there in the August sunshine.

.   .   .   .   .

Like most Spanish towns, the capital of Majorca belonged to children. Six weeks after the arrival of the armed crusaders, they seemed to own it even more thoroughly, for little mobilized marble-players, armed with wooden guns, marched gravely through the empty streets, with a few of the bigger ones at the head of the procession.

'They're playing at soldiers,' I said. But when their big brothers came back each night from some mysterious expedition, when nearly everyone in the island had stumbled over a corpse some time or other, at the roadside, a corpse crawling with flies with the top of its head blown off, with its back propped up against the hedge, and half its blood-pink brains ceremoniously deposited on its belly—why then a hero becomes a policeman, and isn't a soldier any more.

And so we saw our erstwhile marble-players join the auxiliary police. We saw them exchange their heroic little rifles for rubber truncheons, with lead in the end of them.

This may sound comic—laugh at it as much as you please—but still, terrorism is always terrorism, and if you lived the life of a suspect—that is to say, of fair game for the police—in the days of Maximilian Robespierre, a life in constant danger of being ended by even the vaguest denunciation, *you* would have shivered at the marching by of keen thirteen-year-old *Carmagnoles*.

But I don't in the least want to make you shiver. All I want is to make you think, because I myself have been forced to do so. I didn't altogether realize myself at first. Supposing that I had landed at Barcelona in August 1936, and I had met a brand of urchins armed with knuckle-dusters, marching through the streets of that city, all singing the

International—you can guess what I should have said to that! But I should have merely regarded as mischievous little boys the very same young gentlemen, brandishing the same weapons, if only they had been shouting: 'Down with the Reds,' rather than: 'Down with the—parsons!' That's how it is. We can't control certain of our reflexes.

But now I have come to think of them both with equal pity.

CECIL GERAHTY

In Guareña

from *The Road to Spain*, 1937

It was some time before I grasped the cause of loud crashes which were occasionally heard. Then I saw soldiers smashing doors with the butt ends of their rifles while they carried out a systematic house-to-house search. After a short time only the firing at the station remained, the only noise from the town being the occasional breaking-in of a door.

I descended again into the town and made my way to the square, which seemed to be developing into some sort of headquarters. On the way I noticed some bloody footprints leading from a closed door, so I fetched a Civil Guard and asked him to break it down so that we could see what had happened inside.

The scene within was almost too dreadful to describe. The floor was swimming with blood, and everything in the house was wrecked. Lying by the bed was the body of an old lady of seventy-six, her head half chopped off and her poor broken arms lying unnaturally as if trying to reach the bodies of her son and grandson, who were lying beaten to death beside her. I could find no trace of a gunshot wound on either of them, but they were both terribly disfigured by blows which had rained on them from head to foot.

In the half-light of the shuttered room I could hardly keep my feet on the bloody floor as I groped my way back to the open air.

In the street again two men, their eyes looking half insane with hysterical fear, seized me by the hand explaining volubly that they had just been released from prison. They seemed to be unable to grasp for sure that they were talking to friends and not foes, and were panicking for a friendly voice and safety. They told me that they had been in prison for weeks expecting death at any moment and had only just been released. They were very anxious to get somewhere where there was no risk of meeting their late enemies or of being mistaken for Reds by any of the soldiers who were clearing up the town. I could quite understand their anxiety, as the soldiers who had just witnessed scenes such as I have described were in no mood for half-hearted measures with any of the perpetrators they could lay their hands on.

I saw a large building on which was chalked '*Casa del Pueblo*', in other words the town hall of the Red occupation. This struck me as a glorious opportunity to get hold of evidence of their methods. I found a back door open and made my way in. Above all I was struck by the dreadful fuggy smell. Several of the rooms were dormitories packed with bedsteads which had been stolen from the shops. Banana-skins, olive-stones, remains of ham, and eggshells were everywhere. There is something peculiar about this smell. One gets it in the churches that have been occupied by the Reds as well as their houses, but in this building it seemed to be concentrated and left me with the impression that I should never be near a real Anarchist again without my nostrils warning me of his presence.

I soon found the desk of the Red president. Paper was still in his typewriter, and he had evidently been typing when the alarm took place as the orders for the current day were begun. I have beside me as I write a large meat-chopper which was on his desk, and which was possibly the actual weapon or a similar one to that used on the poor old lady. There were a thousand printed copies of a list of twenty-eight names, headed 'Should the following be placed at liberty?' A space on which to put a cross as in a ballot paper was in front of each name—literally a ballot of death.

Some of the documents were headed 'THE REPUBLIC OF GUAREÑA', bearing witness to the influence of Russian agitators. On the door was an amusing paper which stated that danger approaching by various roads would be signalled by the church bell in the following way: one toll indicating one road, two tolls another road, and so on.

Beside the desk were suit-cases filled with loot such as jewellery, silver, cutlery, and small arms. In my nervousness I am afraid I must have slipped an old Cordoba silver cigar-case into my hip pocket, as I found it there some time later.

Not having much time to spare, I stuffed what papers I could lay my hands on into my shirt and went back to the street.

As I retraced my steps to the Square I saw a weeping mother supported by some of her neighbours, crying out for vengeance. Her own daughter had been dragged away from her literally by the feet to probably an unspeakable death at the hands of the retreating Reds.

From time to time shots and screams betokened another capture. On one of these occasions I saw a woman trying to get at the prisoner and being held back screaming that he was the man who had murdered her husband.

By eleven o'clock the town itself had been cleared up and all the prisoners safely secured. Ten of these had been caught red-handed at their dreadful work, and were shut up handcuffed in the building that was being used as town hall. They were to be shot at twelve o'clock, so I interviewed the officer in charge and asked if I might question them before this took place. He raised no objection, so I had them brought to me one at a time.

The first man I spoke to was a rough-looking customer at the best of times, but it was soon clear that he was still very drunk and had no idea of the predicament he was in; in fact he still thought he was enjoying last night's party when he was shot. The second man was a schoolmaster. I explained that I merely wished to give him an opportunity of letting the world know what ideals he was about to die for, explaining that I had no influence whatever as regards his fate. He insisted on trying to argue that he had had nothing to do with the dreadful crimes committed, but as the result of patient questioning it became quite apparent that his callousness, even from his own admissions, was such that he could watch the most dreadful kind of murder without feeling it his duty to interfere. When finally they were shot I believe he was the only one for whom I had no feeling of regret.

Among the others was one man who interested me particularly. In appearance he was something a little above the average peasant. I should think he was probably a small freeholder who raised cattle. I asked him how on earth he had got himself into this position, and he explained that everybody had told him that (although he realized it was a very dreadful thing to have to do) the killing of landowners and capitalists would lead to a wonderful and happy new Spain. When I asked him who had given him this information he seemed to have been more particularly affected by the wireless than anything else. He explained that night after night they listened to the recital of triumphs of the Red forces everywhere. It was fresh news to him to learn that the anti-Reds were in the neighbourhood at all. When I asked him what radio he listened to I found that he had never realized that it was just somebody talking to him through a machine. He looked upon it as something of an oracle, the voice of God, that could not be wrong. The whole thing struck me as being terribly pathetic.

I asked him, as he had now lived for several months under the regime of these people, what sign of the promised good times he had observed, to which he replied, 'Nothing—nothing but terrible things.' He had no desire to escape his fate. He had the stoic Spanish indifference to death, his attitude being rather that he had backed the wrong horse and could not grumble at losing his stake. He went off to his death with less fuss than I make going to the dentist.

   . . . . .

Released from the horrors of the last few months, free once again to enquire after missing relatives and friends, groups of the few remaining inhabitants were strolling about the square, a dull look of misery on their faces, and as an ominous crackle of rifle-shots came from the cemetery wall neither their expression nor their stride changed. One life for them was over and a new one was about to spring, or rather creep, from the old one.

The sun was now getting low, and counter-attacks were expected during the night, so I decided to remain no longer. My road passed the cemetery wall, where a crumpled heap bore silent witness to the wages of sin.

WAR STORIES

CYRIL CONNOLLY
'The House of Arquebus—Part One'

from *Night and Day*, 12 August 1937

Doodles is our Cairn, with lovely crinkly ears. 'So young and so untender,' Dad says sometimes as he prods him with his evening slipper, and I'm sure if he could answer back he would say 'So young, my lord, and true.' He is the smallest but not the least important member of the House of Arquebus, so I have begun with him. Dads is the head. He is Philip Arquebus and I expect not unknown to you. He calls himself a 'blurbie' but he is a good deal more than that—author, essayist, talker, quoter, no mean cricketer and philosopher, an earl's great great nephew through Granny, and literary adviser to some publishers, and 'the famous critic', too, of course. And he wields no mean skittle either. And then there's Mums whom we all adore—a very special person. And Uncle Pat—Mum's brother, who's been 'staying' with us for the last two years, who's been a judge or something in Jamaica or somewhere, and Granny—Dad's mother—a real old Edwardian, and Baby—my young sister who goes to a psycho-school—and my brother Chris who's at Cambridge and terribly Left. All his friends are communist and one of them is CP! And myself, 'the girl Felicity' as Dad calls me—but better known as Fellow. I've often tried to describe myself. Chris is much easier, he's square and solid, but also rather tortured and always running his fingers through his hair. I'm rather elusive and faun-like, a Slade-school Primavera Uncle Pat described me as, but we don't listen to him very much. Love in the Valley, according to Granny. Mariella in *Dusty Answer*, I think, but with a good deal of Roddie too. But it's silly to think about oneself. I realize that as a family we are rather special—happier, cleverer and better-looking than most—good heavens, I've forgotten my elder sister, Jan, who's married to Jeff Crace! He's something the wrong side of Temple Bar. A stockbroker, in fact, but they don't live with us.

Since I do, though, I've decided to keep a diary, or rather Journal, because I think the doings and sayings of a family like ours, with Dads a public figure etc. and Granny a link with the past, and Mums so special, will be worth remembering some day and incidentally be worth a hundred down and twelve per cent. if anything should happen to him.

Best-looking boy friend, Hugo.

Most interesting b.f., Lambert.

Hugo is a Young Conservative and very necessary to any Berkeley Buttery side. Lambert was very well-known at Oxford. My girl friend is called Cecily.

Family politics—The Ruling Caste: Granny; Dads; Me;? Baby. The Ruled: Uncle Pat; Doodles; Chris; the Craces. The Administration: Mums.

Also—four servants and Nurse.

Of course the governed kick against the traces quite a bit. Uncle Pat is an escapist and Chris tries to be cold and rebellious and writes furious letters to Lackstrop, who's a don. And Doodles gets lost on the Heath. But we're essentially a happy family, and all thoroughly binworthy —which is something in these standardized times. Like all happy families, we don't talk at meals unless there are visitors, but I took down some conversation at dinner last night. The dining-room is rose, with a shiny mahogany table and lots of silver and candles. It looks out on the garden. The only house in Hampstead Leigh-Hunt didn't live in, according to Dads. There is just the faintest suspicion of spring, a premonition of green on the privet. The bulbs look rather impertinent, and everything seems to say 'Just you wait!'

Dads: 'Well, Chris, not gone to Madrid yet?'

Chris: 'If that's a joke, I don't think it's very funny.'

Mums: 'Chris!'

Dads: 'And if it's not a joke?'

Chris: 'Then I'll try and oblige you by going now.'

Dads: 'Master Chris doesn't feel very well, Fawcett, you can take his place away.'

Mums: 'Chris! Come back!'

Miss Saint-Gothard to Uncle Pat: 'And who do you think are going to win?'

Dads: 'I only hope Cambridge's loss will prove Madrid's gain.'

The B.F.: 'No business of mine of course, but I shouldn't think they'd let your brother past the frontier.'

Me (oil on troubled waters): 'All one can say is that everything one likes is going to go, whatever happens.'

Miss Saint-Gothard: 'How I agree!'

Jeff Crace: 'Depends on how much one likes Rio Tinto.'

Miss Saint-Gothard: 'And Rioja. And Valdepeñas!'

The B.F.: 'And Lalanda and Belmonte.'

Humble Self: 'And Goya and Greco.'

Dads (finding his form): 'There used to be a posada, the inn of the beekeepers, in a certain hidden valley near a small town which I'm not going to mention because, if the fascists don't spoil it, I know one of you would, where they sold me a brandy from Queen Isabel's reign that was paradise to young limbs that had crossed the arrête and walked through the chestnut woods from Roncesvalles. Wines of Navarre! Woods of the Val d'Arasas! What do they care about isms and ologies—what do ists and ologists care about them?'

Miss Saint-Gothard and Mums: 'Bravo?'

B.F.: 'What, politically, is your father?'

Dads: 'I usually describe myself as a liberal rather liable to pink deviations.'

Miss Saint-Gothard: 'I'm a socialist.'

Humble Self: 'I'm just frightfully Left, I'm afraid.'

B.F. and Jeff C.: 'Come, come!'

Humble Self: 'But I think the most wonderful people are people like Mums, who still manages not to be anything.'

Sister: 'And it gets harder every day.'

Mums: 'Well, somebody has got to look after you all, and happy families have large appetites.'

B.F.: 'An army marches on its stomach.'

Dads: 'Well, here's to our quarter-master-general.'

Miss Saint-Gothard: 'I think it's much more likely to march on mine.'

General merriment. Miss Saint-Gothard is finding her form. She's so crisp. That's what I want to be like when I'm fifty, a nice clean stick of celery. Though she's not really one of the family, not in the know. Uncle Pat, for instance, doesn't get a second glass of wine ever—Fawcett sees to that—and, when you know, it makes his dinner manners much more comical. And there's Chris stealing down the stairs with a suitcase, silly boy; he puts his finger to his lips as he goes by. I feel so much older than him tonight. It doesn't seem fair to let him go. 'Why, there's Chris!' I cry. He looks quite odious for a moment. 'Oh, do come in,' says the male parent. 'Have some dinner, won't you? And bring your luggage.' 'We've all missed you,' from Miss Saint-G. 'Is your headache better?' (Mums). 'I don't want any dinner, thank you, and I don't enjoy sitting for hours over a meal in any case.' 'Perhaps you'd like a soap-box.' When Dads gets

in a shrewd blow like that there's not much to say. Uncle Pat makes one
of his Eyeless in Gaza noises. Chris goes out and is tiresomely careful *not*
to slam the door. 'Supposing he does go?' says the B.F. 'How's the
exchequer, Mrs Arquebus?' says Dads. 'He had nine and elevenpence
when Nurse turned out his suit this morning.' 'And I've locked his
passport up—he won't get farther than Cook's. I think somehow before
the night is out we shall be a united family again.' Dads *can* be sweet.

JEAN-PAUL SARTRE

'The Wall'

'A Story of the Spanish Civil War'
Transl. C. A. Whitehouse
from *Life and Letters Today*, Winter 1937

They pushed us into a great white room, and I began to blink because the
sun hurt my eyes. Then I saw a table with four fellows behind it, civilians,
looking at some papers. The other prisoners had been herded into the
back of the room and we had to cross right over to join them. There were
several I knew, and some others who must have been foreigners. The two
in front of me were fair, with round heads. They looked alike—
Frenchmen, I supposed. The smaller one kept hitching up his trousers.

It lasted nearly three hours; I was dazed and light-headed, but the
room was well heated and I thought it rather pleasant. For the last
twenty-four hours we hadn't stopped shivering. The guards brought the
prisoners to the table, one by one. The four men there asked them their
name and profession. For the most part they didn't pursue the inquiry,
but sometimes they asked, 'Did you take part in the blowing-up of the
munitions?' Or, 'Where were you on the morning of the 9th, and what
were you doing?' They didn't listen to the answers—or at least, so it
seemed. They were merely silent a moment, looking straight ahead; then
they began to write on their papers.

They asked Tom if it were true that he served with the International
Brigade: Tom couldn't deny this because of the papers they had found in
his coat. They didn't question Juan, but after he had given his name, they
wrote for a long time.

'It's my brother José, who's an anarchist,' Juan said. 'You know he's
not living here any more. I don't belong to any party. I've never had
anything to do with politics.' They didn't reply.

'I haven't done anything,' Juan repeated. 'Why should I foot the bill?'

His lips trembled. A guard silenced him and led him away. It was my turn.

'Your name is Pablo Ibbieta?'

I told them it was.

The man looked at his papers and said,

'Where is Ramon Gris?'

'I don't know.'

'You hid him in your house from the 6th to the 19th.'

'No.'

They wrote for a bit, then the guards took me out. In the passage Tom and Juan were waiting for me between two guards. We set off.

'Now what?' Tom asked one of the guards.

'What?' said the guard.

'Is that an examination or a trial?'

'It was a trial,' said the guard.

'Well? What will they do with us?'

The guard replied dryly, 'The sentence will be made known to you in your cells.'

Actually our 'cell' was one of the hospital cellars. It was terribly cold because of the draughts. We had shivered the whole night long and by day it was scarcely any better. I had spent the five preceding days in a hiding-place in the archbishop's palace—a kind of medieval trap-dungeon. I hadn't been cold, but I was lonely, and that puts you on edge in the long run.

In the cellar was a bench and four palliasses. When they had brought us back we sat down and waited in silence. After a time, Tom said,

'We're done for.'

'I think so too,' I said, 'but I don't think they'll touch that youngster.'

'They've nothing against him,' said Tom. 'He's the brother of a combatant, that's all.'

I looked at Juan. He didn't seem to be listening.

'You know what they do at Saragossa?' Tom went on. 'They lay the chaps down on the road and run lorries over them. A deserting trooper from Morocco told us about it. They say it saves bullets.'

'It doesn't save petrol,' I remarked. I was annoyed with Tom; he shouldn't have said this.

'Then there are officers walking up and down with their hands in their pockets, smoking cigarettes. Do you think they'd finish a chap off? Not they! They let them scream. Sometimes for an hour. The black trooper told me he was nearly sick the first time.'

'I don't think they do that here,' I said. 'Unless they're really short of ammunition.'

Daylight was coming in through four vent-holes and through a round opening on the left, in the ceiling, through which you could see the sky. It was through this round hole, normally covered by a trap-door, that they shot the coal into the cellar. Just under the hole was a big heap of coal-dust. Since the outbreak of war the patients had been evacuated from the hospital and the coal lay there unused; it even got rained on, because they had forgotten to close the trap.

I wasn't exactly cold, but I had no more feeling in my shoulders and arms. From time to time I had the impression there was something missing, and I would begin to look around for my coat; and then I would notice that they hadn't given me a coat. It was rather painful. They had taken away our clothes to give to their soldiers, and had only left us our shirts and those thin cotton trousers that patients wear in the heat of summer.

Tom shivered, then began to do some physical jerks. Presently he came and sat down near me, blowing hard.

About eight o'clock an officer entered with two Phalangists. He was holding a sheet of paper.

'What are their names?' he asked the guard.

'Steinbock, Ibbieta, and Mirbal.'

The officer put on his spectacles, and looked at his list. 'Steinbock . . . Steinbock . . . here we are . . . You're condemned to death. You will be shot to-morrow.'

He gave another look.

'And the others too.'

'That can't be right,' said Juan. 'Not me!'

The officer gazed at him in astonishment.

'What's your name?' he asked.

'Juan Mirbal.'

'Well, your name's down,' replied the officer, 'you are sentenced to death.'

'I haven't done anything,' said Juan.

The officer shrugged his shoulders and turned to Tom and me.

'You are Basques?'

'No.'

He looked annoyed.

'They told me there were three Basques here. I'm not going to waste my time running after them. Well, you won't be wanting a priest, of course?'

We didn't even reply. He said, 'A Belgian doctor will be along presently. He has permission to spend the night with you.'

He saluted and went out.

'What did I tell you,' said Tom. 'We're for it.'

'Yes,' I said, slowly. 'But it's lousy for that kid.'

I just said that to be fair, but I didn't really like him. His face was too soft, and fear and suffering had disfigured it and distorted its features. Three days before, he was nice-looking in a rather mawkish way, but now he looked like an old woman; and I thought he would never be young again, not even if they set him free. He didn't say any more, but he had grown grey: his hands and his face were grey. He sat down again, and his round eyes stared at the ground. Tom was a kind soul; he wanted to take his arm, but the youngster shook him off, making a face.

'Let him be,' I said. 'Can't you see he's going to howl?'

Tom obeyed, reluctantly. He would have liked to comfort the boy, to avoid the temptation of thinking about himself.

'Have you bumped any fellows off?' he then asked. I didn't answer; I was wondering if one suffered much; I was thinking of the bullets; I imagined their burning shower through my body. After a time, Tom stopped talking, and I looked at him out of the corner of my eye. I saw that he had grown grey, that he too looked wretched, and I said, 'It's the beginning.'

It was nearly dark. A wan light filtered through the vent-holes and the coal-heap made a big splodge beneath the sky. I saw a star through the hole in the ceiling; the night would be cold and fine.

The door opened, and two guards came in. They were followed by a fair man in a Belgian uniform. He saluted us and said, 'I'm a doctor. I have permission to assist you in these painful circumstances.'

He had a pleasant, refined voice.

'What have you come to do?' I asked.

'I'm at your service. I will do my very best to lighten these last hours.'

'Why have you come to us? There are others. The hospitals are full of them.'

'I have been sent here,' he replied, vaguely. 'Oh! you'd like a smoke, I expect. I've some cigarettes and cigars.'

He offered us some English cigarettes and some Spanish cigars, but we refused them. I looked him straight in the face and he seemed uneasy.

'You haven't come here out of pity,' I said. 'Besides, I know you, I saw you with the fascists in the barrack-yard the day I was arrested.'

I was going to go on, but suddenly something surprised me: the presence of this doctor all at once ceased to interest me. Usually when I come to grips with a man I don't let go, but now I shrugged my shoulders and looked away. A little later on I raised my head. He was looking at me with a strange look. The guards were sitting on a palliasse. Pedro, the long thin one, was twiddling his thumbs; the other was shaking his head from time to time to keep himself awake.

'Would you like a light?' Pedro suddenly asked the doctor.

The doctor nodded. He looked about as intelligent as a block of wood, but probably he was quite kind-hearted. Pedro got up and returned with a paraffin lamp which he set on one end of the bench. It gave a poor light, but was better than nothing. The night before they had left us in the dark. I gazed at the round patch of light thrown up on the ceiling. It fascinated me. Then suddenly I woke up; the patch vanished, and I felt crushed beneath an enormous weight. It was neither the thought of death, nor fear: it was unnameable. My cheeks were burning and my head ached.

I shook myself and looked at my two companions. Tom had buried his head in his hands, and I could see his fat, white neck. Young Juan was much less composed: his mouth was open and his nostrils quivered. The doctor went over to him and put his hand on his shoulder as if to comfort him; but his eyes remained cold. Then I saw the Belgian's hand slip slyly down Juan's arm to his wrist. Juan sat still, indifferent. The Belgian took his wrist between three fingers with a detached air, and at the same time drew back a bit to hide Juan from me. But I leant forward and saw him pull out his watch and consult it a moment without leaving go of the youngster's wrist. After a little, he let the hand flop and went and stood over against the wall; then, as if he had suddenly remembered something important to note down, he took a little book from his pocket and scribbled a few lines. 'The dirty dog!' I thought, angrily, 'if he comes near me, I'll give him a sock in the jaw.'

He didn't come, but I felt him looking at me. I raised my head and returned his gaze. He said in an impersonal tone,

'Don't you think it freezing down here?'

He looked cold: almost purple.

'I'm not cold,' I replied.

He went on staring at me. Suddenly I realized, and put my hands to my face; it was drenched with sweat. I passed my fingers through my hair: it bristled with perspiration. At the same time I noticed that my shirt was wet and sticking to my skin. I had been dripping for at least half an hour, without feeling a thing. But it hadn't escaped that Belgian swine; he had seen the drops running down my cheeks, and had thought that it was almost a pathological case of terror. While he had felt quite normal and proud because he was cold! I wanted to get up and punch his nose; but I had hardly made a move when my shame and anger vanished. I sat back on the bench, unmoved.

'Are you a doctor?' Young Juan suddenly asked the doctor.

'Yes,' replied the Belgian.

'Does one suffer . . . long?'

'When? Oh! Why no!' said the Belgian in fatherly tones. 'It's soon over.' (Just as though he were soothing a paying patient!)

'But I thought . . . they said that they often have to take two rounds . . .'

'Yes, sometimes,' said the Belgian, nodding his head. 'Sometimes it does happen that the first shot doesn't touch the vital organs.'

'Then they have to reload their rifles and take fresh aim?' Juan thought a moment, then added in a hoarse voice, 'It must take a time!'

I got up and walked over to the coal-heap. Tom started and gave me a dirty look; I got on his nerves because my shoes squeaked. I wondered if my face was as fearful as his: I saw that he was sweating too. The sky was superb; no light crept into the quiet corner and I had only to lift my head to see the Great Bear. But it was no longer the same as before. The night before last I was able to see from my episcopal dungeon a big piece of the sky, and every hour of the day had recalled a different memory. In the morning when the sky was a hard, light blue, I thought of the bathing-beaches round the Atlantic; at midday, I saw the sun, and I thought of a bar in Seville where I used to drink sherry and eat anchovies and olives; in the afternoon I was in the shade, and I thought of the deep shade that extends over one half of a bullring when the other half sparkles in the sun. It was really painful to see the whole world reflected in the sky. But now I could look up as long as I wished; the sky held no more memories. And I preferred it that way. I came back and sat near Tom.

A long time passed.

Tom began to speak in low tones. He always had to talk, otherwise he couldn't shape his ideas. He was doubtless afraid at seeing me as I was, grey and sweating. We were alike, and worse than mirrors to each other. He was looking at the Belgian, that *living* man.

'Can you understand it?' he asked. 'I can't.'

Then I too began to speak softly. I was looking at the Belgian.

'Well, what's the matter?'

'Something's going to happen that I can't understand.'

'You'll understand all right presently,' I sniggered.

'It isn't clear,' he persisted. 'I want to be brave, but I must at least know . . . Listen, they take us into the court-yard, the chaps line up in front of us, . . . how many?'

'I don't know. Five, or eight—not more.'

'All right. Say eight. They'll shout "Present" and I shall see eight rifles pointing at me . . . I believe I shall want to shrink into the wall . . . I shall push the wall as hard as I can, with my back, and the wall will resist . . . like in a nightmare . . . I can imagine all that . . .'

'That'll do,' I said, 'so can I.'

'It must be devilish painful. They aim at your eyes and mouth, you know, to disfigure you . . . I can feel the wounds already. I've had pains in my head and neck for the last hour. Not real pains—it's worse than that. Pains I shall feel to-morrow . . . And then what?'

I understood perfectly what he wanted to say, but I didn't want to appear to understand.

'And then,' I said, harshly, 'you'll be sucking dandelion roots!'

He began to talk to himself, but his eyes never left the Belgian. The latter did not appear to be listening. I knew what he had come to do, though; he wasn't interested in our thoughts; he had come to watch our bodies—our bodies that were dying a living death.

Tom went on mumbling in a distracted kind of way. He talked, of course, to stop himself from thinking. I agreed with him, naturally, and could have said all that he was saying: it is not natural to die. And, since I was going to die, nothing seemed natural any longer—neither the coal-heap, the bench, nor Pedro's ugly face. Only, I didn't like to think the same thoughts as Tom. I gave him a side glance, and, for the first time, he looked queer to me. Death was in his face. My pride was injured. I had lived beside Tom, had listened to him, spoken to him, and yet I knew that we had nothing in common. And now we were as alike as twin brothers, simply because we were going to pass on together. Tom took my hand without looking at me.

'Pablo, I wonder . . . I wonder if it is really true that we shall be wiped out?'

I freed my hand and said,

'Look out, you dirty pig!'

There was a pool between his feet and drops were dripping off his trousers.

The Belgian came over.

'Are you ill?' he asked, with false concern.

Tom did not reply. The doctor looked at the pool, but said nothing.

'I don't know what it is,' said Tom wildly, 'but I'm not afraid, I swear I'm not afraid!'

The Belgian did not answer; he was making notes.

We watched him, young Juan as well. We three watched him because he was alive. He had the movements of a living being, the cares of a living being; he was shivering in this cellar as living beings shiver; he had an adaptable and well-nourished body. We three were no longer conscious of our bodies—not in the same way, at any rate. We were just three beings robbed of life, watching and sucking his life, like vampires.

He finally went over to young Juan. He stroked Juan's head and neck. The youngster let him do it without taking his eyes off him; then, suddenly, he seized the doctor's hand and looked at it in a funny way. He was holding it between his own. I had a shrewd idea of what was going to happen and Tom had too: but the Belgian couldn't make it out, and smiled in an indulgent fashion. Presently Juan put the big fat hand up to his mouth as though to bite it. The Belgian hastily shook himself free and staggered back against the wall. He looked at us with horror for a moment; it must have dawned on him that we were no longer men like himself. I began to laugh and one of the guards started up in surprise; the other was sound asleep.

I felt tired, but over-excited. I didn't want to think about the dawn, about death. But as soon as I tried to think of something else I saw guns levelled at me. I must have lived my execution twenty times over. Once I thought I was a goner; I expect I fell asleep for a moment. They were dragging me towards the wall and I was struggling; I begged for mercy. I woke with a start and looked at the Belgian. I was afraid of having shouted in my sleep, but he was smoothing his moustache and hadn't noticed anything. I think I could have slept a little had I wished; I had been up for forty-eight hours and was worn out. But I didn't want to lose two hours of life. They would have woken me up at dawn; I should have followed them, dazed with sleep; and I should have passed out without a word. I didn't want to do that, I didn't want to die like a dumb animal; I wanted to understand. Also, I was afraid of having nightmares. I rose and walked up and down; and to take my mind off the present, I began to think of the past. A host of memories surged back, helter-skelter—some good, some bad—or at least I should have called them bad before this. There were faces and stories. I saw the face of a little *novillero*, who got gored at Valencia during the festival; I saw the face of one of my uncles, and that of Ramon Gris. I remembered certain episodes: how I had been out of work for three months in 1926: how I had nearly died of hunger. I remembered a night I had slept on a bench in Granada; I hadn't eaten for three days, I was furious, and hadn't wanted to die. That made me smile. How eagerly had I pursued happiness, women, freedom. And for what? I wanted to free Spain; I admired Pi y Margall; I had stuck to the anarchist movement, had spoken at public meetings, I had taken everything seriously, as though I were immortal. Just then the whole of my life seemed spread out before me and I thought, 'It's a bloody lie.' It was worthless because it was over. I wondered how I could ever have gone out and about and chased after women. I shouldn't have lifted a finger had I thought I was going to die like this. My life was before me, clapped shut like a book, and yet all it contained was unfinished. For a moment I tried to judge it. I wanted to say: it's been a fine life. But you couldn't judge it, it was just a sketch. I had no regrets, although there were heaps of things I might have regretted: the taste of sherry, or those summer bathes in a little creek near Cadiz. But death had taken the zest from recollection.

Suddenly the Belgian had a fine idea.

'Look here,' he said, 'if the military authorities allow it, I'll undertake to write a little note to any of your friends.'

Tom groaned. 'I've no one.'

I didn't answer. Tom looked at me curiously for a second, then said, 'You're not going to let Concha know?'

'No.'

I hated that tender participation. It was my fault, of course, for telling him about Concha the night before; I should have kept it to myself. I was with her a year. Yesterday evening, I would have given my right hand to see her again just for five minutes. That's why I had spoken of her; it was stronger than I. And now I didn't want to see her; I had nothing to tell her. I shouldn't even have wanted to hold her in my arms. I was afraid of my body because it had grown grey and sweaty—and I thought maybe I should have been afraid of hers. Concha would cry when she learnt of my death; for months she wouldn't want to go on living. Yet it was I who had to die; and I was alone.

Tom was alone too, but not in the same way. He was sitting astride the bench and was looking at it with a kind of astonished smile. He put out his hand and touched the wood carefully, as if he were afraid of breaking something; then he withdrew his hand quickly and shuddered. I too thought that things had an odd look: they were less distinct and dense than usual. I had only to look at the bench, the lamp, the heap of coal-dust, and I felt I was going to die. Naturally, I couldn't think my death clearly, but I saw it on all sides—in objects and the way they had receded. They held themselves at a discreet distance, like people talking in hushed tones around a death-bed. When Tom touched that bench, he had touched his own death.

It would have left me unmoved in my present condition if they had come and announced that I could go quietly home, that my life was spared; a few hours or a few years of waiting are alike when you have lost the illusion of eternity. In one sense, I was calm: I didn't cling to anything. But it was a ghastly calm—because of my body, my body which I saw with the body's eyes and heard with the body's ears, but it was no longer I. It sweated and trembled by itself; I no longer recognized it. I was obliged to touch it and look at it, as if it were someone else's body.

The Belgian pulled out his watch and consulted it.

'It's half-past three,' he said.

The dirty dog! He must have said that on purpose. Tom jumped; he hadn't realized the lapse of time. Night had shrouded us in a dark, shapeless mass; I hardly realized when it had begun.

Young Juan began to howl. He wrung his hands, crying, 'I don't want to die, I don't want to die!'

He ran the entire length of the cellar with his arms in the air, then collapsed on to a palliasse and sobbed. Tom watched him with mournful eyes, but no longer wanted to comfort him. Indeed, it hardly seemed worth while: the youngster made more noise than we, but he was suffering less. For one solitary second I too wanted to cry, but just the opposite happened: I looked at the lad, I saw his shaking shoulders, and I felt inhuman. I couldn't be sorry for others or for myself. I said: I want to die decently.

Tom had risen; he stationed himself just under the round opening and began to watch the daylight. But it was still dark when I heard him say,

'Can you hear them?'

'Yes.'

People were marching about the court-yard.

'What are they up to? They can't shoot in the dark.'

Then all was silent again.

'It's daylight,' I said to Tom.

Pedro got up and blew out the lamp.

'Bloody cold,' he remarked to his companion.

The cellar had grown quite grey. We heard some shots in the distance.

'They're beginning,' I said to Tom, 'they must be doing it round the back.'

Tom asked the doctor for a cigarette. I didn't want one—neither tobacco nor drink. After that the firing never left off.

'Just listen to 'em!' said Tom.

He wanted to add something, but stopped, looking at the door. It opened and a lieutenant came in with four soldiers. Tom dropped his cigarette.

'Steinbock?'

Tom made no answer. Pedro pointed to him.

'Juan Mirbal?'

'The one on the palliasse.'

'Get up,' said the lieutenant.

Juan didn't budge. Two soldiers took him by the armpits and stood him on his feet. But as soon as they let go he slumped down. The soldiers hesitated.

'He's not the only one who's feeling ill,' remarked the lieutenant. 'You two will just have to carry him and we'll fix him up out there.'

He turned to Tom.

'Come on now!'

Tom went out between two soldiers; two others followed, carrying Juan by the shoulders and legs. He hadn't fainted; his eyes were wide open and tears were coursing down his cheeks. When I made to go too, the lieutenant stopped me.

'Are you Ibbieta?'

'Yes.'

'You are to wait here—they'll come for you presently.'

They went out. The Belgian and the two jailers went out as well, and I was left alone. I didn't understand what was happening to me, but I should have preferred them to have done with it at once. I listened to the rounds of shooting which were going off at almost regular intervals; at each one I started. I wanted to shout and tear my hair. But I gritted my teeth and buried my hands in my pockets because I wanted to stay decent.

After an hour they came to fetch me. They took me to the first floor and into a little room that smelt of cigar smoke and in which the heat seemed stifling. Two officers were sitting in arm-chairs, smoking, with papers on their laps.

'Is your name Ibbieta?'

'Yes.'

'Where is Ramon Gris?'

'I don't know.'

The one who questioned me was short and fat. His eyes were hard behind his glasses.

'Come here,' he said.

I approached. He got up and took me by the arms and gave me a look which should have made me sink through the floor; at the same time he pinched my biceps with all his might. It wasn't to hurt me; it was all in the game! He wanted to dominate me. He also thought it necessary to blow his fetid breath full in my face. We stayed a moment in this position. I felt rather like laughing: it takes a lot more than that to intimidate a man who is going to die. It didn't work at all. He pushed me away violently and sat down again.

'It's your life against his,' he said. 'We'll let you go if you tell us where he is.'

These fellows, all decked out with riding-whips and high boots, they too were doomed to die. A bit later than I, perhaps, but not much. And here they were busying themselves looking for names on their little lists, and running after other men to imprison or kill them; they had views on the future of Spain and on other subjects! Their activities seemed mildly shocking and grotesque. I couldn't put myself in their place. I thought they were mad.

The little man was still looking at me and drumming his boots with his whip. His every movement was calculated to make him seem like a fierce live beast.

'Well, then? You understand?'

'I don't know where he is. I thought he was in Madrid.'

The other officer raised a white, indolent hand. This movement, too, was rehearsed. I saw through all their little tricks and was stupefied that there were still men who could act like this.

'You've a quarter of an hour to think it over,' he said slowly. 'Take him to the wash-house and bring him back in a quarter of an hour. If he still refuses, he will be shot immediately.'

They knew what they were about. I had spent a whole night waiting, then they had made me wait an extra hour in the cellar while they were shooting Tom and Juan; and now they were going to shut me up in the wash-house. They must have made their plans overnight; they must have thought that nerves wear out in the long run, and hoped to get me like that.

They were mistaken. I sat down in the wash-house on a stool because I felt very weak; and I began to think. But not about their proposal. Naturally, I knew where Gris was: he was hiding in his cousin's house, a mile from the town. But I knew that I should not betray that hiding-place, unless they tortured me (but they didn't seem to have thought of that!). All that was absolutely taped; it was definite, and ceased to interest me. What I did want to know was the reason for my conduct. I would rather die than hand over Gris. Why? I didn't even like Ramon Gris any more. My friendship for him had died a little before the dawn, at the same time as my love for Concha, at the same time as my desire for life. Of course, I should always think well of him; he was tough. But it wasn't for that that I was accepting to die for him; his life had no more value than my own; no life had any more value. They were going to stand a man up against a wall and shoot at him until he was dead: it was all the same whether that man were I, Ramon, or another. I realized that he was more useful than I to the Spanish cause, but now I didn't care a hang for Spain or for anarchy; nothing had any importance. And yet, I could save my skin by handing over Ramon Gris, and I was refusing to do it! I thought it rather comical: it was sheer obstinacy.

'I must be obstinate,' I thought. And a kind of light-heartedness came over me.

They arrived to fetch me and take me back to the officers. A rat scurried off from under our feet and that amused me. I turned to one of the officers and said,

'Did you see that rat?'

He did not reply. He was morose and took himself seriously. I wanted to laugh, but didn't, because I was afraid that if I started I shouldn't be able to stop. The officer had a moustache.

'You'll have to chop off that moustache, old top,' I cried.

He gave me a kick, but without much conviction and I was silent.

'Well!' said the fat little man. 'Have you thought it over?'

I eyed them curiously, as if they were rare insects.

'I know where he is,' I said. 'He is hiding in the cemetery. In a tomb or in the grave-diggers' shed.'

It was just for a joke. I wanted to see them get up, buckle on their belts, and bustle round giving orders.

They jumped to their feet.

'Come on. Molès, go and ask Lieutenant Lopez for fifteen men. As for you,' the little man said, 'if you've told the truth, I've only one word to say. But you'll pay for it dearly if you're having us on.'

They went out in a great stir, and I waited peacefully with the guards. I smiled from time to time when I thought of the figure they were going to cut. I felt dazed and malicious. I pictured them lifting the stones, opening up tombs one after another!

After half an hour, the short fat officer came back alone. I thought he was going to give the order for my execution. The other must have stayed behind at the cemetery.

He looked at me, but he was neither sheepish nor annoyed.

'Put him into the main courtyard with the others,' he said. 'After the military operations the ordinary tribunal will decide his fate.'

I thought I had misunderstood.

'Then they're not . . .' I said, 'they're not going to shoot me?'

'Not now, at any rate. Afterwards, perhaps—but that doesn't concern me.'

I still didn't understand.

'But why . . . ?' I asked.

He shrugged his shoulders without replying and the soldiers led me away.

There were about a hundred prisoners in the main courtyard, women, children, and a few old men. I began to walk round the centre lawn, still not understanding what had happened. I was bewildered. At midday they gave us lunch in the refectory. Two or three fellows hailed me. I must have known them, but did not reply. I did not even realize where I was.

Towards evening, a dozen or so fresh prisoners were pushed into the yard. I recognized Garcia, the baker.

'You lucky dog!' he cried. 'I didn't think to see you alive!'

'They sentenced me to death,' I replied, 'then they changed their minds—I don't know why.'

'They arrested me at two o'clock,' said Garcia.

'Why?' Garcia didn't meddle with politics.

'I don't know,' he said. 'They arrest anyone who thinks differently from them.'

He lowered his voice.

'They've got Ramon Gris.'

I began to tremble.

'When?'

'This morning. He quarrelled and left his cousin's house on Tuesday. There were plenty of people who would have sheltered him, but he didn't want to be beholden to anyone. He said: "I would have gone to Ibbieta's, but since they've taken him up, I'll go and hide in the cemetery."'

'In the cemetery?'

'Yes. Naturally, they went over there this morning—it was bound to happen. They found him in the grave-diggers' shed. He fired on them and they had to bring him down.'

'In the cemetery!'

Everyone began to turn round, and I found myself sitting on the ground. I laughed so much that tears came into my eyes.

ANDRÉ MALRAUX

Days of Hope

from *Days of Hope* (*L'Espoir*), transl. Stuart Gilbert and Alastair Macdonald, 1938

Langlois, slightly wounded in the head, had been able to drag himself clear, limping on one foot; the other was sprained. Saïdi and Scali were lying among the splintered ruins of the tapering box which had been the cockpit. Beneath the dome of the overturned lower turret was Mireaux, his limbs sticking out from under the boss, the top of which was grinding into his broken shoulder as in an engraving of some ancient torture scene; right in among the wreckage, was the bomber, lying flat. Obsessed by the ever-present danger of fire, all who had strength to do so were shouting for help, their cries echoing through the mountain stillness.

Pujol and Langlois had freed Scali and Saïdi. Then Pujol had begun to extricate the bomber, while Langlois tried to lift the turret which was crushing Mireaux. At last he managed to tip it over, with a fresh crash of steel and mica which startled the wounded lying in the snow, then died away.

Gardet had seen a hut and went off towards it, shoring up his broken jaw with the butt of his revolver. (He did not dare to use his hand, and blood was still pouring from his chin.) A peasant who had seen him in the distance had taken to his heels. The hut was nearly a mile away, empty except for a horse; it eyed him, hesitated, and began to whinny. 'My face must be a god-awful mess,' Gardet thought. 'Still, a living, unrequisitioned horse must mean that we're in Republican territory . . .' The hut was warm after the snow outside, and he felt a desire to lie down and sleep. Nobody came. Gardet picked up a shovel that was in a corner, with his free hand; it would help to get Saïdi out when he got back to the plane, and it would help him to walk. He was finding it difficult to see clearly, except just at his feet. His upper eyelids were swelling. He found his way back by following the trail of blood in the snow, and his footprints, blurred and elongated at the spots where he had fallen.

As he walked he remembered how a third of the *Canard* had been built of old parts from another machine, paid for out of a joint international proletarian subscription, which had been brought down on the Sierra: the *Commune de Paris*.

Just as he reached the plane, a little boy aproached Pujol. 'If we're among fascists, we're done for,' the pilot was thinking. Where were the revolvers? Machine-guns don't lend themselves to suicide.

'Which are you, here?' Pujol asked. 'Reds or Franco?'

The boy—an inauspiciously sly-seeming brat with ears that stuck out and a parting right on the top of his head—looked at him without answering. Pujol began to realize how extraordinary he must look. He had put on his red-feathered hat again, unconsciously, and was still wearing it; his face was only shaved on one side, and the blood was trickling down over his white overalls.

'Which is it, tell me!'

He moved towards the boy, who backed away from him. Threats would do not good. And there was no chewing-gum left.

'Republicans or fascists?'

They could hear the noise of water in the distance, and the cawing of rooks in flight above them.

'There's all sorts here,' the boy answered, looking at the plane. 'Republicans and fascists.'

'What about the syndicate?' Gardet shouted.

Pujol had an inspiration.

'Which is the most important? the UGT? The CNT? Or the Catholics?'

Gardet was walking towards Mireaux, on the boy's right, and the boy could only see his back with the little wooden rifle slung across it.

'The UGT,' the child said at last, with a smile.

Gardet turned round. His face was still supported by the revolver-butt; it had been slashed wide open from ear to ear. The lower part of the nose was hanging down, and the blood, which was now flowing quietly after its first violent uprush, was congealing on the leather flying-coat which Gardet wore outside his overalls. The lad gave a shriek and fled, scuttling sideways like a cat.

Gardet helped Mireaux to gather his spread-eagled limbs together and got him into a kneeling position. When he leant forward his face began to burn, and he tried to keep his head erect as he helped him up.

'We are on our own ground!' Pujols said.

'I must be looking the hell of a sight!' Gardet said. 'Did you see how that kid beat it?'

'You're crazy!'

'Ain't surprising after that slosh on the napper!'

'Look! There's people coming.'

Some peasants were making for them now at last, led by the one who had run away when he saw Gardet. Now that he was no longer alone he had found the courage to return. The explosion of the bomb had brought out the whole village, and the boldest of them were approaching.

'Frente Popular!' Pujol shouted, hurling his red-feathered hat into the middle of the heap of twisted steel.

The peasants started to run. They seemed to have guessed that the crashed plane was one of theirs, for they were practically unarmed; perhaps one of them had caught sight of the red wingbands while the plane was still in the air. Gardet saw the reflecting-mirror hanging still in place amid the jumble of joists and wire, in front of Pujol's seat. 'If I look at my mug now, I'll kill myself,' he thought.

When the peasants were near enough to see the pile of frayed and twisted steel, the battered engines, the propeller bent double like an arm and the bodies lying in the snow, they stopped. Gardet went towards them. They stood waiting in a bunch, absolutely still, as if they were awaiting some catastrophe. The women were wearing black scarves round their heads. 'Look out!' said the peasant leading them; he had noticed that Gardet's broken jaw was supported by a revolver. Reverting instinctively to their former habits at the sight of the blood, the women began to cross themselves. Then, looking towards the bodies in the snow rather than at Gardet and Pujol, who had also started to walk towards them, one of the peasants raised his clenched fist; and one after another, all saluted with their fists the wrecked plane and the bodies which they imagined to be those of dead men.

'There's no need for all that,' Gardet muttered. Then, in Spanish: 'Give us a hand.'

They returned to the other wounded. Directly the peasants realized that only one of the bodies in the snow was dead, they began to bustle round them with clumsy affection.

'Wait a bit!'

Gardet began to organize things. Pujol was showing great activity, but nobody was obeying him. Gardet was in command, not because he was the actual commander but in virtue of his face-wound. 'If Death in person were to arrive on the scene, he'd have everybody at his beck and call!' he thought. Somebody must go for a doctor. A long way; but it couldn't be helped. Moving Scali, Mireaux, and the bomber looked like being difficult; but, he reflected, they're used to broken legs in the mountains. Pujol and Langlois could walk. Himself too, if it came to the worst.

They started the journey down to the village, a little group of men and women dwarfed by the snow. Before losing consciousness Gardet glanced once more at the mirror. It had been smashed to pieces when the plane crashed; there had never been a mirror in the wreckage.

*   *   *

Magnin could see the first improvised stretcher coming into view. Four peasants were shouldering it. Four others followed close behind. They were carrying the bomber.

He looked more like a case of long-standing tuberculosis than a man with a broken leg. The deep-cut furrows in his face increased the tensity of expression in the eyes to the maximum, and the bullet-head with the small moustache had now an air of high romantic dignity.

Mireaux came next. He had changed, too, but in another way. In his case pain had brought back the look of childhood.

'It was snowing when we started down!' he said when Magnin shook his hand. 'A damn' queer show!' He smiled, and closed his eyes again.

Magnin went on, with the bearers from Linares following. It must be Gardet in the next litter; a dressing covered almost the entire face. Only the eyelids could be seen—swollen to bursting point, pale mauve in colour, and so distended that they almost met—between the flying-helmet and a flat bandage. The nose underneath seemed to have disappeared. Seeing that Magnin wanted to say something, the front two bearers lowered their end to the ground before the others, and for a moment the airman's body lay aslant, like a tragic bas-relief Armageddon.

Direct contact was impossible. Both Gardet's hands were under the blanket. Between the lids of the left eye, Magnin fancied he could distinguish a faint line.

'Can you see?'

'Not too well. Just about see you, old chap!'

Magnin felt an impulse to take him in his arms and hug him.

'Anything we can do?'

'Tell the old woman to bloody well stop fussing round with that soup! And listen, when do we reach the hospital?'

'You'll get to the ambulance in an hour and a half. Hospital this evening.'

The stretcher got under way again, with half Valdelinares behind it. As Scali's stretcher went past Magnin, an old woman with a black handkerchief over her hair approached with a cup and gave him some soup. She was carrying a basket containing a thermos flask and a Japanese cup, her most treasured possessions, very likely. Magnin pictured the rim of the cup slipped beneath the turned-up bandage on Gardet's face.

'Better not to give any to the man who's wounded in the face,' he said to her.

'It was the only chicken in the village,' she answered gravely.

'Even so!'

'You see my boy is at the front, too—'

Magnin watched the rest of the peasants and stretchers go past, with the coffin bringing up the rear. It had taken less time to make than the stretchers: a matter of habit . . . The peasants had tied one of the buckled machine-guns from the plane on to the lid.

The bearers changed over every twenty-five minutes, but without putting the stretchers down. Magnin was amazed at the contrast between the women's appearance of extreme poverty and the thermos flasks that several were carrying in their baskets. One of them approached him, pointing at Mireaux.

'How old is he?'

'Twenty-seven.'

She had been following the stretcher for some minutes with a confused idea of being helpful, and there was a precise and gentle tenderness in her movements, a way of propping up the shoulders of the wounded man whenever the bearers had to choose their footing carefully over a steep stretch, in which Magnin recognized the changeless maternal instinct.

The valley was taking them steadily down. On one side the expanse of snow rose until it met the grey, disconsolate waste of sky; on the other, dreary-looking clouds were sailing past the peaks.

The men were maintaining an unbroken silence. Once more a woman approached Magnin.

'What are they, the foreigners?'

'One Belgian. One Italian. The rest are French.'

'Are they the International Brigade?'

'No, but they're the same thing.'

'The one who is . . .'

She pointed vaguely towards his face.

'French,' Magnin said.

'Is the dead one French, too?'

'No, Arab.'

'An Arab? Who'd have thought of it! An Arab—my word!'

She went off to spread the news.

Magnin moved up from the rear of the procession to Scali's stretcher; he was the only one who could do anything except lie flat. In front of him, the path led down in even zigzags to a small frozen stream where Langlois was waiting. Pujol had moved back to the rear. On the far side of the water the path turned at right-angles. The stretchers were about two hundred yards apart. Langlois, their outlandish advance-guard with the bristling mane of hair, was more than half a mile away; a ghost-like figure on his donkey, blurred by the mist which was beginning to rise from the valley. Behind Scali and Magnin there was only the coffin. The stretchers were crossing the stream one by one; seen from the side, the cortège looked like a long, moving fresco painted on the cliff-wall.

'Do you know,' Scali began, 'I used to . . .'

Magnin cut him short:

'Look at that: what a picture!'

Scali did not pursue his story. No doubt it would have got on Magnin's nerves as much as his comparison of the scene before them with a picture got on Scali's.

In the days of the first Republic a Spaniard courting his sister, who neither encouraged nor discouraged his advances had taken her once to his country house in Murcia. The house was a fantastic product of the end of the eighteenth century, with cream-coloured columns against a background of orange walls, stucco decorations freaked with tulips, and box hedges in the garden tracing a palm-like motif beneath the garnet-red roses. One of its former owners had built a miniature shadow theatre, holding thirty people; the magic lantern was already working when they entered, and the silhouettes were visible on the tiny screen. The Spaniard had been successful; she had slept with him that night. Scali had been jealous of that supremely fanciful tribute.

As he approached the mountain stream below, he thought of the four loggias, gold and salmon-pink, which he had never seen. A house full of floral designs, with plaster busts between the dark leaves of the orange-trees. His stretcher crossed the stream and turned the corner. The bulls came into view again opposite. The Spain of his youth—love, make-believe, and misery! Now Spain was that twisted machine-gun on an Arab's coffin and birds numbed with cold crying in the ravines.

*   *   *

The mules in front were vanishing round another corner, following the original direction again. The new line of descent led straight to Linares; Magnin recognized the apple tree.

What forest was that on which the rain was beating down, on the far side of the rock, where the path turned? Magnin coaxed his mule to a trot, went past all the others, and arrived at the turning. No rain; it was the sound of the streams which the cliff wall had screened from him as a rock-wall hides a landscape, and which could not be heard from the other slope. The sound was rising from Linares, as though the ambulances and the new lease of life which lay before them were sending up this insistent rustling, as of a high wind on leaves, from the far depths of the valley. Night had not fallen yet, but the light was failing. Like an equestrian statue, Magnin was sitting askew on his saddleless mule, gazing at the little apple tree surrounded by its dead fruit. Langlois's bristling crest of blood-stained hair came into view in front of the branches. In the silence suddenly grown murmurous with the sound of rippling water, the ring of decaying fruit seemed to typify the passage from life to death that not only was the doom of men but was an immutable law of the universe. Magnin's eyes wandered from the tree to the ageless ravines. One after another, the stretcher were going past. Branches reached forward on either side over the swaying stretchers, as above Langlois's head; above the corpse-like smile of Taillefer, the childlike face of Mireaux, Gardet's flat bandage, and Scali's lacerated lips; above each blood-stained body gently borne along by comrades' hands. The coffin went by, with its machine-gun twisted like the branch of a tree. Magnin moved on again.

Without his quite knowing why, the deep gorges into which they now were plunging, as if into the bowels of the earth, seemed imbued with the same agelessness as the trees. He thought of the quarries in which prisoners were left to die in former days. But that shattered leg which the muscles barely held together, that sagging arm, that obliterated face, that machine-gun on a coffin, all these were the results of risks voluntarily accepted, sought after. The solemn, elemental progress of that line of stretchers had something as compelling about it as the pale rocks that merged into the lowering sky, something as fundamental as the apples scattered on the ground. Birds of prey were crying again, close beneath the clouds. How many years had he to live, still? Twenty?

'What made that Arab airman join in?'

One of the women was approaching him again, accompanied by two others.

Up above the birds were wheeling through the air with rigid wings, like so many aeroplanes.

'Can they really give people new noses now?'

The path widened steadily as the valley approached Linares; the peasants were walking beside the stretchers now. The black-clothed women, scarves on their heads and baskets on their arms, were still bustling around the wounded, moving from one to another. The men were keeping pace with the stretchers, without ever getting in front of them; walking abreast of each other, holding themselves with the stiff erectness of those who have been carrying a weight on their shoulders. At each changeover, the new bearers abandoned their stiff walk as they took up the shafts with affectionate care, moving off again to the accompaniment of the grunts which tell of physical strain, as if anxious to mask the

betrayal of their emotions which their solicitude conveyed. Their attention concentrated on the stones which obstructed the path, thinking only
of the necessity not to jolt the stretchers, they moved steadily forward,
slowing up a little on the steeper inclines. And the steady rhythm of
their tread over the long pain-fraught journey seemed to fill the vast
ravine down which the last cries came floating from the birds above,
with a solemn beat like a funeral drum. But it was not death which
haunted the mountains at that moment; it was triumphant human
will.

They were beginning to be able to make out Linares at the bottom of
the valley, and the stretchers were drawing closer together; the coffin was
level with Scali. The machine-gun had been tied on where a wreath
would normally have been laid; the whole procession recalled a funeral
as precisely as that twisted machine-gun recalled the wreath which it
replaced. Near the Saragossa road down below, around the fascist
planes, the trees in the dark forest were still burning in the fading light.
Well, those planes would never reach Guadalajara now. And all that long
line of black-clothed peasants, the women with their hair hidden beneath
the scarves which they had worn from time immemorial, seemed to have
more of the character of an austere triumphal progress than a rescue
party bringing home wounded men.

The gradient was easy now. Leaving the path, the stretchers spread
out across the grass, and the hillmen scattered out fanwise. Children
were running up from Linares; a hundred yards from the stretchers they
moved aside, to let them pass, and followed on behind. The road
followed the fortifications up to the gate; its cobbles, set edgewise, were
more slippery than the mountain path.

The whole town was massed behind the battlements. Night had not
yet fallen, but there was little daylight left. Though there had been no
rain, the cobbles were moist and shining, and the bearers picked their
way carefully. In the houses which projected above the battlements
lamps were glimmering.

The bomber still headed the line. The women on the battlements
looked at him gravely, but without surprise; only the face of the wounded
man appeared above the blanket, and it showed no sign of injury. Scali
and Mireaux likewise. Langlois gave them a shock; with a bleeding
bandage round his head, and toes sticking into the air (he had removed
the shoe from his sprained foot), he looked like Don Quixote. Was this
how war in the air ended, war in its most romantic form? The atmosphere
grew tenser when Pujol went past; there was still light enough for
observant eyes to see the large blood-stains on his leather coat. When

Gardet arrived a hush so profound fell upon the crowd that the noise of the distant mountain torrents suddenly became audible.

All the other wounded could see; and all, even the bomber, had made an effort to smile when they saw the crowd. Gardet did not look at them; he was alive, but that was all. From the battlements the crowd could make out the bulky coffin behind him. Covered with a blanket up to his chin, and with the bandage under his flying-helmet lying so flat that it was impossible that there could be any nose beneath it, this stretcher was the visible incarnation of the peasants' immemorial conception of war. And nobody had forced him to fight. For a moment they hesitated; not knowing what to do, but determined to make some gesture. Then, as at Valdelinares, they silently raised their clenched fists.

It had begun to drizzle. The last stretchers, the peasants from the mountains, and the last mules were advancing between the vast background of rocky landscape over which dark rain-clouds were massing, and the hundreds of peasants standing motionless with raised fists. The women were weeping quietly, and the procession seemed to be fleeing from the eerie silence of the mountains, its noise of clattering hoofs and clogs linking the everlasting clamour of the vultures with the muffled sound of sobbing.

*   *   *

The ambulance set out.

Through the driver's communicating-window Scali could see square patches of the nightbound countryside. Here and there a section of the ramparts of Sagunto showed up, and cypresses, black and massive in the misty moonlight (that self-same mist which favoured night-bombing raids); ghostly white houses, emblematic of peace; sheen of oranges in their dark groves. Shakespearian orchards, Italian cypresses . . . 'On such a night as this, Jessica . . .' Yes, there still was happiness in the world. On the stretcher above him the bomber was groaning at every jolt.

There was no room for thoughts in Mireaux' brain. He was in a high fever, fancied himself struggling to keep afloat in scalding water.

The bomber was thinking of his leg.

Gardet thinking of his face. Gardet had been a great lover.

Magnin was listening to Vargas over the telephone.

'It's the decisive battle, Magnin. Bring everything you can, as best you can.'

'The controls of the *Marat*'s rudder are pretty well smashed.'

'Do what you can.'

GRAHAM GREENE

The Confidential Agent

from *The Confidential Agent*, 1939

He turned up the collar of his mackintosh and went up on to the cold and foggy deck where the gulls were mourning, blowing over his head towards Dover. He began to tramp—up and down beside the rail—to keep warm, his head down, the deck like a map marked with trenches, impossible positions, salients, deaths: bombing planes took flight from between his eyes, and in his brain the mountains shook with shell-bursts.

He had no sense of safety walking up and down on this English ship sliding imperceptibly into Dover. Danger was part of him. It wasn't like an overcoat you sometimes left behind: it was your skin. You died with it: only corruption stripped it from you. The one person you trusted was yourself. One friend was found with a holy medal under the shirt, another belonged to an organisation with the wrong initial letters. Up and down the cold unsheltered third-class deck, into the stern and back, until his walk was interrupted by the little wooden gate with a placard: 'First-Class Passengers Only.' There had been a time when the class distinction would have read like an insult, but now the class divisions were too subdivided to mean anything at all. He stared up the first-class deck: there was only one man out in the cold like himself: collar turned up, he stood in the bow looking out towards Dover.

D turned and went back into the stern, and again as regular as his tread the bombing planes took off. You could trust nobody but yourself, and sometimes you were uncertain whether after all you could trust yourself. *They* didn't trust you, any more than they had trusted the friend with the holy medal; they were right then, and who was to say whether they were not right now? You—you were a prejudiced party; the ideology was a complex affair: heresies crept in ... He wasn't certain that he wasn't watched at this moment. He wasn't certain that it wasn't right for him to be watched. After all, there were aspects of economic materialism which, if he searched his heart, he did not accept ... And the watcher—was he watched? He was haunted for a moment by the vision of an endless distrust. In an inner pocket, a bulge over the breast, he carried what were called credentials, but credence no longer meant belief.

He walked slowly back—the length of his chain ... He came up to the barrier—'First-Class Passengers Only'—and looked through. The other man was approaching through the fog, walking the longer length of his chain. D saw first the pressed trousers, then the fur collar, and last the face. They stared at each other across the low gate. Taken by surprise they had nothing to say. Besides, they had never spoken to each other; they were separated by different initial letters, a great many deaths —they had seen each other in a passage years ago, once in a railway station and once on a landing field. D couldn't even remember his name.

The other man was the first to move away; thin as celery inside his thick coat, tall, he had an appearance of nerves and agility: he walked fast on legs like stilts, stiffly, but you felt they might fold up. He looked as if he had already decided on some action. D thought: he will probably try to rob me, perhaps he will try to have me killed. He would certainly have more helpers and more money and more friends. He would bear letters of introduction to peers and ministers—he had once had some kind of title himself, years ago, before the republic . . . count, marquis . . . D had forgotten exactly what. It was a misfortune that they were both travelling on the same boat and that they should have seen each other like that at the barrier between the classes, two confidential agents wanting the same thing.

The siren shrieked again and suddenly out of the fog, like faces looking through a window, came ships, lights, a wedge of breakwater. They were one of a crowd. The engine went half speed and then stopped altogether. D could hear the water slap, slap the side. They drifted, apparently, sideways. Somebody shouted invisibly—as though from the sea itself. They sidled forward and were there: it was as simple as all that. A rush of people carrying suitcases were turned back by sailors who seemed to be taking the ship to pieces. A bit of rail came off, as it were, in their hands.

Then they all surged over with their suitcases, labelled with Swiss Hotels and *pensions* in Biarritz. D let the rush go by: he had nothing but a leather wallet containing a brush and comb, a tooth-brush, a few oddments. He had got out of the way of wearing pyjamas: it wasn't really worth while when you were likely to be disturbed twice in a night by bombs.

The stream of passengers divided into two for the passport examination: aliens and British subjects. There were not many aliens; a few feet away from D the tall man from the first class shivered slightly inside his fur coat: pale and delicate, he didn't seem to go with this exposed and windy shed upon the quay. But he was wafted quickly through—one glance at his papers had been enough. Like an antique he was very well authenticated. D thought without enmity: a museum piece. They all on that side seemed to him museum pieces—their lives led in big cold houses like public galleries hung with rather dull old pictures and with buhl cabinets in the corridors.

D found himself at a standstill. A very gentle man with a fair moustache said, 'But do you mean that this photograph is—yours?'

D said, 'Of course.' He looked down at it: it had never occurred to him to look at his own passport for—well, years. He saw a stranger's face—that of a man much younger and, apparently, much happier than himself: he was grinning at the camera. He said, 'It's an old photograph.' It must have been taken before he went to prison, before his wife was killed, and before the air raid of December 23 when he was buried for fifty-six hours in a cellar. But he could hardly explain all that to the passport officer.

'How old?'

'Two years perhaps.'

'But your hair is quite grey now.'

'Is it?'

The detective said, 'Would you mind stepping to one side and letting the others pass?' He was polite and unhurried. That was because this was an island. At home soldiers would have been called in: they would immediately have assumed that he was a spy, the questioning would have been loud and feverish and long drawn out. The detective was at his elbow. He said, 'I'm sorry to have kept you. Would you mind just coming in here a moment?' He opened the door of a room. D went in. There was a table, two chairs and a picture of King Edward VII naming an express train 'Alexandra': extraordinary period faces grinned over high white collars: an engine-driver wore a bowler hat.

The detective said, 'I'm sorry about this. Your passport seems to be quite correct, but this picture—well—you know you've only to look at yourself, sir.'

He looked in the only glass there was: the funnel of the engine and King Edward's beard rather spoilt the view: but he had to confess that the detective was not unreasonable. He did look different now. He said, 'It never occurred to me—that I had changed so much.' The detective watched him closely. There was the old D—he remembered now: it was just three years ago. He was forty-two, but a young forty-two. His wife had come with him to the studio: he had been going to take six months' leave from the university and travel—with her, of course. The civil war broke out exactly three days later. He had been six months in a military prison: his wife had been shot—that was a mistake, not an atrocity: and then . . . He said, 'You know war changes people. That was before the war.' He had been laughing at a joke—something about pineapples: it was going to be the first holiday together for years. They had been married for fifteen. He could remember the antiquated machine and the photographer diving under a hood; he could remember his wife only indistinctly. She had been a passion, and it is difficult to recall an emotion when it is dead.

'Have you got any more papers?' the detective asked. 'Or is there anyone in London who knows you? Your Embassy?'

'Oh no, I'm a private citizen—of no account at all.'

'You are not travelling for pleasure?'

'No. I have a few business introductions.' He smiled back at the detective. 'But they might be forged.'

He couldn't feel angry: the grey moustache, the heavy lines around the mouth—they were all new: and the scar on his chin. He touched it. 'We have a war on, you know.' He wondered what the other was doing now: he wouldn't be losing any time. Probably there was a car waiting. He would be in London well ahead of him—there might be trouble. Presumably he had orders not to allow anyone from the other side to interfere with the purchase of coal. Coal used to be called black diamonds before people discovered electricity. Well, in his own country it was more valuable than diamonds, and soon it would be as rare.

The detective said, 'Of course your passport's quite in order. Perhaps if you'd let me know where you are staying in London . . .'

'I have no idea.'

The detective suddenly winked at him. It happened so quickly D could hardly believe it. 'Some address,' the detective said.

*   *   *

People set down their wine and listened—as if it were poetry. Even the girl stopped eating for a while. The self-pity of it irritated him: it was a vice nobody in his country on either side the line had an opportunity of indulging.

> I don't say you lie: it's just the modern way.
> I don't intend to die: in the old Victorian way.

He supposed it represented the 'spirit of the age,' whatever that meant: he almost preferred the prison cell, the law of flight, the bombed house, his enemy by the door. He watched the girl moodily: there was a time in his life when he would have tried to write her a poem—it would have been better stuff than this.

> It was just day-dreaming—I begin to discern it:
> It was just a way of talking—and I've started to learn it.

She said, 'It's muck, isn't it? But it has a sort of appeal.'

A waiter came over to their table. He said, 'The gentleman by the door asked me to give you this, sir.'

'For somebody who's just landed,' she said, 'you make friends quickly.'

He read it: it was short and to the point, although it didn't specify exactly what was wanted. 'I suppose,' he said, 'you wouldn't believe me if I told you I had just been offered two thousand pounds.'

'Why should you tell me if you had?'

'That's true.' He called a waiter. 'Can you tell me if that gentleman has a chauffeur—a big man with something wrong about his eye?'

'I'll find out, sir.'

'You play it fine,' she said, 'fine. The mystery man.' It occurred to him that she'd been drinking too much again. He said, 'We'll never get up to London if you do not go carefully.'

The waiter came back and said, 'That's his chauffeur, sir.'

'A left-handed man?'

'Oh, stop it,' she said, 'stop it.'

He said gently, 'I'm not showing off. This has nothing to do with you. Things are going so fast—I had to be sure.' He gave the waiter a tip. 'Give the gentleman back his note.'

'Any reply, sir?'

'No reply.'

'Why not be a gentleman,' she said, 'and write "Thank you for the offer"?'

'I wouldn't want to give him a specimen of my handwriting. He might forge it.'

'I give up,' she said. 'You win.'

'Better not drink any more.' The singing woman had shut down—like a wireless set the last sound was a wail and a vibration; a few couples began to dance. He said, 'We have a long drive in front.'

'What's the hurry? We can always stay the night here.'

'Of course,' he said. 'You can—but I must get to London somehow.'

'Why?'

'My employers,' he said, 'wouldn't understand the delay.' They would have time-tabled his movements, he knew for certain, with exactly this kind of situation in mind—the meeting with L and the offer of money. No amount of service would ever convince them that he hadn't got, at some level, a price. After all, he recognised sadly, *they* had their price: the people had been sold out over and over again by their leaders. But if the

only philosophy you had left was a sense of duty, that knowledge didn't
prevent you going on . . .

The manager was swinging his monocle at Rose Cullen and inviting
her to dance; this, he thought gloomily, was going on all night—he would
never get her away. They moved slowly round the room to the sad stiff
tune: the manager held her firmly with one large hand splayed out on her
spine, the other was thrust, with rather insulting insouciance it seemed to
D, in his pocket. He was talking earnestly, and looking every now and
then in D's direction. Once they came into earshot and D caught the
word 'careful.' The girl listened attentively, but her feet were awkward:
she must be more drunk than he had imagined.

D wondered whether anybody had changed that tyre. If the car was
ready, perhaps after this dance he could persuade her . . . He got up and
left the restaurant; L sat over a piece of veal, he didn't look up, he was
cutting the meat up into tiny pieces—his digestion must be rotten. D felt
less nervous; it was as if the refusal of the money had put him into a
stronger position than his opponent. As for the chauffeur, it was unlikely
that he'd start anything now.

The fog was lifting a little: he could see the cars in the courtyard—half
a dozen of them—a Daimler, a Mercédès, a couple of Morrises, their old
Packard and a little scarlet cad car. The tyre had been fixed.

He thought, if only we could leave now, at once, while L is at his
dinner, and then heard a voice which could only be L's speaking to him in
his own language. He was saying, 'Excuse me. If we could have a few
words together . . .'

D felt a little envious of him as he stood there in the yard among the
cars—he looked established. Five hundred years of inbreeding had
produced him, set him against an exact background, made him at home,
and at the same time haunted—by the vices of ancestors and the tastes of
the past. D said, 'I don't think there's much to talk about.' But he
recognised the man's charm: it was like being picked out of a party by a
great man to be talked to. 'I can't help thinking,' L said, 'that you don't
understand the position.' He smiled deprecatingly at his own statement,
which might sound impertinent after two years of war. 'I mean—you
really belong to us.'

'It didn't feel like that in prison.'

The man had an integrity of a kind: he gave an impression of truth. He
said, 'You probably had a horrible time. I have seen some of our prisons.
But, you know, they are improving: the beginning of a war is always the
worst time. After all, it is no good at all our talking atrocities to each
other. You have seen your own prisons. We are both guilty. And we shall

go on being guilty, here and there, I suppose, until one of us has won.'

'That is a very old argument. Unless we surrender we are just prolonging the war. That's how it goes. It's not a good argument to use to a man who has lost his wife . . .'

'That was a horrible accident. You probably heard—we shot the commandant. What I want to say'—he had a long nose like the ones you see in picture galleries in old brown portraits: thin and worn, he ought to have worn a sword as supple as himself—'is this. If you win, what sort of a world will it be for people like you? They'll never trust you—you are a bourgeois—I don't suppose they even trust you now. And you don't trust them. Do you think you'll find among those people—the ones who destroyed the National Museum and Z's pictures—anyone interested in your work?' He said gently—it was like being recognised by a State academy—'I mean the Berne M S.'

'I'm not fighting for myself,' D said. It occurred to him that if there had not been a war he might have been friends with this man: the aristocracy did occasionally fling up somebody like this thin tormented creature interested in scholarships or the arts, a patron.

'I didn't suppose you were,' he said. 'You are more of an idealist than I am. My motives, of course, are suspect. My property has been con-fiscated. I believe—' he gave a kind of painful smile which suggested that he knew he was in sympathetic company—'that my pictures have been burnt—and my manuscript collection. I had nothing, of course, which was in your line—but there was an early manuscript of Augustine's *City of God* . . .' It was like being tempted by a devil of admirable character and discrimination. He couldn't find an answer. L went on, 'I'm not really complaining. These horrible things are bound to happen in war—to the things one loves. My collection and your wife.'

It was amazing that he hadn't seen his mistake. He waited there for D's assent—the long nose and the too sensitive mouth, the tall thin dilettante body. He hadn't the faintest conception of what it meant to love another human being: his house—which they had burnt—was probably like a museum, old pieces of furniture, cords drawn on either side the picture gallery on days when the public were admitted. He appreciated the Berne M S. very likely, but he had no idea that the Berne M S. meant nothing at all beside the woman you loved. He went fallaciously on, 'We've both suffered.' It was difficult to remember that he had for a moment sounded like a friend. It was worth killing a civilisation to prevent the government of human beings falling into the hands of—he supposed they were called the civilised. What sort of a world would that be? a world full of preserved objects labelled 'Not to be touched': no religious faith, but a lot of Gregorian chants and picturesque ceremonies. Miraculous images which bled or waggled their heads on certain days would be preserved for their quaintness: superstition was interesting. There would be excellent libraries, but no new books. He preferred the distrust, the barbarity, the betrayals . . . even chaos. The Dark Ages, after all, had been his 'period.'

He said, 'It isn't really any good our talking. We have nothing in common—not even a manuscript.' Perhaps this was what he had been painfully saved from by death and war; appreciation and scholarship were dangerous things: they could kill the human heart.

L said, 'I wish you would listen.'

'It would waste our time.'

L gave him a smile. 'I'm so glad,' he said, 'at any rate, that you finished your work on the Berne M S. before this—wretched—war.'

'It doesn't seem to me very important.'

'Ah,' L said, 'now that is treachery.' He smiled—wistfully; it wasn't that war in his case had killed emotion: it was that he had never possessed more than a thin veneer of it for cultural purposes. His place was among dead things. He said whimsically, 'I give you up. You won't blame me, will you?'

'What for?'

'For what happens now.' Tall and brittle, courteous and unconvincing, he disengaged himself—like a patron leaving an exhibition of pictures by somebody he has decided is, after all, not quite good enough: a little sad, the waspishness up the sleeve.

MOVING PICTURES

CLAUDE SIMON

The Side of a Railway Carriage

from *Les Géorgiques* (Les Éditions de Minuit,
Paris, 1981, transl. John Fletcher)

The side of a railway carriage, photographed at a slight angle, occupies
the whole length of the picture. It is one of those massive cars, of Belgian
make, which travelled on the wide-gauge tracks of the companies set up
with foreign capital in Spain at the turn of the century. Even in peacetime these trains had something sad about them which was not
due solely to their dirtiness. The carriages and their windows were
indeed always thickly coated with a greasy soot which came off on one's
hands, and the locomotive whistles made a sound at once plaintive and
lugubrious, with a double note which recalled those trains of the
wild west, slowly pushing their way through herds of bison as they
crossed vast distances as arid and barren as the plateaus of Aragon or
Castille.

Of course these foreign companies had been nationalised along with
all the others, and clearly visible on the side of the carriage, written in
chalk or white paint, are the initials of the two main trade unions, the
U G T and C N T, as well as inscriptions glorifying the Iberian Anarchist
Federation.

Strangely, the black and white snapshot gives a better idea than a
colour photograph could of the greyish, remarkably dusty appearance of
these carriages, although, in fact, they were not exactly greyish but a
muddy brown. The impression conveyed by the mournful wailing of the
locomotive and this unusual dirtiness was reinforced by the perfunctory,
brutal nature of their construction, a utilitarian, robust quality, con-
forming no doubt to the directives of the Belgian bankers; and the
profusion of bolts, screws and rivets which nothing had been done to
conceal, as well as the solid girders of their underframes, gave them, like

certain conventual or military vehicles, something at once penitentiary, metallurgical, funereal and barbaric.

From the narrow windows sealed in thick bands of copper (soot does not cling to it as it does to the paintwork of the carriages but deposits itself on it in the form of fine granules under which the yellow metal can be seen, and a quick wipe is enough to make it shine, as happens where the fingermarks are edged by black streaks of soot crushed and dampened by sweat from sticky hands—in other places, where a finger has simply touched, there is a fingerprint with its concentric, graphite rings) . . . from the narrow windows, then, the torsos of young men lean out, in shirtsleeves or overalls, reminiscent of those rowdy groups such as sports teams seen returning from a match on a Sunday evening, standing in train doorways and bellowing victory slogans and bawdy songs punctuated by animal cries. Despite its narrowness three of them are pressed together in one of the rectangles from which the slimmest seems to be squeezed out as far as his waist, with his head raised and thrown back, his arm raised too, as if he were brandishing at head height a flask or other object (weapon? posy?) which cannot be seen because the right hand side of the photograph cuts off his arm just below the wrist.

Most of the carriage's occupants look at the camera and two of them show off their rifles, which they hold at a sloping angle, the barrels pointing skywards out of the windows. They all have thick, black, shiny, oily hair combed backwards, except for one, prematurely balding, who has only two tufts on the sides and a quiff in the middle, his high clear forehead visible above a shy, gentle, almost childlike face which could be that of a restaurant waiter or barber's assistant. The webbing straps of his cartridge pouches stand out against the white shirt he is wearing. There is also something vulnerable and childlike in the way he brandishes his rifle and raises his fist, which instead of presenting palm forwards he shakes in a boyishly threatening gesture.

The window next to his is occupied only by a single militiaman whose head and shoulders are all that are visible, perhaps because he is kneeling or crouching on the floor of the compartment, with his body concealed by the side of the carriage as if he were shielding behind armour plating. He is older than his companions and indifferent to the general excitement; he shows no interest in the photographer but stares at a point on the platform in front and slightly to the left of himself. In his right hand he is holding one of those heavy, flat, shiny black pistols seen in gangster films. It is almost as if he has just pressed the trigger on which his forefinger is still bent and that he is watching carefully the enemy he has just shot. The breech and barrel of the weapon hide the lower part of his face seen in semi-profile and bar it with a thick black line running from slightly under the ear and ending up like a sort of moustache on the upper lip. To the right of the barrel's mouth a cloud of smoke curls away in a whitish blur in front of the militiaman standing at the next window. In fact, it drifts up from the end of a lighted cigarette held between the index and middle fingers of the left hand which the man dangles outside the door. This individual has thick crinkly hair which looks as if it has been piled up in dense waves above his low forehead. His features are of a mediterranean type, sharp, hard and regular with a straight nose, and his eyes are hidden by the patches of shadow cast by his eyebrows; he has a concentrated, grim, even slightly histrionic expression, no doubt exaggerated for the benefit of the photographer (that is of the public who will eventually see the photograph) engaged in taking the picture. No friends or relatives seem to have come to see the men off. Above the top of the carriage the iron vaulting supporting the sooty glass roof can be seen, its massive beams studded with rivets.

JOHN SOMMERFIELD

'War Picture'

from *Volunteer in Spain*, 1937

Rain was falling, a thin, cold drizzle, and on the pavements the women covered their heads with their black shawls. It was curious to march through streets, to march in daylight, and see ordinary people walking about.

Gradually the streets became emptier, traffic ceased. We were entering a strange territory. Further on was the war—soldiers, an open space, and then more soldiers, with death in between. We had left the normal life of the town behind. Here was something in between the two, partaking of both, yet with a strange character of its own. Blocks of flats, half-gutted by shells, were still tenanted. Within bullet range men and women ate meals, washed their faces, lay down to sleep at night.

We came to a broad, straight avenue, tree-bordered, with tall blocks of flats at either side. Many of the trees were uprooted or broken, lampposts leaned drunkenly and sprawled across pavements; shell-holes in the road were full of water; the litter of smashed buildings was everywhere. But little cafés and shops still seemed to be carrying on some kind of miserable, hunted existence; women went by carrying home for their fires wood gleaned from the wreckage of neighbours' houses. There was something both horrible and pitiful in the way these people clung to their homes in this desolate region.

At the end of the avenue was a cross-roads, an open space, a triangular patch of ground stuck with ruined trees. On two sides were big barricades made of cobble-stones, with machine-guns set up beside them.

We halted. The wide roads were littered with broken glass and branches of trees, scattered bricks, cartridge-cases, wet, shapeless, burnt objects; from a burst water-main a stream gushed noisily upwards at the raining sky. Tall houses exhibited gaping wounds through which showed smashed furniture; rooms ripped in half exposed the melancholy relics of murdered homes. Bullets plopped intermittently against bricks, every wall was pitted with their marks.

By the barricade stood militiamen, cloaked in soaked blankets. An indescribably horrible air of desolation brooded over everything. It was quiet now, the fighting almost over.

By the open space lay two dead Fascists, one in the gutter, his head smashed open against the kerbstone, the brains slopping out. A big, lean dog with a famished look came up to the corpse, sniffed, and began to lap at the mess of brains. One of the guards drew his automatic and put three bullets into the dog. It lay coughing over the corpse, not yet dead. The guard ran forward, his head held down, and finished the dog off with his rifle-butt.

He stopped when he passed us, looked apologetic, and said in bad French, 'It has to be done. They get the taste for human flesh. It is bad . . .' His keen Spanish face, edged with black beard, smiled deprecatingly. Sure, we said. We understand. And he looked relieved and went back to his post.

And we stood there waiting, steel-helmeted, hung about with arms and ammunition, gas-masks dangling on our chests, a hundred and forty soldiers, the machine-gun company of the Marty Battalion of the International Brigade; and the rain came down, the broken water-main gushed continuously, the tall buildings gaped their wounds, and from the corpse in the gutter the blood and brains washed slowly away, mingling with those of the dead dog.

It was as good a war picture as I could think of.

STEPHEN SPENDER

'War Photograph'

from *New Statesman & Nation*, 5 June 1937

I have an appointment with a bullet
At seventeen hours less a split second
—And I shall not be late.

Where the sun strikes the rock and
The rock plants its shadowed foot
And the breeze distracts the grass and fern frond.

There, in the frond, the instant lurks
With its metal fang planned for my heart
When the finger tugs and the clock strikes.

I am that numeral which the sun regards,
The flat and severed second on which time looks,
My corpse a photograph taken by fate;

Where inch and instant cross, I shall remain
As faithful to the vanished moment's violence
As love fixed to one day in vain.

Only the world changes and time its tense
Against the creeping inches of whose moon,
I launch my wooden continual present.

The grass will grow its summer beard and beams
Of light melt down the waxen slumber
Where soldiers lie dead in an iron dream;

My corpse be covered with the snow's December
And roots push through skin's silent drum
When the years and fields forget, but the whitened bones remember.

GUSTAV REGLER

Black-and-White

from *The Owl of Minerva* (transl. Norman Denny), 1959

The next day [Hemingway] brought with him Joris Ivens, the Dutchman with whom I had made the film in Moscow. I greeted him with considerable reserve, remembering where we had last worked together. Did he propose to make another film of self-deception? It would be hard on my Spaniards.

But the smiling Ivens was full of stories. He had been visiting villages behind the lines where they were in the throes of dividing up the land. 'I've been filming it,' he said, tapping his small camera, the same which he had used on the Red Square. 'Wonderful faces!' He made a sign in the air. 'They've grown young—and you've grown younger, too,' he said, and at once regained my confidence; for what he meant was, younger since the great betrayal in the east; grown younger and with faith renewed by the peasant people for whom we were fighting. I felt that I wanted to show him the front at once. He said that Hemingway was going to write a commentary for his film—'and you and the peasants will be the heroes, you, the nameless, and they who until yesterday were landless.' He was once more as convincing as the dykes of his homeland.

He filmed the bursting of shells from a dangerously short distance, and said that he intended to follow these with explosions of a different kind, which were to make it look as though the shells in this war had tapped new springs, causing water to flow through land that for centuries had been neglected by its wealthy owners. The owners were gambling away their money in Hendaye, and Ivens intended to go there and film them as they were, overfed and weary with idleness. He was still not afraid of plain black-and-white. 'The world *is* black and white!' he said. 'Look!' And he produced photographs out of his case of peasants kissing the soil that was at last to be rendered fruitful again—seared and wrinkled faces now wreathed in a new smile. 'Faces like the earth itself,' he said.

When we awoke the moon was still shining.

'There won't be a dawn attack,' I said.

Ivens already had his camera ready.

'I wanted to show you another picture,' he said, as though our last night's conversation had not been interrupted. He handed me one that he had taken a few days before in Madrid.

It was a picture of the open space in front of an hotel, under a bright sun. Beside a black hole in the plaster a man lay with his face to the ground in a dark pool—and at once I was painfully reminded of the artilleryman on the Chemin des Dames who had drunk his own blood with his last gasping breaths.

'They deliberately only shoot one shell a day into the town,' said Ivens. 'Cunning, isn't it? They want to keep everyone in a state of fear. Naturally the Madrid people take no notice, and then someone cops it when he's engaged in some harmless occupation. Hemingway will explain it. It's all so simple, so clear-cut—a truly vulgar death that they want to inflict on Spain.'

'I've known that ever since Badajoz,' I said.

Ivens stood up.

'And now I'm going to photograph the peasants, over there behind Arganda. Perhaps I shall be able to get some of the ones who dare to come out and do their ploughing at night. That will be another symbol of the dirtiness of this war—ploughing in secret, as though it were a crime!'

GEORGE BARKER

'Elegy on Spain'

from *Collected Poems 1930–1955*, 1957

Dedication to the photograph of a child
killed in an air raid on Barcelona

O ecstatic is this head of five-year joy—
Captured its butterfly rapture on a paper:
And not the rupture of the right eye may
Make any less this prettier than a picture.
O now, my minor moon, dead as meat
Slapped on a negative plate, I hold
The crime of the bloody time in my hand.

Light, light with that lunar death our fate;
Make more dazzling with your agony's gold
The death that lays us all in the sand.

Gaze with that gutted eye on our endeavour
To be the human brute, not the brute human:
And if I feel your gaze upon me ever,
I'll wear the robe of blood that love illumines.

I

The hero's red rag is laid across his eyes,
Lies by the Madrid rock and baptizes sand
Grander than god with the blood of his best, and
Estramadura is blazing in his fallen hand.
All of a fallen man is what is heaven's;
Grievance is lowered to a half-mast of sorrow,
Tomorrow has no hand in the beat of his breath, and after
Laughter his heart is hollow.

For a star is against him, that fallen on his forehead,
Forward is blocked by the augury of our evil.
Sin is a star that has fallen on our own heads.
Sheds us a shower of chlorine, the devil's revel;
Evil lifts a hand and the heads of flowers fall—
The pall of the hero who by the Ebro bleeding
Feeds with his blood the stones that rise and call,
Tall as any man, 'No pasaran!'

Can the bird cry any other word on the branch
That blanches at the bomb's red wink and roar,
Or the tall daffodil, trodden under the wheel of war,
But spring up again in the Spring for will not stay under?
Thunder and Mussolini cannot forbid to sing and spring
The bird with a word of determination, or a blossom of hope.
Heard in a dream, or blooming down Time's slope.

But now for a moment which shall always be a monument
Draw like a murder the red rag across those eyes.
Skies in July not drier than they are,
Bare of a tear now that pain, like a crystal memorial,
Is their memorials scattered over the face of Spain.
Together this hero and the ghost of the Easter Irish,
Brother and sister, beaten by the fist of the beast,
Water tomorrow with the tears and blood of slaughter.

2

Go down, my red bull, proud as a hero,
Nero is done with, but the Hungerford Hundred,
The Tolpuddle Martyr, the human hero,
Rises and remains, not in loss sundered;
Plundered, is proud of his plenitude of prizes.
Now spiked with false friendship, bright with blood,
Stood did my bull in the pool of his passion,
Flashing his sickle horn as he sinks at the knees.

Peace is not angels blessing blood with a kiss;—
Is the axis pinning Spain through the breast
To the water-wheel that makes a nation a martyr
To the traitor who wheels the whips of gold and steel.
O bold bull in the ring, old ox at the wheel,
Sold for a song on the lips of a Hitler,
No halter shall hold you down to the bloodly altar
Longer than life takes to rise again from slaughter.

This flower Freedom needs blood at the roots,
Its shoots spring from your wounds, and the bomb
Booming among the ruins of your houses, arouses
Generation and generation from the grave
To slave at your side for future liberation.
Those who die with five stars in their hands
Hand on their ghosts to guard a yard of land
From the boot of the landlord and the band of war.

Drop, drop that heavy head, my less and more than dead,
Bled dry a moment, tomorrow will raise that hand
From the sad sand, less than death a defeat.
Beaten by friend, not enemy, betrayed, not beaten,
Laid let that head be, low, my bull, stunned,
Gunned from the royal box by a trigger pull.
Bigger no courage is than the blood it can spill.

Not in a wreath I write the death in a ring,
But sing a breath taken by heroes, a respite:
No fight is over when Satan still straddles a man;
Then the real battle begins which only ends
When friends shake hands over the break of evil.

O level out the outrageous crags of hate
To those great valleys where our love can slant
Like light at morning that restores the plant!

O Asturian with a burst breast like an aster,
Disaster sports blooms like that in many places;
Graces the grave of a nation with human pain.
Spain like a sleeping beauty finds her kiss
Is the lips of your wounds awakening her again
To claim her freedom from the enclosing chain.
Silence the blackbird, take away the tree,
He will not need them until he is free.

At evening is red the sky over us all.
Shall our fiery funeral not raise tomorrow also?
So shall the order of love from death's disorder
Broader than Russia arise and bring in the day.
Sleep gives us dreams that the morning dissolves,
But borne on death we reach the bourne of dreams.
Seems blood too bitter a bargain to pay for that day?
Too bitter a bargain, or too far a day?

Draw then the red sky over his eyes, and Sleep
Keep Orion silent above him, and no wind move
Love's leaves covering him at the French border.
The marauder snuffles among his guts for a night:
Right is capsized: but Spain shall not drown,
For grown to a giantess overnight arises,
Blazes like morning Venus on a bleeding sea,
She, he, shall stretch her limbs in liberty.

3

Madrid, like a live eye in the Iberian mask,
Asks help from heaven and receives a bomb:
Doom makes the night her eyelid, but at dawn
Drawn is the screen from the bull's-eye capital.
She gazes at the Junker angels in the sky
Passionately and pitifully. Die
The death of the dog, O Capital City, still
Sirius shall spring up from the kill.

Farewell for a day my phoenix who leaves ashes
Flashing on the Guernica tree and Guadalajara range.
Change is the ringing of all bells of evil,
Good is a constant that now lies in your keeping
Sleeping in the cemeteries of the fallen, who,
True as a circling star will soon return
Burning the dark with five tails of anger.

What is there not in the air any longer,
Stronger than songs or roses, and greater
Than those who create it, a nation
Manhandling god for its freedom? lost,
O my ghost, the first fall, but not lost
The will to liberty which shall have liberty
At the long last.

So close a moment that long open eye,
Fly the flag low, and fold over those hands
Cramped to a gun: gather the child's remains
Staining the wall and cluttering the drains;
Troop down the red to the black and the brown;
Go homeward with tears to water the ground.
All this builds a bigger plinth for glory,
Story on story, on which triumph shall be found.

STEPHEN SPENDER

'The Bombed Happiness'

from *New Statesman & Nation*, 4 February 1939

Children, who extend their smile of crystal,
And their leaping gold embrace,
And wear their happiness as a frank jewel,
Are forced in the mould of the groaning bull
And engraved with lines on the face.

Their harlequin-striped flesh,
Their blood twisted in rivers of song,
Their flashing, trustful emptiness,
Are trampled by an outer heart that pressed
From the sky right through the coral breast
And kissed the heart and burst.

This timed, exploding heart that breaks
The loved and little hearts, is also one
Splintered through the lungs and wombs
And fragments of squares in the sun,
And crushing the floating, sleeping babe
Into a deeper sleep.

Its victoried drumming enters
Above the limbs of bombed laughter
The body of an expanding State
And throbs there and makes it great,
But nothing nothing can recall
Gaiety buried under these dead years,
Sweet jester and young playing fool
Whose toy was human happiness.

HERBERT READ

'Bombing Casualties in Spain'

from *Collected Poems*, 1966

Dolls' faces are rosier but these were children
their eyes not glass but gleaming gristle
dark lenses in whose quicksilvery glances
the sunlight quivered. These blench'd lips
were warm once and bright with blood
but blood
held in a moist bleb of flesh
not spilt and spatter'd in tousled hair.

In these shadowy tresses
red petals did not always
thus clot and blacken to a scar.
These are dead faces.
Wasps' nests are not so wanly waxen
wood embers not so greyly ashen.

They are laid out in ranks
like paper lanterns that have fallen
after a night of riot
extinct in the dry morning air.

STEPHEN SPENDER

'Pictures in Spain'

from the *Spectator*, 30 July 1937

Before we left Minganilla—a village between Valencia and Madrid,
where we were banqueted and, after the banquet, danced to by the
children whilst the women without their men stood round weeping—a
woman took me to her house, showed me photographs of her two sons,
both on the Madrid front, and insisted on giving me half a dozen
sausages, about half of all she had, because she felt certain that I would
be hungry before we reached Madrid. Then we of the International
Writers' Congress got into our cars, and, as my car waited for the
'caravan' to start, one old beggar woman pressed forward from the
crowd to ask me for some money. I was about to give her a few
coppers when a boy leapt forward and exclaimed, with a passionate
gesture, 'No, no, give her nothing. The Spanish people do not accept
charity.'

This little incident lives in my mind with several others which go to
impress on me what I can only call the seriousness of the people's
movement in Spain. Another is my surprise when I saw for myself that
the University City—with the Government buildings only separated
from those taken by the rebels by yards—is still used as a place of
learning, for in half-ruined class rooms, their walls perforated with
bullets, the soldiers attend classes.

The welcome given to the International Writers' Congress, by the people of small villages, by soldiers in the trenches, by a deputation of tramway workers in Madrid, by the common people in the streets, in cafés, in barber shops, in bars, if they happened to realise that one was a member of the Congress, were all signs that the Spanish people have acquired that passion for education and popular culture which goes with a fundamental revolutionary change in a nation's life. It was our good fortune to symbolise popular culture for them, and this explains the great welcome which we received.

To me, perhaps the strangest of my impressions of Madrid was that of the interior of a great and massively built church on the outskirts of the city—looking over, I think, that part of the front which is called the Caso del Campo—where a vast collection of treasures from the palaces and churches of Madrid has been collected. The domed, gloomy, vast interior of the church, with its congregation of royal coaches, rood screens, crucifixes, candelabras, tapestries, ceramics, was like a meeting of all the centuries in a solemn fancy-dress ball, not of people but of objects. Our little party from the Congress walked round, feeling as out of place as a member of the audience on a stage set. We made M. Julien Benda sit in a royal coach, which suited him well, M. Egon Kisch looked handsome in an eighteenth-century wig, but apart from these courageous isolated attempts we did not succeed in adapting ourselves to our surroundings. Myself, I made no attempt to take the plunge back into the past. On the contrary, I thought in terms of making films of these stage properties, particularly one propaganda film, to show that the Republic cares for Spain's art treasures.

In this church all the lesser works of art from the palaces and churches of Madrid have been collected. Along the passages, in vaults and in chapels, there were placed thousands of canvases, a varied and unequal collection of ceramics, ivory crucifixes, antiqué watches, jewelry, fans, and in one vault so many images of saints that we could only make our way through them along the narrow gangway which they had discreetly left. Our guide explained that this vault had been the home of what Franco refers to as the 'Quinta Columna' of his allies in Madrid. But some of the French writers lifted their fists in vigorous response to one Saint Anthony, whose clenched hand was raised in an eternal '*Salud.*' There are traitors in both camps.

Everything in this collection was catalogued, giving the name of the palace or church from which it was taken, as well as its number in the depositary. Among the pictures catalogued here and in the cellars of Madrid, taken from private collections, are 27 Grecos, 8 Rubens, 13 Zurbaranes, 51 Goyas, 9 Titians, 6 Tintorettos, 6 Tiepolos, &c. Many pictures and many valuable first editions and manuscripts have now been brought to light for the first time.

Other pictures and treasures are in bomb-proof and damp-proof cellars of Madrid. The pictures from the Prado are in the vaults and cellars of Valencia, each of them packed so as to protect it from the damp. I was assured by members of the Government that nothing from these collections has been destroyed or (as has been said) given to the Russian Government in exchange for aeroplanes. The only pictures going abroad are those lent to Paris for the Exhibition of Spanish Art. I saw some of the pictures that are soon to be shown in Paris in the chapel of a seminary at Valencia. The chapel itself was strongly built, but the main arches under which the pictures lay in packing cases had been further strengthened by piles of sandbags placed above pillars of reinforced concrete.

It is true that at the beginning of the Civil War anarchists burned churches and buildings in Spain which they saw not as things of beauty but as symbols of tyranny and superstition. Yet even in these early days, they removed and collected the treasures of art from the churches, which have been saved. Maria Therésa Lèon, the wife of the great poet Rafael Alberti, told me that when the Government made an appeal that art treasures should be saved, they were embarrassed by the quantity of stuff, some of it good, some trash, which was brought to them. Naïvely and eagerly the people look on the art treasures of Spain as their own heritage. The spirit in which, during a terrible siege, under bombardments, in a time of penury and hunger, the Junta del Tesoro Artístico in Madrid collected and arranged and catalogued meticulously the objects which we saw in that great church shows the same seriousness as that of the boy who passionately forbade me to give money to a beggar, as that of the women in Minganilla who received us with tears and asked one of us to speak to them in Spanish, just to show that we understood their fate (*suerte*). A people who speak in the language of war and armaments are looking ahead a month, perhaps a year, to victory. But a people who educate the soldiers in the trenches, who collect the art treasures of the nation because they have become the concern of the whole democracy, are looking forward not a month or a year, but to a future in which whole generations are liberated not by guns, but by the great tradition of Spanish painting and literature.

GRAHAM GREENE
Last Train from Madrid

Review of *The Last Train from Madrid* (USA Paramount, 1937),
from *Night and Day*, 8 July 1937

As for *The Last Train from Madrid*, it is probably the worst film of the
decade and should have been the funniest. Emotional and uplifting
dialogue ('I don't want to die, Senorita. I'm young, I want to live. My
father kept a farm . . .'). Mr Lionel Atwill ('a grand old trooper', as Miss
Lejeune would say) playing the Madrid Commandant, full of sternness
and duty and tenderness ('You will be tried by court martial tomorrow',
and his warm encouraging paw falls like a headmaster's on the prisoner's
shoulder): all we still need for a really good laugh are the presence of the
Dean of Canterbury and the absence of actual war. For there is
something a little shocking about these noble self-sacrifices and heroic
deaths—the eyes close always of their own accord—in front of a
back-projection of ruined Madrid itself, about the facetiousness of the
screen journalist in a screen air raid mingled with news-shots of the
genuine terror.

ERNEST HEMINGWAY

'The Heat and The Cold: Remembering Turning the Spanish Earth'

from *Verve*, Paris, Spring 1938

Afterwards when it is all over, you have a picture. You see it on the
screen; you hear the noises and the music; and your own voice, that
you've never heard before, comes back to you saying things you'd
scribbled in the dark in the projection room or on pieces of paper in a hot
hotel bedroom. But what you see in motion on the screen is not what you
remember.

The first thing you remember is how cold it was; how early you got up
in the morning; how you were always so tired you could go to sleep at any
time; how hard it was to get gasoline; and how we were always hungry. It
was also very muddy and we had a cowardly chauffeur. Nothing of that

shows on the screen except the cold when you can see the men's breath in the air in the picture.

What I really remember clearest about that, the cold part of the picture, is that I always carried raw onions in the pockets of my lumberman's jacket and would eat them whenever I was really hungry much to the disgust of Joris Ivens and John Ferno. No matter how hungry they were they would not eat raw spanish onions. It has something to do with their being Dutchmen. But they would always drink out of the large, flat, silver flask of whiskey which was always empty by four o'clock in the afternoon. The greatest technical discovery we made at that time was to carry a bottle to refill the flask with and the greatest non-technical discovery we made was Warner Heilbrun.

After we met Heilbrun, who was medical officer for the twelfth International Brigade, we always had gasoline, his gasoline. All we had to do was to get out to a brigade hospital to eat well and fill with gasoline. He always had everything marvellously organized. He furnished us with transport. He took us to attacks, and a big part of the film that I remember is the slanting smile, the cap cocked on the side, the slow, comic Berlin Jewish drawl of Heilbrun. When I would go to sleep in the car coming back from somewhere to Madrid at night Heilbrun would tell Luis his chauffeur to take a short way out to the hospital at Moraleja. When I would wake it would be to see the gates of the old castle and at three in the morning we would have a hot meal in the kitchen. Then, when all the rest of us were dead with sleep, Heilbrun would do his work; the work he did so well, so intelligently, so painstakingly, so delicately and skillfully, and always with the languid air of doing nothing.

The big part of that section of the picture, for me, is Heilbrun. But he doesn't show in it and he and Luis now are buried in Valencia.

Gustav Regler shows in the picture. You see and hear him make a speech, a fine speech, and again you see him, not speech making, but in the line under fire, very calm, very cheerful and a good officer pointing out an immediate objective just before a counter-attack. Regler was a big part of the picture that I remember.

Lucasz shows just for a moment bringing up the Twelfth Brigade to deploy along the Arganda road. You do not see him late at night on that great party on the first of May in Moraleja playing the tune he only played so very late at night on a pencil held against his teeth; the music clear and delicate like a flute. You only see a little glimpse of Lucasz when he was working.

After the cold part of the picture I remember the hot part very well. In the hot part you ran with cameras, sweating, taking cover in the folds of the terrain on the bare hills. There was dust in your nose, and dust in your hair and in your eyes, and you had the great thirst for water, the real dry-mouth that only battle brings. Because you had seen a little war when you were young you knew that Ivens and Ferno would be killed if they kept on because they took too many chances. And your moral problem was always to get clear how much you were holding them back from necessary and just prudence, based on experience, and how much was simply the not so pretty prudence of the burnt monkey who dreads the hot soup. That part of the film that I remember was all sweat and thirst and blowing dust; and in the film I think that shows a little.

So now when it is all over you sit in a theater and suddenly the music comes and then you see a tank come riding like a ship and clanking in the well remembered dust and your mouth dries again. When you were young you gave death much importance. Now you give it none. You only hate it for the people that it takes away.

Death is still very badly organized in war, you think, and let it go at that. But it is a remark you would like to make to Heilbrun, who would grin, and to Lucasz, who would understand it very well. So if it's all the same to you I won't go to see the *Spanish Earth* any more. Nor will I write about it. I don't have to. Because we were there. But if you weren't there I think you ought to see it.

ANTHONY POWELL

'A Reporter in Los Angeles— Hemingway's Spanish Film'

from *Night and Day*, 19 August 1937

The film was billed for 8.15. We called up that morning to reserve seats but were told that this would not be necessary. However, brisk booking was in progress when we arrived in Los Angeles at about seven o'clock in the evening. After what turned out to be an indiscreet dinner of clam chowder, sea-food à la Bernstein, and Sonoma Valley chablis, we crossed Pershing Square, where bums cluster in the twilight under sub-tropical vegetation, and began forcing our way into the Philhar-monic Auditorium. There was a large crowd trying to get in. Outside the neon lights said:

Inside there were 3,000 or more people. A disbelief in private property had induced a number of old-fashioned socialists, and one gentleman who announced himself as a Cuban fascist, to sit in seats which had in fact been reserved by other people. By the time these wreckers had been liquidated it was nearly nine o'clock. Many of the audience had to find accommodation on the stairs of the gangway.

Two kinds of pamphlet lay about on the seats. After reading the one in red advertising *We From Krondstadt* the man next door handed me the yellow one and said: 'This should be good too.' It advertised a meeting of protest on the anniversary of the outbreak of the Spanish Civil War. 'Did you come last time?' 'No, what was it?' 'Well, they had a loyalist flying ace.' He returned to the *Western Worker*. Over his shoulder I read the headline: STOOGES OUTGAG UNIONS IN SACRAMENTO. The audience were getting restive and occasional outbursts of clapping settled down to a regular tattoo. A sort of compère came on to the stage and begged for a little patience. It appeared that there were still people who wanted to get in. The man next door said: 'Are you Canadian or English?' 'English.' 'I like the English,' he said; 'I've been to London several times. I saw Sir Oswald Mosley. Woolwich was the part that appealed to me. I've been in the East too. To your face—to your face, mark you—the Japanese are the politest race in the world. And after them the English. A Camel?' 'Thanks.' We just had time to light them before the compère appeared again and requested everyone to stop smoking. My friend threw his cigarette away. The reputation of the Old Country was in my hands and I followed his example. The lights went out and the show began.

Spanish Earth was directed by Ernest Hemingway and Joris Ivens. Precisely who did what was not stated, but presumably Mr Ivens, who is a professional movie man, was responsible for the actual shooting and Mr Hemingway wrote the treatment and the commentary. The film opened with a sequence of shots showing Spain in time of peace, through which the commentator was accompanied with bursts of Spanish music. Now, no voice but a Spanish voice can be heard above Spanish music; but on the other hand no music can entirely drown a determined commentator. The ensemble was not successful. Later on, however, victory went to the commentator, who held his own throughout the greater part of the film, with occasional lapses, as when *Giovanezza* ushered in some Italian prisoners.

There followed scenes in the line, in besieged Madrid, or at the Left's headquarters at Valencia. *Spanish Earth* is frankly propaganda, but not up to the Russian standard. It is true the Russians made theirs after the fighting was over; but I suspect that with the Spanish material at hand one of the big-shot Soviet directors would make something distinctly more effective.

Mr Hemingway's film was either too ham or not nearly ham enough. There were good shots of air-raids and troops training or on the march; but we continually cut back to one of those impassive peasant faces, the backbone of propaganda films all the world over. This particular old-timer was engaged in making a gully to bring water to Madrid. Like all his kind, he just got it fixed in time. Then there was the boy writing home. We were shown Juan's letter, the lorry on which Juan goes on leave, Juan drilling the village boys, etc. Later there was a close-up of some art treasures—an eighteenth-century edition of *Don Quixote* and an oil painting attributable to a disciple of Carlo Dolce—being rescued from a bombardment.

At the close of the film Mr Hemingway himself came on the stage and read an account of the war and made an appeal for ambulances. He wore a dark-blue suit and leant on the lectern, straddling out his left leg awkwardly. What he read had no very personal touch about it, except perhaps when he referred to a shell's direct hit on a tram: 'Two persons were taken to hospital, the rest removed with shovels.' He spoke with dignity, but it was evident that he was in a highly nervous state. The audience received him with loud applause. When he had finished, and Mr Ivens had said a few words, the compère appeared again and took a collection. The compère's manner and methods would have cleared any hall in England in ninety seconds, but I believe they were the traditional ones of American preachers beginning 'Is there anyone here who will give one hundred dollars?' and working down to dimes and nickels.

Spanish Earth is said to have been run off for Twentieth Century Fox, and it seems likely that if they do not take it on one or other of the big companies will mother it. But the Spanish war will be a picnic compared with Mr Hemingway's battle with the Hollywood bosses to keep the film as he likes it. There are rumours that he has already had one brush in the Green Hills of Beverly with a director best known for his comic-opera fantasias, whose criticisms were too astringent.

The fact is, *Spanish Earth* has the documentary interest attached to any good newsreel of contemporary danger. As a film, it will not make movie history. It asks to be judged by severe standards because its pretensions are considerable. Mr Hemingway has an immense talent and it is no doubt remarkable to get a shot of men going into action; but should the commentator say: 'These men's faces are something a little different from anything you have ever seen before; they are men going into action' when the shot is too blurred to distinguish the faces of the men at all? Why make a claim to which the photography shouts a denial?

The American Press has strange habits. The showing of this film was obviously an important event in local life. When Jean Harlow died some weeks before, half-a-dozen pages were devoted to her biography. The crowd standing in awed reverence in front of her former 'gorgeous residence' was described as vast. Quite by chance I happened to pass the house on the day of her funeral. The street was empty as far as the eye could see. On the lawn a bored policeman, looking like one of Mr Wyndham Lewis's self-portraits, sat on a kitchen chair.

Yet the newspapers scarcely mentioned *Spanish Earth* or Mr Ernest Hemingway.

GRAHAM GREENE
'News Reels'

from the *Spectator*, 29 September 1939

War always seems to surprise somebody; a year after Munich trenches which were begun that autumn are still being dug on the common outside; even the news-reel companies have been caught unprepared. They must have expected the temporary closing of the cinemas; they must have been prepared for censorship, and yet, like the newspapers, they have to rely on Germany as their chief source of supply—an admirable picture of the siege of the Westerplatte, and another of the war in Poland. What have they got ready for us from the home front, and how have their commentators risen to the great occasion? One remembers what Hemingway did for *Spanish Earth*, and one hopes . . . Even a war of nerves has its heroic angle.

As we fumble for our seats the too familiar voice, edgeless and French-polished, is announcing: 'The Queen has never looked prettier.' Royalty is inspecting something or other: 'Royal interest inspires them to redoubled efforts.' Women bus-conductors climb aboard: 'For men passengers it will make going to work almost a pleasure'; they wave holiday-girl hands. Mr and Mrs Chamberlain walk in the Park; complete strangers take off their hats—an odd custom. The Duchess of Kent, instead of going to Australia, makes splints: 'We never thought we would live to be grateful to Hitler.' Very slowly we approach the violent reality; the Expeditionary Force marches to the coast, whippet tanks move through the woodlands, and the voice remarks something about 'shoulder to shoulder in this death struggle for liberty'. Surely by now we should realize that art has a place in propaganda; the flat and worthy sentiment will always sound hypocritical to neutral ears beside the sharp and vivid statement. There was much that Hemingway had to slur over in his commentary: his cause was far more dubious than ours, but the language was much more effective. Let us hope that Germany is not employing a commentator of his standard, for I cannot believe that neutral opinion—or home opinion if it comes to that—will be impressed by the kind of words we listen to—shoulder to shoulder, liberty, baby-killers . . .

BERNARD GUTTERIDGE

'Spanish Earth'

from *New Writing*, Christmas 1939

Now we can walk into the picture easily
To be the unknown hero and the death;
We who have watched these things as stunts
And held our startled breath.

In Hampshire or in Yorkshire these same moving arms
Like pendulums across the marching fours
Are lifted, work; they will not wait;
Death does not make them pause.

Eyes are another signature of Spanish death.
This evening in the cinema will kill
This man we watch direct his troops;
A man whose eyes are still

Searching the landscape for his dying countrymen
In buildings burning fast as celluloid,
Impotent here in the empty city
Italian bombs destroyed.

Over the mud I have watched the broken wild duck
Chucked down from the railing wind. Now I climb
Memory as from Norfolk swamps
And wars and wars fill time—

Destroying all the countries, all the incidents
Clasped in my childhood's wishes like my toys
And present past and future seem
These marching, dying boys.

Perhaps we shall be killed: there is no life secure.
Yet they want so little, water for crops,
Schools for the children, hospitals.
The shooting never stops.

ANTHONY BLUNT

'Picasso Unfrocked'

from the *Spectator*, 8 October 1937

There is something pathetic in the sight of a talented artist struggling to cope with a problem entirely outside his powers. This is the feeling aroused by the new series of etchings produced by Picasso as his contribution to the struggle in Spain. The *Sueño y Mentira de Franco* unquestionably expresses a genuine hatred for the Spanish rebels, and if it does nothing else it shows that Picasso's heart is in the right place. But the questions remain: Where is his brain? and where are his eyes?

The work consists of two plates of etchings, with nine scenes on each, accompanied by a poem, printed (in the English edition) in Spanish, French and English. To describe the etchings in detail is impossible. But the general impression which they convey is clear cut. They have the same nightmare atmosphere as the Guernica mural, and the conventions are in many ways the same as those which the artist has used for bull-fights and for all the private paintings of the last years. They are undeniably terrifying. Obscene polyps, in mitre, coronet, or mantilla, hack at statues, prance on tight-ropes, ride on a charger which turns into pig or Pegasus, pray to financial monstrances, are tossed by bulls. The other sheet is more allusive in matter and even less clear in rendering. The same symbols persist in part. Polyp and Pegasus and bull are there, but in greater confusion. Most moving in a far simpler way is a single figure of the corpse of a woman, relatively realistically conceived, lying, half-absorbed into the ground, against a blasted landscape. In the last four of the series the style becomes frantic. Arms, eyes, and heads are contorted in a scrawl of horror. Frightening they certainly are.

And this is Picasso's contribution to the Spanish civil war. It is not surprising that his offering should be of this kind. For Picasso has spent the whole of his life in the Holy of Holies of Art, served by the chosen, refining more and more his mystical rites, so that for the initiate they grew in significance, but for the world they became ever more remote and unreal. And now the earthquake which is shaking the world has brought the carefully constructed temple toppling down, and the inhabitants of it are thrown out into the open air and find themselves in a real world full of unpleasantness. But the light in the Sanctum was so dim and the atmosphere so rarified, that priests and devotees blink and choke, and cannot understand what is going on around them. In panic they call for bell, book and candle, and try to conjure the horror with the old hocus-pocus. But alas! the new ills are real and can only be cured by real means. In his new etchings and poems Picasso seems to be aware of what is going on around him, but not of its real meaning. And, indeed, how could he be? For so many years he has been unaccustomed to looking anything in the face, that when he needs to do so he does not know how to set about it. What he does is to register horror—genuine, but useless horror. Useless, because all that these etchings will do is to make certain of the devotees feel that at last they have made contact with reality, that after all this is life, whereas they have not really stepped a yard outside their old circle. The etchings cannot reach more than the limited coterie of aesthetes, who have given their life so wholly to the cult of art that they have forgotten about everything else. The rest of the world will at most see and shudder and pass by. For the etchings to perform a more important function two things would have been necessary: that Picasso should have seen more than the mere horror of the civil war, that he should have realised that it is only a tragic part of a great forward movement; and that he should have expressed this optimism in a direct way and not with circumlocution so abstruse that those who are occupied with more serious things will not have time or energy to work out all its implications. It may be that if the first condition was fulfilled the second would follow automatically.

In the religious half-light of the temple Picasso looked a giant. Now, in a harsher glare, and up against more exacting standards, he appears as a pigmy. And remember what Michelangelo said to an artist who was showing him his sculpture in the studio and arranging the light to the greatest advantage: 'Don't bother about that. It is by the light of the market place that it will be judged.'

HERBERT READ

from the *Spectator*, 15 October 1937

Sir,—I do not wish to raise the general issues of modern art which Mr Blunt and I have more than once debated in public without reaching agreement, but there are one or two questions of fact in connexion with his attack on Picasso which call for correction. Picasso is not so detached from the Spanish struggle as Mr Blunt tries to make out. Not only has the Spanish Government given him the highest recognition in its power (the directorship of the Prado Museum), but more recently invited him to paint the great mural which dominates the Spanish pavilion at the Paris Exhibition. Here is the best kind of evidence of the close co-operation and mutual understanding which exist between the artist and the democratic government of his native country. This painting is virtually in the market-place, where Mr Blunt wishes to see all art, and hundreds of thousands of people have seen it and, as I can testify from personal observation, accepted it with the respect and wonder which all great works of art inspire. As for the series of etchings referred to by Mr Blunt, *Sueño y Mentira de Franco*, reproductions of these are to be issued in the form of postcards and will thus become available even to the poorest people.

There is no evidence at all that modern art is necessarily unpopular, or non-popular. At the present moment, for example, Mr McKnight Kauffer's magnificent *décor* for the ballet *Checkmate* is meeting with the approval of a popular audience at Sadler's Wells, where if Mr Blunt were to venture into the cheaper seats he would find none of the superior abuse which might emanate from the stalls. It is only too evident to anyone who knows the real facts that the particular form of opposition to modern art adopted by Mr Blunt comes from middle-class doctrinaires who wish to 'use' art for the propagation of their dull ideas. That the drab realism which these philistines have enforced in Russia and Germany should become the art of a country like Spain is happily a contradiction of its innate artistic spirit too improbable to entertain seriously.

One further point: Mr Blunt tries to discredit Picasso by picturing him as the idol of a set of emasculated aesthetes. But on the contrary the people associated with Picasso, either as personal friends or as disinterested supporters of his art, have had rather more experience of the actual horrors of war than Mr Blunt and other ideologists of his generation.—Yours faithfully,

Herbert Read

ANTHONY BLUNT

from the *Spectator*, 22 October 1937

Sir,—Mr Read calls attention to several important facts about Picasso, some of which were unknown to me, but which do not seem to me to affect the thesis which I put forward, namely, that Picasso's art is a highly specialised product, an essentially private art, which is therefore not easily applied to public problems.

The Spanish Government has so genuine a respect for the arts that it is anxious to honour all its artists, and therefore rightly honours Picasso, who is by far the best known of living Spanish painters. The publication of the etchings in postcard form in itself proves nothing. To estimate their real appeal it will be necessary to know how widely they are selling, and to what sort of public.

I could almost resent Mr Read's suggestion that I wish to use art for some end. I have never tried to do more than analyse forms of art and to say that a particular painting is the product of a certain set of circumstances, and is therefore likely to appeal to one kind of person and not to another. I have never said that Picasso is a bad artist. I have said that his painting is not a popular art, but the last refinement of a private art produced by certain conditions, and that therefore, in relation to events like the Spanish civil war it has not the far-reaching importance which it seems to have for the specialists.

Mr Read is confident that realism will never flourish in Spain. Its appearance in Russia is evidently no argument to him, but the fact that it has been developed in Mexico may seem to him more relevant. There it has been directly evolved by the people who took part in the revolutionary movements, and is widely and enthusiastically enjoyed by peasants and workers.

Finally let me say that I never intended to insult any of Picasso's friends or supporters. I have no doubt that, as Mr Read says, many of them have experienced the horrors of war. Indeed that fact confirms me in my view. For the horrors of war might well compel a sensitive intellectual to take refuge in the sort of private art which Picasso has cultivated, and, when the pressure of external events again proves too strong, drive him to the despair shown in the latest etchings. I cannot reproduce the etchings to show the tone of despair which characterises them, but the same effect can be produced by quoting from the translation of the poem with which Picasso accompanies them: 'fandango of shivering owls souse of swords of evil-omened polyps scouring brush of hairs from priests' tonsures standing naked in the middle of the frying-pan—placed upon the ice cream cone of codfish fried in the scabs of his lead-ox heart . . .' Surely this is a specialised kind of poetry, and the product of a rarefied atmosphere.—Yours faithfully,

Anthony Blunt

WILLIAM COLDSTREAM

from the *Spectator*, 22 October 1937

Sir,—I read with interest Mr Blunt's article on Picasso and Mr Herbert Read's criticism of it.

To me the important point implicit in Mr Blunt's article was that Picasso belongs to a generation of painters more than ordinarily detached from any generally understandable point of view and concerned rather with studio experiment than communication to the unspecialised spectator.

Many feel that communications between the better painters and any wide public have for some time been broken down and that this comparative isolation of the artist has had a devitalising effect on his work. This was the most interesting aspect of Mr Blunt's article to me and I should have been interested to hear Mr Read's opinion on it.—Yours, &c.,

William Coldstream

HERBERT READ

from the *Spectator*, 29 October 1937

Sir,—The point common to Mr Blunt's and Mr Coldstream's letters, and incidentally to the former's criticism of Barbara Hepworth's sculpture which appears in the same issue of *The Spectator*, is that the modern artist has lost 'contact with life,' and that if only he would give up his 'isolation' he would have a million-wide public instead of, as at present, a circle of a few thousand—a 'happy few.'

I would like to ask what exactly Mr Blunt and Mr Coldstream mean by this phrase 'contact with life.' From my knowledge of the lives of Picasso and Barbara Hepworth, I should say that they both led extremely full and varied lives, in intimate contact with their friends, their children, their fellow-workers and all the associates and activities which artists in all ages have normally had. I can only suspect that by 'contact with life' your correspondents mean something like 'contact with a political party,' or 'contact with a particular section of workers' (for the artists in question already have full contact with their fellow-workers in the craft they practise). It is for Mr Blunt or Mr Coldstream to show that the very specialised kind of contact they have in mind has had, in this age or any other, any beneficial effect on art.

As for the example of Mexico, quoted by Mr Blunt, I submit that it is irrelevant, for it takes no account of the quality of the art. I do not wish even to suggest that your art critic is prepared to judge art by its quantitative appeal, for what then would be the use of art criticism? We could decide everything by vote.—Yours faithfully,

Herbert Read

ROLAND PENROSE

from the *Spectator*, 29 October 1937

Sir,—I have followed with great interest the correspondence resulting from the article in which Mr Blunt criticised the recent work of Picasso for the Spanish Government, claiming to unfrock Picasso's activities and expose the fool's paradise in which he and his admirers have laboured for so long. After Mr Read's very comprehensive reply Mr Blunt covers his retreat from this unwarranted attack by coining a new phrase. Picasso's art, he writes is, 'an essentially private art,' and he goes on to draw a distinction between popular and private art which merely adds to his confusion, for even if such a distinction were possible he spoils his case by admitting that Picasso is 'by far the best known of living Spanish painters.' Moreover, it can no more be possible to exclude 'private' experience and emotion from the arts than from love. In both cases it is the personal emotion which renders them universal. In dealing with Picasso's reactions to public events Mr Blunt quarrels with the lack of optimism. The appalling anguish of Guernica expressed in the great mural is apparently not healthy propaganda for the cause. But Mr Blunt forgets that the mural is exhibited amidst the gaiety of the Paris exhibition where it makes an overwhelming contrast to its surroundings; whereas the postcards with their fantastic caricatures of Franco and their bitter humour are meant for Spain and the world in general. It may be that the Spaniards have a very acute sense of the right propaganda in the right place. It would be of little use to disguise the sufferings of the Spanish people with starry-eyed platitudes; 'the print which the foot leaves in the rock,' to quote a part of Picasso's poem which Mr Blunt omits, is more worthy of expression by a painter of such penetrating vision.—Yours faithfully,

Roland Penrose

ANTHONY BLUNT

from the *Spectator*, 5 November 1937

Sir,—In his letter Mr Read defines the types of people with whom the contemporary artist associates so clearly that he exactly confirms the point which I had been trying to make. Picasso and Barbara Hepworth, he says, have contact with their friends, their children, and their fellow workers—by which I suppose he means fellow artists. He goes on to say that these are the contacts which artists have had in all ages. And this is where I quarrel with him. Artists have, of course, always had these contacts. Before the nineteenth century, however, they did not limit themselves to such a small group of interests, but also interpreted —though not necessarily consciously or directly—the situation in the world around them. I cannot clearly quote an exhaustive list of such cases, but two, of rather different kinds, will illustrate my point. Michelangelo—and Mr Read may again say that I am not taking into account the quality of the art—took an active interest in the religious questions and reforms of his time, which was the form in which changes of attitude towards the world then clothed themselves; and the artists of the early fifteenth century in Florence were often men of importance in the public administration of the city, both Brunelleschi and Ghiberti being members of different governing bodies. The modern artist, on the other hand, has only been aware of his immediate friends and studio associates. By 'contact with life' I am very far from meaning contact with any one political party, but merely awareness of what is taking place outside one's own room and studio. This awareness can even be achieved in spite of the most wicked political opinions—witness the case of Balzac.

Mr Penrose finds a contradiction in the two statements that Picasso's art is private (an idea which he flatteringly describes as novel) and that Picasso is a well-known artist. But Picasso can be well known and yet only have contact with a small public in the sense that only a few people understand and enjoy him. As for the question of private art, I do not, of course, wish to *exclude* personal emotion from works of art, though I think that its importance is constantly overemphasised at the present time. I demand only in the case in question that the emotion should be commensurate with its object (the Spanish war), that it should be supported by a true understanding of this object, and that it should be expressed in a manner intelligible to more than the happy few.—Yours faithfully,

Anthony Blunt

STEPHEN SPENDER

'Guernica'

Picasso's *Guernica*, at the New Burlington Gallery
from the *New Statesman & Nation*, 15 October 1938

André Gide writes in *Verve* that *Guernica* fails because it is *excentric*, it breaks away from its centre, or has no centre. Other critics complain that it is neither expressionist nor abstract, but falls between two stools; that it is terrifying without producing any sensation of pity; and so on. All these criticisms are attempts to answer the question whether or not this picture is a great masterpiece. Otherwise, they could not be criticisms at all, but just descriptions, which so far from being *against* it, might well be an account of its merits.

Guernica affects one as an explosion, partly no doubt because it is a

AMERICANS IN SPAIN

NEW ENGLAND FIGHTS FOR SPANISH DEMOCRACY

" . . . so that this Government of the people, by the people, for the people, shall not perish from the earth"

Price—ANY DONATION TO THE ABRAHAM LINCOLN BATTALION

Written by:
OTIS HOOD AND PHIL FRAN

MARCH 1937 SIXPENCE
ARTICLES STORIES POEMS DRAWINGS

★ ON GUARD FOR SPAIN!
By Jack Lindsay

LORCA: POET OF SPAIN. By A. L. Lloyd
SPANISH DIARY: John Sommerfield

DICKENS, THE RADICAL. By T. A. Jackson
Randall Swingler • Fred Urquhart • Mark Benney

II CONGRESO INTERNACIONAL DE ESCRITORES PARA LA DEFENSA DE LA CULTURA

VALENCIA MADRID BARCELONA

Writers and writing take sides

(*Top left*) Captain Tom Wintringham in his new uniform

(*Above*) Wounded ambulance-man Wogan Philipps catches up on his Spanish ('I'm so glad Wogan is not to drive an ambulance again'—Virginia Woolf, to Rosamond Lehmann, 20 August 1937)

(*Bottom left*) John Cornford, on leave from Spain, at Dartington, September 1936

Come and See:

"THE DEFENCE OF MADRID"

Film record of the glorious International Column halting the Fascists at the very gates of Madrid! German-Italian warplanes, tanks and troops stopped at last by the heroic soldiers of the International brigades, who came from every corner of the earth to save the Spanish people from the horrors of a foreign invasion. Remember Abyssinia!

Come and Hear:

DAVID FREEMAN (Chairman)
JOHN SOMMERFIELD (Back from Madrid)
LEAH MANNING and
Prof. J. B. S. HALDANE

AT

Hampstead Town Hall
(HAVERSTOCK HILL)

WEDNESDAY, FEBRUARY 10th
8.30 p.m.

ADMISSION FREE

LIMITED NUMBER OF RESERVED SEATS AT 1/- EACH

WELCOME

The British Battalion of the

INTERNATIONAL BRIGADE

at

Hampstead Town Hall
HAVERSTOCK HILL

Tuesday, November 8
AT 8 O'CLOCK

MAURICE ORBACH in the Chair
WILFRID ROBERTS, M.P.
JOHN PARKER, M.P.
with the Commander of the British Anti-Tank Section
of the Brigade

HUGH SLATER

The Spanish Government fights on without the help of our countrymen, but our responsibility still persists :

To the Spanish people who need food, medical supplies, and arms;

To the Brigaders, their dependants and their widows, who merit our fullest support.

Hampstead Spanish Relief Committee
78 Haverstock Hill, N.W.3

Printed by the Farleigh Press (T.U. all depts.), 17-29 Cayton Street, London, E.C.1

(*Above and right*) Returned International Brigaders John Sommerfield and Hugh Slater speak for the cause

Julian Bell (in pith helmet) and Richard Rees, with their ambulance in Spain, July 1937

(*Above*) Spain makes Ernest
Hemingway scratch his head,
1 May 1938 (and is that Hugh
Slater on his left?)

(*Right*) Stephen Spender, in an
ambulance-man's issue leather
jacket, befriends a child, Calle
Lista, Madrid, March 1937

Charlotte Haldane catches up at last with her volunteer son

Spanish militia-woman Maria Petra, sketched by English militia-woman Felicia Browne

Winifred Bates tends
Republican wounded

(*Below*) Nan Green types and
a militiaman slumbers

Partido Socialista Unificado de Cataluña

Servicio especial de los
Extranjeros

Las portadoras del presente las compañeras Sylvia Taunssud Warner y
Valentine Ackland estan controoladas por nuestro servicio.
Rogamos de darlos todas facilitades.

Barcelona 28 de Septiembre 36

responsable per el servicio

GENERALITAT DE CATALUNYA

CONSELL DE SANITAT DE GUERRA

Hom nomena Miss Valentine Ackland
per el carrec de la primera Unidad Sanitaria Británica

Barcelona, 28 de Septiembre del 1936

PEL CONSELL DE SANITAT
DE GUERRA

Signa: Dr. MIAS.

Sylvia Townsend Warner

PRIMERA
AMBULANCIA
INGLESA
EN ESPAÑA

Safe-conduct pass from the Catalan Communist Party and Identity Cards of the Republican Medical Services, issued to Sylvia Townsend Warner and Valentine Ackland

George Orwell, head and shoulders above his POUM comrades, proves there was a Lenin Barracks in Barcelona, for all Claude Simon's scepticism (see Introduction)

picture of an explosion. If one attempts to criticize it, one attempts to relate it to the past. So long as a work of art has this explosive quality of newness it is impossible to relate it to the past. People who say that it is *excentric*, or that it falls between two stools, or that it is too horrible, and so on, are only making the gasping noises they might make if they were blown off their feet by a high-explosive bomb. All I can try to do is to report as faithfully as possible the effect that this very large and very dynamic picture makes on me.

In the first place, it is certainly not realistic in the sense that Goya's etchings of another tragedy in Spain are realistic. *Guernica* is in no sense reportage; it is not a picture of some horror which Picasso has seen and been through himself. It is the picture of a horror reported in the newspapers, of which he has read accounts and perhaps seen photographs.

This kind of second-hand experience, from the newspapers, the news-reel, the wireless, is one of the dominating realities of our time. The many people who are not in direct contact with the disasters falling on civilization live in a waking nightmare of second-hand experiences which in a way are more terrible than real experiences because the person overtaken by a disaster has at least a more limited vision than the camera's wide, cold, recording eye, and at least has no opportunity to imagine horrors worse than what he is seeing and experiencing. The flickering black, white and grey lights of Picasso's picture suggest a moving picture stretched across an elongated screen; the flatness of the shapes again suggests the photographic image, even the reported paper words. The centre of this picture is like a painting of a *collage* in which strips of newspaper have been pasted across the canvas.

The actual figures on the canvas, the balloon-like floating head of a screaming woman; the figure throwing arms up in despair; the woman running forwards, and leaving behind one reluctant, painful, enormous, clumsy leg; the terror of a horse with open mouth and skin drawn back over the teeth; the hand clutching a lamp and the electric lamp glowing so that it shows the wires, as though at any moment the precious light may go out; the groaning bull, the woman clutching her child, a complex of clustered fingers like over-ripe fruit; all this builds up a picture of horror, but to me there is grandeur in the severed arm of a hero lying in the foreground, clutching the noble, broken, ineffective sword with which he has tried to ward off the horrors of mechanical destruction; and there is pity in the leaves of the little plant growing just above this hand.

Picasso uses every device of expressionism, abstractionism and effects learnt from *collage*, to build up the horror of *Guernica*. Diagonal lines of light and shade in the background, suggest searchlights and confusion, and the violent contrasts of the faces revealed in a very white light suggest the despair of light and darkness in air raids; despair of the darkness because it is too complete and you are lost; despair of the light because it is too complete and you are revealed to the enemy raiders.

The impression made on me by this picture is one that I might equally get from a great masterpiece, or some very vivid experience. That, of course, does not mean that it *is* a masterpiece. I shall be content to wait some years before knowing that. But it is certainly worth seeing. And if you don't like, or resist, or are overwhelmed by explosions, there are the sixty-seven studies for *Guernica*, some of them quite unlike anything in the picture itself, which are certainly amongst the most beautiful and profound drawings Picasso has ever made.

RUTHVEN TODD

'Joan Miró'

from *Poets of Tomorrow: First Selection*, 1939

Once there were peasant pots and a dry brown hare
Upon the olive table in that magic farm;
Once all the showmen were blown about the fair
And none of them took hurt or any harm;
Once a man set his fighting bull to graze
In the strict paths of the forgotten maze.

This was that man who knew the secret line
And the strange shapes that went
In dreams; his was the bewitched vine
And the crying dog in the sky's tent.

Once he had a country where the sun shone
Through the enchanted trees like lace,
But now it is troubled and happiness is gone
For the bombs fell in that fine place
And the magician found when he had woken
His people killed, his gay pots broken.

WOMEN WRITING SPAIN

VIRGINIA WOOLF
The Educated Man's Sister

from Three Guineas, 1938

But the educated man's sister—what does 'patriotism' mean to her? Has she the same reasons for being proud of England, for loving England, for defending England? Has she been 'greatly blessed' in England? History and biography when questioned would seem to show that her position in the home of freedom has been different from her brother's; and psychology would seem to hint that history is not without its effect upon mind and body. Therefore her interpretation of the word 'patriotism' may well differ from his. And that difference may make it extremely difficult for her to understand his definition of patriotism and the duties it imposes. If then our answer to your question, 'How in your opinion are we to prevent war?' depends upon understanding the reasons, the emotions, the loyalties which lead men to go to war, this letter had better be torn across and thrown into the waste-paper basket. For it seems plain that we cannot understand each other because of these differences. It seems plain that we think differently according as we are born differently; there is a Grenfell point of view; a Knebworth point of view; a Wilfred Owen point of view; a Lord Chief Justice's point of view and the point of view of an educated man's daughter. All differ. But is there no absolute point of view? Can we not find somewhere written up in letters of fire or gold, 'This is right. This wrong'?—a moral judgement which we must all, whatever our differences, accept? Let us then refer the question of the rightness or wrongness of war to those who make morality their profession—the clergy. Surely if we ask the clergy the simple question: 'Is war right or is war wrong?' they will give us a plain answer which we cannot deny. But no—the Church of England, which might be supposed able to abstract the question from its worldly confusions, is of two minds also. The bishops themselves are at loggerheads. The Bishop of London maintained that 'the real danger to the peace of the world today were the pacifists. Bad as war was dishonour was far worse.' On the other hand, the Bishop of Birmingham described himself as an 'extreme pacifist . . . I cannot see myself that war can be regarded as consonant with the spirit of Christ.' So the Church itself gives us divided counsel—in some circumstances it is right to fight; in no circumstances is it right to fight. It is distressing, baffling, confusing, but the fact must be faced; there is no certainty in heaven above or on earth below. Indeed the more lives we read, the more speeches we listen to, the more opinions we consult, the greater the confusion becomes and the less possible it seems, since we cannot understand the impulses, the motives, or the morality which lead you to go to war, to make any suggestion that will help you to prevent war.

But besides these pictures of other people's lives and minds—these biographies and histories—there are also other pictures—pictures of actual facts; photographs. Photographs, of course, are not arguments addressed to the reason; they are simply statements of fact addressed to the eye. But in that very simplicity there may be some help. Let us see then whether when we look at the same photographs we feel the same things. Here then on the table before us are photographs. The Spanish Government sends them with patient pertinacity about twice a week.* They are not pleasant photographs to look upon. They are photographs of dead bodies for the most part. This morning's collection contains the photograph of what might be a man's body, or a woman's; it is so mutilated that it might, on the other hand, be the body of a pig. But those certainly are dead children, and that undoubtedly is the section of a house. A bomb has torn open the side; there is still a birdcage hanging in what was presumably the sitting-room, but the rest of the house looks like nothing so much as a bunch of spillikins suspended in mid air.

Those photographs are not an argument; they are simply a crude statement of fact addressed to the eye. But the eye is connected with the brain; the brain with the nervous system. That system sends its messages in a flash through every past memory and present feeling. When we look at those photographs some fusion takes place within us; however different the education, the traditions behind us, our sensations are the same; and they are violent. You, Sir, call them 'horror and disgust'. We also call them horror and disgust. And the same words rise to our lips. War, you say, is an abomination; a barbarity; war must be stopped at whatever cost. And we echo your words. War is an abomination; a barbarity; war must be stopped. For now at last we are looking at the

* Written in the winter of 1936-7.

same picture; we are seeing with you the same dead bodies, the same ruined houses.

Let us then give up, for the moment, the effort to answer your question, how we can help you to prevent war, by discussing the political, the patriotic or the psychological reasons which lead you to go to war. The emotion is too positive to suffer patient analysis. Let us concentrate upon the practical suggestions which you bring forward for our consideration. There are three of them. The first is to sign a letter to the newspapers; the second is to join a certain society; the third is to subscribe to its funds. Nothing on the face of it could sound simpler. To scribble a name on a sheet of paper is easy; to attend a meeting where pacific opinions are more or less rhetorically reiterated to people who already believe in them is also easy; and to write a cheque in support of those vaguely acceptable opinions, though not so easy, is a cheap way of quieting what may conveniently be called one's conscience. Yet there are reasons which make us hesitate; reasons into which we must enter, less superficially, later on. Here it is enough to say that though the three measures you suggest seem plausible, yet it also seems that, if we did what you ask, the emotion caused by the photographs would still remain unappeased. That emotion, that very positive emotion, demands something more positive than a name written on a sheet of paper; an hour spent listening to speeches; a cheque written for whatever sum we can afford—say one guinea. Some more energetic, some more active method of expressing our belief that war is barbarous, that war is inhuman, that war, as Wilfred Owen put it, is insupportable, horrible and beastly seems to be required. But, rhetoric apart, what active method is open to us? Let us consider and compare. You, of course, could once more take up arms—in Spain, as before in France—in defence of peace. But that presumably is a method that having tried you have rejected. At any rate that method is not open to us; both the Army and the Navy are closed to our sex. We are not allowed to fight. Nor again are we allowed to be members of the Stock Exchange. Thus we can use neither the pressure of force nor the pressure of money. The less direct but still effective weapons which our brothers, as educated men, possess in the diplomatic service, in the Church, are also denied to us. We cannot preach sermons or negotiate treaties. Then again although it is true that we can write articles or send letters to the Press, the control of the Press—the decision what to print, what not to print—is entirely in the hands of your sex. It is true that for the past twenty years we have been admitted to the Civil Service and to the Bar; but our position there is still very precarious and our authority of the slightest. Thus all the weapons with which an educated man can enforce his opinion are either beyond our grasp or so nearly beyond it that even if we used them we could scarcely inflict one scratch.

Women Take Sides on the Spanish War

from *Authors Take Sides on the Spanish War*, 1937

For the Government

Valentine Ackland

Fascism is symptomatic of the sick man's will to self-destruction: artists live to resist this will, they express the fight of the living people for life, against death.

I stand with the People and Government of Spain. Against Fascism always. Against confused thinking and cowardice. For the artist's most important qualities of reason and tenacious courage.

Pearl Binder

To-day the future of European Culture is being decided on Spanish soil. All sincere writers must support the legal Spanish Government in its heroic struggle for learning and liberty against the dark forces of General Franco.

Ralph Fox was one of us.

Margaret Cole

The cause of the war in Spain, and the actions of Fascist Powers with regard to it, have made it clear to everyone who cares for democracy, liberalism, or culture, that Fascism is determined to wipe these out by every possible means, both of brutal violence and lying propaganda. Those who doubt should read or listen to the speeches of the rebel generals and their foreign supporters: this should be enough for anyone who cares at all for civilisation.

Storm Jameson

It ought to be impossible to find any writer willing to admit that he is for Franco and Fascism. This hideous war, which is murdering Spain and may let war loose again over the whole of Europe, is the deliberate act of the two Fascist dictators, and avowed by them as such. It is an act they

will not hesitate to repeat. Civilisation, the civilisation of the mind
and the heart, is threatened with utter ruin by this doctrine which
exalts violence and uses incendiary bombs to fight ideas. For any
writer to support it is plain treachery and worse, if there is anything
worse.

Rosamond Lehmann

With all my mind and heart I am against Franco and Fascism, and for the
legal Government and the people of Republican Spain. As a mother, I
am convinced that upon the outcome of the struggle in Spain depends
the future, the very life of my children. Up till now a pacifist in the fullest
sense, I have come to feel that non-resistance can be—in this case, is—a
negative, a sterile, even a destructive thing.

Fascism, whose main principle is the sacrifice of the People to the
State, must in the last analysis attack what are called the humanities.
Culture, which has been violently destroyed in Italy and Germany, is in
mortal danger even here, even in England. Not only as an international-
ist, but as an English writer, I must choose to bear my part in the defence
of culture against Fascism.

Rose Macaulay

Against Franco.

Ethel Mannin

I am for the Legal Government of Spain inasmuch as I am against
Franco and Fascism, and that passionately, but with the defeat of Franco
I hope for very much more than a mere Republican Spain (with the old
bourgeois capitalist Government still in power)—for the establishment
of a Workers' State, not on Communist (U S S R) lines, but C N T-F A I
(Anarcho-Syndicalist).

Naomi Mitchison

There is no question for any decent, kindly man or woman, let alone a
poet or writer, who *must* be more sensitive. We have to be against Franco
and Fascism and for the people of Spain, and the future of gentleness
and brotherhood which ordinary men and women want all over the
world.

Willa Muir

I am against Franco and on the side of Republican Spain, because I
desire to see individuals growing up undistorted by economic or other

pressure, free to develop creatively in a creative environment that fosters new life. For that reason I am against capitalism in general.

Christina Stead

Franco, the traitor, image of his caste, with eighty per cent of the army and desperate foreign allies expected to win back Spain for the landlords in three days. The resistance of Spain's Republican Government is a guarantee of the eventual victory of the common peoples against these sterile powers: but to shorten their struggle, we must expose the Fascists' allies at home and abroad.

Helen Waddell

I detest Fascism, in Spain or elsewhere, in any of its disguises. I still believe in a God who is the father of mankind: and I abhor the Moloch of the Sovereign State. Any creed, religious or political, that will torture a man's body to coerce his mind is gangrenous: but the torturer and the tortured have shirts of many colours.

I endorse every word of your letter but one: 'unavenged'. That the signatories should still, in 1937, be speaking of vengeance is a nightmare: a return to Carthage, or Versailles.

Sylvia Townsend Warner

I am for the people of Spain, and for their Government, chosen by them and true to them.

And I am against Fascism, because Fascism is based upon mistrust of human potentialities. Its tyranny is an expression of envy, its terrorism is an expression of fear.

Rebecca West

I am for the legal Government of Republican Spain against Franco, since Spain herself, at a properly conducted election, chose that Government and rejected the party which now supports Franco.

I am also against Fascism: the reforms of Diocletian were a work of genius and made many people temporarily happy, but failed in the end and added greatly to human misery. I see no reason why this inferior modern copy of them should succeed.

Antonia White

I am against Fascism and any form of government or society which is based on fear, violence, and the suppression of free enquiry.

Amabel Williams-Ellis

I am for the Republican Government of Spain, and against Franco and all other Fascist leaders.

Neutral?

Ruby M. Ayres

Uninformed interference in international politics is more to be dreaded than any anticipated danger resulting from the conflict in Spain.

As a professional writer I dread amateurs.

Vera Brittain

As an uncompromising pacifist, I hold war to be a crime against humanity, whoever fights it and against whomever it is fought. I believe in liberty, democracy, free thought and free speech. I detest Fascism and all that it stands for, but I do not believe that we shall destroy it by fighting it. And I do not feel that we serve either the Spanish people or the cause of civilisation by continuing to make Spain the battle-ground for a new series of Wars of Religion.

Vita Sackville-West

The reason I did not respond to your previous questionnaire still holds good. It is that I dislike Communism and Fascism equally; and, in fact, cannot see any difference between them, except in their names. It seems to me that they each bully and oppress the individual; and, through the individual, Society at large. That is chiefly why I cannot make up my mind to take either side in the Spanish quarrel, which is really a quarrel between Communism and Fascism in Europe, not only in Spain.

One point in your questionnaire strikes me as ambiguous. You stress 'the *legal* Government' of Spain, as the Government you wish to support. Is this because it is the *legal* Government, or because it is a Communist Government? If because it is the *legal* Government, then you ought also to be prepared to support Hitler or Mussolini in the event of a rebellion against them. Yet I do not think you would do so?

Therefore what you really mean is that you want to see Communism established in Spain as well as in Russia, and you do not care a snap of the fingers whether a Government is 'legal' or not. If so, why not have said so frankly? I hate these subterranean forms of propaganda—and wish you could have avoided them if your convictions are sincere and therefore respect-worthy.

Against

Eleanor Smith

I was delighted to receive your unprejudiced brochure.

Naturally, I am a warm adherent of General Franco's, being, like all of us, a humanitarian.

The destruction of so many beautiful objects, and the massacre of so many innocent persons, makes one pity profoundly the ignorant red masses—subsidized by Russia—in Spain.

Do you not agree?

VALENTINE ACKLAND

'Instructions from England (1936)'

from *The Penguin Book of Spanish Civil War Verse*, ed. V. Cunningham, 1980

> Note nothing of why or how, enquire
> no deeper than you need
> into what set these veins on fire,
> note simply that they bleed.
>
> Spain fought before and fights again,
> better no question why;
> note churches burned and popes in pain
> but not the men who die.

ROSAMOND LEHMANN

'Books for Spain'

from the *New Statesman & Nation*, 21 August 1937

Sir,—Any one of your readers who has been ill—by which I mean every one of your readers—knows the pleasure, not to say the necessity, of books during the period of convalescence. In Spain, the Spanish

Medical Aid Committee have now established at least four permanent hospitals, crowded with wounded from the International as well as from Spanish Brigades. These wounded are badly in need of books; and an effort is being made to collect good libraries for them. Books of the following categories are required: political; elementary scientific; fiction (including detective stories); historical; and books on simple technical subjects such as carpentry, electric fittings, etc. Some new German and French books (for patients who do not speak English) would be much appreciated; also Spanish grammars. If any of your readers are willing to give books, these would be very gratefully received and sent straight out to Spain by the Committee of the Spanish Medical Aid, 24, New Oxford Street, W C1; or should there be too much difficulty and distress attached to the despatching of parcels, the S M A would, if informed, collect books from London and near-London addresses.

Perhaps it is scarcely necessary to add a reminder that the wounded in Spain are as likely as we are to find dull books dull and bad books bad; and to beg that such volumes as sink the owners' spirits should be allowed to remain in the spare room, the box room, the cupboard in the passage.

Rosamond Lehmann

Spanish Medical Aid
Committee,
24 New Oxford Street, W C 1

VIRGINIA WOOLF
Remembering Julian

30 July 1937; from Quentin Bell, *Virginia Woolf: A Biography*, 1973

I am going to set down very quickly what I remember about Julian, —partly because I am too dazed to write what I was writing: & then I am so composed that nothing is real unless I write it. And again, I know by this time what an odd effect Time has: it does not destroy people—for instance, I still think perhaps more truly than I did, of Roger, of Thoby: but it brushes away the actual personal presence.

The last time I saw Julian was at Clive's, two days before he went to Spain. It was a Sunday night, the beginning of June—a hot night. He was

in his shirtsleeves. Lottie* was out, & we cooked dinner. He had a
They   peculiar way of standing: his gestures were, as they say,
reminded   characteristic. He made sharp quick movements, very
one of a   sudden, considering how large & big he was, & oddly
sharp winged   graceful. I remember his intent expression; seriously
bird—one of   looking, I suppose at toast or eggs, through his specta-
the snipe   cles. He had a very serious look: indeed he had grown
here in   much sterner, since he came back from China. But of the
the marsh   talk I remember very little; except that by degrees it
turned to politics. L. & Clive & Julian began to talk about Fascism, I
daresay: & I remember thinking, now Clive is reining himself in with L.:
being self restrained: which means there's trouble brewing. (I was
wrong, as L. told me afterwards.) Julian was now a grown man: I mean,
he held his own with Clive & L.: & was cool & independent. I felt he had
met many different kinds of people in China. Anyhow, as it was hot, &
they talked politics, V[anessa]. & A[ngelica]. & I went out into the
Square, & then the others came, & we sat & talked. I remember saying
something about Roger's papers, & telling Julian I should leave them to
him in my will. He said in his quick way, Better leave them to the British
Museum. & I thought, That's because he thinks he may be killed. Of
course we all knew that this was our last meeting—all together—before
he went. But I had made up my mind to plunge into work, & seeing
people, that summer. I had determined not to think about the risks,
because, subconsciously I was sure he would be killed; that is I had a
couchant unexpressed certainty, from Thoby's death I think; a legacy of
pessimism, which I have decided never to analyse. Then, as we walked
towards the gate together, I went with Julian, & said, Won't you have time
to write something in Spain? Won't you send it us? (This referred of
course to my feeling, a very painful one, that I had treated his essay on
Roger too lightly.) And he said, very quickly—he spoke quickly with a
suddenness like his movements—'Yes, I'll write something about Spain.
And send it you if you like.' Do I said, & touched his hand. Then we went
up to Clive's room: & then they went: we stood at the door to watch them.
Julian was driving Nessa's car. At first it wouldn't start. He sat there at
the wheel frowning, looking very magnificent, in his shirt sleeves; with an
expression as if he had made up his mind & were determined, though
there was this obstacle—the car wouldn't start. Then suddenly it jerked
off—& he had his head thrown slightly back, as he drove up the Square

* Lottie Hope, who had once been the Woolfs' servant, now worked for Clive Bell
at 50 Gordon Square.

with Nessa beside him. Of course I noted it, as it might be our last meeting. What he said was 'Goodbye until this time next year.'

We went in with Clive & drank. And talked about Julian. Clive & L. said that there was no more risk in going to Spain than in driving up & down to Charleston. Clive said that only one man had been hurt by a bomb. And he added, But Julian is very cool, like Cory [Clive's brother] & myself. It's spirited of him to go, he added. I think I said, But it's a worry for Nessa. Then we discussed professions: Clive told us how Picasso had said, As a father, I'm so glad my son does not have one. And he said, he was glad Julian should be a 'character'; he would always have enough money to get bread and butter: it was a good thing he had no profession. He was a person who had no one gift in particular. He did not think he was born to be a writer—No he was a character, like Thoby. For some reason I did not answer, that he was like Thoby. I have always been foolish about that. I did not like any Bell to be like Thoby, partly through snobbishness I suppose; nor do I think that Julian was like Thoby, except in the obvious way that he was young & very fine to look at. I said that Thoby had a natural style, & Julian had not.

.   .   .   .   .

I was so anxious to do everything to stop him from going that I got him to meet Kingsley Martin once at dinner, & then Stephen Spender, & so never saw him alone—except once, & then only for a short time. I had just come in with the *Evening Standard* in which *The Years* was extravagantly praised, much to my surprise. I felt very happy. It was a great relief. And I stood with the paper, hoping L. would come & I could tell him when the bell rang. I went to the top of the stairs, looked down, & saw Julian's great sun hat (he was amazingly careless of dress always—would come here with a tear in his trousers) & I called out in a sepulchral voice 'Who is that?' Whereupon he started, & laughed & I let him in. And he said What a voice to hear, or something light: then he came up; it was to ask for Dalton's telephone number. He stood there; I asked him to stay and see Leonard. He hesitated, but seemed to make up his mind that he must get on with the business of seeing Dalton. So I went & looked for the number. When I came back he was reading the *Standard*. I had left it with the review open. But he had turned, I think to the politics. I had half a mind to say, Look how I'm praised. And then thought No, I'm on the top of the wave: & it's not kind to thrust that sort of thing upon people who aren't yet recognised. So I said nothing about it. But I wanted him to stay. And then again I felt, he's afraid I shall try to persuade him not to go. So all I said was, Look here Julian, if you ever want a meal, you've only to ring us up. Yes he said rather doubtingly, as if we might be too busy. So I

insisted. We can't see too much of you. And followed him into the hall, &
put my arm round him & said You can't think how nice it is having you
back. & we half kissed; & he looked pleased & said Do you feel that? And
I said yes, & it was as if he asked me to forgive him for all the worry; and
then off he stumped, in his great hat and thick coat.

When I was in that horrid state of misery last summer with the proofs
of *The Years*, in such misery that I could only work for 10 minutes & then
go & lie down, I wrote him my casual letter about his Roger paper, & he
only answered many weeks later to say he had been hurt, so hadn't
written: & then another letter of mine brought back the old family
feeling. I was shocked at this, & wrote at once, in time to catch him before
he started home, to say don't let us ever quarrel about writing, & I
explained & apologised. All the same, for this reason, & because of his
summer journey, & also because one always stops writing letters unless
one has a regular day, we had one of those lapses in communication
which are bound to happen. I thought, when he comes back there'll be
time to begin again. I thought he would get some political job & we
should see a lot of him.

This lapse perhaps explains why I go on asking myself, without finding
an answer, what did he feel about Spain? What made him feel it
necessary, knowing as he did how it must torture Nessa, to go? He knew
her feeling. We discussed it before he went to China in the most intimate
talk I ever had with him. I remember then he said how hard it was for her,
now that Roger was dead; & that he was sorry that Quentin was so much
at Charleston. He knew that: & yet deliberately inflicted this fearful
anxiety on her. What made him do it? I suppose its a fever in the blood of
the younger generation which we can't possibly understand. I have never
known anyone of my generation have that feeling about a war. We were
all C O's in the Great war. And though I understand that this is a 'cause',
can be called the cause of liberty & so on, still my natural reaction is to
fight intellectually: if I were any use, I should write against it: I should
evolve some plan for fighting English tyranny. The moment force is
used, it becomes meaningless & unreal to me. And I daresay he would
soon have lived through the active stage, & have found some other,
administrative, work. But that does not explain his determination . . .

NAN GREEN

Death on the Ebro

from unpublished Memoir, 'A Chronicle of Small Beer'

We crossed the Ebro by night, one night after the first of the troops. With Crome and his Adjutant, we drove down steep hairpin bends through the dusty dark, but all along the route we could hear and sometimes see, the local peasants laying down swathes of branches to fill up the potholes, and hacking away at the rocky sides to make the corners more manoeuvrable for heavy vehicles. We just made it by dawn.

It was a scene of desolation, with still unburied bodies lying by the roadside, shattered dwellings and huge piles of jettisoned material, papers, suitcases, bedding, even rifles, showing the haste with which the enemy had made his get away. We set up our first HQ at (I think) Flix, in the buildings of a power station where the (German) technicians had left us some well-built slit trenches in which to take refuge when the bombardment began, which it soon did. We were too near a pontoon bridge, and all the bridges were bombed throughout the hours of daylight; we could not get enough work done in the circumstances and moved away from the river bank to a relatively undamaged farmhouse where, in addition to our HQ, we had a 'first emergency' operating theatre, supplied with electricity by a small temperamental generator nursed with immense skill and care by Kozar. Now my job grew intensive. Each day the doctors in charge of four front line dressing stations sent in their lists of the day's casualties; my job was to type these out, classify them into various categories (head wounds, leg wounds, amputations and so on; the base hospitals to which they were sent, the weapons which had caused their injures—mortars, shells, bullets and others) and to turn these figures periodically into graphic form, with the aid of a box of water-colours and some drawing instruments. The casualty lists were sent off every day at four o'clock to the higher command, where they would be co-ordinated with those from other divisions and matched to reports from base hospitals which revealed how long, for instance, it took for a man with a compound fracture of the tibia to work through his treatment and get back into action, or the urgent need for more tin helmets (of which there were shockingly few). There were a lot of casualties; an avalanche of work descended with which we could barely cope (though I still went on making tea) and for an agonising few moments every day I scrutinised for George's name.

We had daily air raids and were sometimes under shell fire. An illustration of the terrible handicap under which the whole army was fighting (due to the criminal policy of 'Non-Intervention') is that when planes came over we had no need to identify them as the enemy or 'ours'. A glance at the sky was enough. If it was one of ours, the sky was full of bursts of anti-aircraft fire, while if it was one or more of theirs—and they often came in formation—an occasional puff of smoke was all that could be seen.

The peasant family to whom the farm belonged had moved to a village further in the rear. Two or three times a week the farmer and one or two daughters used to risk their lives by trudging several miles, making their way over a road-crossing that was constantly being shelled, to keep their irrigation ditches clear and thus save their vegetable harvest. One day, for some reason, we received an issue of shoes, among which there was a pair of woman's shoes, leather, which were too small for me. I gave them to the farmer's daughter. The next time they were due to visit us, the whole family came, including their small, dignified granny, who was carrying in her apron four new laid eggs for me. They had all come under fire to satisfy Spanish obligation by making a return gift.

There were almost forty of us—doctors, orderlies, stretcher bearers, drivers and office staff. I begged some flour from the cookhouse and a small frying pan from Kozar: there was no milk but with flour, water and four eggs I made thirty-eight pancakes (a sort of miracle of the Feeding of the Five thousand) each with a tiny sprinkling of sugar, on which we feasted.

The bridges across which all our supplies reached us were under incessant bomb attacks. Sometimes all of them were damaged and could not be repaired for hours or as much as two days, though the fortification units slaved heroically. One of the most urgent requirements was blood for the transfusion service (then in its infancy). Being fortunate to be a Universal Donor, and a sedentary worker, I was recruited to give some of my blood by direct transfusion, an unforgettable experience. Lying down beside a seriously wounded man, on the point of death, I watched as the colour came back into his lips, his breathing improved and he turned back towards life. Nowadays the transfer of blood is a far more scientific business and the simple grouping used at that time has become immensely more complex (I wasn't given even a Schick Test, there wasn't time). During those early days of the Ebro campaign I actually gave 200cc of my blood three times in little over two weeks. I felt no ill-effects, except that my legs seemed rather heavy for a day or two afterwards. On each occasion I received (by regulation) a *vale*—a piece of paper entitling me to a tin of condensed milk and an egg. Neither was available. But on the third occasion Kozar, sitting by his generator, had seen someone running to fetch me to the operating theatre and by the time I emerged he had managed to snare a rabbit and was cooking it in his little frying pan. It was so fresh that the heart, lying in a saucer beside him, was still beating. Dear Kozar, yet another of the quite underserved benefactors who have adorned my life.

Its first onslaught over, the 15th Brigade got a few days' rest. I visited the British Battalion, a raggle-taggle bunch of weary men, scattered over an arid hillside. George was there, unharmed. We spent two evenings together and one whole night, on a louse-infested sofa. I was taken to see Sam Wild, the Commander of the Battalion. Dear, gruff old Sam's first greeting was 'Ave you etten?' (pure Lancashire hospitality). He told me that George had been 'mentioned in despatches'.

They went back into the lines, where the British won the name of the 'Shock Battalion' for its part in the near successful attack on Hill 481 outside Gandesa.

But the long, slow, desperate and heroic retreat of the Spanish People's Army battling against the overpowering superiority of the Fascists, aided by German and Italian troops and war material in growing force, had begun. We lost ground. There were a few hours when our hospital and HQ were actually between our own and the enemy lines. We had to retire quickly, back towards the river where we set up in yet another derelict farmhouse, not far from a railway tunnel which had been converted into a hospital, for safety from the air.

Crome was replaced by a medical chief from the crack 5th Regiment (the Communist regiment which had throughout covered itself with glory and was a byword for courage and military efficiency). Enrique Bassadone was a contrast to the easy-going but nevertheless highly efficient Crome, who had a devastating irreverence for bureaucracy, and liked to surround himself with eccentrics and oddballs. Highly professional, with a batman to keep his spotless uniform in order and wait on him at table, Enrique didn't approve of women and always addressed me in the third person—to which I naughtily replied in the second person, the universal habit in Republican Spain.

At this time we received the news that the Republican Government had decided, in view of the endless shilly-shallying in the League of Nations about foreign troops 'on both sides'—equating with the utmost cynicism the comparatively few volunteers who had come to Spain to risk their lives in the fight against Fascism with the armies of conscripted men from Germany, Italy and Portugal—not to mention the aeroplanes etc.

which they brought with them—to call this bluff by withdrawing *all* the members of the International Brigades and sending them home, and proposing a proportional withdrawal. This, disregarding the fact that a great many of the volunteers had no home to go to, having come from Fascist countries to return to which would be to court imprisonment and death.

We were to be sent home. George had sustained a slight headwound, which was soon stitched up and healed, but the hospital to which he had been sent wanted to keep him for treatment of the suppurating sores on his legs (we all suffered from them in various degrees). Learning of the coming withdrawal George had insisted on returning to the Battalion to take part in the final action with his British fellow-soldiers. He came through our HQ with a note stating that he had been discharged from hospital *at his own request.* We spent an hour or two together eagerly discussing which of us would reach England first, and how it would come about; who would see the children first—and we agreed that George should not shave off his beard until they had seen it, because Grandpa Green had told us they were fascinated by the idea of a bearded Daddy. The 22nd September had been fixed for the withdrawal of the British Battalion; our little group in the Divisonal HQ (mostly drivers, mechanics, American and Canadian) was to engage in training their Spanish successors and we had no date fixed for our departure. George was convinced that the British and French governments, seeing what was at stake in their own interests after Munich, must now take steps to release the vast stores of military supplies which were being held up at the French frontier in the name of 'Non-Intervention'. He was joyous at going back into the lines for his final swipe at the Fascist enemy, and sent me a note on his return to the Battalion, repeating the conviction that the desperately-wanted war supplies must 'even now' be pouring in.

The 22nd September came and went. Though I was still at the front, I sighed with relief that George was not on the casualty lists I had studied daily with dread.

On the night of the 23rd, two chaps came and wakened me.

'George is *missing*,' they said.

Due to an unexpectedly severe enemy attack, the British had been asked to spend one more day in helping to repulse it in the Sierra de Pandols. In spite of desperate resistance, they had been forced to retire and when the time came to call the roll, George did not answer.

I didn't say anything. I pulled up the sheets around my suddenly icy-cold shoulders and lay down, trying to grasp the thunderbolt. It must not, it could not be true. 'Missing' meant 'He might be alive, he might be dead' and this thought began to repeat itself in my mind as if a needle had been dropped on a gramophone and had stuck in the groove. My dear colleagues next morning made a pact among themselves not to leave me alone for a second and established a sort of rota for the purpose. It was too kind. I would have liked to be on my own and try to come to terms with the situation. I *must not* weep. I *must* cherish hope. He-might-be-alive-he-might-be-dead repeated itself with bewildering monotony in my waking thoughts for the rest of my stay in Spain and for the following months, gradually changing to despair. We left the front, our handful of internationals, a couple of weeks later, having handed over our jobs to our Spanish successors. We drove back across the river in an open *camion* and I recall the sudden surprise and delight I felt as we drove through our first village on the far side, to see women in the streets! I hadn't seen another woman for weeks, and wished I could get down and embrace them—there you are, my sisters, my dear ones, weep with me! We stopped in Asco, where I began to telephone all the hospitals to which casualties might have been sent, spending hours shouting down crackling, buzzing, intermittently silent lines. Eventually I had an answer that raised a faint hope. At some hospital they said they had a Georges Crey not too seriously wounded, a Frenchman. Could it be a mistake? I must go and find out!

I do not remember how I got to Barcelona. But there I received the tenderest sympathy and most practical help from Peter Kerrigan, at that time the correspondent of the *Daily Worker*. Dear Peter facilitated my journeys to five hospitals—the one I'd hoped for denied all knowledge of any Georges Crey at all. There was nothing to do but to go home.

The Catalan chauffeur who drove me and one of the English nurses (Margaret Findlay or Dorothy Rutter?) to the border was preoccupied with worry about his little son, who was sick. At the French guardpost I begged and pleaded to be allowed to enter France, buy some condensed milk and cross back to the Spanish end—about 20 yards—to give it to him; it was surely harmless to introduce sealed tins of condensed milk into Spain? The guard refused. We made our way to a café for a meal. I ate two bits of a white roll and some fresh butter (neither of which we had tasted for months) and then was absolutely unable to get another morsel down. In Toulon I bought a pair of shoes, my *alpargatas* being almost worn out. Then took the train—I don't even remember whether for Calais or Le Havre.

How was I going to tell Grandpa Green? How—and what—was I going to tell the children? 'He is missing,' I told Grandpa, and the sharing of the burden with him seemed to make it heavier rather than lighter. But it was comforting to be with him. We went to Summerhill the next day (a Sunday). A. S. Neill was at the station—he usually went there to meet parents on Sundays. I told him, and then hastened to the school to find my darlings. 'Daddy isn't coming just yet, we don't quite know where he is,' was the best I could do. But some child had overheard me speaking to Neill and half an hour later Frances came to me and said, 'Sally says Daddy is *missing*. I don't want him to be missing!' I must give them hope but I mustn't give them too much hope . . . one doesn't tell lies to one's children, but what is the truth here? He-might-be-alive-he-might-be-dead . . .

That afternoon there was a tea-party, someone's birthday I think. I sat and watched my two eat their jelly, sandwiches and cake. In between every spoonful or mouthful Martin looked across at me with such blazing love in his bright brown eyes—so like the look in his father's grey ones when he used to sit beaming at me in the early days of our marriage, saying 'I'm doting on you!'—that I could hardly bear it. Frances refused to admit to herself that her father might not come back. She buried it inside herself where it began to canker. She experienced an adult grief but had no outlet for it.

Summerhill had been good for them and good *to* them. And when the time came for me to tell Neill that I by myself could not pay their fees and must take them away, there came another stupendous kindness. He offered to keep the two of them for the fees of one. Yet another of those fantastic acts of generosity that I have received all my life. My debt to Neill is unrepayable.

I went right on working for Spain—'merely changing the front and the weapons' as the International Brigaders put it. The war was not yet lost. The fight was still going on. Food, medical supplies, everything was needed more than ever, and the political struggle, 'Save Spain—Save Peace', more urgent still. My daytime job was the National Joint Committee for Spanish Relief. I shared a small basement flat in Blooms-bury with Winifred Bates and together we formed a voluntary group: 'British Medical Units from Spain' in which we organised all the nurses, doctors and others who had returned, to speak at meetings, to hold meetings, to raise funds and write to the press, local and national. A deputation of nurses set off to visit Mrs Chamberlain, to ask her intervention on behalf of Spanish women and children. She was not at Downing Street, so they took taxis and went to Chequers, where they found *barricades* at the entrance to the drive. They had informed the press, which made headlines of the story. Angela Guest, always original and daring, by herself upset a tin of red paint on the steps of No 10

Downing Street, to represent the blood of the Spanish people. This made press headlines. The struggle became more and more desperate and now doubt began to creep in as to its outcome . . .

Doubt meanwhile was stealthily coming over my spirit. As the days wore on and there was no news I began to know in my heart that if George had been alive he would somehow by now have managed to communicate with me, though I invented all sorts of fantasies to keep alive the fragile flame of hope. (Could he be a prisoner, seriously ill or blinded and unable to write . . . ?) I was an embarrassment to my friends, who did not know whether to console me or offer hope. In my youthful intolerance I had declared that funerals were superstitious nonsense but now I knew, and have since realised even more strongly, that a funeral is a necessity for those left behind, enabling them to give vent to their grief and to draw a line under a stage of life after which one must get on with it in a new way, come what may. But I had nothing to come to terms with. Was I a widow or a wife? When must I begin to tackle life without my other half?

The long nightmare came to an end. Early in March, when the end was drawing near in Spain and the exodus from Catalonia was about to begin, I got an official letter from the Republican Government telling me that George had died on 23rd September. Winifred, who watched me open it, told me afterwards that she knew what it contained because my face went grey. What I built up in the next few hours was the determination not to show that I was shattered: for the sake of the children, who must discover that I could now cope with being both father and mother to them, and for the sake of George, upon whom no blame must fall. Pride, pride in his having given his life for the cause we all held dear must be the keynote.

Letters of condolence arrived, few but precious. Wogan Philipps wrote that 'knowing George had altered the whole course of his life'. The Musicians' Union presented me with a cheque for £60 and a despatch case inscribed, on a little metal label, with recognition of the work he had done for the Union. Paddy O'Daire gripped my hand and said 'He was a great guy'. These and others were of immense comfort.

Now I could tell the children. Frances, poor sweet, could not accept the news. She continued to tell her schoolmates fantasies about the cake she was going to bake for her Daddy when he came back . . . She became actually ill, ran a mysterious high temperature, and Neill sent for me. The very day I got there, Neill, with characteristic wisdom, had sent a girl to play with her in bed who was an orphan. Conversation turned to fathers. 'I haven't got a father,' said Sally. 'That's funny, neither have I,' said Frances . . . I had brought her something she wanted—a 'grass skirt' in which to dance like a Caribbean girl. She looked at it and wept. 'What is the matter,' I said. 'Don't you want it after all?' She burst into tears and flung herself into my arms, saying 'I only want Daddy.' Now we were able to cry together.

Martin, I think, with the resilience of a younger child who had not grasped what it meant, actually took longer to work the loss out of his system (if he ever did). Two years later I found him in bed, one night, staring at the ceiling. 'What's up, can't you get to sleep?' I asked. 'I am *trying to remember Daddy*,' he replied.

SYLVIA TOWNSEND WARNER

'Waiting at Cerbère'

from *Poems for Spain*, 1939, ed. Stephen Spender and John Lehmann

And on the hillside
That is the colour of peasant's bread
Is the rectangular
White village of the dead.

No one stirs in those streets.
Out of those dark doorways no one comes.
At the tavern of the Black Cross
Only the cicada strums.

And below, where the headland
Strips into rock, the white mane
Of foam like a quickened breath
Rises and falls again;

And above, the road
Zigzagging tier on tier
Above the terraced vineyards,
Goes on to the frontier.

SYLVIA TOWNSEND WARNER

'Benicasim'

from *Left Review*, March 1938

Here for a little we pause.
The air is heavy with sun and salt and colour.
On palm and lemon-tree, on cactus and oleander
a dust of dust and salt and pollen lies.
And the bright villas
sit in a row like perched macaws,
and rigid and immediate yonder
the mountains rise.

And it seems to me we have come
into a bright-painted landscape of Acheron.
For along the strand
in bleached cotton pyjamas, on rope-soled tread,
wander the risen-from-the-dead,
the wounded, the maimed, the halt.
Or they lay bare their hazarded flesh to the salt
air, the recaptured sun,
or bathe in the tideless sea, or sit fingering the sand.

But narrow is this place, narrow is this space
of garlanded sun and leisure and colour, of return
to life and release from living. Turn
(Turn not!) sight inland:
there, rigid as death and unforgiving, stand
the mountains—and close at hand.

[*Original footnote.*] At Benicasim on the east coast of Spain is the Rest
Home for the convalescent wounded of the Spanish People's Army, and
the Villa dedicated to Ralph Fox, supported by the Spanish Medical Aid.

SYLVIA TOWNSEND WARNER

'The Drought Breaks'

from *Life and Letters Today*, Summer 1937

Rafaela Perez went a step or two into the street, pulling her shawl closer around her. A drizzling rain fell out of the winter sky, by midnight that rain would be snow. A cat came along, nosing in the gutters. It would not find much there, this was a poor street and the poor had no food to throw away.

In the rich quarter there was feasting and waste. The German soldiers, the Italian soldiers, were eating as they had not eaten for years. Last week a German lieutenant, tipsy, very affable, had said to her in his halting, clumsy syllables, 'Spain, fine country. Much eating, much wine. Pouf!' And he had distended himself, and thumped his stomach, smiling candidly, showing his bright young teeth. '*De nada*,' she had said—'It's nothing'—the conventional phrase with which one puts off a thanks or a commendation. For it did not do to give no answer at all, one must at all costs seem civil to these invaders. And she had gone on scrubbing the floor of the café, wringing out the cloth stinking of chloride of lime.

Now the cat was licking up rain-water. It would not find anything else, drink water if one can fill the belly no other way. Curious to think at all about a cat, curious to be so attentive to a grey cat slinking through the grey dusk. Ah, but life was so empty, so hideously empty, one would think of anything now, of a cat, of a cobweb.

Two days after the town was taken by the Nationalists her husband had been shot. They had not even troubled to find the gun in the chimney, the bullets padded in the mattress. His Trades Union card had been enough. One glance at it, and they were driving him out of the house, up the narrow street towards the church. A dozen other similar groups converged thither: a man, struggling, or walking in silence (Diego had walked demurely, without a word, without a glance back), and about him the soldiers and Civil Guards, and, trailing after, a woman, two women, a woman with her children. There, by the church, the firing squad was waiting, trim and powerful. And so—and so—the men were lined up against the wall, and the word was given to fire.

The bloodstains were still on the church wall and the flies buzzing round them when the church was solemnly re-sanctified. New confessionals, new hangings, new pictures and images, arrived in furniture vans and were carried in. Then had come the procession, soldiers and choir-boys, the bishop under a canopy, priests and gentlefolk and more soldiers. They, the people of the quarter, must kneel on the cobbles while the procession went by. Inside the church everything was smart and fresh, there was a smell of incense and of flowers and of varnish from the new confessionals. Outside there was the stain of blood and the smell of blood. The religious people came clustering and buzzing back as fast as bluebottles, as though they, too, came wherever there was a smell of blood. And now, more than ever, it was impossible to escape them, impossible to say them nay, whether they came demanding alms or children.

If one's husband had been shot, then one's children must be taken also.

'Holy Church,' said the Reverend Mother, her black robes seeming to fill the room, her eyebrows bristling, 'Holy Church will not leave these innocents where they can be contaminated. You have three children, I think. See that they are ready by eight to-morrow morning.'

The convent was far away, at the other end of the town, a heavy building with barred windows, a garden surrounded by a high wall topped with spikes. For many days the mothers of the lost children haunted there, hanging about, watching the barred windows and the spiked wall; for though there was no chance of seeing the children one might perhaps hear a voice on the other side of the wall. But there were never any voices. Twice a day one could hear a clatter of small feet, marching, marching. And so, after a time, one lost hope, did not go so often, did not go at all.

Every week the nuns came round to collect the money. They knew to a peseta how much one earned. 'Your children are well. They want no other mother than the Mother of God. But they cannot be kept for nothing. We ask you in the name of the Lord and his little ones.' Then the hand would glide out of the sleeve and the downcast eyes would scan the pesetas.

From the loud-speaker further up the street came the accustomed sound of the hour. A drunken vaunting voice, Queipo de Llano's, saying that Madrid would fall in a couple of days, that Valencia had been bombed, that the Catalans would not fight, that everywhere the Reds were falling back, without food, without arms, without hope. Then would come the singing, and the shouts of *Arriba España!*

It was four months and twenty-one days since the children had been taken away, and now she was standing in the rain, looking at a cat—no, looking where the cat had been, for it had long ago sneaked on its way. The street was dark and silent, as though dead. Indeed, it was half-dead, depopulated. This neighbour dead, that neighbour in prison, that neighbour gone off. People would be there in the evening, and in the morning they would have disappeared, leaving no word, no trace.

The wireless brayed on, presently there would be the national music, humstrum of guitars, snap of castanets. In the cafés of the rich quarter the foreigners would lean back in their chairs, wag their heads, stir their haunches, eye the prostitutes trailing past, say to themselves, 'We are in Spain.'

Later still, a noise not broadcast, there would be cries, hooting laughter, rattle of a volley. Every night, even now, they were shooting in the prisons.

In the Calle de Rosas no one stirred. Those who were left in the tall houses sat, cold and scattered, like the last leaves on a winter tree. The houses were so much colder, being half-empty: no steps on the stairs, no smells of cooking, never a laugh or a song, not even a quarrel to liven up the air.

She shook her head and sighed. Like an echo there came the noise of the wind awaking in the mountains.

The voice on the wireless bragged on. Madrid had again been bombed, a sally of the Reds had been wiped out with great slaughter, five hundred prisoners had been taken on the Basque front, an ammunition dump had blown up. One did not listen, but yet one heard. One did not look at the placards, but yet one saw. One pulled one's shawl over one's ears, turned away one's eyes; yet through one's mind marched the newly-arrived battalions, one saw their grand equipment, one heard their strong marching and the words of command shouted in foreign tongues. A scrap of newspaper, wrapped round a bit of salt fish or a handful of olives, jabbed at one's eyes with a threat or a sneer.

And yet Diego had said that it was good to know how to read, good to take an interest in the affairs of the country.

Sometimes out of her stagnating cold misery a flash of rancour would explode like a marsh-gas. If Diego had been content to work and to eat, like other men!—then, though this had come, though there had been hunger and cold and terror, there would still have been husband and children, a clue to living; and the church wall would have been only what it had been, a wall much thicker than those of the flimsy tenements around it.

The wind was rising, desolate among the stone crags. *Arriba España!* chorused the voices on the wireless, a wolfish pack-howling. Overhead a window opened softly, a head peered out.

'Rafaela! Is that you? What is it, what are you waiting for?'

'Nothing.'

Without comment the head withdrew, the window was closed again. There was nothing to wait for. She must go in, chew her slow supper, lie down cold on the bed. The wind blew stronger, its voice among the mountains trembled with intensity, it was like a wild singer. The wind throbbed, came closer with its throbbing voice.

Ah! What was that?—that rending crash of sound, and after-rattle, and another and another crash? What were these jarring wings over the city?

Windows opened, doors opened, the street was full of voices. Blind Adela was wailing. 'It's them! Mother of God, it's them! They're going to bomb us now!'

'No! It's us, it's us! They're *ours*!'

She tore off the dripping shawl, waved it upwards in greeting, turning up her face, her heart, to the death falling from the air, as though to a greeting from the dead, as though to a greeting from life.

All around were voices, voices hushed, broken, excited; gasps, cries caught back, questions and exclamations. It was like the noise of earth, thirsty with long drought, clucking with parched lips as it drinks the rain.

CHARLOTTE HALDANE

'Passionaria'

from *Left Review*, April 1938

You are the great figurehead
At the prow of the ship: Spain
Forging forward

You are stalwart, strong;
Long generations of sturdy miners
Have forged you—iron is in your blood.

You are good. You have stood
Always in the vanguard, leading,
Hands held out to uphold
Children and women above this sea
Of hatred and of blood.

You are wise. In your eyes
That smiled at me so lovingly
I saw and understood
Also the buried tears.
Crystallised toil and struggle,
Years of hardship, privation, sorrow,—

But never for yourself alone,
Never to moan in solitude,
But ever surrounded and uplifted by your comrades,
The valour of your people,
The honourable, proud, and noble unknown
Of whom you were one, and are still

The indomitable will. Now a leader among them
Great carved woman at the prow
Who knows sorrow; suffers hate; feels love:
Whose eyes and hands and voice have moved
Thousands into battle-line:

In you I salute, Comrade Dolores,
Spain, forging a new world for us too!

ETHEL MANNIN

Spanish Struggles

from *Comrade O Comrade: Or, Low-Down on the Left*, 1947

Outside the hall, and in the entrance, enthusiastic and persistent comrades of various political denominations were attempting to sell their various papers and pamphlets and distribute handbills.

'To-day's *Worker* one penny!'

'The Truth about the Spanish Struggle, twopence!'

Anarchists trying to sell *Spain and the World*, I L P-ers trying to sell *The New Leader*, Pacifists trying to sell *Peace News*—to a crowd intent on the lifting of the arms embargo so that more Spaniards could be killed by Spaniards. There was an atmosphere of eagerness and excitement.

Linn found a seat for Larry at the back of the hall and left him; she was stewarding, and continually in demand by other stewards, all with paper rosettes of the Republican colours pinned to their bosoms. The hall was packed, from floor to ceiling, and people were standing along the sides. The platform was draped with red and yellow bunting.

Larry sat and looked at the various leaflets which had been thrust into his hands, but all he could see, imposed upon the slogans about ending non-intervention and lifting the arms embargo, was Jackie's eager brown face upturned to his as she said, 'We'll go riding together one day—and I'll tell you about the moated grange.' It sounded like a fairy castle to him.

The meeting began on time. It was quite a distinguished platform— an assortment of well-known Communists, and various hardly less distinguished 'fellow-travellers'—a well-known actress, a well-known poet, a distinguished cleric, authors, male, female, and intermediate.

The chairman, a Party member, rattled off a set piece about the struggle of the Spanish people against Franco being part of a world-wide struggle—the struggle of the forces of progress against the forces of reaction—fight between capitalists, clerical and feudal owners against the exploited workers, class struggle between rich and poor, exploiters and exploited—Spanish war one sector of international struggle between Fascism and Democracy—call upon—distinguished poet—read translation he has made of one of the poems of a distinguished Spanish anti-Fascist poet—afterwards read one of his own poems—Mr Rer-rer-rer—Clap-clap-clap.

The distinguished poet, clad in classy tweeds, heaved up languidly from his chair and in a bored, classy tone murmured that he would first read the perm in the original Spanish. The perm expressed the struggle of the anti-Fascist masses against the military clique and the Church.

Lifting his voice a little he read the Spanish verses, and everyone assumed intelligent expressions. A few nodded and faintly smiled at various points to indicate that they understood Spanish.

'I will now read the translation I have made of this perm.'

At that everyone looked even more intelligent and the distinguished poet's cultural accents droned on. At the conclusion of the translation everyone clapped vigorously.

'Now I will read you a perm of my own. I have called it "No More the Castanets"' He read this in a rather more lively tone.

> No more the castanets,
> All that is finished.
> Plough all such insignia
> Of the bourgeoisie
> Into the blood-soaked ground.

> Now the machine-gun blooms
> With crimson flowers
> Under the orange tree.
> No more the castanets,
> The soul of Spain is free!

This was received with such tremendous applause that the poet was induced to give an encore. He obliged with 'A Song of Deliverance.'

> The Falangists say
> They look into the sun;
> But the sun blinds them;
> Only eagles can look into the sun;
> You are the eagles, comrades,
> You have the burning vision,
> You are the free.

There was another surge of applause, but before the poet could be induced to recite another of his own unaided works the chairman intervened to thank Mr Rer-rer-rer and called upon Miss Rer-rer-rer, the celebrated actress, to speak to us.

The celebrated actress smiled, shifted her furs to the back of her shoulders, waited for a spotlight which was not forthcoming, and came gracefully down-stage amid prolonged applause.

Her speech was brief but impassioned. She did *feel*, she said, with *heart* and *mind*, deep in her heart, deep in her brain—sense of *exultation*—as a mother of *sons*—facing the future—triumph of Fascism return to Dark Ages—brave Spanish people fighting for us all against forces of evil —Spain unconquerable—they shall not pass—*no pasaran!*

She lifted a rapt face to the gallery, tears in her eyes, and the applause was terrific.

'Silly bitch!' murmured the young man next to Larry. 'Always plays to the gallery—can't resist it even at a public meeting—'

When the applause had finally subsided the chairman said he had some messages to read. He read messages from Louis Aragon, Heinrich Mann, Ramon Sender, Pablo Neruda, Mulk Raj Anand, and various others, all amid tumultuous applause. Some of the messages were cultural in tone, others purely political. When all this was over the chairman called upon Comrade Rer-rer-rer, organising secretary rer-rer-rer, to speak to us.

Comrade Rer-rer-rer was a thick-set little man with a self-confident manner and a very loud voice. He made a very violent and very long speech, the burden of which was that the British Government policy of non-intervention in Spain was a very bad thing, and that British workers must *act*. (Loud applause.) British Labour and Trade Union leaders supporting the National Government's policy of non-intervention (cries of 'Shame!')—Popular Front government in Spain—Arms for Spain —British policy—British workers—Call upon all present—gallant comrades in Spain—non-intervention—lift arms embargo—

It went on and on and on. It rushed out upon the audience wave upon wave, first one great wave of words, and then another and another and another. His voice was so loud that those on the platform and in the first few rows of the audience could not hear the words; the noise deafened and stupefied them. Every now and then he would reach a peak, and surely, it seemed, this was the end; at this peak he must surely stop; the rest would be anti-climax. But at the crest of the wave he plunged down again, only to come up again in another wave. The chairman kept glancing at the watch he had laid on the table—though he faced a large clock on the front of the gallery—and finally, in despair, took a slip of paper and printed on it, large and bold and clear, T I M E. He pushed the slip to the edge of the table, and the entire platform was all agog to see would the speaker pick it up. There was a moment when he turned to the table and their hearts leapt up, but he turned to the table only to bang a clenched fist down on it, and the scrap of paper went flying . . . 'This, too, must pass,' the chairman said in the bitterness of his soul, and 'he can't go on for ever' said the audience in its hidden heart.

When he finally came to an end, when chairman and audience were least expecting it, the chairman called upon another comrade to make an appeal, and the audience sank back in relief, exhausted, and fumbled in handbags and pockets. It was so much easier to sit and deliver than to be harangued till they felt they would die of it.

The young man next to Larry muttered, 'Lot of dam' lies! Why don't they admit that the whole red racket in Spain is subsidised by Russia —that is to say by the Jews?'

Larry regarded the young man with interest. He was small and pale and was wearing, Larry noticed, a black shirt.

Larry answered him, amiably, with his pleasant smile. ' 'Tis the Jews is after causin' all the trouble, is it?' This was new to him and he was interested.

The pale young man turned his angry face to Larry. 'You're Irish, aren't you—Southern Irish?'

'I am so.'

'That means you're Catholic—and anti-Red?'

'Ah, I wouldn't be knowin' at all! 'Tis very hard to go against the

Church when you're brought up to it, but if the Spanish people wanted the kind of government they had, I'm thinkin', 'twas no business of General Franco and the rest to go chargin' in upsettin' things, stirrin' up trouble and plungin' the country in this terrible war! And 'tis not all Reds that do be against Franco, I'm told.'

'Whoever told you that is lying!' the young man snapped.

'Ah, no,' Larry cried, quickly, as the picture of Jackie and Mary flashed before him. 'They could be mistaken, perhaps, God help them, but it's not lyin' they'd be!'

'Who were your informants?'

'One was a lady writer is a member of something called the ILP. The other is a young lady agin all governments!'

'Both Reds!' the young man insisted, angrily.

'How can they be?' Larry was bewildered once more. 'They're both against the Communists!'

'The ILP is Marxist,' the young man pointed out. 'It supported the Bolshevisk Revolution—engineered by the Jews! The Anarchists are not Marxists but they're trouble-makers. They've no use for the Soviet Union, it's true, but they're cranks, and dangerous ones. The most dangerous of them is in London now—an old Jewess they call "Red Emma." And you try to tell me the Anarchists are not Reds along with the rest! A different brand of Reds, if you like, but Reds all the same. In this country no one takes the Anarchists seriously, but in Spain they're an infernal nuisance. They hate the Communists, but they work in with that other Marxist lot, the POUM. There's nothing to choose between any of them! Behind it all is international Jewry!'

''Tis all very confusin' for a gossoon and a galoot like meself,' said Larry, 'but if your honour would be tellin' me—what have the Jews to do with it, at all?'

'I've told you,' the young man replied, impatiently, waving the collecting-box away as it approached him, and pushing it past Larry as well. 'I've already told you that the real rulers of Russia are the Jews. As a good Catholic, and therefore as a good anti-Red, you ought to know that! The Jews are behind the Communists everywhere.'

Larry tried to touch-bottom in the sea of confusion.

SIMONE WEIL
'Letter to Georges Bernanos (1938?)'

(transl. Valentine Cunningham) from *Écrits Historiques et Politiques*, Paris 1960

Monsieur,

However silly it might be to write to a writer who is continually, by the nature of his profession, inundated with letters, I can't stop myself from doing just that now that I've read *Les Grands Cimetières sous La Lune*. Not that this is the first time a book of yours has impressed me. The *Journal d'un curé de campagne* is to my mind the most beautiful of your books, at least of those I've read. It is, truly, a great book. But despite my loving other books of yours, I never had any reason for being a pest and putting my feelings into a letter. But with this latest book it's a different matter. I have had an experience myself which echoes yours—to be sure, one more abbreviated, less profound, sited elsewhere and on the face of it, but only on the face of it, burdening the spirit in a different way.

I am not a Catholic. However—and what I am about to say must doubtless seem presumptuous to every Catholic, coming from a non-Catholic, but I can't put it any differently—nothing Catholic, nothing Christian has ever appeared alien to me. I sometimes tell myself that if only there were a notice on church doors saying that entry was forbidden to anybody who enjoyed an income somewhat above the ordinary, I would convert straightaway. From infancy my sympathies were directed towards groups that made much of their origins beyond the pale of the social high-ups—until I realised that it's the nature of such groups to discourage all one's sympathies. The last one to inspire a certain confidence in me was the Spanish CNT. I had travelled a bit—only a bit—in Spain before the civil war, but enough to experience the love that it's hard not to feel for the Spanish people. I perceived the anarchist movement to be the natural expression of the Spaniards' greatnesses and blemishes, of their most legitimate and least legitimate aspirations. The CNT and the FAI were an amazing stew, to which anybody and everybody was admitted. In consequence you found in them immorality, cynicism, fanaticism, cruelty, but also love, the spirit of brotherhood, and above all that demand on honour that is so fine among the humble of the earth. These qualities were all cheek by jowl. It seemed to me that those people who came to these organisations inspired by idealism outnumbered the ones animated by a relish for violence and disorder. In July 1936 I was in Paris. I do not like war. But what has always horrified me most in war is the position of those who find themselves behind the battle-lines. When I realised that, try as I might, I could not stop myself from participating morally in this war, that's to say hoping every day, every hour, for the victory of one side and the defeat of the other, I put it to myself that Paris was the rear, and I got on the train for Barcelona with every intention of enlisting. This was at the beginning of August 1936.

An accident compelled me to cut short my stay in Spain. I spent a few days in Barcelona. After that I went deep into rural Aragon, on the banks of the river Ebro, about 15 kilometres from Saragossa, at the very spot where Yagüe's forces recently crossed the river. Then I visited the palace at Sitges that had been transformed into a hospital. Then I went back to Barcelona. All in all, about two months. I left Spain against my will, and with the intention of returning. In the event I decided, without compulsion, not to go back. I ended up not feeling any more the interior necessity to take part in a war which was no longer what it had seemed to me at the beginning; a war of starving peasants against landed proprietors and a clergy in league with those proprietors, had turned into a war between Russia, Germany and Italy.

I recognised that stench of civil war, of blood and terror, which your book gives off: I had breathed it myself. I have to say that I neither saw nor heard anything that quite matches the ignominy of some of the stories you tell, those murders of old peasants, those *Ballilas* pursuing aged people and beating them up with coshes. However, what I did come across was quite sufficient for me. I just missed watching the execution of a priest. As we waited for it I was wondering whether I was simply going to look on or whether I would get myself shot by trying to intervene. I still don't know what I would have done if a fortunate chance had not impeded the execution.

So many stories crowd into my pen . . . But they would take too long. And what would be the good of that? Just one will suffice. I was in Sitges when the militia-men returned, beaten, from the expedition to Majorca. They had been decimated. Out of forty young lads who had left Sitges, nine were dead. This was only found out when the remaining thirty-one returned. On the following night, nine punitive sorties were made and nine Fascists, or so-called Fascists, were bumped off, and all in that tiny town where, in July, nothing at all had gone on. Among the nine there was a baker whose crime, they told me, was that he had belonged to the local branch of the old Catalan citizens' defence group. His old dad, whose only child and sole support this was, went mad. Let me tell you something else: in Aragon, an international band of twenty-two fighters from all countries captured, in a slight engagement, a lad of fifteen who was fighting as a Falangist. As soon as he was brought in, still shaking from the sight of comrades being killed at his side, he said he had been conscripted against his will. They searched him and found on him a holy medal of the Virgin and a Falangist membership card. They sent him to Durruti who was leader of the column, and he, having expatiated for a whole hour on the beauties of the Anarchist ideal, offered him a choice between dying and enlisting straightaway in the ranks of those who had taken him prisoner and against his former comrades. Durruti gave the child twenty-four hours to think things over. At the end of twenty-four hours the kid said no and was shot. And yet Durruti was in some senses an admirable man. The death of this tiny hero has never stopped weighing on my conscience, even though I only learned about it after the event. And here's something else. In a village that the Reds and the Whites had each won and lost, won again and lost again goodness knows how many times, the Red fighters who eventually got the definitive upper hand found hiding in the cellars a handful of haggard, scared, famished creatures. Among them were three or four young men. The fighters argued in this fashion: if these young fellows stayed behind and waited for the Fascists instead of going with us the last time we pulled back, it's because they are Fascists. So they shot them there and then, after which they gave the rest something to eat and fancied themselves extremely humane. One final story, this time from behind the lines. Two Anarchists on one occasion told me how they and some comrades had captured two priests. With a revolver they killed one of them on the spot, right in front of the other one, then they told that one he could go. When he had gone twenty paces they shot him down. The person who told me this story was quite astonished not to see me laugh.

In Barcelona they killed an average of fifty men a night in punishment raids. Proportionally this was many fewer than on Majorca, since Barcelona is a city of around a million people. Moreover three days of murderous street-fighting had taken place there. But numbers are perhaps not the main thing in such matters. The real point is how murder is regarded. I never observed anybody, neither among the Spaniards nor among the French who had come to fight or just to look around—these latter being usually dim and inoffensive intellectuals—I never came across anybody who professed, even privately, any repulsion, or disgust or merely disapprobation on account of the blood that was being spilled to no purpose. You speak of fear. Yes, fear played its part in these butcherings. But where I was, I never observed fear in the role you attribute to it. One comradely meal-time some men who all seemed bold enough to me—I had personally witnessed the bravery of one of them—recounted with the hearty cheer of brothers-in-arms how they had killed some priests or some 'Fascists'—which is one of those very elastic terms. I had the feeling, for my part, that when the temporal and spiritual authorities have excluded a category of human beings from among those whose lives have worth, then nothing comes more naturally to man than killing. When you know that you can kill with no risk of punishment or blame, you kill. At the very least you surround the killers with encouraging smiles. Should you by chance feel a little disgust to start with, you keep it quiet and soon stifle it altogether for fear of appearing short on virility. A kind of enticement sets in, an intoxication impossible to resist except with a strength of spirit that I am bound to judge exceptional, given that I never came across it anywhere. On the other hand I have met peaceable Frenchmen, for whom up until then I had never felt any contempt, people who would not have considered doing any killing for themselves, but who wallowed in this blood-soaked atmosphere with visible delight. I shall never again be able to feel any respect for them.

An atmosphere of this kind soon obscures the very purpose of the struggle. For that purpose can only be formulated in terms of the public good, the good of men—and men have lost their value. In a country where the poor are, by a very large majority, peasants, the well-being of the peasants must be an essential ambition of every party of the far-left. And at the start this war was perhaps above all a war over how the land should be shared out. But, you know, these magnificent poverty-stricken peasants of Aragon, who have remained so proud despite every humili-ation, were not even an object of curiosity for the militia-men. No acts of insolence, no injuries, no brutality were perpetrated—at least I never saw any, and I do know that robbery and rape were capital offences in the anarchist columns—but still an abyss separated the men with the weapons from the unarmed population, a gulf just like the one that separates the rich from the poor. You sensed it in the rather humble, cringing, fearful attitude on the one side, and in the confidence, the offhandedness, the condescension on the other.

One sets out as a volunteer, with notions of sacrifice; one stumbles into a war which looks just like a war for mercenaries, only with many more cruelties and far less sense of the respect that's due to the enemy.

I could prolong reflections of this kind indefinitely, but I have to call a halt. From the start of my Spanish experiences and in all the time I've been attending to and reading every kind of observation about Spain, I have come across nobody who has been submerged in the atmosphere of the Spanish war and remained uninfected by it—except you alone. You are a Monarchist, a disciple of Drumont—but what is that to me? You are incomparably closer to me than my comrades in the Aragon militias —those comrades that, in truth, I loved.

What you say about nationalism, about war, about the foreign policy of France after the war has all likewise found a lodging in my heart. I was ten years old when the Treaty of Versailles was signed. Up until then I had been a patriot with all the enthusiasm children display in wartime. The desire to humiliate the conquered enemy which broke out everywhere at that time (and in the years that followed) in such a repellent fashion, cured me of that naïve patriotism once and for all.

I'm afraid I've pestered you with a dreadfully long letter. It only remains for me to say how much I admire you.

Mlle Simone Weil,   3, rue Auguste-Comte, Paris VIeme

PS   I put my address down quite automatically. I'm sure, in the first place, that you must have far better things to do than reply to letters. What's more, I'm going to be in Italy for a couple of months, and a letter from you sent to me there would probably get intercepted.

PRIVATE FACES IN THAT PUBLIC PLACE

JOHN CORNFORD

'A Letter from Aragon'

from *Left Review*, November 1936

This is a quiet sector of a quiet front.

We buried Ruiz in a new pine coffin,
But the shroud was too small and his washed feet stuck out.
The stink of his corpse came through the clean pine boards
And some of the bearers wrapped handkerchiefs round their faces.
Death was not dignified.
We hacked a ragged grave in the unfriendly earth
And fired a ragged volley over the grave.

You could tell from our listlessness, no one much missed him.

This is a quiet sector of a quiet front.
There is no poison gas and no H E.

But when they shelled the other end of the village
And the streets were choked with dust
Women came screaming out of the crumbling houses,
Clutched under one arm the naked rump of an infant.
I thought: how ugly fear is.

This is a quiet sector of a quiet front.
Our nerves are steady; we all sleep soundly.

In the clean hospital bed my eyes were so heavy
Sleep easily blotted out one ugly picture,
A wounded militiaman moaning on a stretcher,
Now out of danger, but still crying for water,
Strong against death, but unprepared for such pain.

This on a quiet front.

But when I shook hands to leave, an Anarchist worker
Said: 'Tell the workers of England
This was a war not of our own making,
We did not seek it.
But if ever the Fascists again rule Barcelona
It will be as a heap of ruins with us workers beneath it.'

FRANZ BORKENAU

Spanish Journal

from *The Spanish Cockpit: An Eye-Witness Account of the Political and Social Conflicts of
the Spanish Civil War*, 1937

11 p.m.   *Barcelona*

Again a peaceful arrival. No taxi-cabs, but instead old horse-cabs, to
carry us into the town. Few people in the Paseo de Colon. And, then,
as we turned round the corner of the Ramblas (the chief artery of
Barcelona) came a tremendous surprise: before our eyes, in a flash,
unfolded itself the revolution. It was overwhelming. It was as if we had
been landed on a continent different from anything I had seen before.

The first impression: armed workers, rifles on their shoulders, but
wearing their civilian clothes. Perhaps 30 per cent. of the males on the
Ramblas were carrying rifles, though there were no police, and no
regular military in uniforms. Arms, arms, and again arms. Very few of
these armed proletarians wore the new dark-blue pretty militia uniforms.
They sat on the benches or walked the pavement of the Ramblas, their
rifles over the right shoulder, and often their girls on the left arm. They
started off, in groups, to patrol out-lying districts. They stood, as guards,
before the entrances of hotels, administrative buildings, and the larger
stores. They crouched behind the few still standing barricades, which

were competently constructed out of stones and sand-bags (most of the barricades had already been removed, and the destroyed pavement had been speedily restored). They drove at top speed innumerable fashionable cars, which they had expropriated and covered, in white paint, with the initials of their respective organizations: CNT-FAI, UGT, PSUC (United Socialist-Communist Party of Catalonia), POUM (Trotskyists), or with all these initials at once, in order to display their loyalty to the movement in general. Some of the cars simply wore the letters UHP (Unite, proletarian brothers!), the slogan glorified by the Asturias rising of 1934. The fact that all these armed men walked about, marched, and drove in their ordinary clothes made the thing only more impressive as a display of the power of the factory workers. The anarchists, recognizable by badges and insignia in red and black, were obviously in overwhelming numbers. And no 'bourgeoisie' whatever! No more well-dressed young women and fashionable señoritos on the Ramblas! Only working men and working women; no hats even! The Generalitat, by wireless, had advised people not to wear them, because it might look 'bourgeois' and make a bad impression. The Ramblas are not less colourful than before, because there is the infinite variety of blue, red, black, of the party badges, the neckties, the fancy uniforms of the militia. But what a contrast with the pretty shining colours of the Catalan upperclass girls of former days!

The amount of expropriation in the few days since 19 July is almost incredible. The largest hotels, with one or two exceptions, have all been requisitioned by working-class organizations (not burnt, as had been reported in many newspapers). So were most of the larger stores. Many of the banks are closed, the others bear inscriptions declaring them under the control of the Generalitat. Practically all the factory-owners, we were told, had either fled or been killed, and their factories taken over by the workers. Everywhere large posters at the front of impressive buildings proclaim the fact of expropriation, explaining either that the management is now in the hands of the CNT, or that a particular organization has appropriated this building for its organizing work.

In many respects, however, life was much less disturbed than I expected it to be after newspaper reports abroad. Tramways and buses were running, water and light functioning. At the door of the Hôtel Continental stood an anarchist guard; and a large number of militia had been billeted in the rooms. Our driver, with a gesture of regret, explained that this obviously was no longer an hotel but a militia barrack, but the manager and the anarchist guards at once retorted that not all the rooms were occupied by militia-men, and that we could stay there, at somewhat reduced rates. So we did, and were well cared for, as to food and service.

All the churches had been burnt, with the exception of the cathedral with its invaluable art treasures, which the Generalitat had managed to save. The walls of the churches are standing, but the interior has in every case been completely destroyed. Some of the churches are still smoking. At the corner of the Ramblas and the Paseo Colon the building of the Cosulich Line (the Italian steamship company) is in ruins; Italian snipers, we are told, had taken cover there and the building had been stormed and burnt by the workers. But except for the churches and this one secular building there has been no arson.

These were the first impressions. After a hasty dinner I went out again, in spite of warnings that the streets would not be safe after dark. I did not see any confirmation of this. Life, as usual in Barcelona, was even more seething after nine o'clock at night. True, the turmoil now abated earlier than in peace times, and long before midnight streets were empty.

Now when I went out the streets were full of excited groups of young men in arms, and not a few armed women as well; the latter behaving with a self-assurance unusual for Spanish women when they appear in public (and it would have been unthinkable before for a Spanish girl to appear in trousers, as the militia-girls invariably do) but with decency. Particularly numerous groups gathered before the fashionable buildings now requisitioned as party centres. The enormous Hôtel Colon, dominating the splendid Plaza de Cataluña, has been taken over by the PSUC. The anarchists, with an eye for striking contrasts, have expropriated the offices of the Fomento del Trabajo Nacional, in the fashionable Calle Layetana. The Trotskyists have settled down in the Hôtel Falcon, on the Ramblas. A tremendous group of cars and motor-lorries, with one or two armoured cars, was standing before the door of their newly acquired offices, and a group of young people in arms was standing about, in excited and eager discussion.

.   .   .   .   .

Among this POUM group, exactly as among the young people gathering at the doors of the Colon (the Socialist-Communist Party centre), there are Germans, Italians, Swiss, Austrians, Dutch, English, a few Americans, and a considerable number of young women of all these nations; the latter sharply contrasted, by their unconcerned behaviour and by the absence of any sort of male chaperoning, from their Spanish sisters, even those who wear arms. All languages are spoken and there is an indescribable atmosphere of political enthusiasm, of enjoying the adventure of war, of relief that sordid years of emigration are passed, of absolute confidence in speedy success. And everybody is friends with everybody in a minute, knowing that in twenty-four or forty-eight hours one will have to separate again, when the next transports to the front send people towards different sectors.

On my way home I saw the burning of a church, and again it was a big surprise. I imagined it would be an act of almost demoniac excitement of the mob, and it proved to be an administrative business. The burning church stood in a corner of the big Plaza de Cataluña. Flames were devouring it rapidly. A small group of people stood about (it was about 11 p.m.) silently watching, certainly not regretting the burning, but as certainly not very excited about the matter. The fire-brigade did service at the spot, carefully limiting the flames to the church and protecting the surrounding buildings; nobody was allowed to come near the burning church—in order to avoid accidents—and to this regulation people submitted with surprising docility. Earlier church burnings must have been more passionate, I suppose.

14 August

By the afternoon of the 13th our car was at last completely repaired, and we reached Leciñana, the centre of the larger of the two POUM columns on the Saragossa front. We were received with great friendliness by its leader, Grossi, and offered every chance to see what was going on. The position here is the same as in Alcalá; a few hundred militia crowded in the village, a few advance-guards ahead, but no contact with the next village, occupied by Catalan troops. Grossi took us at once to the advance-guards. They were posted about half a mile ahead of the village, on a group of hills. In the heat of the afternoon the staff officers did not want to walk. I myself thought it would have been a safer way than to drive up to the advance-guards, but we went in two cars through the open, dusty plain and so quiet was the front that there was not the slightest danger in doing so under the eyes of the enemy, although they hold the next village and could easily see the cars. Some of the advance-guards are hidden behind rocks, some have dug themselves shallow trenches, without barbed wire. Every picket has a machine-gun, camouflaged with branches. They had not been relieved for five days (!) but their life was not altogether uncomfortable; they had their mattresses with them in their trenches! Leciñana had been taken by a night surprise attack last week and very little fighting had occurred since.

Back in Leciñana, Grossi put the relief of the advance-guards into effect. The whole column, consisting of four *centurias* (hundreds), was summoned to the Plaza, and Grossi addressed them with a short speech from a balcony, saying that things must be put in better order, and that the advance-guards should now be relieved. One hour later he himself led the relief and stayed out with them for a whole night. The gathering in the Plaza was more picturesque than military. There was not the slightest sign of military discipline, not even a serious attempt to form orderly ranks. There were very few uniforms, but a multi-coloured mosaic of the most varied costumes which would have been a delightful sight for an artist, less delightful for an officer. What is worse, there is evidently not the slightest attempt to get this incoherent mass organized, disciplined, and trained. There would be ample opportunity for this, as the zone behind the front provides an ideal training ground, and the militia-men, in the long intervals between operations, have nothing to do and are desperately bored. Grossi is of a type somewhat crude, but *au fond* very appealing, and certainly he possesses the personal allegiance of his column. He is evidently courageous and, being an Asturias miner, is an old hand at revolution, and knows how to handle the masses psychologically. But he is deficient as an organizer, and has no conception of the job of warfare. There is obvious rivalry between him and his military adviser. This is a very common state of affairs, which of course results in a considerable amount of disorder. Soldiers, lacking any reasonable occupation, squatted about in the tavern.

There we found, among the militia-men, the one militia-woman of the column. She was not from Barcelona, but a native of Galicia, had been married before to an *asalto*, and then divorced him, and she had now followed her lover to the front. She was very good-looking but no special attention was given her by the militia-men, for all of them knew that she was bound to her lover by a link which is regarded among the revolutionaries as equivalent to marriage. Every single militia-man, however, was visibly proud of her for the courage she seems to have displayed in staying in an advanced position under fire for many hours with only two companions. 'Was it an unpleasant experience?' I asked 'No, solo me da el enthusiasmo' ('To me it is only inspiring'), replied the girl with shining eyes: and from her whole bearing I believed her. There was nothing awkward about her position among the men. One of them who was playing an accordion started *La Cucaracha*, and she immediately began the movements of the dance, the others joining in the song. When this interlude was over, she was again just a comrade among them. The whole position of this isolated girl among a crowd of men was the more remarkable because of the complete isolation of the militia-men from the village girls, who in accordance with the strict Spanish tradition refused even to speak to strangers. Some of the nurses were less strict in their moral principles.

I passed the night in the deserted house of an enemy of the Government, with some foreign volunteers. The house was in a horrible condition. All the cupboards were broken, and their contents—linen, books, clothes, religious objects, children's toys, etc.—had been roughly thrown on the floors all over the house, giving it the appearance of having been sacked, though no actual sacking seems to have occurred. It was uncomfortable for the militia-men themselves, but they did nothing to tidy things up. This lack of order in their quarters must be an element of demoralization.

The morning was rather an exciting one. First a militia-man was fired on and a nervous but unavailing search was made throughout one section of the village. The militia-man believed, rightly or wrongly, that he had been fired at by a hidden 'fascist'. Then three enemy planes flew overhead, and the whole column, together with half the village, crowded most inopportunely to the Plaza to watch them. Grossi, having returned from his night watch, ordered out the machine-guns, but they had nothing to do, as for the first time for many days the rebels did not bomb the village, but only flew over it. As far as I could make out, their previous daily bombardment had been utterly ineffectual. In the village there was only the mark of one hit, and one would not have recognized this as the mark of a bomb without being told, it was so shallow. Obviously the enemy bombing material was of very poor quality. But a peasant had been killed a few days before by a bomb, while quietly harvesting in no-man's-land, and the women still wept for him: 'Oh, señor, what a terrible war! They have killed one of our men in the field.' This was the one casualty which had occurred in Leciñana for many days.

There was a group of deserters from the rebel camp in Leciñana. They were all regular soldiers who had been caught up in the revolt during the period of their military service, and all of them had been socialists or anarchists before becoming soldiers. There seemed to be many such deserters all over the front, all of them previously belonging to some revolutionary organization. Ordinary prisoners were everywhere shot immediately. The deserters had to run this risk in order to live up to their political convictions; when they arrived in the Government lines they had to establish their identity as members of an anti-fascist organization. The deserters talked at length about the rebel leaders' distrust of the regular soldiers, and their reluctance to bring them into the front lines. No pressure, however, seemed to be exerted in the rebel camp to force soldiers to participate in religious services.

On the way back we passed through the village of Alcubierre, which had been taken by the Catalans, then retaken by the insurgents, and taken again by the Government forces. The rebels, after having recaptured it, had, I was told, shot all the most active anarchists and socialists—eight to ten altogether. It was about the same number as had been executed by the Government forces during their occupation.

We arrived in Barcelona late at night, with the exception of Mr J. Cornford, who had enlisted in Leciñana.

.   .   .   .   .

26 August

One remarkable aspect of the streets becomes more conspicuous with time: the changed position of women. Young working-class girls in hundreds and perhaps thousands are walking up and down the streets, and are especially to be seen in the elegant cafés of the Alcalá and the Gran Via. They collect for the 'International Red Help', an organization 'in favour of the victims of class war', here mostly working for the wounded and for the relatives of the victims of the civil war; it was sponsored originally all over the world by the Comintern, but is run in Spain by socialists and communists jointly. There is no collecting either in Barcelona or in Valencia, whereas the couples of girls (they never go alone; walking through the streets completely unchaperoned would still be unthinkable for any decent Spanish girl), well dressed in working-class fashion, who ask everybody for a contribution, are almost a nuisance in Madrid, or at least would be were they not so pleasant to look at. They enjoy it enormously; for most of them it is obviously their first appearance in public, and now they are even allowed to talk to foreigners and sit down at their ease in the cafés for a chat with the militia-men.

The revolutionary tribunal, which is starting its activities to-day, will limit its trials to such cases as fall under established civil or military law; this means that practically only cases of mutiny will come before it. But there is an enormous number of other cases: priests, nobles, and innumerable people of the Right wing who have taken no part in military activity but have either been caught conspiring against the Government or are suspected of having done so. All those cases are outside the competence of the revolutionary tribunal. In the first days of the rebellion the anarchists suggested that every single member of a Right-wing party should be shot; they have the lists, and there are 42,000 members of Gil Robles's Catholic Accion Popular alone. They have been convinced of the inexpediency of this cruel folly, but no one thinks of limiting executions to such cases as might be convicted of high treason by way of regular trial. What happens is that investigation committees of the three proletarian groups in Madrid, communists, socialists, and anarchists, cooperate. Each of them has a list of suspects, and when they arrest one they ask the two other parties their opinion. If they all agree, then the man is either executed or released. If they disagree, closer investigation ensues. It is certainly a rough and ready manner of dealing with an insoluble problem.

DAVID GASCOYNE
Barcelona Diary

from Journal 1936–1937, 1980

We got our visas, and then I went back to the hotel in Montparnasse where I was staying with the Penroses. I forget how we spent the evening. Next morning, we left from the Gare du Quai d'Orsay for Toulouse, which we did not reach till late in the afternoon. We spent the night in an old hotel there, which I remember had a curious shell-stuck grotto in the lounge. After dinner wandered about the deserted streets for a while, cobblestones, an ancient arcaded square. Next morning, the Penroses, the Zervos', a young painter friend of their's, Fernandez, who had also joined us, and I all drove to the Toulouse airfield and boarded the 'plane for Barcelona. It was the first time I had ever flown. We flew over Carcassonne and the Pyrenees. On our arrival we were greeted cordially by people from the Propaganda Ministry.

We stayed at a comfortable small hotel just off the top of the Ramblas, near the Plaza de Cataluna. I was to get a job at the Propaganda Ministry, translating news bulletins during the day, and broadcasting them, in English, from a studio in the Ministry of Marine, near the port, every evening at 6 o'clock. Stephen Spender, in his autobiography *World Within World*, has written of his surprise at hearing my voice coming from a loudspeaker attached to a lamp-post at a street-corner. My parents also heard the broadcasts, which were in several languages, as they were intended to be heard all over Europe.

I was very excited by the atmosphere in Barcelona in the streets on the first Sunday morning after our arrival, the universal dancing of the traditional *sardana*, the goodwill and optimism everywhere. That afternoon, we went to my first and only bullfight, which was a rather depressing affair, in aid of the families of bull-fighters who had gone to the Front to fight, and as the toreadors who were left were naturally not much good, and the spectacle seemed to me to consist of protracted, clumsy slaughter, while the shadow of the arena-terrace crept gradually across the ring, for this was late October, and surely bull-fighting ought to be seen, if at all, in blazing sunlight. After it was over, we had a brief encounter with a remarkable character, whose name unfortunately escapes me now, but who was locally very famous in his time for his peculiar wit and wisdom, the quintessence of the unique spirit of Catalonia, a man who was reputed to have had a crucial influence on Picasso, and later Dali, Bunuel, Miro and many others . . . (As far as I know, this important though perhaps now forgotten figure, never wrote or published anything, but, like Socrates, influenced people purely by his conversation and ideas, which were, as I said, peculiarly Catalan in their anarchy, destructiveness and irony).

Another occasion at this time which much impressed me was a free public poetry-reading by Rafael Alberti and his beautiful wife, also a poet, in a quite large Barcelona theatre, which was packed with a wildly enthusiastic and very largely working-class audience.

Christian Zervos was in Barcelona with us at the invitation of the Propaganda Minister, Mirravitles,* to collect material for a new work on Catalan Art, based on newly-discovered works which had been dis-covered shortly after the outbreak of the War, in the houses of exiled, executed Fascists, now requisitioned by the Government and also in churches, cathedrals etc; and one day we all went with him to look over a very old convent which had been abandoned by the nuns at a moment's notice (of their own free-will, we were told), at the beginning of the conflict, and was to be seen just as it had been left. This was a very odd experience. There was not much in the way of art to be found, but the primitive, mediaeval conditions everywhere, the dirt, dust, tawdriness, and, in the refectory, the remains of a last frugal, apparently interrupted meal, all made a deep, somewhat macabre, impression on me.

Later, we went with the Zervos' and Fernandez, to Gerona, where some wonderful old tapestries of the Apocalypse had been discovered, which had not been seen by anyone from outside for centuries. (Photos of these were later reproduced in Zervos' definitive and still respected book on Catalan Art). We also saw there, by the way, the machine-guns which had been placed on the turrets of the cathedral by the local clergy, to protect their property from the faithful . . .

It was so cold in Gerona that I caught a bout of *grippe* there, and had to

---

* Who was later to be shot by the Francoists at the end of the War.

stay in bed at the hotel for a few days, during which time I was looked after most devotedly by Valentine P., who read to me some new French translations she had made from the work of Lorca, who had then only recently been murdered.

What I saw of the Anarchists in Barcelona I found on the whole very sympathetic, though this sympathy was not at all approved of by the young English girl Communist who was my colleague at the Ministry. In spite of the United Front, supposed to join together all left-wing factions against Franco, which was proclaimed at about the time we arrived there (it did not last much longer than a fortnight), I came to find that the Communists hated the Anarchists and the POUM (Trotskyists) much more than they hated the Fascists, and I think this was the beginning of my disillusionment with Communism as a means of creating a better world. (At the time, of course, I was still a more or less 'active' member of the CP).

During my short stay in Spain, I came to form a rather unexpected friendship with a young Yugoslav journalist whose name was Vladimir Djedier. He later became well-known as a Resistance fighter and a friend and biographer of Tito; though he was subsequently, I'm afraid, disgraced, and even possibly sent to prison for a time. Just then, he had only recently returned from an assignment following Edward VIII and Mrs Simpson in the now famous yacht trip round the Adriatic, had taken many news-photographs, and was able to give me a detailed account of the whole affair, which was the first I had heard about it, as it was all still being hushed up in England at the time. This Yugoslavian friend and I used frequently to meet and chat in cafés on the Ramblas in the evenings (there are one or two wonderful sherry bars there). And one night we set out together on a tour (as 'voyeurs' rather than as clients) of all the brothels in the Barrio Chino. This was another memorable evening. Also, as one might imagine, a rather dismal one, as all the 'houses' (we visited at least a dozen of them) were monotonously similar and, with their down-floor waiting-rooms, where the semi-clad girls sat around desultorily on benches waiting for someone from among the long queue of brutish-looking working-men to choose one of them,—all walled with tiles and with the manageresses seated in raised, glass-fronted cash-desks dealing out numbered disk-tokens, and with their sanded floors, —reminded one more than a little of butcher-shops.

At the end of my Barcelona stay, my Yugoslav friend was to travel back to Paris with me.

A first encounter for me at this time was with Tristan Tzara. I had not met him in Paris while I was there collecting material for my little

Introduction to Surrealism the year before (he was then already estranged from André Breton and the others) and he had taken exception to my repeating in the book an anecdote told by Breton referring to an early collection of his poems as *Twenty Elucubations of a Police-agent*; even going so far as to threaten me and Cobden-Sanderson with prosecution if we did not remove the offending passage, and also remove the translation of part of his 'L'Homme Approximatif' which had appeared in the appendix of translated surrealist poems at the end of the first printing. This was done and no further action was taken. Now he suddenly appeared in Barcelona, at the head of a deputation accompanying a brand-new Ambulance Unit, subscribed for by, I think, the Front Populaire (at any rate, largely the CP), and to my surprise and with a certain reluctance, I found myself being introduced to him. To my relief he turned out to be perfectly amiable, most reconciliatory, and we were later to meet again quite often in Paris.*

A feature of the city which I must mention at some place in this account is the architecture of Gaudi. This I naturally found altogether extraordinary, and at one time or another I must have seen every building of his still then existing in the Catalonian capital. One of them, with a façade resembling an undulating sea-shore after the tide had receded, with wrought-iron balconies arranged across it to look like skeins of abandoned sea-weed, I used to see every day from the top of the tram taking me to and from the Propaganda Ministry. Another well-known building, still preserved, I believe, as a sort of Gaudi museum, being entirely filled with furniture and household objects of his design, I visited one evening with the Penroses and Zervos, and we had drinks there. At that time Gaudi was little-known outside Spain, though nowadays† universally recognized as one of the great pioneers of modern architecture, and his buildings, particularly the Cathedral of the Holy Family, and also the fantastic rambling park in the hilly suburbs of Barcelona, made a great impact on my imagination.

Talking of the suburbs of Barcelona reminds me of a visit I made with Roland Penrose one evening to a man then (and perhaps still) considered to be the finest poet then writing in the Catalan language, Foix (I'm afraid the Christian name at present escapes me). Rather oddly, this poet made his living as a pastry-cook, owning a rather expensive *patisserie* in one of the richer quarters of the city. He was a charming man and generous

---

* As recorded in *Paris Journal 1937–9*, and also on several later occasions, up until a few days before his death.

† i.e., in the 1970s.

host, and it would have been a pleasant enough evening had it not been interrupted from time to time by the sound of gunfire from close at hand. Apparently these shots were being fired by militia hunting for suspected Fascists thought to be hiding in the gardens of nearby houses. Foix himself was politically quite neutral, but the whole district he lived in was regarded as more or less hostile to the Republicans, and the poor man was naturally more than a little nervous as to the fate of himself and family, and we left him feeling more than a little disturbed . . .

Finally, I must record what was, apart from everything to do with the War, probably the most interesting event that happened to me while I was there. This was a visit our party paid to the apartment of Picasso's sister, married to a prominent Barcelona doctor, where Picasso's mother, a wonderful old lady of about 80, was then staying. I could not speak much Spanish, but her face and gestures were so expressive that I felt I could understand everything she was saying. She talked about Pablo's childhood and youth, and the great gift he had displayed so early. She told us how her husband, a Barcelona art-teacher who had first met her on a sketching holiday in another part of Spain, had one day, when Picasso (his mother's maiden name, by the way) was about 12 or 14, made up his mind to set his son a test to decide on his future, whether he was to earn his living as a whole-time painter or not. Pablo was to paint a picture, and if the result was good enough, then he was to be allowed to become a professional artist. The subject chosen was a still life, a dead pigeon. When it was finished, naturally everyone was very impressed and Picasso had passed the test more than successfully: it was of the bird lying on its back, '. . . and you should see the fragile little claws stretching up in the air,' the old lady exclaimed, 'so wonderfully pathetic and expressive!' Whereupon she showed us the picture. Indeed, the whole apartment, which overlooked the grounds of another convent, (this one, I think, reassuringly unevacuated), was full of a marvellous small collection of early Picasso drawings and paintings.

Not long after this, I had to return to England, leaving the Penroses and the Zervos' behind, as I had two reasons to prevent me from staying longer. One was that I had to take back with me a collection of Spanish War posters that were needed in London for an exhibition that was soon to be held in aid of supplies (not armaments, of course, unfortunately) for the anti-fascists, presided over by Fenner Brockway. And the other was that I had a previous engagement in Oxford to talk to an undergraduate literary society about Surrealism (this seemed rather irrelevant to the Civil War, but I think when the occasion arrived, I was able to include a certain amount of attention to that subject, too).

I travelled back to England with, as far as Paris, as I have mentioned, my Yugoslav journalist friend; and armed with a letter of introduction to Picasso from Christian Zervos (who had devoted a great many of his *Cahiers d'Art* to Picasso's work.) The idea was that I should take Picasso direct reassuring direct news about his mother's and sister's existence in Barcelona. We arrived at the Paris railwaystation late in the evening, and I said goodbye to Vladimir D, unfortunately for the last time. That night I slept in a room of the Zervos' suite in a big hotel-apartment building, above the old Pergola club, just off the Blvd. St Germain. The next morning about 11, I set out for the rue de la Boëtie, where Picasso was then still living, in a flat above the Rosenburg Gallery. It was on the top floor and I went up by lift, to find Picasso waiting for me at the lift-gates outside his apartment. I spent about an hour in conversation with him. He was extremely friendly and delighted to have news of his mother and sister and nephews about whom we talked for a while. We talked about other things as well, of course, chiefly the War, but unfortunately not much about painting, as far as I can remember, which was easy to understand, as it was at this period, about eight months before *Guernica* finally put an end to the block, that Picasso was quite unable to paint anything for a while. He seemed depressed and anxious about Spain (everyone knows of his violent hatred of Franco), and I also remember him expressing worry about his son Paulo, whose political affiliations did not quite seem to please him. This was also the time when Picasso for a while took to writing poetry, of a kind peculiar to himself, (short, unpunctuated passages of prose, full of colour adjectives), some examples of which I translated and which were later published in my friend Roger Roughton's magazine *Contemporary Poetry and Prose*.

JOHN CORNFORD

'Letters to Margot Heinemann'
(November–December 1936)

from *John Cornford: A Memoir*, ed. Pat Sloan, 1938

Letter of 21st November
It's a long time since I've written, but I simply haven't had the chance, as the last ten days we've been at the front just by Madrid, in the open all day. This is real war, not a military holiday like the Catalan affair. We

haven't done any fighting yet: we are a group with a French machine-gun company which has been in reserve most of the time. I'm writing in the sunlight in a valley full of oaks, with one section leader twenty yards away explaining the Lewis gun to a group of French. But though we haven't yet fought, we've been having a sample of what's to come this winter. Three times heavily and accurately bombarded by artillery—and there are first-class German and Italian gunners.

But the main trouble is the cold. It freezes every night, and we sleep in the open sometimes without blankets. The trouble is that the offensive on Madrid became so hot that we were called out before our training was over, and without proper equipment. But our International Brigade has done well. Continuous fighting, heavy losses, many of them simply due to inexperience, but we've been on the whole successful.

The Fascist advance guard got very close to Madrid: but as I've always said, their main trouble is shortage of men, and they can't make a concerted advance: they push forward in alternate sectors. And we've given the head of their advance a hell of a hammering.

I don't know what the press is saying over in England: but Madrid won't fall: if we get time to organize and to learn our guns, we shall do very well.

Now as to our personnel. Less good news. Our four best Lewis gunners were sent up with an infantry section. One is in hospital with two bullets in the guts. Steve Yates (ex-corporal in the British army, expelled and imprisoned for incitement to mutiny) is missing, believed 90 per cent certain dead. Worst of all, Maclaurin, picked up dead on his gun after covering a retreat. He did really well. Continuously cheerful, however uncomfortable, and here that matters a hell of a lot. Well, it's useless to say how sorry we are; nothing can bring him back now. But if you meet any of his pals, tell them (and I wouldn't say it if it weren't true) he did well here, and died bloody well.

Then worse still, our section leader, Fred Jones, he was a tough, bourgeois family, expelled from Dulwich, worked in South American Oil. Has been three years in the Guards, a hell of a good soldier, unemployed organizer, etc. Did magnificently here. Kept his head in a tough time after our captain got killed, and was promoted to section leader. Then on a night march got caught in some loose wire when a lorry passed, hurled over a bridge, and killed. We didn't see what happened: and to give some idea of the way we felt about him, after his death none dared to tell the English section for several hours. Well, we shall get along somehow. But that's a hell of a way to have your best man killed.

Bernard* has been doing fine. Worked terribly hard as liaison man and political delegate because of his knowledge of French: and he hasn't much reserve of physical strength. Two nights running he fainted from the cold, but hasn't made any complaints. There's a tough time ahead, and those that get through will be a hell of a lot older. But by Christ they'll learn a lot.

There's little enough else to say. Everyone here is very tired by the cold nights, often sleepless, a bit shaken and upset by our losses, depressed. And its's affected me a bit, though I'm getting a thick skin. If I'd written a few hours ago you'd have got a different kind of letter. For five weeks I scarcely missed you, everything was so new and different, and I couldn't write but formal letters. Now I'm beginning to wake up a bit, and I'm glad as I could be that the last few days I had with you were as good as they could be. I re-read your letter to me yesterday, and I was proud as hell. And as you say there, the worst won't be too hard to stand now. I don't know what's going to happen, but I do know we're in for a tough time. And I am glad that you are behind me, glad and proud. The losses here are heavy, but there's still a big chance of getting back alive, a big majority chance. And if I didn't, we can't help that. Be happy, darling. Things here aren't easy, but I never expected them to be. And we'll get through them somehow, and I'll see you again, bless you, darling.

John

I felt very depressed when I wrote this. Now I've eaten and am for the moment in a building. I feel fine. Warm. I'll get back to you, love, don't worry. God bless you.

Letter of 8th December

Darling,

There is an English comrade going back, and this is my first chance of an uncensored letter. Remember that a good deal is not for publication. Excuse incoherence, because I'm in hospital with a slight wound and very weak. I'll tell you about that later.

I'll assume none of my letters have yet got through, as I've had no answers. First of all about myself. I'm with a small English group in the Machine Gun Company of the French Battalion of the First International Brigade. Luckily we are in the best company, the machine gunners; and in the best section of that, a Franco-Belgian section.

* Bernard Knox.

Now, as to the English blokes. Amongst the good blokes, Bernard, who is political delegate, replacing me because I did not speak enough French to get things done. He's been ill, and suffers terribly from the cold, but has borne up really well. John Summerfield [sic], tough and starting like me with no military training, has become a good soldier, and a good scrounger which is very important in a badly equipped army. David Mackenzie, a Scots student: age 19: first-class rifle shot and machine gunner: intellectual and writes good verse. A very good buy is Edward Burke of the *Daily Worker.* Ex-actor, looks like a sap, always loses everything, but has a queer gift for understanding machinery, became a good machine gunner in no time, was put *pro tem* on a trench gun, promoted to section leader he did well on a really nasty bit of the front line.

We had about a month's training at Albacete and La Rada. We English did badly, we were a national minority very hard to assimilate, mucked about between one station and another, starting work on one kind of gun and then having it taken away from us, taking part in manoeuvres which those that didn't speak French couldn't understand. When we at last got down to work with the machine gunners our training was interrupted almost before we started, and we were switched through to the front. That was early in November. We were put in general reserve in the University City, thought we could rest and take it easy. The first morning we were heavily shelled with 75's. I did quite well that day. The section leader, Fred Jones, was away, and so confident that all was quiet that he hadn't appointed a successor. I took charge on the moment, was able to get all the guns—we then had four—into position, and rescued one which the gunmen had deserted in a panic. But there was no attack after all.

Then in reserve in the Casa del Campo: a big wood, ex-royal forest, rather Sussexy to look at: but behind to the right a range of the Guadarama, a real good range with snow against a very blue sky. Then a piece of real bad luck. Maclaurin and three other Lewis gunners were sent up to the front. The French infantry company they were with was surprised by the Moors. The Lewis gunners stayed to cover the retreat. Mac was found dead at his gun, Steve Yates, one of our corporals, an ex-soldier and a good bloke, was killed too. Another, wounded in the guts. It's always the best seem to get the worst.

Then for the first time up to the front. We advanced into position at exactly the wrong time, at sunset, taking over some abandoned trenches. The Fascists had the range exact and shelled us accurately. Seven were killed in a few minutes. We had a nasty night in the trenches. Then back into reserve. The main trouble now was the intense cold: and we were sleeping out without blankets, which we had left behind in order to carry more machine-gun ammunition. Worse still to come; we had to make a night march back. There was a lorry load of wounded behind us. The lorry driver signalled, but wasn't noticed and got no answer. The four lines were so indeterminate that he thought we were a Fascist column and accelerated past us. Someone put up a wire to stop the car. The wire was swept aside, caught Fred Jones by the neck, hauled him over the parapet and killed him. Fred was a really good section leader: declassed bourgeois, ex-guardsman unemployed organizer, combination of adventurer and sincere Communist: but a really powerful person and could make his group work in a disciplined way in an army where there wasn't much discipline. That day the French redeemed their bad start by a really good bayonet attack which recaptured the philosophy building. We were in reserve for all this.

Then a spell of rest behind the lines. Back at the front in a really comfortable position in the philosophy and letters building. This was our best front line period. Comfortable, above all warm, and supplies regular. A great gutted building, with broken glass all over, and the fighting consisted of firing from behind barricades of philosophy books at the Fascists in a village below and in the Casa Velasques opposite. One day an anti-aircraft shell fell right into the room we were in. We were lucky as hell not to be wiped out completely: as it was there were only three slightly wounded, I gathering a small cut in the head. After the night in the rather inefficient but very nice Secours Rouge Hospital, where the amateur nurses wash your wounds like scrubbing the floor, I came back, feeling all right, but must have been a bit weak from loss of blood. Then came two heavy days work trench-digging in the frozen clay. The afternoon of the second day I think I killed a Fascist. Fifteen or sixteen of them were running from a bombardment. I and two Frenchmen were firing from our barricades with sights at 900: We got one, and both said it was I that hit him, though I couldn't be sure. If it is true, it's a fluke, and I'm not likely to do as good a shot as that again. Then back again into reserve. The first day we were there, David Mackenzie and I took a long walk towards the Guadarama. When I came back my wound began to hurt again: this morning I was very weak, a kind of retarded shock, I think, and am now in hospital for the time being.

Well, that's how far we've got. No wars are nice, and even a revolutionary war is ugly enough. But I'm becoming a good soldier, longish endurance and a capacity for living in the present and enjoying all that can be enjoyed. There's a tough time ahead but I've plenty of strength left for it.

Well, one day the war will end—I'd give it till June or July, and then if I'm alive I'm coming back to you. I think about you often, but there's nothing I can do but say again, be happy, darling, And I'll see you again one day.

Bless you,

John

RALPH FOX
'Letters from Spain'

from *Ralph Fox: A Writer in Arms*, ed. John Lehmann, T. A. Jackson, C. Day Lewis, 1937

Albacete, 7 December, 1936

Life has gone by very slowly and somewhat monotonously since I arrived here. The French who came with me have departed for a nearby village, and the friends who came yesterday are about to join them. So I remain on alone, all because some people think it would be nice if I put on a pair of red tabs, which is the last thing I want to do.

This little town is very quiet, and one knew far more in London about what is happening in Spain. Indeed I never was so cut off in my life from the great world.

What is happening here is really the greatest thing since 1917. Victory means the end of Fascism everywhere sooner or later, and most likely sooner. In any case, the very fact of the resistance has wakened up the Democratic forces, encouraged them and weakened the enemy to an extent we don't quite yet realize. So however hard one's work may be, and exasperating, we do feel it counts, is history, and must be effective. When this job is over, life will be easier for everyone.

Albacete, 10 December

Still stuck in this place, though all the boys are now at another village where I hope to join them soon. This is a funny little town, rather like the Russian provincial town of ten years ago. Little two-storey houses, mostly of an early nineteenth-century character, narrow streets, cobbles and lots of mud. At night and at early morning there are strong frosts, in the daytime, blue skies and lots of sun. It is a pretty healthy climate. The Spanish militia are interesting to watch. Dressed in every variety of uniform or no uniform at all, with all kinds of arms, no particular march discipline, but tough, wiry looking fellows. If some genius could arise to organize them they would certainly play hell with Franco, a revolutionary General Gordon perhaps.

The position at the front is interesting and many things which seemed so odd and inexplicable at home, are clearer here. However, in general we had the right ideas about things at home. I don't know when the stalemate will break, but it should not be long. I am sure it is still true that one severe defeat for the Fascists would win the war. Not at once of course, but their morale, already weakened, won't stand defeat.

The whole atmosphere is revolutionary, the very streets full of the people, few signs of any bourgeoisie, and out of all this talking, gesticu-latory, variegated crowd, the energy of the workers will surely create something firm and stable in the end. The Party here grows daily, though their difficulties are naturally enormous. We want more and quicker volunteers—no limit, but good stuff essential.

Albacete, 11 December

The comrade coming on leave is bringing this letter to you. This is a most wonderful experience. We left Paris in two special coaches, and all the way across France people were greeting us with clenched fists, not even waiting for us to salute first, but knowing where we were going and wishing us 'bonne chance.' The defence of Madrid has saved Europe. The spirit in France is quite different to what it was a few weeks ago.

In Barcelona we marched through the town, passed the Party and Anarchist headquarters, greeted everywhere by the people . . .

Our little army is of every nation, French, Belgians, Germans, and Poles predominating. I have talked to Ukrainians from Poland, fellows who have been soldiers nearly all their lives, happy at last to be fighting for something worth while.

For years, the Liberal bourgeoisie has talked about a League of Nations' army to impose Peace on the world. Well, we have created the first International Army to fight for Peace and Freedom. At present I am on the staff at the Brigade Headquarters here. Hanging around makes me fed up, but they promise that as soon as the English are all here I shall join as Political Commissar.

Albacete, 18 December

I am now doing much more interesting work as Political Commissar at the base for English people. I have the job of educating the political workers for our force as they come, and look forward to it immensely. But it is all very topsy turvy—five or six hours' sleep at the best, and meals if and when one can.

Still it is, when we really get our men going, to be such work as we never did before in our lives, any of us. I am a general nurse, mother, teacher, and commander to all the English as they pass through, and it is wearing. It will be some time before we go to the front.

CHRISTOPHER CAUDWELL
(Christopher St John Sprigg)
'Last Letters of a Hero'

from *News Chronicle*, 28 June 1937 (subsequently reprinted as part of a pamphlet appealing for funds for a Sprigg Memorial Ambulance in Spain)

Extract from a letter, 9 December 1936

I expect it will be a surprise to you, but I am leaving for Spain the day after tomorrow. You know how I feel about the whole mad business of war, but you know also how I feel about the importance of democratic freedom.

The Spanish People's Army needs help badly; their struggle, if they fail, will certainly be ours tomorrow and, believing as I do, it seems clear where my duty lies . . . I am going out as a driver in a convoy of lorries and we shall make the journey by road through France.

Postcard from Perpignan, 17 December

Just arrived at the frontier. Convoy had engine trouble all through France. Spain tomorrow. *Salud!*

Extract from a letter, 30 December

Just a line to let you know that we delivered the lorries safely at [*name censored*] and have now been drafted into the British Unit of the International Brigade. At the moment, we are at a training-centre, but do not expect to stay here long.

My letters will be very sketchy from now on, and do not be surprised if you do not hear from me at all for a fairly long time.

Extract from a letter, 7 January, written to the brother of a
fallen comrade in the International Brigade

I am writing to you because I have only just heard the news of your brother's death—though I gather that it must have been known to you soon after it happened.

I want to pass on the sympathy with your mother and you that all the English-speaking battalion here feels; and above all I want to tell you of the tremendous pride and admiration the whole International Brigade feels for those few English comrades, including your brother, who were with the Thaelmann Battalion of the Brigade from the very start.

In [*name censored*] I met the German under whose command your brother served soon after the casualties had occurred, and although he was a reserved kind of man, he was so moved by them that he was going up to every Englishman to explain in his broken English what admiration the whole Battalion felt for them. [*Name censored*] asked the same man why the casualty rate among the English portion of his unit was so high, and he answered, 'Because every one of them was a hero.'

I think you can understand what that means, coming from the commander of the Battalion which played such a vital part in the early days of the Madrid fighting.

Extract from a letter, 14 January, from Albacete

Our training is almost over now. It has been extraordinarily interesting; the International Brigade in its composition and organisation is so entirely different from any ordinary army.

Our commandant is thoroughly at home in this Spanish fighting, which is about as different as possible from that of the Great War; a very extended front, continual flanking movements and a very mobile type of fighting.

At Madrid, of course, there is a certain amount of digging-in. A feature of this war is the tremendous use of machine-guns—far eclipsing the last war, so I am told. In this connection we are handicapped by shortage of ammunition due to the Arms ban. We are also short of artillery and aeroplanes.

English recruits are coming out fairly well now and we are already forming an English Battalion. Of course, we are tremendously outnumbered in the Brigade by the Germans and the French and the Italian sections.

Extract from a letter, 30 January, from Albacete

We expect to move off very soon.

We've been here so long now, waiting for new drafts to arrive to bring us up to battalion strength—that I am almost beginning to feel an old soldier, and already act as machine-gun instructor to our group.

England seems centuries away, and we are yearning to get to the Front. No rifles yet—the arms shortage is acute here—but we should get them very soon now and will then move off.

Extract from a letter, 7 February, from Albacete

This is only a short note, written in haste. I may not find time to write again for some time. You will understand why. So until I write again, all the very best to you both.

Five days after writing that letter he was killed in action outside Madrid. One of his comrades, himself wounded, wrote this letter describing how he died:

On the first day Chris' [*sic*] section was holding a position on a hill crest. They got it rather badly from all ways, first artillery, then machine-gunned by aeroplanes, and then by ground machine-guns. The Moors then attacked the hill in large numbers and as there were only a few of our fellows left, including Chris, who had been doing great work with his M G, the company commander—the Dalston busman—gave the order to retire.

Later, I got into touch with one of the section who had been wounded whilst retiring, and he told me that the last they saw of Chris was that he was covering their retreat with the advancing Moors less than 30 yards away. He never left that hill alive, and if any man ever sacrificed his life that his comrades might live that man was Chris.

When I come out of hospital I will try to obtain further details for you, but I am afraid it may prove a little difficult, as out of the 600 men of his battalion who went into that engagement less than 200 are now left.

Caption to photo at head of News Chronicle page:

(Christopher St John Sprigg was killed on February 12 while fighting with the International Brigade among the olive groves of Madrid. Though only 29 when he died, he had a remarkable record of literary achievement. Under the name of Christopher Caudwell he had published seven novels and several aviation text books. His last book, *Illusion and Reality*, was published posthumously. Here the *News Chronicle* prints extracts from his last letters.)

JULIAN BELL

'Letters'

from *Julian Bell: Essays, Poems & Letters*, ed. Quentin Bell, 1938

To John Lehmann

8 Fitzroy Street,
WI.
June 6 [1937]

Dear John

Just off to Cordoba with the Medical Aid, as a driver. Perhaps you'll be coming out? I'm getting Y's stories translated, and must arrange if I can to have them sent you for *New Writing*. I hope you'll look at them sympathetically. My own proposals comprise one small book, polemical and likely to cause annoyance if only I can get it read.

Love

Julian

To Vanessa Bell

Perpignan
Thursday, June 10 [1937]

Dearest Nessa

Alas, no certain address till we get to Valencia—and in general it's likely to be some time between letters. It's been a stiffish drive, but not bad fun. We celebrated the sight of the Pyrenees with a smash, the man in front of me in the convoy coming off at a corner and turning clear over. By miracle, he wasn't hurt at all, and his engine and chassis were sound. I've spent my afternoon delivering French rhetoric to hurry ... In general, I'm the only one of the convoy who talks fluent French—none of us talks decent Spanish! It's really rather fun—very like last year's journey to Fa-tsien-lu. Some of the country looks lovely, and we must see it again in peace. In general, I'm enjoying life a lot. Wheeler is a really sensible leader, and all's boy-scoutish in the highest. I'll send you the address the second I have it.

Love

Julian

P S—My particular love to Angelica.

To Vanessa Bell

Villa Esther,
90 Maria Blasco,
Alboraya,
Valencia.
Sunday, June 13 [1937]

Dear Nessa

This is the best approximate address I can do: don't use it for anything that matters being lost. We shan't get definite orders for some days. Meanwhile, an amusing queer journey, and here picnic in a seaside villa: a goodish bull-fight to-day, bathing, the human race—all very entertaining. So far, war has meant nothing worse than hard driving. Spain down the coast is still, to appearances, a charming, peaceful country: posters and troops a bit, but masses of leisurely civilians.

Wogan* has apparently been wounded and will almost certainly be repatriated . . .

I find Spanish tolerably easy to understand, but when I try to talk it find myself bogged in Chinese. And what else? I'm extremely content: it's the sort of life that suits me. There are too many minor events, and really I'm too stupid to write good letters. Will you ring Rosamond and say that if I see Wogan I'll write to her at once, but at present I've no news she won't have.

I think perhaps one of the reasons one enjoys war and travel is getting back into male society. I've never used and heard such foul language, for one thing. As a military and political education it's by no means bad: one sees a number of things at first hand one had only read about before: one being driving through Valencia in almost pitch darkness. Still, it's all very definitely a picnic. Perhaps I shall change my mind a bit if there's real danger or real boredom.

One piece of luck is, belonging to a thoroughly nice team: my special 'mate' being an odd fish who wants to write and has a passion for sailing: he's also an expert engineer.

---

* Wogan Philipps.

Do remember to bother Eliot on my behalf: I should very much like to get my say said now, when a lot of my panics seem to be coming true.

I will try to write to you longer and better letters, and I'll try to write to other people, tell them. But somehow one can't in this social, exterior life: there isn't the leisure and privacy of China. But it's a very good life to live.

News about the war is plentiful and contradictory, and not really worth repeating. Once again, I'll try to write more, and to more people. But it's an unpropitious atmosphere.

Love
Julian

PS—15th?
Since writing I've had one day's work buying eggs in the mountains, with Spaniards, and to-day am hanging about waiting for orders—just like war—and China; of which I'm for ever being reminded. Just this very agreeable Mediterranean holiday, plenty of queer incidents go on happening, particularly the drive yesterday, when I broke a passenger's nose on the windscreen, thanks to my infernally fierce brakes. I spent the day talking Spanish, and making fast progress—though with regrettable lapses into pure Chinese.

At the moment my fate waits on Churchill's return: I expect it will be Cuenca, at first, anyway.

Tell Q his friend U . . . is here, convalescing typhoid: would he—Q—collect any introductions he can for me from his Left friends.

And really that's all—just this preposterous holiday, the more I think about it the sillier it all seems.

Love
Julian

PPS—I'll send my new address when I know it.
Don't send letters here until a few days after getting this.

To Vanessa Bell

Madrid
June 22 [1937]

My dear Nessa
There's really no time at all for writing, (or so I thought—now probably too much), except when, as now, there's nothing to do but wait about—while someone else's telephone call comes through. I'm hoping, eventually, to work at the Madrid Hospital—so far I've been there some

three hours. Fortunately I've partnered myself, more or less, with Rees,* who's nice and competent. The whole affair is very like my last year's journey, really—more variety and comedy, but not so tough. Also a similar out-of-the-worldness—not much news now that's much use —you must have far more in London. What we do hear doesn't sound nice.

On the other hand, the people are often charming and almost always amusing—also in what they say about each other. It would be superb to write it up, but almost impossible, I fancy, politics apart. Also it's extremely instructive, about organisations.

The country is lovely—as you'll remember—and singularly unmilitarised: true, one is stopped fairly often by guards, but they're all extremely friendly. Madrid is utterly fantastic in the way it keeps the war on one edge and a fairly ordinary civil life going on—you can take the metro to the front, etc.

I've been going about with two old friends—a Reuter's man, American, who was at Taviton Street, and Portia Holman, whom I'll try to get to ring you.

I go on back at the Madrid Hospital, I hope my future home, at the end of a very hard two-days' driving, about 500 miles between Rees and myself . . .

And will you tell all my friends that I shall write as and when I have time, and give them my love.

It's utterly impossible to give the full fantastic effect of it all. But I find it perpetually entertaining and very satisfactory. And though I have begun to realise what a pleasure ordinary life will be, I don't feel I've more than touched the possibilities of this.

Tell Q that so far I've only hearsay about technique: I'll see what I can tell him later.

My Spanish improves, but still has awful fade-outs into Chinese. Good night—I'm very sleepy, and goodness knows what will happen to-morrow. But it's a better life than most I've led.

Love
Julian

To Vanessa Bell

July 1 [1937]

Dear Nessa

There is a sudden crisis here—at last—and rumours of an attack. As far as I am concerned it consists mainly of sitting about, since the infernal

---

* Sir Richard Rees.

Chevrolet ambulance I now have to drive is, approximately, in order.

So far it's all an uneventful life of minor events: poor Richard, however, had his dose of horrors, evacuating badly wounded patients to a rear hospital about a hundred miles off. It was a grim story—not possible to write.

All else that's happened has been a furious struggle to keep our house from a transport corps: French is a really useful accomplishment here: my Spanish also improves. It's all the oddest out-of-the-world business you can imagine: my military instincts are being badly shocked, both on a large and a small scale, but it will be a satisfaction if we really do see something at first hand, and may calm my impatience with the whole business. Not that it's an unsatisfactory life, if it weren't for the consciousness of a war going on. But it does inhibit a good deal of one's mind—the constant small events, and the company of people with whom one has only a certain amount in common. Really intimate relations, for some reason, aren't possible: I don't even know Richard well.

I continue with another crisis—the interval punctuated by a 12-hours' drive—midnight to midday—evacuating lightly wounded some fifty miles over very bad roads. I've discovered that I can fall asleep with my eyes open—or pretty near.

I've the worst forebodings for the military results of anything so public as our present operation. But at least it does mean, personally, excitement and events. I'm also getting very angry over organisation. One thing—I do think I'm being a real use as a driver, in that I'm careful and responsible and work on my car—a Chevrolet ambulance, small lorry size. Most of our drivers are wreckers, neglect all sorts of precautions like oiling and greasing, over speed, etc. Any really good and careful drivers out here would be really valuable.

The other odd element is the Charlestonian one of improvising materials—a bit of carpet to mend a stretcher, e.g.—in which I find myself at home.

I don't know what will happen to this—I expect continue in a few days, after another false alarm.

No, all clear and morning.

Love

Julian

SECOND THOUGHTS

GEORGE ORWELL
'Letter to Rayner Heppenstall'

from *Collected Essays, Journalism and Letters*, ed. Sonia Orwell and Ian Angus, 1968

The Stores
Wallington
Nr Baldock, Herts
31 July 1937

Dear Rayner,

. . . We had an interesting but thoroughly bloody time in Spain. Of course I would never have allowed Eileen to come nor probably gone myself if I had foreseen the political developments, especially the suppression of the POUM, the party in whose militia I was serving. It was a queer business. We started off by being heroic defenders of democracy and ended by slipping over the border with the police panting on our heels. Eileen was wonderful, in fact actually seemed to enjoy it. But though we ourselves got out all right nearly all our friends and acquaintances are in jail and likely to be there indefinitely, not actually charged with anything but suspected of 'Trotskyism'. The most terrible things were happening even when I left, wholesale arrests, wounded men dragged out of hospitals and thrown into jail, people crammed together in filthy dens where they have hardly room to lie down, prisoners beaten and half starved etc. etc. Meanwhile it is impossible to get a word about this mentioned in the English press, barring the publications of the ILP, which is affiliated to the POUM. I had a most amusing time with the *New Statesman* about it. As soon as I got out of Spain I wired from France asking if they would like an article and of course they said yes, but when they saw my article was on the suppression of the POUM they said they couldn't print it. To sugar the pill they sent me to review a very good book which appeared recently, *The Spanish Cockpit*, which blows the gaff pretty well on what has been happening. But once again when they saw my review they couldn't print it as it was 'against editorial policy', but they actually offered to pay for the review all the same—practically hush-money. I am also having to change my publisher, at least for this book. Gollancz is of course part of the Communism-racket, and as soon as he heard I had been associated with the POUM and Anarchists and had seen the inside of the May riots in Barcelona, he said he did not think he would be able to publish my book, though not a word of it was written yet. I think he must have very astutely foreseen that something of the kind would happen, as when I went to Spain he drew up a contract undertaking to publish my fiction but not other books. However I have two other publishers on my track and I think my agent is being clever and has got them bidding against one another. I have started my book* but of course my fingers are all thumbs at present.

My wound was not much, but it was a miracle it did not kill me. The bullet went clean through my neck but missed everything except one vocal cord, or rather the nerve governing it, which is paralysed. At first I had no voice at all, but now the other vocal cord is compensating and the damaged one may or may not recover. My voice is practically normal but I can't shout to any extent. I also can't sing, but people tell me this doesn't matter. I am rather glad to have been hit by a bullet because I think it will happen to us all in the near future and I am glad to know that it doesn't hurt to speak of. What I saw in Spain did not make me cynical but it does make me think that the future is pretty grim. It is evident that people can be deceived by the anti-Fascist stuff exactly as they were deceived by the gallant little Belgium stuff, and when war comes they will walk straight into it. I don't, however, agree with the pacifist attitude, as I believe you do. I still think one must fight for Socialism and against Fascism, I mean fight physically with weapons, only it is as well to discover which is which. I want to meet Holdaway and see what he thinks about the Spanish business. He is the only more or less orthodox Communist I have met whom I could respect. It will disgust me if I find he is spouting the same defence of democracy and Trotsky-Fascist stuff as the others . . .

* *Homage to Catalonia*

GEORGE ORWELL
'Getting Out'

from *Homage to Catalonia*, 1938

The worst of being wanted by the police in a town like Barcelona is that everything opens so late. When you sleep out of doors you always wake about dawn, and none of the Barcelona cafés opens much before nine. It was hours before I could get a cup of coffee or a shave. It seemed queer, in the barber's shop, to see the Anarchist notice still on the wall, explaining that tips were prohibited. 'The Revolution has struck off our chains,' the notice said. I felt like telling the barbers that their chains would soon be back again if they didn't look out.

I wandered back to the centre of the town. Over the POUM buildings the red flags had been torn down, Republican flags were floating in their place, and knots of armed Civil Guards were lounging in the doorways. At the Red Aid centre on the corner of the Plaza de Cataluña the police had amused themselves by smashing most of the windows. The POUM book-stalls had been emptied of books and the notice-board farther down the Ramblas had been plastered with an anti-POUM cartoon —the one representing the mask and the Fascist face beneath. Down at the bottom of the Ramblas, near the quay, I came upon a queer sight; a row of militiamen, still ragged and muddy from the front, sprawling exhaustedly on the chairs placed there for the bootblacks. I knew who they were—indeed, I recognized one of them. They were POUM militiamen who had come down the line on the previous day to find that the POUM had been suppressed, and had had to spend the night in the streets because their homes had been raided. Any POUM militiaman who returned to Barcelona at this time had the choice of going straight into hiding or into jail—not a pleasant reception after three or four months in the line.

It was a queer situation that we were in. At night one was a hunted fugitive, but in the daytime one could live an almost normal life. Every house known to harbour POUM supporters was—or at any rate was likely to be—under observation, and it was impossible to go to a hotel or boarding-house, because it had been decreed that on the arrival of a stranger the hotel-keeper must inform the police immediately. Practically this meant spending the night out of doors. In the daytime, on the other hand, in a town the size of Barcelona, you were fairly safe. The streets were thronged by Civil Guards, Assault Guards, Carabineros, and ordinary police, besides God knows how many spies in plain clothes; still, they could not stop everyone who passed, and if you looked normal you might escape notice. The thing to do was to avoid hanging round POUM buildings and going to cafés and restaurants where the waiters knew you by sight. I spent a long time that day, and the next, in having a bath at one of the public baths. This struck me as a good way of putting in the time and keeping out of sight. Unfortunately the same idea occurred to a lot of people, and a few days later—after I left Barcelona—the police raided one of the public baths and arrested a number of 'Trotskyists' in a state of nature.

Half-way up the Ramblas I ran into one of the wounded men from the Sanatorium Maurín. We exchanged the sort of invisible wink that people were exchanging at that time, and managed in an unobtrusive way to meet in a café farther up the street. He had escaped arrest when the Maurín was raided, but, like the others, had been driven into the street. He was in shirt-sleeves—had had to flee without his jacket—and had no money. He described to me how one of the Civil Guards had torn the large coloured portrait of Maurín from the wall and kicked it to pieces. Maurín (one of the founders of the POUM) was a prisoner in the hands of the Fascists and at that time was believed to have been shot by them.

I met my wife at the British Consulate at ten o'clock. McNair and Cottman turned up shortly afterwards. The first thing they told me was that Bob Smillie was dead. He had died in prison at Valencia—of what, nobody knew for certain. He had been buried immediately, and the ILP representative on the spot, David Murray, had been refused permission to see his body.

Of course I assumed at once that Smillie had been shot. It was what everyone believed at the time, but I have since thought that I may have been wrong. Later the cause of his death was given out as appendicitis, and we heard afterwards from another prisoner who had been released that Smillie had certainly been ill in prison. So perhaps the appendicitis story was true. The refusal to let Murray see his body may have been due to pure spite. I must say this, however. Bob Smillie was only twenty-two years old and physically he was one of the toughest people I have met. He was, I think, the only person I knew, English or Spanish, who went three months in the trenches without a day's illness. People so tough as that do not usually die of appendicitis if they are properly looked after. But when you saw what the Spanish jails were like—the makeshift jails used for political prisoners—you realized how much chance there was of a sick man getting proper attention. The jails were places that could only be described as dungeons. In England you would have to go back to the eighteenth century to find anything comparable. People were penned together in small rooms where there was barely space for them to lie down, and often they were kept in cellars and other dark places. This was not as a temporary measure—there were cases of people being kept four and five months almost without sight of daylight. And they were fed on a filthy and insufficient diet of two plates of soup and two pieces of bread a day. (Some months later, however, the food seems to have improved a little.) I am not exaggerating; ask any political suspect who was imprisoned in Spain. I have had accounts of the Spanish jails from a number of separate sources, and they agree with one another too well to be disbelieved; besides, I had a few glimpses into one Spanish jail myself. Another English friend who was imprisoned later writes that his experiences in jail 'make Smillie's case easier to understand'. Smillie's death is not a thing I can easily forgive. Here was this brave and gifted boy, who had thrown up his career at Glasgow University in order to come and fight against Fascism, and who, as I saw for myself, had done his job at the front with faultless courage and willingness; and all they could find to do with him was to fling him into jail and let him die like a neglected animal. I know that in the middle of a huge and bloody war it is no use making too much fuss over an individual death. One aeroplane bomb in a crowded street causes more suffering than quite a lot of political persecution. But what angers one about a death like this is its utter pointlessness. To be killed in battle—yes, that is what one expects; but to be flung into jail, not even for any imaginary offence, but simply owing to dull blind spite, and then left to die in solitude—that is a different matter. I fail to see how this kind of thing—and it is not as though Smillie's case were exceptional—brought victory any nearer.

My wife and I visited Kopp that afternoon. You were allowed to visit prisoners who were not *incommunicado*, though it was not safe to do so more than once or twice. The police watched the people who came and went, and if you visited the jails too often you stamped yourself as a friend of 'Trotskyists' and probably ended in jail yourself. This had already happened to a number of people.

Kopp was not *incommunicado* and we got a permit to see him without difficulty. As they led us through the steel doors into the jail, a Spanish militiaman whom I had known at the front was being led out between two Civil Guards. His eye met mine; again the ghostly wink. And the first person we saw inside was an American militiaman who had left for home a few days earlier; his papers were in good order, but they had arrested him at the frontier all the same, probably because he was still wearing corduroy breeches and was therefore identifiable as a militiaman. We walked past one another as though we had been total strangers. That was dreadful. I had known him for months, had shared a dug-out with him, he had helped to carry me down the line when I was wounded; but it was the only thing one could do. The blue-clad guards were snooping everywhere. It would be fatal to recognize too many people.

The so-called jail was really the ground floor of a shop. Into two rooms each measuring about twenty feet square, close on a hundred people were penned. The place had the real eighteenth-century Newgate Calendar appearance, with its frowsy dirt, its huddle of human bodies, its lack of furniture—just the bare stone floor, one bench, and a few ragged blankets—and its murky light, for the corrugated steel shutters had been drawn over the windows. On the grimy walls revolutionary slogans —'*Visca* POUM!' '*Viva la Revolución!*' and so forth—had been scrawled. The place had been used as a dump for political prisoners for months past. There was a deafening racket of voices. This was the visiting hour, and the place was so packed with people that it was difficult to move. Nearly all of them were of the poorest of the working-class population. You saw women undoing pitiful packets of food which they had brought for their imprisoned men-folk. There were several of the wounded men from the Sanatorium Maurín among the prisoners. Two of them had amputated legs; one of them had been brought to prison without his crutch and was hopping about on one foot. There was also a boy of not more than twelve; they were even arresting children, apparently. The place had the beastly stench that you always get when crowds of people are penned together without proper sanitary arrangements.

Kopp elbowed his way through the crowd to meet us. His plump fresh-coloured face looked much as usual, and in that filthy place he had kept his uniform neat and had even contrived to shave. There was another officer in the uniform of the Popular Army among the prisoners. He and Kopp saluted as they struggled past one another; the gesture was pathetic, somehow. Kopp seemed in excellent spirits. 'Well, I suppose we shall all be shot,' he said cheerfully. The word 'shot' gave me a sort of inward shudder. A bullet had entered my own body recently and the feeling of it was fresh in my memory; it is not nice to think of that happening to anyone you know well. At that time I took it for granted that all the principal people in the POUM, and Kopp among them, *would* be shot. The first rumour of Nin's death had just filtered through, and we knew that the POUM were being accused of treachery and espionage. Everything pointed to a huge frame-up trial followed by a massacre of leading 'Trotskyists.' It is a terrible thing to see your friend in jail and to know yourself impotent to help him. For there was nothing that one could do; useless even to appeal to the Belgian authorities, for Kopp had broken the law of his own country by coming here. I had to leave most of the talking to my wife; with my squeaking voice I could not make myself heard in the din. Kopp was telling us about the friends he had made among the other prisoners, about the guards, some of whom were good fellows, but some of whom abused and beat the more timid prisoners, and about the food, which was 'pig-wash'. Fortunately we had thought to bring a packet of food, also cigarettes. Then Kopp began telling us about the papers that had been taken from him when he was arrested. Among them was his letter from the Ministry of War, addressed to the colonel commanding engineering operations in the Army of the East. The police had seized it and refused to give it back; it was said to be lying in the Chief of Police's office. It might make a very great difference if it were recovered.

I saw instantly how important this might be. An official letter of that kind, bearing the recommendation of the Ministry of War and of General Pozas, would establish Kopp's bona fides. But the trouble was to prove that the letter existed; if it were opened in the Chief of Police's office one could be sure that some nark or other would destroy it. There was only one person who might possibly be able to get it back, and that was the officer to whom it was addressed. Kopp had already thought of this, and he had written a letter which he wanted me to smuggle out of the jail and post. But it was obviously quicker and surer to go in person. I left my wife with Kopp, rushed out, and, after a long search, found a taxi. I knew that time was everything. It was now about half past five, the colonel would probably leave his office at six, and by tomorrow the letter might be God knew where—destroyed, perhaps, or lost somewhere in the chaos of documents that was presumably piling up as suspect after suspect was arrested. The colonel's office was at the War Department down by the quay. As I hurried up the steps the Assault Guard on duty at the door barred the way with his long bayonet and demanded 'papers'. I waved my discharge ticket at him; evidently he could not read, and he let me pass, impressed by the vague mystery of 'papers'. Inside, the place was a huge complicated warren running round a central courtyard, with hundreds of offices on each floor; and, as this was Spain, nobody had the vaguest idea where the office I was looking for was. I kept repeating: '*El coronel—, jefe de ingenieros, Ejército de Este!*' People smiled and shrugged their shoulders gracefully. Everyone who had an opinion sent me in a different direction; up these stairs, down those, along interminable passages which turned out to be blind alleys. And time was slipping away. I had the strangest sensation of being in a nightmare: the rushing up and down flights of stairs, the mysterious people coming and going, the glimpses through open doors of chaotic offices with papers strewn everywhere and typewriters clicking; and time slipping away and a life perhaps in the balance.

However, I got there in time, and slightly to my surprise I was granted a hearing. I did not see Colonel—, but his aide-de-camp or secretary, a little slip of an officer in smart uniform, with large and squinting eyes, came out to interview me in the ante-room. I began to pour forth my story. I had come on behalf of my superior officer, Major Jorge Kopp, who was on an urgent mission to the front and had been arrested by mistake. The letter to Colonel—was of a confidential nature and should be recovered without delay. I had served with Kopp for months, he was an officer of the highest character, obviously his arrest was a mistake, the police had confused him with someone else, etc., etc., etc. I kept piling it on about the urgency of Kopp's mission to the front, knowing that this was the strongest point. But it must have sounded a strange tale, in my villainous Spanish which elapsed into French at every crisis. The worst was that my voice gave out almost at once and it was only by violent straining that I could produce a sort of croak. I was in dread that it would disappear altogether and the little officer would grow tired of trying to listen to me. I have often wondered what he thought was wrong with my voice—whether he thought I was drunk or merely suffering from a guilty conscience.

However, he heard me patiently, nodded his head a great number of times, and gave a guarded assent to what I said. Yes, it sounded as though there might have been a mistake. Clearly the matter should be looked into. *Mañana*—I protested. Not *mañana*! The matter was urgent; Kopp was due at the front already. Again the officer seemed to agree. Then came the question I was dreading:

'This Major Kopp—what force was he serving in?'

The terrible word had to come out: 'In the POUM militia.'

'POUM!'

I wish I could convey to you the shocked alarm in his voice. You have got to remember how the POUM was regarded at that moment. The spy-scare was at its height; probably all good Republicans did believe for a day or two that the POUM was a huge spying organization in German pay. To have to say such a thing to an officer in the Popular Army was like going into the Cavalry Club immediately after the Red Letter scare and announcing yourself a Communist. His dark eyes moved obliquely across my face. Another long pause, then he said slowly:

'And you say you were with him at the front. Then you were serving in the POUM militia yourself?'

'Yes.'

He turned and dived into the colonel's room. I could hear an agitated conversation. 'It's all up,' I thought. We should never get Kopp's letter back. Moreover I had had to confess that I was in the POUM myself, and no doubt they would ring up the police and get me arrested, just to add another Trotskyist to the bag. Presently, however, the officer reappeared, fitting on his cap, and sternly signed to me to follow. We were going to the Chief of Police's office. It was a long way, twenty minutes' walk. The little officer marched stiffly in front with a military step. We did not exchange a single word the whole way. When we got to the Chief of Police's office a crowd of the most dreadful-looking scoundrels, obviously police narks, informers, and spies of every kind, were hanging about outside the door. The little officer went in; there was a long, heated conversation. You could hear voices furiously raised; you pictured violent gestures, shrugging of the shoulders, bangings on the table. Evidently the police were refusing to give the letter up. At last, however, the officer emerged, flushed, but carrying a large official envelope. It was Kopp's letter. We had won a tiny victory—which, as it turned out, made not the slightest difference. The letter was duly delivered, but Kopp's military superiors were quite unable to get him out of jail.

The officer promised me that the letter should be delivered. But what about Kopp? I said. Could we not get him released? He shrugged his shoulders. That was another matter. They did not know what Kopp had been arrested for. He would only tell me that the proper inquiries would be made. There was no more to be said; it was time to part. Both of us bowed slightly. And then there happened a strange and moving thing. The little officer hesitated a moment, then stepped across, and shook hands with me.

I do not know if I can bring home to you how deeply that action touched me. It sounds a small thing, but it was not. You have got to realize what was the feeling of the time—the horrible atmosphere of suspicion and hatred, the lies and rumours circulating everywhere, the posters screaming from the hoardings that I and everyone like me was a Fascist spy. And you have got to remember that we were standing outside the Chief of Police's office, in front of that filthy gang of tale-bearers and *agents provocateurs*, any one of whom might know that I was 'wanted' by the police. It was like publicly shaking hands with a German during the Great War. I suppose he had decided in some way that

I was not really a Fascist spy; still, it was good of him to shake hands.

I record this, trivial though it may sound, because it is somehow typical of Spain—of the flashes of magnanimity that you get from Spaniards in the worst of circumstances. I have the most evil memories of Spain, but I have very few bad memories of Spaniards. I only twice remember even being seriously angry with a Spaniard, and on each occasion, when I look back, I believe I was in the wrong myself. They have, there is no doubt, a generosity, a species of nobility, that do not really belong to the twentieth century. It is this that makes one hope that in Spain even Fascism may take a comparatively loose and bearable form. Few Spaniards possess the damnable efficiency and consistency that a modern totalitarian state needs. There had been a queer little illustration of this fact a few nights earlier, when the police had searched my wife's room. As a matter of fact that search was a very interesting business, and I wish I had seen it, though perhaps it is as well that I did not, for I might not have kept my temper.

The police conducted the search in the recognized Ogpu or Gestapo style. In the small hours of the morning there was a pounding on the door, and six men marched in, switched on the light, and immediately took up various positions about the room, obviously agreed upon beforehand. They then searched both rooms (there was a bathroom attached) with inconceivable thoroughness. They sounded the walls, took up the mats, examined the floor, felt the curtains, probed under the bath and the radiator, emptied every drawer and suitcase and felt every garment and held it up to the light. They impounded all papers, including the contents of the waste-paper basket, and all our books into the bargain. They were thrown into ecstasies of suspicion by finding that we possessed a French translation of Hitler's *Mein Kampf*. If that had been the only book they found our doom would have been sealed. It is obvious that a person who reads *Mein Kampf* must be a Fascist. The next moment, however, they came upon a copy of Stalin's pamphlet, *Ways of Liquidating Trotskyists and other Double Dealers*, which reassured them somewhat. In one drawer there was a number of packets of cigarette papers. They picked each packet to pieces and examined each paper separately, in case there should be messages written on them. Altogether they were on the job for nearly two hours. Yet all this time they *never searched the bed*. My wife was lying in bed all the while; obviously there might have been half a dozen sub-machine-guns under the mattress, not to mention a library of Trotskyist documents under the pillow. Yet the detectives made no move to touch the bed, never even looked underneath it. I cannot believe that this is a regular feature of the Ogpu routine. One must remember that the police were almost entirely under Communist control, and these men were probably Communist Party members themselves. But they were also Spaniards, and to turn a woman out of bed was a little too much for them. This part of the job was silently dropped, making the whole search meaningless.

That night McNair, Cottman, and I slept in some long grass at the edge of a derelict building-lot. It was a cold night for the time of year and no one slept much. I remember the long dismal hours of loitering about before one could get a cup of coffee. For the first time since I had been in Barcelona I went to have a look at the cathedral—a modern cathedral, and one of the most hideous buildings in the world. It has four crenellated spires exactly the shape of hock bottles. Unlike most of the churches in Barcelona it was not damaged during the revolution—it was spared because of its 'artistic value', people said. I think the Anarchists showed bad taste in not blowing it up when they had the chance, though they did hang a red and black banner between its spires. That afternoon my wife and I went to see Kopp for the last time. There was nothing that we could do for him, absolutely nothing, except to say good-bye and leave money with Spanish friends who would take him food and cigarettes. A little while later, however, after we had left Barcelona, he was placed *incommunicado* and not even food could be sent to him. That night, walking down the Ramblas, we passed the Café Moka, which the Civil Guards were still holding in force. On an impulse I went in and spoke to two of them who were leaning against the counter with their rifles slung over their shoulders. I asked them if they knew which of their comrades had been on duty here at the time of the May fighting. They did not know, and, with the usual Spanish vagueness, did not know how one could find out. I said that my friend Jorge Kopp was in prison and would perhaps be put on trial for something in connexion with the May fighting; that the men who were on duty here would know that he had stopped the fighting and saved some of their lives; they ought to come forward and give evidence to that effect. One of the men I was talking to was a dull, heavy-looking man who kept shaking his head because he could not hear my voice in the din of the traffic. But the other was different. He said he had heard of Kopp's action from some of his comrades; Kopp was *buen chico* (a good fellow). But even at the time I knew that it was all useless. If Kopp were ever tried, it would be, as in all such trials, with faked evidence. If he has been shot (and I am afraid it is quite likely), that will be his epitaph: the *buen chico* of the poor Civil Guard who was part of a dirty system but had remained enough of a human being to know a decent action when he saw one.

It was an extraordinary, insane existence that we were leading. By night we were criminals, but by day we were prosperous English visitors—that was our pose, anyway. Even after a night in the open, a shave, a bath, and a shoe-shine do wonders with your appearance. The safest thing at present was to look as bourgeois as possible. We frequented the fashionable residential quarter of the town, where our faces were not known, went to expensive restaurants, and were very English with the waiters. For the first time in my life I took to writing things on walls. The passage-ways of several smart restaurants had '*Visca* POUM!' scrawled on them as large as I could write it. All the while, though I was technically in hiding, I could not feel myself in danger. The whole thing seemed too absurd. I had the ineradicable English belief that 'they' cannot arrest you unless you have broken the law. It is a most dangerous belief to have during a political pogrom. There was a warrant out for McNair's arrest, and the chances were that the rest of us were on the list as well. The arrests, raids, searchings were continuing without pause; practically everyone we knew, except those who were still at the front, was in jail by this time. The police were even boarding the French ships that periodically took off refugees and seizing suspected 'Trotskyists'.

Thanks to the kindness of the British consul, who must have had a very trying time during that week, we had managed to get our passports into order. The sooner we left the better. There was a train that was due to leave for Port Bou at half past seven in the evening and might normally be expected to leave at about half past eight. We arranged that my wife should order a taxi beforehand and then pack her bags, pay her bill, and leave the hotel at the last possible moment. If she gave the hotel people too much notice they would be sure to send for the police. I got down to the station at about seven to find that the train had already gone—it had left at ten to seven. The engine-driver had changed his mind, as usual. Fortunately we managed to warn my wife in time. There was another train early the following morning. McNair, Cottman, and I had dinner at a little restaurant near the station and by cautious questioning discovered that the restaurant-keeper was a C N T member and friendly. He let us a three-bedded room and forgot to warn the police. It was the first time in five nights that I had been able to sleep with my clothes off.

Next morning my wife slipped out of the hotel successfully. The train was about an hour late in starting. I filled in the time by writing a long letter to the Ministry of War, telling them about Kopp's case—that without a doubt he had been arrested by mistake, that he was urgently needed at the front, that countless people would testify that he was innocent of any offence, etc., etc., etc. I wonder if anyone read that letter, written on pages torn out of a note-book in wobbly handwriting (my fingers were still partly paralysed) and still more wobbly Spanish. At any rate, neither this letter nor anything else took effect. As I write, six months after the event, Kopp (if he has not been shot) is still in jail, untried and uncharged. At the beginning we had two or three letters from him, smuggled out by released prisoners and posted in France. They all told the same story—imprisonment in filthy dark dens, bad and insufficient food, serious illness due to the conditions of imprisonment, and refusal of medical attention. I have had all this confirmed from several other sources, English and French. More recently he disappeared into one of the 'secret prisons' with which it seems impossible to make any kind of communication. His case is the case of scores or hundreds of foreigners and no one knows how many thousands of Spaniards.

In the end we crossed the frontier without incident. The train had a first class and a dining-car, the first I had seen in Spain. Until recently there had been only one class on the trains in Catalonia. Two detectives came round the train taking the names of foreigners, but when they saw us in the dining-car they seemed satisfied that we were respectable. It was queer how everything had changed. Only six months ago, when the Anarchists still reigned, it was looking like a proletarian that made you respectable. On the way down from Perpignan to Cerbères a French commercial traveller in my carriage had said to me in all solemnity: 'You mustn't go into Spain looking like that. Take off that collar and tie. They'll tear them off you in Barcelona.' He was exaggerating, but it showed how Catalonia was regarded. And at the frontier the Anarchist guards had turned back a smartly dressed Frenchman and his wife, solely—I think—because they looked too bourgeois. Now it was the other way about; to look bourgeois was the one salvation. At the passport office they looked us up in the card-index of suspects, but thanks to the inefficiency of the police our names were not listed, not even McNair's. We were searched from head to foot, but we possessed nothing incriminating, except my discharge-papers, and the carabineros who searched me did not know that the 29th Division was the POUM. So we slipped through the barrier, and after just six months I was on French soil again. My only souvenirs of Spain were a goatskin water-bottle and one of those tiny iron lamps in which the Aragon peasants burn olive oil—lamps almost exactly the shape of the terra-cotta lamps that the Romans used two thousand years ago—which I had picked up in some ruined hut, and which had somehow got stuck in my luggage.

After all, it turned out that we had come away none too soon. The very first newspaper we saw announced McNair's arrest for espionage. The Spanish authorities had been a little premature in announcing this. Fortunately, 'Trotskyism' is not extraditable.

I wonder what is the appropriate first action when you come from a country at war and set foot on peaceful soil. Mine was to rush to the tobacco-kiosk and buy as many cigars and cigarettes as I could stuff into my pockets. Then we all went to the buffet and had a cup of tea, the first tea with fresh milk in it that we had had for many months. It was several days before I could get used to the idea that you could buy cigarettes whenever you wanted them. I always half-expected to see the tobacconists' doors barred and the forbidding notice '*No hay tabaco*' in the window.

McNair and Cottman were going on to Paris. My wife and I got off the train at Banyuls, the first station up the line, feeling that we would like a rest. We were not too well received in Banyuls when they discovered that we had come from Barcelona. Quite a number of times I was involved in the same conversation: 'You come from Spain? Which side were you fighting on? The Government? Oh!'—and then a marked coolness. The little town seemed solidly pro-Franco, no doubt because of the various Spanish Fascist refugees who had arrived there from time to time. The waiter at the café I frequented was a pro-Franco Spaniard and used to give me lowering glances as he served me with an aperitif. It was otherwise in Perpignan, which was stiff with Government partisans and where all the different factions were caballing against one another almost as in Barcelona. There was one café where the word 'POUM' immediately procured you French friends and smiles from the waiter.

I think we stayed three days in Banyuls. It was a strangely restless time. In this quiet fishing-town, remote from bombs, machine-guns, food-queues, propaganda, and intrigue, we ought to have felt profoundly relieved and thankful. We felt nothing of the kind. The things we had seen in Spain did not recede and fall into proportion now that we were away from them; instead they rushed back upon us and were far more vivid than before. We thought, talked, dreamed incessantly of Spain. For months past we had been telling ourselves that 'when we get out of Spain' we would go somewhere beside the Mediterranean and be quiet for a little while and perhaps do a little fishing; but now that we were here it was merely a bore and a disappointment. It was chilly weather, a persistent wind blew off the sea, the water was dull and choppy, round the harbour's edge a scum of ashes, corks, and fish-guts bobbed against the stones. It sounds like lunacy, but the thing that both of us wanted was to be back in Spain. Though it could have done no good to anybody, might indeed have done serious harm, both of us wished that we had stayed to be imprisoned along with the others. I suppose I have failed to convey more than a little of what those months in Spain meant to me. I have recorded some of the outward events, but I cannot record the feeling they have left me with. It is all mixed up with sights, smells, and sounds that cannot be conveyed in writing: the smell of the trenches, the mountain dawns stretching away into inconceivable distances, the frosty crackle of bullets, the roar and glare of bombs; the clear cold light of the Barcelona mornings, and the stamp of boots in the barrack yard, back in December when people still believed in the revolution; and the food-queues and the red and black flags and the faces of Spanish militiamen; above all the faces of militiamen—men whom I knew in the line and who are now scattered Lord knows where, some killed in battle, some maimed, some in prison—most of them, I hope, still safe and sound. Good luck to them all; I hope they win their war and drive all the foreigners out of Spain, Germans, Russians, and Italians alike. This war, in which I played so ineffectual a part, has left me with memories that are mostly evil, and yet I do not wish that I had missed it. When you have had a glimpse of such a disaster as this—and however it ends the Spanish war will turn out to have been an appalling disaster, quite apart from the slaughter and physical suffering—the result is not necessarily disillusionment and cynicism. Curiously enough the whole experience has left me with not less but more belief in the decency of human beings. And I hope the account I have given is not too misleading. I believe that on such an issue as this no one is or can be completely truthful. It is difficult to be certain about anything except what you have seen with your own eyes, and consciously or unconsciously everyone writes as a partisan. In case I have not said this somewhere earlier in the book I will say it now: beware of my partisanship, my mistakes of fact, and the distortion inevitably caused by my having seen only one corner of events. And beware of exactly the same things when you read any other book on this period of the Spanish war.

Because of the feeling that we ought to be doing something, though actually there was nothing we could do, we left Banyuls earlier than we had intended. With every mile that you went northward France grew greener and softer. Away from the mountain and the vine, back to the meadow and the elm. When I had passed through Paris on my way to Spain it had seemed to me decayed and gloomy, very different from the

Paris I had known eight years earlier, when living was cheap and Hitler was not heard of. Half the cafés I used to know were shut for lack of custom, and everyone was obsessed with the high cost of living and the fear of war. Now, after poor Spain, even Paris seemed gay and prosperous. And the Exhibition was in full swing, though we managed to avoid visiting it.

And then England—southern England, probably the sleekest landscape in the world. It is difficult when you pass that way, especially when you are peacefully recovering from sea-sickness with the plush cushions of a boat-train carriage under your bum, to believe that anything is really happening anywhere. Earthquakes in Japan, famines in China, revolutions in Mexico? Don't worry, the milk will be on the doorstep tomorrow morning, the *New Statesman* will come out on Friday. The industrial towns were far away, a smudge of smoke and misery hidden by the curve of the earth's surface. Down here it was still the England I had known in my childhood: the railway-cuttings smothered in wild flowers, the deep meadows where the great shining horses browse and meditate, the slow-moving streams bordered by willows, the green bosoms of the elms, the larkspurs in the cottage gardens; and then the huge peaceful wilderness of outer London, the barges on the miry river, the familiar streets, the posters telling of cricket matches and Royal weddings, the men in bowler hats, the pigeons in Trafalgar Square, the red buses, the blue policemen—all sleeping the deep, deep sleep of England, from which I sometimes fear that we shall never wake till we are jerked out of it by the roar of bombs.

V. S. PRITCHETT

'The Spanish Tragedy'

Review of *Homage to Catalonia* from *New Statesman & Nation*, 30 April 1938

There are many strong arguments for keeping creative writers out of politics and Mr George Orwell is one of them. If these beings toe the party line they are likely to be ruined as writers; if they preserve their independence—and, after all, they have by nature little choice about that—they become an annoyance to the causes they espouse. There are admitted exceptions. Ludwig Renn must be one. But for him there can be nothing strange in the militarised politics of our ideological war; he has been drilling all his life and he has found a peculiar if limited stability and humanity of his own in the fields of obedience.

Not so Mr Orwell of the liberal tradition. He is the typical English anarchist. Man of action first and politician later by exasperation and disgust, he went out to Spain at the beginning of the civil war, joined the POUM militia and left revolutionary Barcelona to stand and shiver in the trenches of Aragon. There he breathed the sour, stale smell of war, collected firewood, brooded over rifles thirty years old, wondered where the ammunition was and where the artillery and the war were too. On the Fascist side there must have been similar questionings. Unexploded shells were carefully collected, reconditioned and fired back: 'There was said to be one shell with a nickname of its own which travelled to and fro daily without exploding.' But some did burst, there were trench raids and snipings—a sniper got Mr Orwell in the neck later on—and meanwhile the POUM pursued its eternal political theme.

Win the war first, as the Communists said; or revolution and war hand-in-hand? Mr Orwell listened and had no patience with the POUM view. He told these eager children (they were hardly youths) that they were talking through their hats, and when he got to Barcelona he planned to join the Communist-controlled International Brigade. POUM smiled. They did not hunt heretics. But the worker's hey-day had passed in Barcelona when Mr Orwell got there; bourgeois democracy had come back with too much accent on the bourgeois for Mr Orwell's zeal, and he ran into the Anarchist rising. Already POUM was under suspicion. The time of lies was following with depressing inevitability upon the revolutionary dawn, and Mr Orwell, rather than take sides against former comrades, became sentimentally pro-POUM and preferred to return to the front and fight the enemy. But for this eccentricity of Mr Orwell's a Fascist sniper would not have caught him in the neck one morning while he was in the middle of a quiet, interesting conversation.

After this Mr Orwell's book becomes an account of the bloody suppression of POUM, and, being constitutionally 'agin the government,' he undertakes POUM's defence. There seems to be no doubt that the wretched POUM got a raw deal. But though he writes with honest indignation about the lies that were spread about men who were fighting the common enemy and has the idealist's attractive and understandable loathing for the grey arguments of expediency, Mr Orwell is, I am afraid, wrong-headed when he carries the defence into the field of high politics and strategy. Without going into the matter at length, it was surely clear from the very moment of foreign intervention—which was at

the beginning of the war—that the Spaniards had tragically but undoubtedly missed the revolutionary tide. Mr Orwell disagrees. Yet what
grounds are there for believing that the democratic moderate line was
unrealistic and even strategically unsound? Is there any reason to believe
that a revolutionary policy would have awakened the vehement support
of the working classes outside of Spain, say that of the ultra-respectable
English Labour party? (Isn't this the thin end of the Trotskyite heresy
against which Mr Orwell defends the POUM?) Is it credible that
without the 'tainted' Russian arms, there would have been any Government Spain left to which revolutionaries behind Franco's lines could
rally? And once Franco had collared the Moors first for a Holy War, what
hope was there of a Moroccan rising, all questions of French feeling
apart? Given the situation, I see no reason to believe in any of these
possibilities. Mr Orwell is kicking against the pricks—an impulse which
is attractive because he is human, honest and lively in a drilled and
unlikeable world, but which is nevertheless perverse.

Still the dilemma of a man who sees the ideal become the equivocal is a
genuine one. He puts it with verve, freedom and tolerance. And his
descriptions of the men he fought with, the acts of strange and monotonous days, the muddled skirmishes and things like the sensations he
had when he was wounded are extremely well done. No one excels him in
bringing to the eyes, ears and nostrils the nasty ingredients of fevered
situations; and I would recommend him warmly to all who are concerned
about the realities of personal experience in a muddled cause.

JOHN LANGDON-DAVIES

A Warning

Review of *Homage to Catalonia*, *Daily Worker*, Spain Weekend Supplement,
21 May 1938

Better than [Allison Peers' *Catalonia Infelix* and *The Spanish Tragedy*] are
some books produced by individualists who have splashed their eyes for a
few months with Spanish blood. Typical is Orwell's *Homage to Catalonia*.
The road to Wigan Pier leads on to Barcelona and the POUM.

The value of the book is that it gives an honest picture of the sort of
mentality that toys with revolutionary romanticism but shies violently at
revolutionary discipline. It should be read as a warning.

In the same way a much greater book is invaluable as a warning. Ramon Sender's *Seven Red Sundays* (a sixpenny Penguin) should be read by anyone who wants to understand the Spanish anarchist mentality.

You cannot understand Spain without understanding Anarchism also, for the superb, lovable human beings of that great movement had to be mentally changed before the power of the people in Spain could be effectively used.

Seven Red Sundays shows you why, just as *Homage to Catalonia* shows you the obstinate few who refuse to change.

W. H. AUDEN

Missing Churches

from *Modern Canterbury Pilgrims*, 1956, ed. James A. Pike

The theological question seemed irrelevant since such values as freedom of the person, equal justice for all, respect for the rights of others, etc., were self-evident truths. However, the liberal humanism of the past had failed to produce the universal peace and prosperity it promised, failed even to prevent a World War. What had it overlooked? The subconscious, said Freud; the means of production, said Marx. Liberalism was not to be superseded; it was to be made effective instead of self-defeating.

Then the Nazis came to power in Germany. The Communists had said that one must hate and destroy some of one's neighbors now in order to create a world in which nobody would be able to help loving his neighbors tomorrow. They had attacked Christianity and all religions on the ground that, so long as people are taught to love a non-existent God, they will ignore the material obstacles to human brotherhood. The novelty and shock of the Nazis was that they made no pretense of believing in justice and liberty for all, and attacked Christianity on the grounds that to love one's neighbor as oneself was a command fit only for effeminate weaklings, not for the 'healthy blood of the master race.' Moreover, this utter denial of everything liberalism had ever stood for was arousing wild enthusiasm, not in some remote barbaric land outside the pale, but in one of the most highly educated countries in Europe, a country one knew well and where one had many friends. Confronted by such a phenomenon, it was impossible any longer to believe that the values of liberal humanism were self-evident. Unless one was prepared to take a relativist view that all values are a matter of personal taste, one could hardly avoid asking the question: 'If, as I am convinced, the Nazis are wrong and we are right, what is it that validates our values and invalidates theirs?'

With this and similar questions whispering at the back of my mind, I visited Spain during the Civil War. On arriving in Barcelona, I found as I walked through the city that all the churches were closed and there was not a priest to be seen. To my astonishment, this discovery left me profoundly shocked and disturbed. The feeling was far too intense to be the result of a mere liberal dislike of intolerance, the notion that it is wrong to stop people from doing what they like, even if it is something silly like going to church. I could not escape acknowledging that, however I had consciously ignored and rejected the Church for sixteen years, the existence of churches and what went on in them had all the time been very important to me. If that was the case, what then?

W. H. AUDEN and CHRISTOPHER ISHERWOOD

Poor Fish

(Valerian's Speech, *On the Frontier*, 1938, Act III, sc. ii)

Well, I can't blame them ... Gone to a demonstration, I suppose, to shout stickjaw slogans with the rest, and listen to their gibbering prophets who promise the millennium in a week.

[*Goes to window*]

You poor fish, so cock-a-hoop in your little hour of comradeship and hope! I'm really sorry for you. You don't know what you're letting yourselves in for, trying to beat us on our own ground! You will take to machine-guns without having enough. You will imagine that, in a People's Army, it is against your principles to obey orders—and then wonder why it is that, in spite of your superior numbers, you are always beaten. You will count on foreign support, and be disappointed, because the international working-class does not read your mosquito journals. It prefers our larger and livelier organs of enlightenment, which can afford snappier sports news, smarter features, and bigger photographs of bathing lovelies. We shall expose your lies and exaggerate your atrocities, and you will be unable to expose or exaggerate ours. The churches will be against you. The world of money and political influence will say of us: 'After all, they are the decent people, *our* sort. The others are a rabble.' A few of the better educated may go so far as to exclaim: 'A plague on both your houses!' Your only open supporters abroad will be a handful of intellectuals, who, for the last twenty years, have signed letters of protest against everything from bi-metallism in Ecuador to the treatment of yaks in Thibet . . .

STEPHEN SPENDER

Letter to Virginia Woolf

(Previously unpublished manuscript letter in Berg Collection, New York Public Library)

2nd April 1937

Dear Virginia,

I have just returned from Spain and have to wait at Cerbère for an hour, so I have bought the only sheet of note paper here and am writing to remind you of your promise to send me your novel . . .

I have travelled through a good deal of Spain—Barcelona, Valencia, Madrid, Albacete and the Morata Front. The total results of my being here are that I like the Spanish People even more than I did before, that I am convinced the revolution is a very real thing, the war a very horrible one and the International Brigade a mixture of both. I am sure that Cyril Connolly is quite wrong to have allowed the revolution to 'go bad' on him as though it were an undergraduate lunch party. It is quite true that the politicians are very divided and quarrelsome but the real war and the real revolution are less an affair of the politicians who happen to be in power than is usual with such things. What I am convinced of is that politicians are detestable anywhere: and being in Spain has taught me more about the lies and unscrupulousness of some of the people who are recruiting at home than of the indiscipline in Spain itself. For example, everything one hears about the International Brigade in England is lies, because the propaganda is conducted by politicians, whether of the *Daily Worker* or of the *Daily Mail*. This has depressed me a good deal, especially as friends of mine are hopelessly caught in this machinery.

Largo Cabollero is about the most hated man in Spain . . .

The really encouraging thing about Spain is really the Spanish people and only the Spanish people ... This must be about the only War in which allies have come to fight in a country and have grown really to love the inhabitants, because I have never heard a word here against the Spanish people. They are so amazingly friendly and generous on every occasion ...

I have not seen Julian Bell at Albacete, so I suppose he has not joined the Brigade. In any case, I hope he will not do so. The qualities required apart from courage, are terrific narrowness and a religious dogmatism about the Communist Party line, or else toughness, cynicism and insensibility. The sensitive, the weak, the romantic, the enthusiastic, the truthful live in Hell there and cannot get away. The political commissars are mostly Scotch Presbyterians who bully so much that even people who were quite enthusiastic Party Members have been driven into hating the whole thing. One man fighting at the Front complained to me bitterly about the inquisitional methods of the Party. Some of these methods are lies, for instance it is a lie to say as the *Daily Worker* does that people can leave the Brigade whenever they like. On the contrary, one is completely trapped there, and illness, nervous breakdown, bad wounds are no excuse for getting away unless one belongs to the Party élite and is sent home as a propagandist to show one's arm in a sling to audiences. Albacete is the ugliest, dreariest place in Spain, full of people who have nothing to do, many of whom are useless for the front but who cannot be sent home, because to send them would be bad for 'morale' ... The war is often terrible, and a man who had been all through the Great War said he had seen nothing more awful than the first four days of fighting at Morata, without trenches or any defence except olive trees. My greatest friend collapsed on the 4th day at Morata. I tried to get him transferred to me as my secretary in Valencia, but this was not allowed. A few days later, in despair he tried to escape from Albacete to which he had been returned. He is now in a Labour Camp, and for that reason this information is very confidential and only for you & Leonard. If it was known that I had told any of the more unpleasant truths about the Brigade, his chances of ever getting away from Spain would be ruined.

For people who can face all this, the Brigade is all right. It has played a very heroic role in this war, though it is not the English, but the Germans & Italians who fight best. The discipline is not so bad as that of Capitalist armies; deserters are not shot, but quite well treated in a camp which is probably less bad than Albacete. Its real vice is the exclusiveness of the C P leaders who are not only unconcerned with Spain but even intolerant of members of the Brigade who are not as fanatical as themselves. I do not think this is an exaggeration. Lack of imagination is awful in life anyway: in war, it is more cruel and destructive even than the enemy. There are people in Albacete who should never never have joined the Brigade. They are wretchedly unhappy and completely trapped. I am going to do all I can to help them, but it is very difficult. The Communist Party dominates the Brigade, and they would regard an appeal to the Spanish Government (which is very merciful) as treachery. One can only appeal to the Party Chiefs. I wrote a report for them on the whole question of deserters and discontent, but I was told that they would be so angry at receiving it that it would only make matters worse—

.   .   .   .   .

Quote this letter to any pacifist or democrat who wants to fight, but please do not mention my name.

It is not that I care for myself but the freedom of my friend depends on this.

Yours affectionately
Stephen

STEPHEN SPENDER

'Ultima Ratio Regum'

from *Collected Poems*, 1955 (first version is 'Regum Ultima Ratio'
New Statesman & Nation, 15 May 1937)

The guns spell money's ultimate reason
In letters of lead on the Spring hillside.
But the boy lying dead under the olive trees
Was too young and too silly
To have been notable to their important eye.
He was a better target for a kiss.

When he lived, tall factory hooters never summoned him
Nor did restaurant plate-glass doors revolve to wave him in
His name never appeared in the papers.
The world maintained its traditional wall
Round the dead with their gold sunk deep as a well,
Whilst his life, intangible as a Stock Exchange rumour, drifted outside.

O too lightly he threw down his cap
One day when the breeze threw petals from the trees.
The unflowering wall sprouted with guns,
Machine-gun anger quickly scythed the grasses;
Flags and leaves fell from hands and branches;
The tweed cap rotted in the nettles.

Consider his life which was valueless
In terms of employment, hotel ledgers, news files.
Consider. One bullet in ten thousand kills a man.
Ask. Was so much expenditure justified
On the death of one so young, and so silly
Lying under the olive trees, O world, O death?

STEPHEN SPENDER

'Port Bou'

from *Collected Poems*, 1955 (first version is 'Port Bou—Firing Practice',
New Writing, Autumn 1938)

As a child holds a pet
Arms clutching but with hands that do not join
And the coiled animal looks through the gap
To outer freedom animal air,
So the earth-and-rock arms of this small harbour
Embrace but do not encircle the sea
Which, through a gap, vibrates into the ocean,
Where dolphins swim and liners throb.
In the bright winter sunlight I sit on the parapet
Of a bridge; my circling arms rest on a newspaper
And my mind is empty as the glittering stone
While I search for an image
(The one written above) and the words (written above)
To set down the childish headlands of Port Bou.
A lorry halts beside me with creaking brakes
And I look up at warm downwards-looking faces
Of militia men staring at my (French) newspaper.
'How do they write of our struggle over the frontier?'

I hold out the paper, but they cannot read it,
They want speech and to offer cigarettes.
In their waving flag-like faces the war finds peace. The famished
    mouths
Of rusted carbines lean against their knees,
Like leaning, rust-coloured, fragile reeds.
Wrapped in cloth—old granny in a shawl—
The stuttering machine-gun rests.
They shout—salute back as the truck jerks forward
Over the vigorous hill, beyond the headland.
An old man passes, his mouth dribbling,
From three rusted teeth, he shoots out: 'pom-pom-pom'.
The children run after; and, more slowly, the women;
Clutching their skirts, trail over the horizon.
Now Port Bou is empty, for the firing practice.
I am left alone on the parapet at the exact centre
Above the river trickling through the gulley, like that old man's saliva.
The exact centre, solitary as the bull's eye in a target.
Nothing moves against the background of stage-scenery houses
Save the skirring mongrels. The firing now begins
Across the harbour mouth, from headland to headland,
White flecks of foam whipped by lead from the sea.
An echo spreads its cat-o'-nine tails
Thrashing the flanks of neighbour hills.
My circling arms rest on the newspaper,
My mind is paper on which dust and words sift,
I assure myself the shooting is only for practice
But I am the coward of cowards. The maching-gun stitches
My intestines with a needle, back and forth;
The solitary, spasmodic, white puffs from the carbines
Draw fear in white threads back and forth through my body.

FRANZ BORKENAU

'The Second Journey'

from *The Spanish Cockpit*, 1937

Barcelona came as a shock, as in August, but in the opposite sense. Then
it had overwhelmed me by the suddenness with which it revealed the real

character of a workers' dictatorship. This time it struck the observer by the clean sweep of all signs of this same dictatorship. No more barricades in the streets; no more cars covered with revolutionary initials and filled with men in red neckties rushing through the town; no more workers in civilian clothes, but rifles on their shoulders; as a matter of fact, very few armed men at all, and those mostly *asaltos* and *guardias* in brilliant uniforms; no more seething life around the party centres and no large car-parks before their entries; and the red banners and inscriptions, so shining in August, had faded. There was still no definitely 'bourgeois' element visible in the streets. Certainly the really rich people, if there are any, did not appear in public. But the Ramblas, the chief artery of popular life in Barcelona, were far less clearly working-class now than then. In August it was dangerous to wear a hat: nobody minded doing so now, and the girls no longer hesitated to wear their prettiest clothes. A few of the more fashionable restaurants and dancehalls have reopened, and find customers. To sum it up, what one calls the petty-bourgeois element, merchants, shopkeepers, professional men, and the like, have not only made their appearance, but make a strong impress upon the general atmosphere. The Hôtel Continental, where I had stayed in August, one of a few journalists among a large crowd of billeted militia, had entirely resumed its pre-revolutionary aspect. The militia had been removed, the rooms were full of paying and fairly well-dressed guests, and business in this particular hotel seemed to be excellent.

·   ·   ·   ·   ·

The revolutionary terrorism of July, August, and September in Spain was the thing called 'mass terrorism'; the word carrying the double signification of terrorism exerted by the masses themselves, not by an organized police force, and against a very great number, a 'mass' of victims. It has its close analogies in the Paris massacres of September 1792, and in the massacres of the year 1918 in Russia. Let us remember 1792 in Paris and compare it with 1936 in Barcelona. In Paris the volunteers massacred the prisoners before going to the front; so they did in Barcelona. They performed the massacres at a moment of supreme danger for the cause of the revolution, while the enemy approached Paris, and in the conviction that the massacre was the best means of avoiding a rising or counter-revolution in the city while they were away at the front. It was exactly the same in Barcelona. The massacre was performed without any real rule of law, with extreme ruthlessness and cruelty, but without any of the more refined tortures so characteristic of certain police régimes. Terrorism in Paris in 1792, exactly as in Barcelona in 1936, was by no means organized by a body specially created for the purpose, or, for that matter, by any organization at all. True, political groups have always backed the thing: in 1792 Danton and his group, in Russia in 1918 the Bolsheviks, in Barcelona the anarchists. But it was not performed by the party organizations but by the masses in action themselves. From this one might be inclined to conclude that it was aimless, that it struck by chance. How could nondescript masses know whom to strike? But this is not quite true. The mass only strikes, not so much at people who have perpetrated or tried to perpetrate any definite *act* against the régime, but at people who, by their station in life, are supposed to be the natural enemies of the régime which these masses defend. In Russia as in Spain and as in France the aristocrats were killed as aristocrats, the priests as priests, and in Russia and Spain the bourgeois as bourgeois; in all these cases, moreover, those individuals who were known to belong to organizations inimical to the régime. Guilt, in these outbreaks of mass terrorism, was not constituted by criminal actions but by opinions publicly displayed and by certain stations in life in general. There were certainly a great number of mistakes, even in the sense of the aims of the terrorist movement itself. But in general it was not difficult to strike precisely at those people who were aimed at. In strict contrast to a regular police régime mass terrorism obtains its aims the better the more it is decentralized. Local people are more likely to know about the political attitude and the social standing of people than any improvised central organization could possibly be.

The ruthlessness in the killing, the wild exultation of the killers over the destruction of their enemies, the irregularity of the procedure, or rather the complete lack of anything like a procedure, the execution of people not guilty of any offence, have made mass terrorism an object of horror not only for those who have lived through it but even more for later generations. But precisely on account of its characteristics mass terrorism can hardly become an efficient instrument of feud inside the revolutionary camp itself.

. . . Not the sailors of Kronstadt and the exasperated peasants but the GPU have exterminated dissident socialists and communists. These persecutions have been put into effect by a centralized police machinery at the disposal of a small circle of rulers. Every revolution seems to undergo, in its course, this transformation from mass terrorism to police terrorism. . . . It came to full strength in Russia in the years after the end of the civil war. In Spain, where the properly revolutionary processes have been so quickly superseded by something entirely different, it has made great strides in the few months since the beginning of the civil war.

What are the characteristics of the second form of terrorism compared with its first form? There is contrast at every point. Instead of the revolutionary masses themselves the agents of the new terrorism are police forces. Sometimes the revolutionary police have arisen mainly out of the revolutionary ranks; in other cases, and especially to-day in Spain, it is simply the old police force, purged, as much as possible, from openly counter-revolutionary elements, and replenished with elements from the governing parties. But, in Spain at least, the bulk of the new personnel is identical with the bulk of the old, and so is their attitude; they are simply serving the new legal Government. The notion of guilt is reintroduced accordingly. The procedure is not the old procedure, rather an emergency procedure including the right of the police to execute without trial; but, apart from a few exceptions, even the police, and even the irregular police forces like 15 Plaza Tetuan, will not execute unless they are satisfied that the accused did not only dislike the Government but has committed some act against it; even committed something sufficient to justify execution, however vaguely the limits of the accused man's responsibility may be defined. Accordingly, there is a tremendous number of arrests, but the number of executions, though still considerable, bears no proportion to them. With the increasing crisis the police had gone half crazy and arrested people at random, for the silliest reasons or by mistake. But, after all, it was not proceeding in such an irresponsible manner with executions. There was an enormous improvement in this respect, mainly due to republican and communist influence, and people who had lived through the mass terrorism of the first months were particularly appreciative of the change.

But there are other aspects of the matter. Terrorism had ceased to be exercised by the masses and had ceased to be directed against definite classes. With that repression became an instrument of the ruling group against all dissentients. Repression was not limited to the Trotskyists. One day I learnt that a personal friend I had known for many years, of whose genuine socialist convictions there was not the slightest doubt, and who was very far indeed from being a Trotskyist, was in serious danger simply because he had been, in the past (!) a dissident communist. The anarchist with whom I shared my cell was in deadly fear because he had edited a paper for propaganda among communists—and I do not think he was in the least unjustified in his general ideas about what might happen to him, though in this concrete case he proved to be mistaken. One day I was introduced to a man who had been simply critical of certain technical aspects of the work of the international brigades—and, as far as I could judge, was right in his criticisms, which were obviously prompted by a deep concern for the republican cause—and who had to use all sorts of tricks in order to escape persecution and get out of Spain. In general the political commissars of the international brigades are in the habit of supposing that every man who leaves the brigade in order to take up work in another capacity—not under direct communist control —is a deserter, and treat him accordingly.

The police already acts as a GPU, whose chief business it is to hunt dissidents. The man who was trembling every hour to see himself arrested, tried, possibly executed, was in August the aristocrat, the priest, the industrialist, the rich merchant, the wealthy peasant. To-day, besides direct agents in the pay of Franco, he is the man who disagrees with communist policy, even on minor items. In August it was the man who, through his social status, was an adversary of the lower classes. In February it was the man who, through his opinions, was not even an adversary but a critic of the official policy of the Communist Party . . .

The intention of the totalitarian States is . . . to enforce complete unity of life and thought in every matter concerning the State, and to make every matter concern the State. Mass terrorism, far apart from the Catholic Inquisition as it is in many other respects, is nearer to it in this one aspect than to the totalitarian régime. The masses too want to terrorize in the first place the decided and active enemies of the régime as a whole; they are less concerned with dissensions inside the revolution- ary camp. Revolutionary periods under mass terrorism have been, accordingly, times of intense dissension and freedom of thought— within the limits of the fight against the *ancien régime.* But wherever the totalitarian police appears every class of individuality, of intellectual, artistic, or, in a general sense, creative effort, is certain to be strangled. One must certainly feel relief in seeing the number of the victims decrease—Mussolini and Hitler have both boasted of the small number of victims of their revolutions—and those classes which have been the object of mass terrorism will be particularly grateful. But civilization is bound to perish, not simply by the existence of *certain* restrictions on the expression of freedom of thought, for which there can be ample justifica- tion—but by the wholesale submission of thinking to orders from a party centre.

Moreover, in a civil war like that of Spain, no organization, efficient as it may be otherwise—and the Spanish Seguridad is not even efficient —can work without the free support of the people. And it remains to be seen whether the police methods applied by the Seguridad will not, in the end, prove a serious drawback for the Spanish republicans, because they strangle that popular enthusiasm which can only evolve in an atmosphere of freedom—if not for everybody, then at least for those various shades of opinion that prevail among the adversaries of Franco themselves.

GEORGE ORWELL
'Spanish Nightmare'

Review of *The Spanish Cockpit*, by Franz Borkenau. *Time & Tide*, 31 July 1937.
Collected Essays, Journalism and Letters, ed. Sonia Orwell and Ian Angus, 1968

Dr Borkenau has performed a feat which is very difficult at this moment for anyone who knows what is going on in Spain; he has written a book about the Spanish war without losing his temper. Perhaps I am rash in saying that it is the best book yet written on the subject, but I believe that anyone who has recently come from Spain will agree with me. After that horrible atmosphere of espionage and political hatred it is a relief to come upon a book which sums the situation up as calmly and lucidly as this.

Dr Borkenau is a sociologist and not connected with any political party. He went to Spain with the purpose of doing some 'field work' upon a country in revolution, and he made two trips, the first in August, the second in January. In the difference between those two periods, especially the difference in the social atmosphere, the essential history of the Spanish revolution is contained. In August the Government was almost powerless, local soviets were functioning everywhere and the Anarchists were the main revolutionary force; as a result everything was in terrible chaos, the churches were still smouldering and suspected Fascists were being shot in large numbers, but there was everywhere a belief in the revolution, a feeling that the bondage of centuries had been broken. By January power had passed, though not so completely as later, from the Anarchists to the Communists, and the Communists were using every possible method, fair and foul, to stamp out what was left of the revolution. The pre-revolutionary police-forces had been restored, political espionage was growing keener and keener, and it was not long before Dr Borkenau found himself in jail. Like the majority of political prisoners in Spain, he was never even told what he was accused of; but he was luckier than most in being released after a few days, and even (very few people have managed this lately) saving his documents from the hands of the police. His book ends with a series of essays upon various aspects of the war and the revolution. Anyone who wants to understand the Spanish situation should read the really brilliant final chapter, entitled 'Conclusions.'

The most important fact that has emerged from the whole business is that the Communist Party is now (presumably for the sake of Russian foreign policy) an anti-revolutionary force. So far from pushing the Spanish Government further towards the Left, the Communist influence has pulled it violently towards the Right. Dr Borkenau, who is not a revolutionary himself, does not particularly regret this fact; what he does object to is that it is being deliberately concealed. The result is that public opinion throughout Europe still regards the Communists as wicked Reds or heroic revolutionaries as the case may be, while in Spain itself—

It is at present impossible . . . to discuss openly even the basic facts of the political situation. The fight between the revolutionary and non-revolutionary principle, as embodied in anarchists and Communists respectively, is inevitable, because fire and water cannot mix . . . But as the Press is not even allowed to mention it, nobody is fully aware of the position, and the political antagonism breaks through, not in open fight to win over public opinion, but in backstairs intrigues, assassinations by Anarchist bravos, legal assassinations by Communist police, subdued allusions, rumours . . . The concealment of the main political facts from the public and the maintenance of this deception by means of censorship and terrorism carries with it far-reaching detrimental effects, which will be felt in the future even more than at present.

If that was true in February, how much truer it is now! When I left Spain in late June the atmosphere in Barcelona, what with the ceaseless arrests, the censored newspapers and the prowling hordes of armed police, was like a nightmare.

CYRIL CONNOLLY

'A Spanish Diary'

from the *New Statesman & Nation*, 20 February 1937

I have just spent a further three weeks in Spain, visiting Aragon, Catalonia, Valencia, Alicante and Murcia. The impressions which follow are open to contradiction and will probably be contradicted; but so far as possible they are unbiased and the result of checking up on many conversations with many different kinds of people. Spain is a country where it is impossible to get accurate figures about anything important and where rumours gather force in proportion as the censorship grows more severe. There have been considerable changes in the political, economic, and military situations since I was there in December and I should describe them as all for the worse, though not irremediably for the worse. The outstanding political fact is the greatly increased power of the moderate elements in the Government backed up officially by the Communists, whose policy is to support a bourgeois democratic Spain against what they consider the premature revolutionary activities of the Anarchists and the POUM. Their reasons for this are: (1) that it fits in with Stalin's foreign policy elsewhere, which is to do nothing to weaken the anti-Fascist democracies, who might be less able to defend themselves in war if extremists have provoked internal dissensions; (2) that only by presenting England and France with authentic evidence of a legitimate and moderate government in power in Spain will they win over those fearful and hesitant countries, and possibly deflect Mussolini from his threat not to tolerate a Red Catalonia; (3) that it also enables the numerically weak Communist Party to get power through supporting the Liberals and the Marxian Socialists, using the vast bulk of the UGT as a hermit crab takes possession of a winkle; and (4) that it enables them to attack, on patriotic grounds, their ideological enemies, the anarchists of the CNT and the Trotskyites of the POUM. (I see Mr Croyle was criticised for calling the POUM Trotskyite. Their leader Nin was Trotsky's secretary and perhaps this is how the conception has arisen.)

* * *

The Communists and Socialists say 'First win the war, then attend to the revolution.' The younger Anarchists and the POUM say, 'The war and the revolution are indivisible and we must go on with both of them simultaneously. If you postpone the revolution how are we to know you are in good faith?' The Anarchist Ministers try to hold a balance between them, while they advance their giant scheme to fuse the CNT with the UGT into a huge proletarian combine of syndicated workers, which would get on with the war, guarantee the revolution, get rid of the friction between the parties, and permit both the FAI and the Communists to disappear as separate political entities. The Communists naturally oppose this. The position of the POUM is the most precarious, for they are severely condemned by the Communist and Socialist press on charges of being Trotskyites, and hence Fascists, of running away in battle and undermining the Government (from which they have been driven out), of consisting of criminals and the rejected members of other

parties, and of preparing a counter-revolutionary coup. They are defended by the Anarchists with very much less zeal than they are attacked.
In their favour it can be said that they have between eight and ten
thousand men at the front, that no connection with the Trotskyites of the
Russian trials has been proved against them, that they are closely
associated with the Independent Labour Party, whose members find
themselves part of the United Front with the Communists in England,
yet hailed as Fascists by the Communists in Spain, and that the campaign
against them seems to be a price exacted for Russian assistance to the
Government.

The opposition to the Anarchists is more serious, for it is based on a
relative ignorance of the role they have played for seventy years in Spain,
and of their solidarity with the Spanish workers and their hold on the
Spanish character. They are attacked as being either visionaries, half-
wits, or gunmen. Pasionaria referred to them in a public speech as
'analphabetics,' and any reference to them in Valencia is studiously
avoided. The Communists point to their inefficiency. 'Look at the
inaction on the Aragon front. The Fascists could walk through it at any
moment.' The Anarchists reply, 'that is because we have only a few
Mexican rifles and very little artillery and machine-guns—not one
Russian arm has ever reached us—because we are to be denied any
success and our defeat even may be being arranged for, although we
saved Barcelona and supplied the Government with its only popular
hero, Durruti, whom we sent to Madrid.' Thus between twenty and forty
thousand men are immobile on the Northern front at a time when a
victorious counter-attack is desperately needed, and when the troops
opposed to them are clearly demoralised and awaiting reinforcements.

*   *   *

In fact it would be hard to find an atmosphere more full of envy,
intrigue, rumour and muddle than that which exists at the moment in the
capitals of Republican Spain; while Malaga falls and Madrid struggles
heroically, the further one gets from the front, the dimmer grows the
memory of the 19th of July, the louder the mutual accusations and
reproaches of the parties. They are now even jealous of their one hope,
the International Brigade, and it seems useless to clamour for unity of
command when there is no one worthy of it. Here are some notes on
people's conversations. They will show how many different points of
view are permitted.

*   *   *

A German: 'They ask why don't we attack on the Aragon front. I will
tell you. I am in the International Column. There are 12 of us alive out of

my company, and a hundred out of my battalion. If we do decide to attack it is known to the other side almost before we know ourselves. The Spaniards will not attack at night in any case. We have no artillery, few machine-guns, and obsolete 1870 rifles, old German ones bought from Mexico.'

A Hungarian of the POUM: 'Look at those crowds. Look at those women. It's disgraceful. All bourgeois, bargain-basement people, pram-pushers. Is this what I'm fighting for? I tell you we are only at the beginning—yes. There will come a day when father will be killed by son and sister by brother, not just at the front, but here in the streets of Barcelona. At least I hope so. But the Spanish people are like this.' He lights a match and holds it upwards till it goes out.

A High Official (Catalan Left): 'We are all sick of the war in Barcelona. The front is just for people who like fighting, I think. Most people on this side don't know what Communism means, most people on the other don't know what Fascism means. The priests were not Fascist, most of them didn't know about the large sums of money hidden in their churches—only the bishops did—and we got the archbishop out all right. I don't even think Franco is a Fascist.'

Another (Catalan Left): 'This is a very interesting revolution, because it is the only Western revolution since 1789—only do not exaggerate it. We have taken over a few large factories and estates, but we have only socialised transport, hotels, cafés, theatres, cinemas, barbers and boot cleaners—not very much, really. You see we are a nation of *petits bourgeois* and we have naturally left them exactly as they are—no, I should rather describe our present regime as a "capitalism without capitalists".'

English Communist: 'But how can one co-operate with these people? The POUM, of course, are simply Fascists: as for the Anarchists—one can't go bumping people off in 1937! And besides, they're inefficient, anti-militarist, they won't accept officers, they can't keep step. You know Durruti was killed by an Anarchist, they were jealous of his friendship with the Russians: his views were very unpopular. And look at the Aragon front—if the enemy attack they will get to Lerida, and a very good thing too, it will bring people to their senses. That and a stiff bombardment of Barcelona is what we've all been hoping for for two months.'

Spanish Communist: 'I see no reason why the Anarchists and Communists shouldn't be united. The Anarchists are very simple people, they do not realise how long their ideas must take to put into practice. Their Ministers do—and they often turn into Communists when they realise this.'

Anarchist at the 'Shanghai': 'Anarchism with us is very old, very old indeed, and very international—look at me, I drove a tram at the time of the strike in 1933. I arranged some sabotage, I was an idealist—so I escaped to England, and then Belgium. I knew García Oliver, I drove him 8 hours unconscious in my lorry once, after the police had knocked him out. You found him friendly? We of the revolution are like that —besides, who cares about death? A tile might fall on my head at this moment, in any case to die for an ideal is not death.' 'But what about being blinded or lamed for an ideal?' 'Spain would never forget her sons!' 'Would you say there was still a revolution here?' 'Don't you worry about the revolution, the F A I will take care of that—nor about Russia—Oliver sleeps in the Russian Embassy, that is the terms we are on. You worry about England and France; it is they who are deceived about where their interests lie. England and Spain, what couldn't we do together, two rich democracies like ours!'

* * *

I was able to interview the two men of to-morrow, if there is a to-morrow, in the Spanish Cabinet, Juan García Oliver, the Minister of Justice, and Indalecio Prieto, the Minister of Munitions, Marine, and Air.

* * *

Oliver is a man in his thirties, sturdy, good-looking, with one of those stoical, open Iberian faces which reflect the Anarchist blend of idealism and militancy. He was indeed one of the three heroes of the street-fighting in Barcelona. I asked him if the idea of violence was really part of Anarchism or not. 'Certainly not; our ideal is the brotherhood of man. Man first is a beast on four legs, then the family make an agreement to tolerate each other, then that is extended to the tribe, then to the nation, so that it is murder to kill in one's own country and war to kill in another, and ultimately that must apply to all nations. Anarchism has been violent in Spain because oppression has been violent; in England it has not. But Anarchist justice will not be violent; we will consider ignorance of the law as a real excuse. The law has been made by the rich and strong, as in feudal times, and crime can never be suppressed till the economic and cultural level of everybody has been raised. Revolutions fail because they do not raise the country, only the towns. They do not even acknowledge the problem—all culture and education is centred in the towns, in the museums and universities, while people in the country who do not even know their own name are punished for ignorance of the law. I would abolish military service and substitute instead service by which everyone who is well-educated has to spend a year passing on his education to the peasants; the capitalists and the professors are guilty of hoarding culture which must be digested by the whole country in a solid block. People who say 'après moi le deluge,' they are the real criminals. I would like to re-educate Fascist prisoners after the war in reformatories—if a guard uses violence on them he would go to prison himself. I have been 14 years in prison, and I know. There are not many books about Anarchism, because the Spaniards prefer to talk in meetings and act. It was theorising that caused the failure of the Austrian and German democracies. If I had to sum up Anarchism in a phrase I would say it was the ideal of eliminating the beast in man.'

Meanwhile, the blockade goes on, arms and men pile up on one side, petrol, coal, and bread run out on the other. The Atlantic fleet pays courtesy visits to Valencia and Palma, when even a fishing boat can hardly go out a mile for fear of Italian submarines. But what can weak countries like France and England do, when the attitude of Portugal is so profoundly unhelpful?

CYRIL CONNOLLY

'To-day the Struggle'

Review of *War Dance* by E. Graham Howe; *Single to Spain* by Keith Scott-Watson; *The Epic of the Alcazar* by Major Geoffrey Moss; *Spain* by W. H. Auden, from the *New Statesman & Nation*, 5 June 1937

One thing is common to all these books—not just a convenient reviewer's link, but the problem, the *raison d'être* of them all—their obsession with war and fighting and violent death. Professor Howe's concern is how to avoid these things, how we can all avoid them, if we want to, but do we want to? And if not, why not? It seems to me that a great many of us don't, that apart from those whose economic situation makes them desire change, or those whose reasoning process makes them work for it, there exists a large bulk of people who have become, often without knowing it, sensation hunters, whose state of mind reflects unconsciously the hopes and deliberations of the swine of Gadara on the verge of their last migration. They exclaim, 'nothing in the paper,' 'Spain seems very quiet lately,' and their faces would fall, as at the recovery of a sick relative, were someone to succeed in authentically postponing war for fifty years. They are people who have grown up on crises, for whom bad news is better than no news, victims of the war fever which is on the increase twenty years after 1914, which may be universal in thirty. Professor Howe's book is written for them, it is an analysis of the deep psychological causes which originate in the nursery and make us want to hurt each other; 'vicious circle, anxiety, aggressiveness, guilt, forces for war,' are his chapter headings . . .

Single to Spain (a return would have done) is one of the most readable books about the war and one of the very few indeed to be written by someone who has actually fought. The author went out to join the original international brigade when the English numbered only about twenty. He seems a cheery, adventurous young man who chafed very much at first against Communist discipline, and after his first serious action was so horrified at the difference between war in the imagination and in fact that he resigned from the brigade and went to work under Sefton Delmer in Madrid. There he was nearly arrested as a spy, remained to see all except three of his comrades in the Thaelmann battalion wiped out at Boadilla through not receiving the order to retreat, and finally got out of Spain after being hit in his car by a shell, one person in whom the war fever is extinct. He saw the fifty Moors who died of accidentally eating inoculated rabbits in the laboratories of the University City, he saw the Polish company caught by the German bombers.

Twenty men had been hit, some of them were unrecognisable. The bomb splinters had torn them with a macabre humour. One boy lay on his back threshing the air with his leg, where the other should have been was a quivering bloody stump. In the fork of a tree, another was tightly wedged; he was alive and moaning, when the ambulance men touched him, he gave a high-pitched scream, a blue-red tangle of intestines hung from his stomach. We tried to lift one man on to a stretcher—he bent like an old rag doll, his spine had been severed, my arms were soaked in blood. I dared not stop and think or I should go mad. A boy, not more than sixteen, lay grinning at the blue sky as though at a remembered joke, the top of his head was taken off as one opens an egg. Those who were past aid were shot; it was the greatest mercy the ambulance men could have shown.

What is remarkable in Watson's story is the ease with which he is allowed to retire from the Brigade and work for a journalist in Madrid, and the pleasant terms on which his ex-comrades, still fighting, receive him. Such action would be impossible on the other side, and his book is full of flashes of sympathy and intelligence perceived in the people he fought for and the men he fought with, pacifists such as Renn and Marty, publicists like Ralph Bates, Spanish militia women, and belligerent commissars. Yes, a genuine, entertaining, and interesting account of the Spanish war from underneath—but how disillusioned, how utterly fed up with war itself! 'The past two months seemed like a distant nightmare' is what he feels on leaving and he comments often on the sensation of everything happening in a bad dream from which he would suddenly wake up, a sensation also noticed in Malaga by the unfortunate Koestler.

The Epic of the Alcazar is the best book that has come out so far on the other side. To begin with, it is written by a military man and contains a lot of interesting comment on the military operations, including a harrowing account of the tactics by which the Foreign Legion occupy towns and villages, a manoeuvre which apparently can be repeated endlessly since it always produces the same psychological reaction in the defence. No book on Spain is impartial, but Major Moss at least pays a glowing tribute to the attackers of the Alcazar, although he writes to glorify those inside it. He tones down the foreign and Fascist element in Franco's forces, which, since he is writing about the first three months of the war, is perhaps permissible, nor does he fall into the silly error of the author of *Les Cadets de l'Alcazar* and pretend that it was defended by several hundred beardless young officers, animated entirely by patriotism and religious mania. The key to the defence was clearly the six hundred civil guards who formed the backbone of resistance, the two or three extremely intelligent officers at the top, and the handful of Fascists and Carlists who could be used for desperate sallies in search of food. And of course, there was the building itself, a building which seems to have been purposely created exactly for such an occasion, as do so many places in the Spanish civil war. In fact, it is a symptom of war fever that geography seems to make sense only from a military standpoint; streets and squares, farms and sunken fences, knolls and valleys leap into relief, into life in civil war, as in some border ballad, and the Alcazar, with its enormous walls, its tunnels and secret passages, its towers and bastions from which a shot had hardly been fired since the Moors or Charles V first built them, lumbers into its place in history with extraordinary precision. There is everything in the story of the Alcazar, the cosy, ark-like withdrawal into its protection, the first elevated hours of resistance, the gruelling months that follow, the horror of the mines, the hope of relief, the imminence of starvation, and Geoffrey Moss has made a fine and vivid story out of them. The defenders lived for nearly two months on a litre of water a day, one unhusked roll six inches long and the fifteen-hundredth part of a mule or horse. No sweet, no salt, no greens, no tobacco, no light—only roll and mule or roll and horse. Major Moss, who attempts to disprove the massacre at Badajoz (how will he justify Guernica?) makes no mention of the affair of the hostages— Government women brought in from sallies or imprisoned at the beginning—whom Mr Vernon Bartlett and others have alluded to and which puts the defender's refusal to let their women go in a different light. Who were the prisoners he refers to, what happened to them afterwards? Conclusions from the book. Human beings will stand anything. No limit to their endurance. Vast superiority of intelligent military discipline over mere revolutionary enthusiasm—but it must be intelligent. Common factor to both sides, *being Spanish*, both sharing, besieged and besiegers, in their Roman and Iberian heritage of courage, cruelty, stoical patience, and contempt for death. It is easier for them than for us to kill, to endure pain, to die—but while the Spaniards in Watson's book are in every other respect people like ourselves, intelligent, sympathetic, open; inside the Alcazar they are not. Patriotism, militarism, feudalism, faith, not justice and liberty, impregnate those oppressive walls: genii of the Middle Ages, brutal and unenlightened, were stoppered up in that Moorish fortress to be released by the dark race who built it.

Spain is a hundred-line poem by Auden; it is good medium Auden in a good cause—the Spanish Medical Aid. The Marxian theory of history does not go very happily into verse, but the conclusion is very fine. The point of all these books is that war is horrible, but one cannot learn that from the headlines in newspapers, or glimpses of newsreels, one can learn it only by fighting oneself or by observing the disillusion of those who have. By now no one can possibly enjoy fighting in the Spanish war, except perhaps the Moors and the blond Moors. The Rupert Brooke period is over—but no one seems able to stop. I met a great many people in Spain who longed for the war to end and who, perhaps because I was a foreigner, said so freely. When I printed these opinions they didn't correspond with the state of English war fever and caused displeasure here. The more fire I used to eat, the 'better' the article was supposed to be. I don't think this would be the case now. Mr Spender's not very martial muse passes uncriticised in these columns, Mr Koestler's account of the defence of Malaga, a nightmare of Dali-esque intensity, is printed in the *News Chronicle*: we are experiencing a vicarious war-weariness at last. But the war goes on, and it is the fact that war is something which you cannot stop, that renders doubly guilty the callous and obsolete military leaders who began it.

THE LAST FIGHT

JOHN CORNFORD

'Poem'

from *New Writing*, Autumn 1937 (retitled 'To Margot Heinemann', in *John Cornford: A Memoir*, ed. Pat Slaon, 1938)

Heart of the heartless world,
Dear heart, the thought of you
Is the pain at my side,
The shadow that chills my view.

The wind rises in the evening,
Reminds that autumn is near.
I am afraid to lose you,
I am afraid of my fear.

On the last mile to Huesca,
The last fence for our pride,
Think so kindly, dear, that I
Sense you at my side.

And if bad luck should lay my strength
Into the shallow grave,
Remember all the good you can;
Don't forget my love.

'The Will to Live'

Review of *John Cornford, A Memoir*, ed. Pat Sloan, *New Statesman & Nation*, 12 November 1938

Men and women are so deeply influenced by the circumstances which surround them through their adolescence, that during times of rapid change, like the present, generations divided by completely different views of life succeed to each other in less than ten years, instead of thirty. The attitude of young men at the Universities is a good test of this. Since the war, the Universities have seen three different generations. The post-war generation of young men whose adolescence was spent in preparation for fighting in the war, and who were then miraculously released to a life which, having expected death, they did not know what to do with. The 'boom' generation, who were adolescent during the optimistic 'twenties of trade expansion, the League of Nations and the Weimar Republic. Last of all there comes the 'crisis' generation of young men, adolescent since 1929 and brought up in an intensely political, revolutionary and counter-revolutionary atmosphere.

John Cornford was a leader of this youngest generation. Like several of the most promising of his contemporaries, he went to Spain to fight in the International Brigade. He was killed on the day after his twenty-first birthday.

This clear and factual collection of examples of his own writing and essays by those who knew him gives a portrait of a character so single-minded, so de-personalised, that one thinks of him, as perhaps he would wish to be thought of, as a pattern of the human cause for which he lived, rather than as an individual, impressive and strong as his individuality was. His brother says: 'Trying to know him was like standing on a railway embankment and trying to grab an express train.' In Victor Kiernan's account of him at Cambridge, even in Professor Cornford's careful and informative recollections of his childhood, one has the same impression of a person who was driving himself like a powerful machine.

The steam in the engine which Christopher Cornford saw as his brother was Communism, to which he became converted in 1932, the time of the depression, when, it will be remembered, the brothers Esmond and Giles Romilly, both of whom have fought in Spain, were conducting another campaign at another public school. Before he left school, Communism had become his whole life. A group of his contemporaries have contributed simply an account of Cambridge Socialism to this book, instead of any reminiscences, because John Cornford was so completely identified with this movement.

The few years of Cornford's active life as a Communist were an exercise in orthodoxy, both in theory and practice. Until shortly before he died, he had ambitions as a poet; but poetry took second place to political action, or rather, had to grow out of it; when it ceased to do so, the Muse went overboard, like love affairs, *The Waste Land* and everything else.

> All we've brought are our party cards
> Which are no bloody good for your bloody charades.

The last poems he wrote are interesting for the determination with which he was trying to force political lessons into rhyme and imagery:

> Time present is a cataract whose force
> Breaks down the banks even at its source
> And history forming in our hands
> Not plasticine but roaring sands,
> Yet we must swing it to its final source.

These poems are violent and insensitive, yet it is these very defects which make them effective and give them a defiant metallic clang, which does not lack a certain richness, because it is single and strong.

Cornford's own essays are extremely able arrangements of intractable material into a dynamic, if preconceived, pattern. They show the energy of a strong intellectual will and a great intelligence; what is most convincing in them is the single-mindedness of the writer which identifies itself with an objective cause.

How far his disinterestedness could go, is shown by Cornford's death. If he had chosen, he could no doubt have played a leading part in the Socialist movement in this country. All the essays show that he had the rare quality of leadership, great intellectual gifts and a power of organising both himself and others. But he went to Spain, first of all, as he explains in a moving letter to Margot Heinemann, 'with the intention of staying a few days, firing a few shots, and then coming home.' However, he soon discovered that 'you can't do things like that. You can't play at civil war, or fight with a reservation you don't mean to get killed. It didn't take long to realise that either I was here in earnest or else I'd better clear out . . . Having joined, I am in whether I like it or not. And I like it.'

John Cornford was a leader rather than just an original person, because his remarkableness lay in his having qualities that others share, only in a pattern of greater abundance, strength and clarity. Reading this book, one is discovering the potentialities of a generation. Cornford lived for a form of society for which he was also willing to die. When democracy in Spain was threatened, it was natural for him to fight, and in fighting he felt that he was both defending something real and helping to create something new. His spirit was not a resurrection of 1914.

Cornford is immensely significant not merely because he was young and brave, but because he lived and died with the courage of a purpose which reaches far beyond himself and which effectively challenges the barbarism and defeatism of the age we live in. One may feel, as I do, that the pattern of this young hero is over-simplified; his vision of life is impatient and violent, it leaves too many questions unanswered, he burns out too quickly, rushing headlong to his death; but nevertheless it is a pattern which in other lives may take on a greater richness without losing Cornford's power and determination. The spirit of Cornford and some of his comrades rises like a phoenix from the ashes of Spain, which are the ashes of Europe.

RALPH BATES

'My Friend, Ralph Fox'

from *Ralph Fox: A Writer in Arms*, ed. J. Lehmann, T. A. Jackson, C. Day Lewis, 1937

I received the tragic news of Ralph's death just before addressing a Madison Square Garden meeting, here in New York. He was one of my best friends. I mean, outside of all questions of political sympathy, he was a man I naturally delighted to be with. Behind all the enormous panoply of that meeting, the vast hall, the gigantic machine of vulgar yet impressive sound passing out of the organ, booming and wailing across the ceiling, the banners of defiance hung around the balcony, the piles of military clothing, the ambulances—behind all the surging excitement that hung before me, there was the remembrance of my friend as I last saw him sitting at my table in London.

And then, during the meeting, Professor Dewey asked everyone to stand in memory of those who had fallen in defence of the world's liberty. With a noise like—strange how the imagination will not outlive it, childhood's symbols though the mature mind rejects them—with a noise like a rushing wind twenty thousand people stood to the known and the anonymous dead. Ralph was not anonymous to me, nor to thousands present—but it was not the landscape of shattered olive-trees among which he had died that I thought of, but again his boyish laugh and the love of a boyish tale. For that is how we had talked, the five of us, that evening, in London, before we all went off to Spain.

Ralph had been longing to go to China. I say longing, because though he had no trace of romanticism in his nature, he never accepted any idea with a merely intellectual and dry assent. I suppose that China for him, as Spain for me, represented two things, escape and reality. Ralph was one of those magnificent fortunate men who escape into reality. He could not go to China, which he already knew and loved. Instead he met his death in Spain.

I think I described his character correctly in the first improvisatory attempt I made in telling another friend of his death. Standing in a room high above Fifth Avenue I said, to another friend of ours, Rebecca West: 'He was a mature boy,' I said and Rebecca answered, 'I expected to find him quite a young man when I first met him. After that conference I went out and bought all of his books.' That was the effect Ralph always made on people. She was speaking of the International Association of Writers in Defence of Culture at which we were all present. In Defence of Culture! Less than six months later he had died defending it!

At that dinner in my flat we fell into excited argument, as we often did. The writing of an encyclopaedia had been proposed by André Malraux. Ralph was enthusiastic, I less so. 'No, no, no,' I said, 'in less than three months we shall have a Fascist rising in Europe.' I expected the seat of that rising to be France, yet within three weeks it had broken out and André, Ralph and I were all in Spain.

I do not want to write about his books because I cannot regard them as separate from the man. I had enjoyed all of *Storming Heaven* with its intense sincerity and superb direction, *Lenin* and *Genghis Khan*, and his latest and perhaps most beautiful piece of work, *Conversation with a Lama*, all of wise things, expressed his character for me. He was a fine writer and would have done splendid things. He died in Spain, defending the light that no writer may dare to let flicker out.

HUGH (HUMPHREY) SLATER

'How Ralph Fox was Killed'

from *Ralph Fox: A Writer in Arms*, ed. J. Lehmann, T. A. Jackson, C. Day Lewis, 1937

Ralph Fox, the well-known English Communist writer, was killed in the fighting near Lopera in Andalusia, while he was acting as Assistant Political Commissioner to a brigade of the International Legion.

The Fascists had advanced from the direction of Cordova and the Government had thrown special troops into action for a counter-attack. Lopera is the first village in the province of Jean on the road to Cordova. The country is hilly, with gigantic, ragged mountains in the distance. The low hills are covered with olive-groves, planted in endless, symmetrical rows. The most furious fighting was among the trees in the olive-field, covering what is now to be called 'English Crest.' One can imagine how intensely Ralph must have appreciated the beauty of this country.

The counter-attack in which the English-speaking company played a prominent part was made from the bottom of a hill. The Government troops, taking cover behind the olive-trees from the hail of rifle fire from the enemy positions on the crest and also from the dozens of German Junker planes bombing and flying low, machine-gunning with explosive bullets. Ralph Fox was with the brigade commander on the road half-way up the hill, when it became evident that there was an unforeseen possibility of our machine-gunners establishing invaluable positions covering the enemy's right flank. Fox set off running, bending low across some open ground, to organize this manoeuvre. It was a supremely brave thing to do; the bombing and machine-gun fire were at their most intense, and it was almost certain death for anybody to leave cover. Fox knew this, but he considered it necessary to take the risk.

Later the whole front changed, and this open ground became No-Man's Land in the centre of the cross-fire. That night a soldier was instructed to crawl out and bring in the papers from the pockets of our dead. Among the things he collected were Ralph Fox's note-book and a letter addressed to him. The next day a group of comrades were organized to go out at night to identify the bodies, but unfortunately the whole brigade was moved to a new sector that afternoon, and this could not be done.

The military commander with whom Ralph worked said that it was difficult for him to find words to describe Fox's amazing bravery. He said:

'He was an exceedingly brave man, and it was very largely due to his example that we were able to hold the enemy and save as many of our men as we did. I am not just paying a conventional tribute to a dead man when I say that he was a real hero.'

Madrid, 11 January, 1937

W. E. JOHNS
What Waste

from 'The Editor's Cockpit', *Popular Flying*, May 1937

I was shocked to hear of the death of Christopher Sprigg, in Spain, whence he had gone to fight on the side which may, or may not, be right. It matters little to him now. He is not the first man to throw his life away uselessly—I use the word deliberately—for a cause in which he had everything to lose and nothing to gain. I have known Christopher Sprigg since he was a lad of eighteen. Those of you who took *Popular Flying* in its early days knew his work, for he wrote some of the best short air stories that have ever been written. You may remember them, about Mainwaring of Planet Airways. They appeared under the name of Arthur Cave. Since then he has written a number of books, and was rapidly making a name for himself. One of his latest is reviewed in this issue; another is yet to be published. And that will be the last. What a pity! What a tragedy. Above all, what waste. Heavens above, what waste!

DONAGH MACDONAGH
'He is Dead and Gone, Lady . . .
(For Charles Donnelly, RIP)'

from *Ireland Today*, July 1937

Of what a quality is courage made
That he who gentle walked our city streets
Talking of poetry or philosophy,

Spinoza, Keats.
Should lie like any martyred soldier
His brave and fertile brain dried quite away
And the limbs that carried him from cradle to death's outpost
Growing down into a foreign clay.

Gone from amongst us and his life not half begun
Who had followed Jack-o-Lantern truth and liberty
Where it led wavering from park-bed to prison cell
Into a strange land, dry misery,
And then into Spain's slaughter, sniper's aim
And his last shocked embrace of earth's lineaments.
Can I picture truly that swift end
Who see him dead with eye that still repents.

What end, what quietus, can I see for him
Who had the quality of life in every vein?
Life with its passion and poetry and its proud
Ignorance of eventual loss or gain.
This first fruit of our harvest, willing sacrifice
Upon the altar of his integrity
Lost to us; somewhere his death is charted—
Something has been gained by this mad missionary.

LEONARD CROME

The Death of Julian Bell

from *New Statesman & Nation*, 28 August 1937

Sir,—I saw in 'Critic's' column in your paper an obituary notice of Julian Bell, who was recently killed by a Fascist bomb on the Brunete front.

Julian was a member of the British Medical Unit, and was engaged with us in the evacuation of wounded from the front to our stations and hospitals. The conditions of work were the most difficult in our experience. The Government troops had occupied an important sector of Fascist territory, and for almost three weeks, day after day, the enemy were trying to reconquer the lost ground. Bilbao tactics were being used continuously. Villages, towns and fields were sprayed with steel from planes, guns and machine guns. At night whole square kilometres of earth would go up in flames from incendiary bombs.

We in the British Medical Unit have had a very heavy casualty list, and we shall miss sorely some of our best men in our future work. Through shell and machine-gun fire our drivers would take their ambulances time and again, working days and nights for incredible stretches. Only rarely could they avail themselves of the illusory safety of trenches and dug-outs. They have all had their miraculous escapes, but some of them have fallen, and amongst them was Julian.

We all liked him from the first day he joined us. His calm and serenity, his humane intellectualism under the most trying conditions, and the manifest sincerity of his convictions made him one of the most popular men in our group.

Three days before his death the ambulance he was driving was smashed by a bomb. Julian came to me and asked for permission to go out as a stretcher-bearer to the front. He was put in charge of thirty stretcher-bearers and did his work magnificently in one of the most dangerous sectors of the front. A few days later we received a lorry to help us with our evacuation. It was a comparatively quiet day at the front, and Julian took out a party to fill in the dangerous shell-holes on our main evacuation road. He was killed that day, while setting out on one of his trips.

I know that his death was a heavy personal loss to all his friends; we, his comrades, can scarcely spare him in our work.

British Medical Unit,   Leonard Crome
        Spain

MARGOT HEINEMANN

'For R. J. C. (Summer, 1936)'*

from *New Writing*, Autumn 1937

No, not the sort of boy for whom one does
Find easily nicknames, Tommy and Bill,
Not a pleasant bass in the friendly buzz
Of voices we know well,
But not much changing where he goes
Divides talk coldly with the edge of will.

* R. J. C. is John Cornford

When he began, he talked too fast
To be heard well, and he knew too much.
He never had, though learned a little at last,
The sure, sincere and easy touch
On an audience: and his handsome head
Charmed no acquiescence: he convinced and led.

Any movement, going north or south,
Can find a place for charm and open shirts,
The sun-bright hair, the lovely mouth,
But needs as much the force that hurts
And rules our sapphire dreams.
For seeing visions on the evening sky
I can do tolerably well; but I
Can read no blue prints and erect no schemes.

They fear the meddling intellect,
Cold, gritty, loveless, cynical, pedantic—
Rightly, had he no work but to dissect
Romance and prove it unromantic,
Breaking the scenery with his conscious hands.
But we are working towards a richer season,
And mean to plough our lands
With this unfruitful reason.

Thought, which our masters cannot use,
Walks on the slag heaps, wags on broken wires
At the old pit head, hears no news.
Thought rakes the fires
That keep our furnaces at even heat.
Capricious as a starving flame
Frail inspiration flickered till he came
To give the fire a world to eat.

TOM WINTRINGHAM

'Monument'

from *Left Review*, October 1937

When from the deep sky
And digging in the harsh earth,
When by words hard as bullets,
Thoughts simple as death,
You have won victory,
People of Spain,
You will remember the free men who fought beside you, enduring and
    dying with you, the strangers
Whose breath was your breath.

You will pile into the deep sky
A tower of dried earth,
Rough as the walls where bullets
Splashed men to death
Before you won victory,
Before you freed Spain
From the eating gangrene of wealth, the grey pus of pride, the black
    scab of those strangers
Who were choking your breath.

Bring together, under the deep sky
Metal and earth;
Metal from which you made bullets
And weapons against death,
And earth in which, for victory,
Across all Spain,
Your blood and ours was mingled, Huesca to Malaga; earth to which
    your sons and strangers
Gave up the same breath.

Bring to the tower, to its building,
From New Castille,
From Madrid, the indomitable breast-work,
Earth of a flower-bed in the Casa del Campo,
Shell-splinters from University City,

Shell-casing from the Telephonica.
Bring from Old Castille, Santander, Segovia,
Sandbags of earth dug out of our parapets
And a false coin stamped in Burgos by a traitor.

Carry from Leon, from the province of Salamanca,
Where the bulls are brave and the retired generals cowards,
From near the Capital of treason and defeat, bring now
Clean earth, new and untouched, from the cold hills,
And iron from the gate, that shall now be always open
Of Spain's oldest school, where there shall be young wisdom.

From Extramadura, earth from the bullring
Where they shot the prisoners in Badajoz;
And lovely Zafra shall give one of its silver crosses;
Galicia, sea-sand and ship-rivets. From Asturias
Spoil from the pits that taught our dynamiters
To face and destroy the rearing tanks, and a pit-haft
That has cut coal and trenches, and is still fit for work.
From the Basque country, Bilbao, Guernica,
City of agony, villages of fire,
Take charred earth, so burnt and tortured no one
Knows if small children's bones are mingled in it;
Take iron ore from the mines those strangers envied;
And wash your hands, remembering a world that did so.

Navarre shall give a plough share and a rock;
Aragon, soil from the trench by the walnut-tree
Where Thaelmann's first group fought towards Huesca,
And steel from a wrecked car lying by a roadside;
Lukacsz rode in that car.
Catalonia, Spain and not Spain, and our gateway
(For myself a gateway to Spain and courage and love)
Shall bring a crankshaft from the Hispano factory
And earth from Durrutti's grave;
Valencia, black soft silt of the rice fields, mingled
With soil from an orange-grove—also
Telephone-wire, and a crane's chain.
Murcia, a surgeon's scalpel and red earth;
Andalucia, the vast south, shall pay
The barrel of a very old rifle found in the hills

Beside a skeleton; earth
That the olives grow from.
And Albacete, where we built our brigades:
Knife-steel and road-dust.

Take then these metals, under the deep sky
Melt them together; take these pieces of earth
And mix them; add your bullets
And memories of death:

You have won victory,
People of Spain,
And the tower into which your earth is built, and
   Your blood and ours, shall state Spain's
   Unity, happiness, strength; it shall face the breath
Of the east, of the dawn, of the future, when there will be no more
   strangers . . .

August 1937

ROY FULLER

'Poem
(For M. S., killed in Spain)'*

from *New Writing*, Spring 1938 (Fuller's *New And Collected Poems 1934–84* version is
retitled 'To M. S., killed in Spain')

Great cities, where disaster fell
In one small night on every house and man,
Knew how to rub the flesh from fable:
One crying O, his mouth a marble fountain;
In all preserving lava her thigh bones
At compass points, the west and east of love.

The necks bent looking for the geese,
Or over blocks gazing into freedom;

* M. S. is Roy Fuller's Communist friend Maurice Stott, described in Fuller's
Vamp Till Ready: Further Memoirs, 1982

The heads were all alike, short noses, brows
Folded above, the skin a leather brown;
The wrists were thick, the finger-pads worn down,
Oppression built itself in towering stone.

Now uncovered is the hero,
A tablet marks him where his life leaked out
Through grimy wounds and vapoured into air.
A rusty socket shows where in the night
He crammed his torch and kept by flame at bay
Dark, prowling wolves of thought that frightened him.

The poor outlasted rope and crucifix,
We break the bones that blenched through mastic gold.
We excavate our story, give a twist
To former endings in deliberate metre,
Whose subtle beat our fathers could not count,
Having their agile thumbs too far from fingers.

> I fear the plucking hand
> That from our equal season
> Sent you towards the spring
> But left me suavely wound
> In the cocoon of reason
> That preluded your wings.
>
> As the more supple fin
> Found use in crawling, so
> Some new and rapid nerve
> Brought close your flesh to brain,
> Transformed utopia
> To death for human love.
>
> And my existence must
> Finish through your trauma
> The speechless brute divorce
> Of heart from sculptured bust:
> Turn after five acts' drama
> A placid crumpled face.

I see my friend rising from the tomb,
His simple head swathed in a turban of white cloth.
The vault is spotted with a brownish moss,
One corner broken, fallen to the floor,
Whereon I read *Spain* as he advances like
An invalid, changed terribly with pain.

A quiet room holds him, half raised from the bed,
Eyes big and bright, a waxwork and the blood
Of waxworks running down his cheek. Two candles
Rock their light. The bed is moving, tilting,
And slips him rigidly to take a new position
The elbow sharp, the skin a yellow leaf.

The third time he stands against a summer country,
The chestnuts almost black in thunderous air,
The silver-green of willows lining dykes
Choked with flesh. He moves along the furrows
With gestured fingers, spreading death against
The imperishable elements of earth.

What is the meaning of these images?
The wish to leave natural objects richer,
To quicken the chemistry of earth, to be
Immortal in our children. Such desires
Are bodies in a pit, the rotting and bloody
Backwash of a tidal pestilence.

> Take it out, out of my back!
> The scalpel in my dream
> Has extended in a scythe,
> Is passing through the quick,
> Forcing like strychnine
> My body to its curve.

> Eyes open is not waking
> Nor the name and number
> Of distorted figures, and knowledge
> Of pain. It is the breaking
> Before we slumber
> Of the shaping image.

So from the nightmare, from
The death, the war of ghosts,
Those chosen to go unharmed
May join the tall city, the swan
Of changing thoughts
Set sailing by the doomed.

MILES TOMALIN

'Down the Road'

from *Volunteer for Liberty*, January 1940

My letter reached the girl on holiday,
She read it walking down a seaside lane
And felt, instead of me being far away
She walked with me in Spain.

Next walk I took, I fancied she was there,
'You don't hear birds,' I said. 'You may hear shells.
The one that misses us hits someone else,
And now and then it hits him fair and square.

'There's one beside the highway further on,
I saw it happen, and got a cursing too,
Because I told his pal the man was through.

'There wasn't anything he could have done.
Why, the man's blood was thickening on the ground,
The grey had reached his face, and when he spoke
There wasn't any sound.

'Death on an English country road seems huge,
One sight would spoil your holiday,' I said.
'But here one doesn't let one's feelings loose
Even when a man one knew and liked is dead.

'On murder, and all England makes a fuss;
God knows, one cigarette means more to us.
War's crude, oh sure.

But you can tell the smug ones over there
Another hair's breadth, it'll be the same
To walk in England as to walk in Spain.'

(Written in Spain, 1938)

RANDALL JARRELL

'A Poem for Someone Killed in Spain'

from *Blood for A Stranger*, 1942: *Collected Poems*, 1971

Though oars are breaking the breathless gaze
Of the summer's river, the head in the reeds
Has its own success; but time is brimming
From the locks in blood, and the finished heart

Gasps, 'I am breaking with joy—' and joy
Suffuses with its blood the difficult fields
Where the dogs are baying. 'I am not angry,'
Thinks the fox. Nor is death. And the leaves

Of the light summer are too new to joy
To think that their friend is dying, and their whispers
Are not patient but breathless, are passionate
With the songs of the world where no one dies.

JAMES BARKE

The Fight's On Now

from 'Spain: 1938' *The Land of the Leal*, 1939

Andrew was no politician, no profound or scholarly theoretician. But he knew and understood sufficient of the basic class division of society to give him clarity and knowledge, purpose and direction. And when he thought of the peoples of China, of the Abyssinians, the German workers and the Italians and, for the moment, the people of Spain, he felt he was supremely justified in the step he was taking. And he felt too for the first

time in his life that he could repay the debt he owed to his parents and
help as far as one man could to square their account with the Galloway
farmers, the Border laird, the Blackadder days and the horror of the city.

First he broke the news to Chrissie.

'If I get the chance, Chrissie, I'm going to Spain.'

'To Spain—to fight?'

'Yes: in the International Brigade.'

'Andy! you can't leave your mother.'

'There's only one way I can leave my mother, Chrissie—I was
wondering if it would be asking too much of you?'

'When did you make up your mind?'

'To-night—finally.'

'Finally?'

Andrew nodded solemnly.

'You've been fed up for a long time, Andy—I was beginning to wonder
if I had anything to do with it?'

'You know you haven't, Chrissie. But you're right enough about being
fed up. I just wonder if you really understand, Chrissie—it's difficult for
me to explain it. What have I—what have we to live for? Sometimes I
think I would have liked to have been married and to have had
children—but only sometimes. When I think of the mess the world's in
and the financial mess we've been in, I'm glad I haven't. But I can't go on
living like this—not any more. What's in front of us—supposing—and
it's a mighty big supposition—that this system drags on the way it's been
doing? Mother'll die—one of these days—and you and me will be left.
What for? Just to get old and done—and die. But there isn't going to be
any chance of that—we're going to get it in the neck—war, bombing
planes, industrial conscription—but hell anyway we look at it. Well, I'm
not waiting for that. I'm not waiting for anything. The fight's on now—in
Spain—in China—in Czechoslovakia. You understand this as well as I
do. Well, I'm going out to Spain—if they'll have me. If we win there we'll
turn the scales of the whole international situation—we'll be able to start
taking the offensive all along the line. And the Spanish people have got to
win—their fight is our fight. You do understand, don't you, Chrissie?'

.   .   .   .   .

'To-day, where do we stand as Christians?

'We find ourselves at the most crucial turning-point in the world's
history. Everywhere we find the forces of Darkness assuming the
offensive—issuing a life and death challenge to Christianity. Everywhere we find bestial cruelty, hatred, murder, war, torture, envy, greed

and malice. Falsehood is enthroned and deified. The horror of the Appian Way pales to insignificance before the paths of Fascist glory paved with the mangled bodies of little children.

'The pulpit of the Christian Church must never be allowed to become a political rostrum—only too often in the past has it been allowed to become so. Many of you have been perturbed, at times, because you have felt that I have expressed myself of political views. Of course I have political views—the only political views I think a Christian can have. But when I speak to you from the pulpit, I speak to you as a Christian, as a minister of the Gospel, thinking nothing of politics or political parties.

'But I want to make a very special appeal to you this morning.

'I have said that humanity is at the most crucial stage of its history. To-day Christianity is challenged from every side. Can we meet the challenge? Not always, I am afraid. When I visit certain houses in the parish I meet young men and women whose parents are members of this church and they ask me what the Church is doing about Austria, about Czechoslovakia, about China, about Spain.

'And what can I answer? For what is the Church doing about the troubles that beset civilisation? What are you individual Christian men and women doing to relieve the distress and suffering in the world? But this is an old cry. Young people raised the same question during the First World War—and many of them have been lost to the Church since.

'But to-day the situation is much more serious. The whole structure of our civilisation is threatened with destruction. There are nations in Europe to-day that are not only denouncing Jesus Christ because He was a Jew—they are denouncing Christ and Christianity because of Christ's teaching. They are revising the Ten Commandments and re-writing the Sermon on the Mount, they are reviving pagan gods, glorifying murder and torture, they are preparing to drown the last two thousand years in a welter of blood. This evil in the world to-day is the evil of Fascism whose objective is the inauguration of barbarism and violent brute force.

'I appeal to you, in the name of Christ Jesus, to stand together and face this evil, to grapple with it boldly and firmly, to resolve that we would prefer the martyrs' grave rather than deny Christ in this the testing day of our faith.

'Who is on the Lord's side? We must make our decision. I appeal to you, whatever your political beliefs, whether you may be a Conservative like the Duchess of Atholl or a Communist like William Gallacher; a Liberal like Sir Archibald Sinclair or a Labourite like Major Attlee: I appeal to you as Christian men and women to declare that you are for Christ and for all that Christ stands for.

'And let your voices sound as with the sound of trumpets. Gird up your loins and prepare to give battle to the Philistines of Fascism.

'We Scots know what it is to fight for our faith. Our Covenanting forefathers preached the Word with the Bible in one hand and the pistol in the other: nothing could intimidate them. You must remember with pride and glory how in our own parish our Christian forefathers preferred to be rolled down Garran Hill in spiked barrels rather than deny their faith.

'But there is no need, as yet, for you to face the alternative of the spiked barrel. If only every Christian man and woman will unite, sinking all their secular differences in the name of Christ, the Powers of Darkness in the world to-day can be vanquished and overcome and the Light of Christ's Love made to shine again upon the world.

'Bernard Shaw once suggested an epitaph for the Norwegian dramatist Henrik Ibsen. "I come not to call sinners but the righteous to repentance." I call upon you, as Christians, to realise your duty to Christ.

'I began this morning by telling you how Christ was crucified. But to-day the Calvaries darken the sun and Christ is re-crucified ten thousand times.

'And finally I appeal to you in the name of the little children. You may think this is a sentimental plea. If so, then Christ's plea to suffer the children to come unto Him was also sentimental. In Spain and in China, mothers and children are being systematically bombed to death. This deliberate and wholesale destruction of the innocents is something new and terrible in war. The most primitive, the most elementary principles of all religions condemn it. Then how can we professed followers of Christ keep silent?

'Above and beyond all the peoples of the world, we Christians cannot keep silent. Our faith is the highest expression of the human soul and the love of God. How then can we be worthy of our faith if we remain silent and inactive in the face of such horror and barbarity?

'But the expression of sentiments, however pious and noble, cannot avail us. We must have a practical plan of action.

'First we must unite. And our unity must be no narrow unity. We must join with every man and woman of goodwill. And we must give a lead and show an example to those thousands outside the Church who abhor all bloodshed and violence and cruelty as much as we do. We must prove to the world that in us the spirit of the Christian martyr is not dead; we must prove to the world that Christianity is the one supreme force in the world to-day that can save the world from itself. And above all we must prove ourselves in Christ.

'If we fail in this we fail in Christ and there is nothing for us but the darkness of the bottomless pit where the light of the Word may be taken from us.

'There is no middle course. He who is not for us is against us.

'And having achieved unity our voices must penetrate every legislative assembly in the world. Our voices must be raised for Peace, for Justice, for Equality, for Human Decency.'

Jock MacKelvie smiled grimly. Ramsay was making his points well: backed by his sincerity they were obviously getting across. Without that sincerity and the likeable personality of the speaker they would have sounded pretty trite. But he marvelled at Tom's naïve idealism. Obviously he had a long way to go.

The Church still had considerable influence among a section of the people—but he doubted if it was a decisive, or could ever become a decisive influence. The essential spirit of Christianity had rotted away from men's minds—it had no more validity than a dead language. People just didn't believe in the reality of Jesus Christ or of Christ's teaching. Yes, once upon a time men had believed and on the strength of their belief had been prepared to die—and to die painfully. But not now. It would be difficult to find a Christian prepared to risk his skull under a policeman's baton for Jesus Christ—or even to pay an extra penny on the rates. They were a pretty poor bunch. And yet there must be many of them who were prepared to make a stand for the decent things in their religion *because they were the decent things of life.* Yes: if Ramsay could rouse them to a realisation of the dangers that confronted them—if he could awaken their fundamental sense of decency and fairplay. But it would take a bit of doing—would be much worse than trying to rouse the Labour Party. And of course the machine would crush Ramsay if he went too far. The Church machine could be pretty ruthless and effective when it liked. And then there was always the chance that Ramsay would find his philosophical feet. If he did he was the type that would drop the Church without the slighest hesitation. Still, honour where honour was due: Ramsay was a splendid type of fellow and he was doing admirable and heroic work. If he followed up a sermon like this by judicious day-to-day work among the better types in his congregation, he could build up a powerful nucleus for Peace and create the basis of an anti-Fascist movement. And they would need to move for there wasn't such a lot of time to play about in.

'I had a brother. He was not a Christian. He claimed that he was an atheist and a Socialist . . . he denied God and he denied Christ . . . He was in the prime of his life . . . in love with a beautiful and sweet-natured woman. He married that woman and went out to Spain to fight not only for the Spanish people, not only for the defenceless women and children of Spain, but in order that the women and children of Britain might be saved from the horrors of Fascism and open-town bombing. And he hadn't been fighting a week till he was killed.

'I do not mention this to harrow your feelings or to create any sympathy for myself. I mention it so that his example and the example of many hundreds like him may act as a challenge. For such examples of glorious heroism and self-sacrifice must either put us to shame or spur us on to even greater heroism.

'There is no time to lose. Too late, too late may be our cry: and by then it will be too late.

'I refuse to believe that mankind has struggled through the ages, across the plains of time, in order to fulfil a destiny that would shame the most ferocious beasts of brute creation.

'God is not mocked.

'Let us raise high the Cross of Jesus and march before it unto victory, with the blessing of God and the strength of our strong right arm. There is no Evil, no Darkness that can stand against us if we ask His blessing and invoke His aid.'

LEWIS JONES

With the People Till the Last

from 'A Letter from Spain,' *We Live*, 1939

Mary called the Party committee together the following night to make arrangements for the welcome home. There was a full attendance at the meeting, every member alert with subdued excitement. It was decided to organise a demonstration and a mass welcome meeting in the new workmen's hall. Mary agreed to ask the women of the Co-operative and other Guilds to make banners for street decorations. Another Party member, who was also in the town band, stated he knew the latter would turn out in full strength. Harry Morgan, as chairman of the combine, raised the matter in that body, and it agreed to approach all the other organisations in Cwmardy to take part in the welcome home. As a result of all these efforts, a joint committee was formed to take charge of the complete organisation for the day.

Posters were exhibited in the shop windows, leaflets distributed to the houses, and preliminary meetings held in every street. The hall was decorated with red streamers, banners, special Spain prints, and *Daily Worker* posters. The lights were covered with delicate silk so that when they were switched on the whole hall glowed a deep crimson.

Artists belonging to the Party were commissioned to make large canvas paintings of the men who had left Cwmardy for Spain. When these were completed they were fixed on the red plush curtain that backed the stage. Len's wavy hair and big eyes occupied the centre. His picture was painted from a photograph he had taken on one of the marches, and his face looked longer than it actually was in real life.

The intervening days passed like dreams to the members of the Party and the organising committee, but at last the day arrived. The town band was ready to play the battle-hymns of the people. Women had hung banners of every description from their windows and spread long streamers of bunting across the streets, until Cwmardy looked like a lake of waving fire.

The schools were empty of children, all of whom anxiously awaited the street teas that had been organised for them by levies on the wages of the workmen and donations from the Co-operative Society and other organisations.

The men in the pits had already agreed to remain home for the event as a reply to a letter sent to Mary by the chief of police banning any demonstration through the main street.

The people in each street followed the example of Sunny Bank during the unemployed demonstrations, and marched as street contingents, converging on a common point for the mass demonstration through Cwmardy. The police realised it would be impossible to execute their threat and made no attempt to provoke the people.

Long before the train was due the approaches to the railway station were crammed with demonstrators. Most of them heard the train steam in, but very few saw what happened after, until an insistent blare from a motor car urged them to open the ranks for the procession of three cars. The first contained the returned soldiers, with Mary among them. Officials of the committee occupied the other two. The ranks reformed immediately the cars had passed and by the time the latter had reached the Square, they were at the head of a densely packed mile-long stream of people.

The occupants of the cars got out on the Square, the waiting bandsmen formed up before them, the returned soldiers were lifted on unknown shoulders, and, to the deep throb of drums, the march up the hill started.

Mary never knew how the old couple got there, but when her blazing eyes looked round they saw Jim and Shân right behind, the latter waving her arms and shouting at the top of her voice though no one could possibly hear what she said in the deafening tumult that was part of the demonstration.

Mary's heart twitched at the sight and it gave her greater strength to go on, her feet hardly touching the earth till they reached the hall. She managed to get inside, Jim and Shân still following. Those who could not enter were catered for by loud-speakers, which relayed to them every word said in the hall.

Harry Morgan, Mary, Len's parents, and officials of the organising committee surrounded the soldiers on the stage. Harry, who had been elected in charge, beckoned the brigaders to the front, where they stood for many shy minutes listening to the roars of welcome that greeted them back to Cwmardy.

When some measure of order had been restored, Harry called upon them all to sing the Red Flag. The request was heard by the band outside, who immediately struck up the initial chords, which were followed by the massed voices of the people.

When the mighty intonations died down Harry began his speech of welcome. Mary leaned forward, elbow on knee and chin in her hand, the better to follow the proceedings. The faces before her were melted into a huge grey blob framed by the red of the decorations. She heard Harry's piercing voice cut the air with 'Comrades and Friends,' then felt a nudge. She looked around and saw one of the soldiers beckoning her with his finger. Bending back to hear what he wanted, she noticed subconsciously that he carefully avoided her eyes as he handed her a packet.

'This is from Len, Mary, and there's one from me as well. I thought I might just as well bring it with me, since I wrote it.'

The conversation was carried on in a whisper and as soon as he had finished the messenger sat back and fixed his attention on the meeting.

Mary didn't know what to do for some minutes. Her heart was beating into her ribs with an intensity that added to the glow on her cheeks. She felt it would be a sort of sacrilege to read the letters while the speakers were on their feet and before all the eyes in the hall.

Yet all the time she hesitated her whole being demanded that she read them quickly. Her body began to tremble with excitement and, unable to contain herself any longer, she rose quietly and tip-toed off the stage into one of the ante-rooms behind.

This was in darkness, but the many Party meetings held there had taught her where to find the switch. After a little groping she pressed it, and in a moment the room was filled with a glaring light that hurt her eyes after the subdued crimson of the big hall. She paused to ease the quiver of her flesh, all the time looking with intense concentration at the packet in her hand. She was burning to open it, but reluctant to start doing so. At last she pulled herself together and with a haste that made her fingers clumsy tore open the covering and found two mud-stained letters inside.

She recognised Len's writing at a glance and a pathetic half-smile flickered on her face as she remembered the occasions she had twitted him about his terrible scrawl. She pulled the letter from its envelope and began reading to herself. But in a short time her lips began to move, and she read on half aloud.

Dear Mary and All at Home,

I don't know when you had my last letter because postal arrangements are rather wonky, so I'm giving this to one of the boys to make sure that you'll get it, as it looks like he'll be coming home shortly. Well, Mary, I hope everyone at home is O K and that the Party comrades are putting their backs into the campaign to help Spain and save democracy.

Obviously I can't tell you much of what is taking place here, but I have been in this hospital for the last few weeks (just a little scratch) and am going back into the line tomorrow. You will be happy to know Ron is here with me. He was one of the first to come out and has made a name for himself as a fighter and a leader. You can just imagine that the two of us stick together as much as possible. He hasn't changed much since the old days, except that he is perhaps a bit thinner. We are gaining the upper hand now and are beginning a new offensive, of which I am glad.

It's marvellous to see how our boys go into action. You know them all and will remember how they were on the demonstrations and marches, but that is nothing to the way they act out here. It makes me proud of our people and of myself for belonging to them.

But it's strange, Mary (or is it?), that while there are certain differences I could swear sometimes I was still in Cwmardy and that the Fascists are not far away in a strange land, but are actually destroying our birth-place and all it means to us. The men who are dying don't seem to be strangers, but our comrades as we know them at home. The same old hills are somewhere around here, and I know the same old smoke-stack and pit is not far away. The faces I see about me are the same faces as those in Cwmardy. It is only when they speak that I notice any difference.

Yes, my comrade, this is not a foreign land on which we are fighting. It is home. Those are not strangers who are dying. They are our butties. It is not a war only of nation against nation, but of progress against reaction, and I glory in the fact that Cwmardy has its sons upon the battle-field, fighting here as they used to fight on the Square, the only difference being that we now have guns instead of sticks.

Yes, Mary my love. And to-morrow I am happy to go back to them. All our lives we have been together. In our homes, the pit, the streets, the Federation, and the Party. The strikes and demonstrations and marches have led us unerringly to this, the battle-field of democracy.

It is in the nature of things that we can't all come back to Cwmardy, that some of us will be left here with, perhaps, a cross to mark the fact we were once living, but were robbed of life by Fascism.

Yes, that is inevitable, as it is at home that after every action in defence of our rights they stick some of us to rot in prison.

Some of the boys we knew have already gone, but not in vain. They have helped to stamp into the earth an invisible barrier of bodies from which breathes a new spirit of hope and love and invincible courage. Fascism may kill us, Mary, but it can never kill what we die for. No, never! Our very death is creation, our destruction new life and energy and action.

I know, my love, that you appreciate all the possibilities and that whatever happens to me you will carry on building the Party, drawing our masses into a unity that will save Cwmardy for the people. Even as I write I know that you are near and I can almost feel your breath upon my neck as you bend over to read this. I know every throb of that wonderful heart that is too big for your little body.

It seems so long since I touched you with my hands, but I see you in every battle; you are at my side in every action. Remember the day we marched together in the big demonstration, Mary? Well, like that. You are with me wherever I go, whatever I do. And never forget, whatever happens, we were brought together because we belong to the people and it is only the cause of our people can ever part us.

If that should happen, if it becomes necessary, then don't grieve too much, because belonging to the people, you will always find me in the people. Give my love to all the comrades at home. Throw your whole weight into the Party. Tell mam and dad not to worry about me. Sleep happy in the knowledge that our lives have been class lives, and our love something buried so deep in the Party that it can never die.

So-long, Mary, my comrade and love,
Len

A roar of cheering swept from the hall into the little room and Mary raised her head to see what was the matter, but the lights glistening on the tears that filled her eyes blinded her to everything. She felt there was something within her that wanted to escape. It seemed to clog her body and make it hard to breathe. She lifted her hand slowly to the pocket on the left breast of her coat and drew out the red silk handkerchief with its emblazoned hammer and sickle which had been Len's gift to her from Spain. She looked at it dazedly and saw it dancing in her tears.

Equally slowly and methodically she raised it to her eyes and wiped them, then getting a sudden grip on herself she read the letter again before picking up the other.

It felt heavy as lead in her hand as she opened it. Her eyes fixed instantly on one sentence that stood out before her like a neon sign.

We found him lying among a group of Fascists and brought him away from them to bury him with his own people. He had been with them all his life and we left him with them in death.

Mary read this over and over. She could not tear her gaze away from it until something gripped her by the throat and she could not breathe. She sprang to her feet and the grip was released. When she ran headlong from the room she left a moan behind: 'Oh, Len. You are gone for ever.'

She was on the stage before she knew it and the immediate deep silence that followed her entry brought her to a dead stop. Looking around like a woman in a trance, she saw the blur of faces before her, then the weeping form of Shân with Jim pathetically stroking her hair, nearby.

In a flash she knew that the people had been told that Len was dead and she turned her head to see his portrait stand out among the others with its draping of black cloth. Someone caught her arm and led her to a chair near the table, on which she bent her head. When she raised it again the hall was nearly empty and Shân, red-eyed and heaving, was standing near her, with Jim, who kept swallowing hard all the time.

'Come, Mary fach. Our Len have left us for ever, and this is no place for us. Let us go home.'

Mary looked again at the painting and fancied she saw the lips form into a smile and the sad eyes soften with encouragement.

She stared at it for some moments and the feeling grew on her that Len was saying: 'Go, Mary. Follow the people, they are your hope and strength.'

Jumping up, she caught Shân about the shoulders. 'You go home, mam. I can't come yet; the people's day isn't over and I must be with them till the last, as our Len was.'

Shân straightened her body. 'Us will go, Mary, when you come and not before.'

They followed the last figures through the hall doors and found the demonstration getting further away every minute, the smoke from the pit curling round it before dissolving into the air and leaving the scarlet banner dominating the scene. They heard the barely audible strains of the band, and the people singing:

> Then away with all your superstitions,
> Servile masses, arise! Arise!

Mary started to run. 'I must go before they get too far,' she muttered.

Jim and Shân slowly followed, the former shouting, 'Go on, Mary fach. Me and Shân is not quite so quick, but us will be with you at the end.'

Mary stumbled, but kept on her feet. She began mumbling to herself: 'I must catch them up. I must catch them up.' When she reached the tail of the demonstration she thought the beats of her heart were centred in her throat and stumbled again. This time she would have fallen, but eager hands caught her and a cry ran through the ranks towards the front: 'Send the car back. Send a car back.' When it came they placed Mary gently inside and sent it back again to the head of the march.

Jim and Shân limped far behind. He put his arm about her waist. 'Us can never keep step with 'em, Shân fach. Us have got too old. Yes, too old. But never mind, my gel; they have got to come back sooner or later before they can get home, then us can join 'em again.'

Shân halted to get breath. Floating towards them came the voices of the people muted in a common unity:

> Though cowards flinch and traitors sneer,
> We'll keep the red flag flying here.

I REMEMBER SPAIN

LOUIS MACNEICE
And I Remember Spain

from *Autumn Journal*, 1939; *Collected Poems*, 1949

And I remember Spain
　　At Easter ripe as an egg for revolt and ruin
Though for a tripper the rain
　　Was worse than the surly or the worried or the haunted faces
With writing on the walls—
　　Hammer and sickle, Boicot, Viva, Muerra;

With café-au-lait brimming the waterfalls,
　　With sherry, shellfish, omelettes.
With fretted stone the Moor
　　Had chiselled for effects of sun and shadow;
With shadows of the poor,
　　The begging cripples and the children begging.
The churches full of saints
　　Tortured on racks of marble—
The old complaints
　　Covered with gilt and dimly lit with candles.
With powerful or banal
　　Monuments of riches or repression
And the Escorial
　　Cold for ever within like the heart of Philip.
With ranks of dominoes
　　Deployed on café tables the whole of Sunday
With cabarets that call the tourist, shows
　　Of thighs and eyes and nipples.
With slovenly soldiers, nuns,
　　And peeling posters from the last elections

Promising bread or guns
    Or an amnesty or another
Order or else the old
    Glory veneered and varnished
As if veneer could hold
    The rotten guts and crumbled bones together.
And a vulture hung in air
    Below the cliffs of Ronda and below him
His book-winged shadow wavered like despair
    Across the chequered vineyards.
And the boot-blacks in Madrid
    Kept us half an hour with polish and pincers
And all we did
    In that city was drink and think and loiter.
And in the Prado half-
    wit princes looked from the canvas they had paid for
(Goya had the laugh—
    But can what is corrupt be cured by laughter?)
And the day at Aranjuez
    When the sun came out for once on the yellow river
With Valdepeñas burdening the breath
    We slept a royal sleep in the royal gardens;
And at Toledo walked
    Around the ramparts where they throw the garbage
And glibly talked
    Of how the Spaniards lack all sense of business.
And Avila was cold
    And Segovia was picturesque and smelly
And a goat on the road seemed old
    As the rocks or the Roman arches.
And Easter was wet and full
    In Seville and in the ring on Easter Sunday
A clumsy bull and then a clumsy bull
    Nodding his banderillas died of boredom.
And the standard of living was low
    But that, we thought to ourselves, was not our business;
All that the tripper wants is the *status quo*
    Cut and dried for trippers.
And we thought the papers a lark
    With their party politics and blank invective;
And we thought the dark

Women who dyed their hair should have it dyed more often.
And we sat in trains all night
　　With the windows shut among civil guards and peasants
And tried to play piquet by a tiny light
　　And tried to sleep bolt upright;
And cursed the Spanish rain
　　And cursed their cigarettes which came to pieces
And caught heavy colds in Cordova and in vain
　　Waited for the right light for taking photos.
And we met a Cambridge don who said with an air
　　'There's going to be trouble shortly in this country',
And ordered anis, pudgy and debonair,
　　Glad to show off his mastery of the language.
But only an inch behind

　　This map of olive and ilex, this painted hoarding,
Careless of visitors the people's mind
　　Was tunnelling like a mole to day and danger.
And the day before we left
　　We saw the mob in flower at Algeciras
Outside a toothless door, a church bereft
　　Of its images and its aura.
And at La Linea while
　　The night put miles between us and Gibraltar
We heard the blood-lust of a drunkard pile
　　His heaven high with curses;
And next day took the boat
　　For home, forgetting Spain, not realising
That Spain would soon denote
　　Our grief, our aspirations;
Not knowing that our blunt
　　Ideals would find their whetstone, that our spirit
Would find its frontier on the Spanish front,
　　Its body in a rag-tag army.

STEPHEN SPENDER

'Fall of a City'

from *Collected Poems*, 1955

All the posters on the walls,
All the leaflets in the streets
Are mutilated, destroyed, or run in rain,
Their words blotted out with tears,
Skins peeling from their bodies
In the victorious hurricane.

All the names of heroes in the hall
Where the feet thundered and the bronze throats roared
FOX and LORCA claimed as history on the walls,
Are now furiously deleted
Or to dust surrender their gold
From praise excluded.

All the badges and salutes
Torn from lapels and from hands,
Are thrown away with human sacks they wore,
Or in the deepest bed of mind
They are washed over with a smile
Which launches the victors where they win.

All the lessons learned, unlearnt;
The young, who learned to read, now blind
Their eyes with an archaic film;
The peasant relapses to a stumbling tune
Following the donkey's bray;
These only remember to forget.

But somewhere some word presses
In the high door of a skull, and in some corner
Of an irrefrangible eye
Some old man's memory jumps to a child
—Spark from the days of liberty.
And the child hoards it like a bitter toy.

LOUIS MACNEICE
'Today in Barcelona'

from the *Spectator*, 20 January 1939

I was in Barcelona from December 29th till January 9th. The most surprising things I saw were on January 9th—in Toulouse, where I landed by 'plane from Spain: food in the shops and on stalls in the streets, drink in the cafés, well-clad people, the street-lamps lit. It only takes one ten days to find these things surprising.

I had arrived in Barcelona after dark, the streets like limbo but crowded. A feeling of thousands of people circulating round one in the night. That is one thing there is plenty of here—human beings; two and a half millions now against one million before. These people's lives have become very much simplified and assimilated to one another; the topics of conversation are few and universal, money has lost its diversifying force, and everyone, one feels, is by necessity in the same boat. For this reason one feels very much at home in the dark streets of Barcelona. There may be bitter dissensions among the politicians, but the people in the streets, one feels, have become a family party—or, if you prefer it, are in on the same racket—united by material necessities, by hunger, by the fear of sudden death which enhances the values of life. I have never been anywhere where these values were so patent. It would be difficult to be a Hamlet in Barcelona.

The shops are ghosts of shops, only open in the morning, the counters and shelves bare, one object every two yards. The cafés are ghosts of cafés—no coffee, beer, spirits or wine, people making do with coloured water which is called lemonade or with terribly degraded vermouth (yet in one café there was a string quartet). They close at nine and the chairs are piled on the tables. But the people, though thin and often ill, are far from being ghosts of people. Facts in a city at war are necessarily uncertain; how can one know the truth about the Front or unravel the paradoxical knots of Spanish party politics or sort out truth from propaganda? One fact, however, is as clear—and as refreshing—as daylight: the extraordinary morale of these people—their courage, good-humour and generosity.

Their strength, of course, can also be their weakness. Optimism on the Government side has already meant several gains for Franco. Again, while a people must obviously adapt themselves to war conditions, it does not seem altogether desirable that war should become quite so much a habit as it has in Barcelona; one feels the people have almost forgotten about peace and might not know what to do with it if it came. Yet without this confidence and this adaptation to circumstances, Barcelona no doubt would have already given way to Goliath. Her people are essentially non-defeatist; no one this New Year admitted for a moment that Franco's present offensive might succeed. I saw a new *comedor* for children in an industrial district, which is being converted from a theatre and adjacent cinema.

In this, once the great city of cafés and taxis, you now have to get about by walking. And instead of cocktails and seven-course meals there are food-queues, rationing of acorns, a ladleful of lentils for dinner. By ordinary people food cannot be bought though it can be obtained by barter: soap, flints and tobacco are among the best currencies. (I am told that Arabs come into the port and sell soap at 250 pesetas a kilo.) In my hotel (where the bombing commissions stay) we had a privileged access to food—at fancy prices: a dish of chickpeas at 30 to 40 pesetas, horse and chopped swedes at 45, fried sprats (a very rare delicacy) at 60. (A superintendent of a *comedor* gets 400 pesetas a month salary.) People's rations at the moment (they are always decreasing) are as follows: —Bread: 150 grammes per day except on Sundays. Chickpeas (100 gr.) and peas (50) on one ticket, but you only get these once a week or maybe once a month. Oil: ¼ litre, but they have had none now for three months and then it was like machine oil. They have had no fish on ration tickets for two months, no meat for one month. Those who, instead of having ration-cards go to the *comedores*, seem to me to be better off, because as any rate they know what they will get. And the children are considered first; for all that their diet is causing a vast increase in rickets and in skin diseases such as scabies. I should add that the people who work in the *comedores* seem invariably good humoured, kindly and strictly conscientious.

In these extremities statistics are more important than impressions, but here are some snippets from my visit. *The crowing of cocks*: most characteristic sound in Barcelona (as if you were to hear cocks in Piccadilly). Lots of people keep hens or rabbits on their window balconies. *Lack of tobacco*: to give a man a cigarette is to give him the Kingdom of Heaven; I gave a Spaniard three cigarettes one night, and next day he sent me in return a hunk of dry bread wrapped in paper. *Refugee colonies*: often in converted convents, beds in the gloom under towering Gothic arches, old women with eye diseases making jokes about Mr Chamberlain, the children doing eurhythmics. *Schools*: shortage of teachers, but the children clean (though washed in cold water) and happy, the walls often decorated with figures from Walt Disney—the Big Bad Wolf representing Fascism—or with Popeye the Sailor knocking Mussolini for a loop. All the children seem to be natural artists; in some schools they still print their own poems and lino-cuts.

Air raids: The siren is like the voice of a lost soul, but the anti-aircraft defence is beautiful both to hear and to see—balls of cottonwool floating high in the blue day, or white flashes at night. The searchlights also are beautiful, and the red tracer bullets floating in chains gently, almost ineptly, upwards like decorations at a fair. After the raid on the centre on New Year's Eve the streets were heaped with powdered glass, and crowds collected to look at a spatter of black blood-spots fifteen feet high on a wall. During an alarm in Tarragona four girls romped down the square with their arms round each other's necks. *Ruins*: near the cathedral a house six stories high, its face and floors torn away; on the top story a plate-rack fixed to the wall with all its plates unbroken and a shelf with two unbroken bottles. The district to the side of the port, Barceloneta, has been evacuated; all the streets are rubble, and all the houses like skulls. *Irony*: the Banco de Vizcaya still announces stock market prices for July 17th, 1936, and the chemists sell cures for obesity. *Recreation*: every Friday afternoon a crack orchestral concert, well attended, in the enormous Teatro di Liceo; the theatres and cinemas all running; a newsreel showing a fashionable dog show in Moscow. And people still playing pelota. But the Zoo is macabre—a polar bear 99 per cent dead, a kangaroo eating dead leaves.

In the Barcelona air-port I met an American seaman, an ex-member of the International Brigade, short, square and tough, with a face like a gangster. On his lapel he wore the insignia of all the Government parties—to create good feeling, he said. He expressed the greatest admiration for the Spaniards—even, in spite of what some people say, as soldiers. I shared his admiration and, as I flew down from the Pyrenees to a country where money still goes, I felt that my descent into this respectable landscape was not only a descent in metres but also a step down in the world.

GEORGE ORWELL

In My Memory I Live Over

from *Homage to Catalonia*, 1938

When we went on leave I had been a hundred and fifteen days in the line, and at the time this period seemed to me to have been one of the most futile of my whole life. I had joined the militia in order to fight against Fascism, and as yet I had scarcely fought at all, had merely existed as a sort of passive object, doing nothing in return for my rations except to suffer from cold and lack of sleep. Perhaps that is the fate of most soldiers in most wars. But now that I can see this period in perspective I do not altogether regret it. I wish, indeed, that I could have served the Spanish Government a little more effectively; but from a personal point of view—from the point of view of my own development—those first three or four months that I spent in the line were less futile than I then thought. They formed a kind of interregnum in my life, quite different from anything that had gone before and perhaps from anything that is to come, and they taught me things that I could not have learned in any other way.

The essential point is that all this time I had been isolated—for at the front one was almost completely isolated from the outside world: even of what was happening in Barcelona one had only a dim conception —among people who could roughly but not too inaccurately be described as revolutionaries. This was the result of the militia-system, which on the Aragon front was not radically altered till about June 1937. The workers' militias, based on the trade unions and each composed of people of approximately the same political opinions, had the effect of canalizing into one place all the most revolutionary sentiment in the country. I had dropped more or less by chance into the only community of any size in Western Europe where political consciousness and disbelief in capitalism were more normal than their opposites. Up here in Aragon one was among tens of thousands of people, mainly though not entirely of working-class origin, all living at the same level and mingling on terms of equality. In theory it was perfect equality, and even in practice it was not far from it. There is a sense in which it would be true to say that one was experiencing a foretaste of Socialism, by which I mean that the prevailing mental atmosphere was that of Socialism. Many of the normal motives of civilized life—snobbishness, money-grubbing, fear of the boss, etc.—had simply ceased to exist. The ordinary class-division of society had disappeared to an extent that is almost unthinkable in the money-tainted air of England; there was no one there except the peasants and ourselves, and no one owned anyone else as his master. Of course such a state of affairs could not last. It was simply a temporary and local phase in an enormous game that is being played over the whole surface of the earth. But it lasted long enough to have its effect upon anyone who experienced it. However much one cursed at the time, one realized afterwards that one had been in contact with something strange and valuable. One had been in a community where hope was more normal than apathy or cynicism, where the word 'comrade' stood for comradeship and not, as in most countries, for humbug. One had breathed the air of equality. I am well aware that it is now the fashion to deny that Socialism has anything to do with equality. In every country in the world a huge tribe of party-hacks and sleek little professors are busy 'proving' that Socialism means no more than a planned state-capitalism with the grab-motive left intact. But fortunately there also exists a vision of Socialism quite different from this. The thing that attracts ordinary men to Socialism and makes them willing to risk their skins for it, the 'mystique' of Socialism, is the idea of equality; to the vast majority of people Socialism means a classless society, or it means nothing at all. And it was here that those few months in the militia were valuable to me. For the Spanish militias, while they lasted, were a sort of microcosm of a classless society. In that community where no one was on the make, where there was a shortage of everything but no privilege and no boot-licking, one got, perhaps, a crude forecast of what the opening stages of Socialism might be like. And, after all, instead of disillusioning me it deeply attracted me. The effect was to make my desire to see Socialism established much more actual than it had been before. Partly, perhaps, this was due to the good luck of being among Spaniards, who, with their innate decency and their ever-present Anarchist tinge, would make even the opening stages of Socialism tolerable if they had the chance.

Of course at the time I was hardly conscious of the changes that were occurring in my own mind. Like everyone about me I was chiefly conscious of boredom, heat, cold, dirt, lice, privation, and occasional danger. It is quite different now. This period which then seemed so futile and eventless is now of great importance to me. It is so different from the rest of my life that already it has taken on the magic quality which, as a rule, belongs only to memories that are years old. It was beastly while it was happening, but it is a good patch for my mind to browse upon. I wish I could convey to you the atmosphere of that time. I hope I have done so, a little, in the earlier chapters of this book. It is all bound up in my mind with the winter cold, the ragged uniforms of militiamen, the oval Spanish faces, the morse-like tapping of machine-guns, the smells of urine and rotting bread, the tinny taste of bean-stews wolfed hurriedly out of unclean pannikins.

The whole period stays by me with curious vividness. In my memory I live over incidents that might seem too petty to be worth recalling. I am in the dug-out at Monte Pocero again, on the ledge of limestone that serves as a bed, and young Ramón is snoring with his nose flattened between my shoulder-blades. I am stumbling up the mucky trench, through the mist that swirls round me like cold steam. I am half-way up a crack in the mountain-side, struggling to keep my balance and to tug a root of wild rosemary out of the ground. High overhead some meaningless bullets are singing.

I am lying hidden among small fir-trees on the low ground west of Monte Oscuro, with Kopp and Bob Edwards and three Spaniards. Up the naked grey hill to the right of us a string of Fascists are climbing like ants. Close in front a bugle-call rings out from the Fascist lines. Kopp catches my eye and, with a schoolboy gesture, thumbs his nose at the sound.

I am in the mucky yard at La Granja, among the mob of men who are struggling with their tin pannikins round the cauldron of stew. The fat and harassed cook is warding them off with the ladle. At a table nearby a bearded man with a huge automatic pistol strapped to his belt is hewing loaves of bread into five pieces. Behind me a Cockney voice (Bill Chambers, with whom I quarrelled bitterly and who was afterwards killed outside Huesca) is singing:

> There are rats, rats,
> Rats as big as cats,
> In the . . .

A shell comes screaming over. Children of fifteen fling themselves on their faces. The cook dodges behind the cauldron. Everyone rises with a sheepish expression as the shell plunges and booms a hundred yards away.

I am walking up and down the line of sentries, under the dark boughs of the poplars. In the flooded ditch outside the rats are paddling about, making as much noise as otters. As the yellow dawn comes up behind us, the Andalusian sentry, muffled in his cloak, begins singing. Across no man's land, a hundred or two hundred yards away, you can hear the Fascist sentry also singing.

ESMOND ROMILLY

The World Does Not Stop

from *Boadilla*, 1937

There were speeches when we said good-bye to return to Albacete, Valencia, Barcelona and England. Commander Rickard said: 'In the battles of the future, if we know that there are Englishmen on our left flank, or Englishmen on our right, then we shall know that we need give no thought nor worry to those positions.'

We returned to England on January 3. Albacete was just the same, except that it was muddier and dirtier—and the troops now slept on the stone floors without mattresses. Here the first British battalion was being trained. It was part of the section of a thousand Englishmen who, in February, were to hold the most vital positions near the Valencia road under twelve days of the biggest artillery bombardment of the war, then counter-attack and make Madrid's road safe for months—perhaps for good. I might have gone back and joined those men, who are the real heroes of the Spanish struggle. But I did not go. I got married and lived happily instead.

.   .   .   .   .

Yet more and more I see that those three months were not just an adventure, an interlude. The mark which they left is something that does not diminish but grows with time. When we were all together at the castle of El Prado there was a kind of faith which made us feel that we could not ever be destroyed. But seven of those men—including Joe—were killed at Boadilla. They were killed, and forgotten, because they were only important for a day. Then there were other fighters, other martyrs, other sympathies.

There is something frightening, something shocking about the way the world does not stop because those men are dead. Over all this war there is that feeling. It is not something which is specifically due to the fact that one is seeing the struggle of a race of people one loves, that one's friends are fighting, or have died—it is a feeling of the vastness of the thing which has caught up so many separate entities and individualities.

I am not a pacifist, though I wish it were possible to lead one's life without the intrusion of this ugly monster of force and killing—war—and its preparation. And it is not with the happiness of the convinced communist, but reluctantly that I realise that there will never be peace or any of the things I like and want, until that mixture of profit-seeking, self-interest, cheap emotion and organised brutality which is called Fascism has been fought and destroyed for ever.

H. B. MALLALIEU

'Spain'

from *Letter in Wartime And Other Poems*, 1941

Pity and love are no more adequate:
They have not saved ten thousand who are dead,
Nor brought relief to peasants who in dread
Gaze at that sky which held their hope of late:
They have not stifled horror nor killed hate.
Europe is not impatient of her guilt,
But those on whom her tyranny is built,
By love deserted have grown desperate.

Tears are no use. Those who mourn grown mad.
May sanity have strength and men unite
Who in their individual lives are glad
That what remains of peace may yet prove strong.
We have the will, then let us show the might,
Who have foreborne and pitied far too long.

LOOKING BACK

LEON TROTSKY

'The Tragedy of Spain'

from *Socialist Appeal*, 10 February 1939; in *The Spanish Revolution (1931–39)*,
New York, 1973

February 1939

One of the most tragic chapters of modern history is now drawing to its
conclusion in Spain. On Franco's side there is neither a staunch army
nor popular support. There is only the greed of proprietors ready to
drown in blood three-fourths of the population if only to maintain their
rule over the remaining one-fourth. However, this cannibalistic ferocity
is not enough to win a victory over the heroic Spanish proletariat. Franco
needed help from the opposite side of the battlefront. And he obtained
this aid. His chief assistant was and still is Stalin, the gravedigger of
the Bolshevik Party and the proletarian revolution. The fall of the
great proletarian capital, Barcelona, comes as direct retribution
for the massacre of the uprising of the Barcelona proletariat in May
1937.

Insignificant as Franco himself is, however miserable his clique of
adventurists, without honor, without conscience, and without military
talents, Franco's great superiority lies in this, that he has a clear and
definite program: to safeguard and stabilize capitalist property, the rule
of the exploiters, and the domination of the church; and to restore the
monarchy.

The possessing classes of all capitalist countries—whether fascist or
democratic—proved, in the nature of things, to be on Franco's side. The
Spanish bourgeoisie has gone completely over to Franco's camp. At the
head of the republican camp, there remained the cast-off 'democratic'
armor-bearers of the bourgeoisie. These gentlemen could not desert to
the side of fascism, for the very sources of their influence and income
spring from the institutions of bourgeois democracy, which require (or

used to require!) for their normal functioning lawyers, deputies, journalists, in short, the democratic champions of capitalism. The program of Azaña and his associates is nostalgia for a day that has passed. This is altogether inadequate.

The Popular Front resorted to demagogy and illusions in order to swing the masses behind itself. For a certain period, this proved successful. The masses who had assured all the previous successes of the revolution still continued to believe that the revolution would reach its logical conclusion, that is, achieve an overturn in property relations, give land to the peasants, and transfer the factories into the hands of the workers. The dynamic force of the revolution was lodged precisely in this hope of the masses for a better future. But the honorable republicans did everything in their power to trample, to besmirch, or simply to drown in blood the cherished hopes of the oppressed masses.

As a result, we have witnessed during the last two years the growing distrust and hatred of the republican cliques on the part of the peasants and workers. Despair or dull indifference gradually replaced revolutionary enthusiasm and the spirit of self-sacrifice. The masses turned their backs on those who had deceived and trampled upon them. That is the primary reason for the defeat of the republican troops. The inspirer of deceit and of the massacre of the revolutionary workers of Spain was Stalin. The defeat of the Spanish revolution falls as a new indelible blot upon the already bespattered Kremlin gang.

The crushing of Barcelona deals a terrible blow to the world proletariat, but it also teaches a great lesson. The mechanics of the Spanish Popular Front as an organized system of deceit and treachery of the exploited masses have been completely exposed. The slogan of 'defense of democracy' has once again revealed its reactionary essence, and at the same time, its hollowness. The bourgeoisie wants to perpetuate its rule of exploitation; the workers want to free themselves from exploitation. These are the real tasks of the *fundamental* classes in modern society.

Miserable cliques of petty-bourgeois middlemen, having lost the confidence and the subsidies of the bourgeoisie, sought to salvage the past without giving any concessions to the future. Under the label of the Popular Front, they set up a joint stock company. Under the leadership of Stalin, they have assured the most terrible defeat when all the conditions for victory were at hand.

The Spanish proletariat gave proof of extraordinary capacity for initiative and revoltionary heroism. The revolution was brought to ruin by petty, despicable, and utterly corrupted 'leaders.' The downfall of

Barcelona signifies above all the downfall of the Second and Third
Internationals, as well as of anarchism, rotten to its core.

Forward to a new road, workers! Forward to the road of the international socialist revolution!

ARNOLD LUNN

'Afterthoughts on the Spanish War'

from *Come What May: An Autobiography*, 1940

In retrospect the Spanish War seems dwarfed by the scale of the present
tragedy. Spanish Catholicism was at stake in Spain; but it is the future of
Christianity in Europe which is in peril at the moment. And yet, in spite
of the magnitude of the European tragedy, the Spanish war has its
lessons for to-day, and the present trend of Spanish foreign policy has its
moral for all those who are concerned for the future of Christianity.

It is relevant to consider the reasons for the Republican defeat, for we
may still profit by drawing correct deductions from their failure.

The Republicans began the war with almost everything in their favour.
They were in possession of all the great centres of industry. The gold
reserves were in their hands. The Fleet had rallied to their side. The
Nationalist risings in Madrid and in Barcelona had failed. Franco had to
begin the reconquest of Spain from Morocco, across Straits in control of
a hostile fleet.

On the balance the Republicans received as much assistance from
France and Russia as the Nationalists from Germany and Italy.

The Republicans lost because they sacrificed military to political
considerations. The war was regarded as a means to an end, political
revolution. Officers were appointed for political reasons. The army was
'democratised', and the regular officers who remained loyal to the
Republic were regarded with profound suspicion. Now there is no
reason why officers, like priests, should not be recruited from every
social strata; but unless the officer, like the priest, feels himself to be the
representative of a hierarchic tradition, set apart from other men, he will
lack the confidence in himself and the power to impose respect which is
essential in the ordeal of battle. Democratic formulas cannot be applied
in war, which is in essence aristocratic, for leadership in war, to be
effective, must be imposed from above, not dictated from below. There

were many gallant officers in the Republican Army, but there was no sense of hierarchic solidarity. Many a battalion surrendered strong positions and retreated because their officers had no confidence in the staying powers of battalions to the right or to the left.

Many of those who tried to build up the Republican Army have since written books to explain their failure. There is widespread agreement that the Nationalists won because their morale was better, and because the Republican military effort was cramped and hampered by the political control of the Communists. I brought back with me to England a curious collection of pamphlets which I found in trenches captured from the Republicans, among them the notes for a speech delivered in English by a political commissar to an American battalion on the supreme importance of an orthodox interpretation of Dialectical Materialism, and a dreary little pamphlet on the alleged phallic origin of Christianity. 'The rod of Moses was clearly a phallic symbol.' 'Poor devils,' said General Fuller; 'fancy serving out all this dull stuff! What they want is *La Vie Parisienne.*'

Political considerations which hampered the military effort proved even more fatal to the industrial effort. The attempt to eliminate at one fell swoop the 'profit motive' resulted not only in widespread inefficiency but also in universal corruption. The demand for a *levée en masse* and the indiscriminate arming of workers had a disastrous effect on production. It is much more amusing to lounge about with a rifle than to do an honest day's work. Thousands of oranges, the export of which would have procured foreign exchange, were left rotting on the quays because the men who should have been loading them found it more amusing to round up and shoot Fascist suspects.

The peasants, who were angered by the persecution of the Church and infuriated by the incompetence of bureaucratic control, lost heart. It was interesting to contrast the carefully cultivated fields in territory which had been under Nationalist control since the outbreak of the war with the ill-kempt disorder and neglect of the territory captured from the Republicans.

I met at Malta, in March, 1940, an Italian who had helped to organise the anti-Fascist brigades which fought in Spain on the Republican side. 'The principal reason for the Republican defeat', he told me, 'was the insensate savagery of the anarchists. The Spaniards are a cruel race, far more cruel than the Italians. We do not want to kill or to be killed. If we have a revolution in Italy we shall shout a great deal and shoot very little. But in Barcelona they shot a great deal and were very silent. The Spanish anarchist exaggerates the vices of the Spaniard and has none of his virtues, excepting courage. He has no sense. I used to try to convince these fools that they would lose the war if they continued to burn churches and to murder priests. But they were pure fanatics beyond the reach of reason. The Republic needed the support of the peasants, and lost that support by its campaign against the Church, for the Spanish peasant is, and will always be, a Catholic. Let me give you an example from my own experience of Anarchist savagery. We were anxious, for propaganda purposes, that our battalion should be one hundred per cent. Italian, so we sent away two Frenchmen very politely, and asked them to join some other battalion. But when these Frenchmen arrived in Barcelona they were arrested by the Anarchists. "You have been turned out of the Garibaldi battalion because you are Fascists. We shall shoot you." The poor Frenchmen managed to get into touch with the commanding officer of a new Italian battalion which had just arrived in Barcelona, and this man interviewed the Anarchists and begged them to wait until he himself had got into touch with the C O of the battalion at the front. "I'm sure", he said, "that these Frenchmen are telling the truth." But the Anarchists were in a shooting mood, so they refused to wait, and the Italians who turned up next at the front were in a state of frenzied rage. "We would never have come", they exclaimed, "to fight for these savages had we known what they were like." I was nearly shot myself. On my way back to France my papers were examined by the Communist representative at the frontier, who managed to lose them. A few minutes later the representative of the Anarchists turned up and insisted that I was a Fascist. In vain the Communist protested that he had seen my papers, that they were in order, that they had just been mislaid and would turn up again. The Anarchist, who would have welcomed a chance of shooting not only me but the Communist, began to hint that the Communist was trying to pass a Fascist over the frontier. He insisted on going through all my luggage. I was terrified. You see, my wife, though a Catholic, is interested in religion, and had bought an Italian translation of a book which is said to be very interesting—the New Testament. The Anarchist found this book, and my heart sank. But luckily he was a born Catholic and did not recognise it. Of course if it had been full of pious pictures our fate would have been sealed, but it was a Protestant translation and had no pictures, pious or otherwise.'

The Republican leaders did not under-estimate the influence of Catholicism or the folly of the religious persecution, but they were impotent to restrain the Anarchists and Communists. Very few of their supporters in England realised the decisive importance of the religious issue. English Liberals have always assumed that all foreigners are more interested in politics than in religion, and that the majority of foreigners ask for nothing better than to be governed by the nearest available equivalent to Mr Gladstone or Mr Asquith. The English, in general, irrespective of their political views, find it difficult to believe in the power of ideas which they find uncongenial, and in the existence of popular support for leaders such as Hitler, Mussolini or General Franco, whose views are so painfully un-English.

Progressive opinion in England assumed that Franco would have no friends in Spain excepting among priests and aristocrats, and that the people would instinctively rally to the support of a Government which permitted the active persecution of the religion which was still the religion of the overwhelming majority of the Spanish people. Catholicism and Nationalism may be regrettable survivals from a reactionary age, destined to disappear in the enlightened world of to-morrow, but no sound estimate of contemporary Europe is possible which disregards the immense influence of these ancient loyalties.

It was no less shallow to assume that because General Franco accepted the help of Hitler, enemy of Catholicism, his claim to be defending Catholicism was a mere pretext. Nations fighting for existence have always accepted help, where help was available, irrespective of the religious or political views of their allies. England is a Christian country, but we made every effort to secure an alliance with, and should still be prepared to accept help from, Russia. And rightly so, for our objective is the destruction of Nazism, and we may legitimately play off one anti-Christian dictator against another. The criterion in such matters is the objective of the war—the destruction of Spanish Communism in Franco's case, and of German Nazism in our own.

HILAIRE BELLOC

'The Salvation of Spain'

from *Places*, 1942

I have already written of a landscape that shall be ever memorable to me. I mean the central sector of the Catalan Battle as I saw it just before the liberation of Barcelona in the Civil War. That battle was perhaps the ultimate phase, perhaps only the penultimate phase, in the liberation of Spain, the restoration of that which so nearly perished.

I have yet to speak of the man to whose initiative and high talent, integrity, determination and military vision the victory was due.

Here the scene is in the Ebro Valley itself, well up in its middle course, and it will ever be associated in my mind with the spirit that accomplished so great a thing. The physical surroundings, the visual experience, of an event whose roots stand not in the material and passing, but in the permanent, spiritual world, fix and stamp themselves upon a mortal mind. Feats of such a kind as that which was accomplished here belong to the divine story of Christendom, not only to its soil and to its human habitations, but to the mission of Europe—which mission, I take it, has been to found and perpetuate the highest culture, and, happily, the enduring culture, of our race: Christendom.

In that mission Spain has been foremost a battlefield for generation upon generation and its warriors have been the protagonists in the fight. It was in Spain from the Pyrenees to the Straits that the intense enduring warfare for the thrusting back of Islam from the heart of Europe, from western Europe, was accomplished. It is the Spanish blood that was spent in those centuries of effort and of ultimate triumph. The Spanish character and soul was not only moulded, but forged and annealed in that enormous trial.

Of all this we in the north know little. These islands suffered another assault than that of Islam: the assault of the Sea Rovers, the pagans from the north, not supplanters, but mere destroyers, ultimately warred down and tamed, but not until (though few in numbers) they had all but ruined our own extreme province of Christendom which they looted without sense or plan, merely barbaric. Islam, I say, has hardly touched the North, though it is comic to remember one raid, so late as the seventeenth century, in which Corsairs from Barbary set foot for a moment in south Ireland, wherein, for some days (I have heard it said) the call to prayer was heard above an Irish harbour in the south. But that harbour did not remain a Mohammedan foothold. For the rest these islands have not known what was meant by the flood of Islam.

On this account our current history books (which have little value) and, what is more important, our traditions and legends, our corporate memories, retain but slightly and vaguely the endless war which the men of the desert waged against the Cross. On this account also the meaning of Spain is lost to us.

Now in our own day when that meaning has so vividly returned, forming part of actual things before our eyes, they are, through our lack of this historical connection, utterly misunderstood. Spain has saved Europe from Communism and is in process of continuing to do so.

It was my good fortune to meet and speak with the man who has been first and principal in this task. I met him on that very territory, the Marches of the Ebro, wherein Charlemagne first established the Christian bastion against that attack which threatened to destroy, to overwhelm, all the Christian thing. It is into the lifetime and work of Charlemagne, into his apparently ephemeral but profoundly enduring achievement that the last of antiquity flows as into a lake or reservoir of power. It is from that same source that there flow the first streams of the Middle Ages. When Charlemagne was crowned in Rome on that Christmas Day of 800 he set a seal upon the re-establishment of the west.

Already Christendom of the east and of the Mediterranean had been three-quarters overrun by the violent flame. The first Arab charge had had its sequel in the transformation of half our world. From the day when Charlemagne was crowned, although his successors were uncertain and of no continuous dynasty, and although the unity of which he was the lord and symbol seemed to have dissolved in 'the darkness of the death of Charlemagne,' in the dust of feudalism, in the confusion of disputed powers, it was certain that Christendom of the west, the head of the world, was saved. And it was here, in the Ebro Valley, the Emperor fixed a first boundary whence the reconquest of Spain was to go forward. Not even his partial civilizing of the German forests, nor his checking (continued by his German successors) of the Asiatic Nomads, had the significance of this recovered and founded land—the Marches of the Ebro.

I am glad, indeed, that it was within sight of the river, in the palace of a village upon its northern bank, I met General Franco. Nowhere else, not even in Toledo, could I have felt the site of our meeting more filled with the past.

It was one of those great brown buildings which are characteristic everywhere of Spain: monuments which, when you see them from a distance in the plain, their villages surrounding them, you take from their colour to be part of the Iberian earth itself. How many have I not discovered—when, as a younger man, I walked day after day over these immensely open countrysides! They are groups of human dwellings, are these villages, which seem from miles away no more than a natural accident, part and parcel of the endless plain, or of those guardian walls, the sterile mountain ranges. But when you approach them they come alive with the intense spirit of that silent people: their armouries, their shrines, their innumerable carving, their secret but abundant vitality.

The great square building is cubic one might say. For the Cube underlies the building of the Spaniard everywhere. It contains the lines of the great Spanish cathedrals, the Spanish castles and such Spanish palaces as this; for the Cube is a symbol of that solidity and permanence wherein Spain manifests itself.

I was led to the ante-chamber whence I should be ushered into the presence of a man last in succession to those many who on this same general battlefield of Europe have endured, planned and achieved Europe's recovery.

It is not possible to see in their perspective the things of our own time, least of all the things of to-day itself, or even of yesterday. But I can imagine (perhaps a little fantastically) that when the vanguard of the armies which Franco had made from nothing as it were, marched into Barcelona, something had been done on the scale of what was done in the old St Peter's on that Christmas Day nearly 1,140 years ago. We shall see, or rather our distant descendants may see, whether this be so or no. It may be that the entry into Barcelona will mark another turning point and that a remote posterity may perceive it as something even more of a boundary-stone than the Battle of Warsaw. When Barcelona was set free the effort of those who had destroyed Christendom was, in this field at least, at an end.

However this may be, when I entered Franco's presence I entered the presence of one who had fought that same battle which Roland in the legend died fighting and which the Godfrey in sober history had won when the battered remnant, the mere surviving tenth of the first Crusaders, entered Jerusalem—on foot, refusing to ride where the Lord of Christendom had offered Himself up in Sacrifice.

. . . . . .

I will not linger upon that brief experience of mine. I was not there to record for my fellows a personal emotion which perhaps cannot be communicated and which at any rate should not be, but when I had spoken to this man of what he had done for us all and what he meant to us—when I had left him, to retain as I shall ever retain, the impression of those words exchanged in the noble, sombre room of a Spanish palace, majestic as all those proportions are in that land of majesty—I knew that I had experienced something unique. I had been in the air of what has always been the Salvation of Europe—I mean the Spanish Crusade. Worse luck for those who do not understand these things!

GEORGE ORWELL

'Looking Back on the Spanish Civil War'

from 'Looking Back on the Spanish Civil War', *New Road*, 1943,
reprinted in *England Your England*, 1953

I never think of the Spanish war without two memories coming into my
mind. One is of the hospital ward at Lerida and the rather sad voices of
the wounded militiamen singing some song with a refrain that ended—

Una resolucion,
Luchar hast' al fin!

Well, they fought to the end all right. For the last eighteen months of the
war the Republican armies must have been fighting almost without
cigarettes, and with precious little food. Even when I left Spain in the
middle of 1937, meat and bread were scarce, tobacco a rarity, coffee and
sugar almost unobtainable.

The other memory is of the Italian militiaman who shook my hand in
the guardroom, the day I joined the militia. I wrote about this man at the
beginning of my book on the Spanish war,* and do not want to repeat
what I said there. When I remember—oh, how vividly!—his shabby
uniform and fierce, pathetic, innocent face, the complex side-issues of
the war seem to fade away and I see clearly that there was at any rate no
doubt as to who was in the right. In spite of power politics and journalistic
lying, the central issue of the war was the attempt of people like this to
win the decent life which they knew to be their birthright. It is difficult to
think of this particular man's probable end without several kinds of
bitterness. Since I met him in the Lenin Barracks he was probably a
Trotskyist or an Anarchist, and in the peculiar conditions of our time,
when people of that sort are not killed by the Gestapo they are usually
killed by the GPU. But that does not affect the long-term issues. This
man's face, which I saw only for a minute or two, remains with me as a
sort of visual reminder of what the war was really about. He symbolizes
for me the flower of the European working class, harried by the police of
all countries, the people who fill the mass graves of the Spanish
battlefields and are now, to the tune of several millions, rotting in
forced-labour camps.

When one thinks of all the people who support or have supported

* *Homage to Catalonia*

Fascism, one stands amazed at their diversity. What a crew! Think of a programme which at any rate for a while could bring Hitler, Pétain, Montagu Norman, Pavelitch, William Randolph Hearst, Streicher, Buchman, Ezra Pound, Juan March, Cocteau, Thyssen, Father Coughlin, the Mufti of Jerusalem, Arnold Lunn, Antonescu, Spengler, Beverley Nichols, Lady Houston, and Marinetti all into the same boat! But the clue is really very simple. They are all people with something to lose, or people who long for a hierarchical society and dread the prospect of a world of free and equal human beings. Behind all the ballyhoo that is talked about 'godless' Russia and the 'materialism' of the working class lies the simple intention of those with money or privileges to cling to them. Ditto, though it contains a partial truth, with all the talk about the worthlessness of social reconstruction not accompanied by a 'change of heart'. The pious ones, from the Pope to the yogis of California, are great on the 'change of heart', much more reassuring from their point of view than a change in the economic system. Pétain attributes the fall of France to the common people's 'love of pleasure'. One sees this in its right perspective if one stops to wonder how much pleasure the ordinary French peasant's or working-man's life would contain compared with Pétain's own. The damned impertinence of these politicians, priests, literary men, and what-not who lecture the working-class socialist for his 'materialism'! All that the working man demands is what these others would consider the indispensable minimum without which human life cannot be lived at all. Enough to eat, freedom from the haunting terror of unemployment, the knowledge that your children will get a fair chance, a bath once a day, clean linen reasonably often, a roof that doesn't leak, and short enough working hours to leave you with a little energy when the day is done. Not one of those who preach against 'materialism' would consider life livable without these things. And how easily that minimum could be attained if we chose to set our minds to it for only twenty years! To raise the standard of living of the whole world to that of Britain would not be a greater undertaking than the war we have just fought. I don't claim, and I don't know who does, that that wouldn't solve anything in itself. It is merely that privation and brute labour have to be abolished before the real problems of humanity can be tackled. The major problem of our time is the decay of the belief in personal immortality, and it cannot be dealt with while the average human being is either drudging like an ox or shivering in fear of the secret police. How right the working classes are in their 'materialism'! How right they are to realize that the belly comes before the soul, not in the scale of values but in point of time! Understand that, and the long horror that we are enduring becomes at least intelligible. All the considerations are likely to make one falter—the siren voices of a Pétain or of a Gandhi, the inescapable fact that in order to fight one has to degrade oneself, the equivocal moral position of Britain, with its democratic phrases and its coolie empire, the sinister development of Soviet Russia, the squalid farce of left-wing politics—all this fades away and one sees only the struggle of the gradually awakening common people against the lords of property and their hired liars and bumsuckers. The question is very simple. Shall people like that Italian soldier be allowed to live the decent, fully human life which is now technically achievable, or shan't they? Shall the common man be pushed back into the mud, or shall he not? I myself believe, perhaps on insufficient grounds, that the common man will win his fight sooner or later, but I want it to be sooner and not later—some time within the next hundred years, say, and not some time within the next ten thousand years. That was the real issue of the Spanish war, and of the last war, and perhaps of other wars yet to come.

I never saw the Italian militiaman again, nor did I ever learn his name. It can be taken as quite certain that he is dead. Nearly two years later, when the war was visibly lost, I wrote these verses in his memory:

> The Italian soldier shook my hand
> Beside the guard-room table;
> The strong hand and the subtle hand
> Whose palms are only able
>
> To meet within the sound of guns,
> But oh! what peace I knew then
> In gazing on his battered face
> Purer than any woman's!
>
> For the flyblown words that make me spew
> Still in his ears were holy,
> And he was born knowing what I had learned
> Out of books and slowly.
>
> The treacherous guns had told their tale
> And we both had bought it,
> But my gold brick was made of gold—
> Oh! who ever would have thought it?
>
> Good luck go with you, Italian soldier!
> But luck is not for the brave;
> What would the world give back to you?
> Always less than you gave.

Between the shadow and the ghost,
Between the white and the red,
Between the bullet and the lie,
Where would you hide your head?

For where is Manuel Gonzalez,
And where is Pedro Aguilar,
And where is Ramon Fenellosa?
The earthworms know where they are.

Your name and your deeds were forgotten
Before your bones were dry,
And the lie that slew you is buried
Under a deeper lie;

But the thing that I saw in your face
No power can disinherit:
No bomb that ever burst
Shatters the crystal spirit.

JASON GURNEY

You Are Legend

from *The Last Crusade*, 1974

There is no longer any point in trying to untangle the web of lies and confusions which lay behind that ghastly Civil War. It arose out of total confusion and chaos. There were individuals on both sides who committed every possible form of cruelty and beastliness. And nobody, from either side, came out of it with clean hands. We, of the International Brigades, had wilfully deluded ourselves into the belief that we were fighting a noble Crusade because we needed a crusade—the opportunity to fight against the manifest evils of Fascism, in one form or another, which seemed then as if it would overwhelm every value of Western civilization. We were wrong, we deceived ourselves and were deceived by others: but even then, the whole thing was not in vain. Even at the moments of the greatest gloom and depression, I have never regretted that I took part in it. The situation is not to be judged by what we now know of it, but only as it appeared in the context of the period. And in that context there was a clear choice for anyone who professed to be opposed to Fascism. The fact that others took advantage of our idealism in order to destroy it does not in any way invalidate the decision which we made.

The last word lies with the speech of Dolores Ibarruri—*La Pasionaria* —fish pedlar, miner's widow and Member of Parliament, made at the final stand-down parade of the International Brigades at Barcelona on 15th November, 1938.

'Mothers! Women! When the years pass by and the wounds of war are staunched: when the cloudy memory of the sorrowful, bloody days returns in a present of freedom, love, and well-being: when the feelings of rancour are dying away and when pride in a free country is felt equally by all Spaniards—then speak to your children. Tell them of the International Brigades. Tell them how, coming over seas and mountains, crossing frontiers bristling with bayonets, and watched for by ravening dogs thirsty to tear at their flesh, these men reached our country as Crusaders for freedom. They gave up everything, their loves, their country, home and fortune—fathers, mothers, wives, brothers, sisters and children and they came and told us: "We are here, your cause, Spain's cause, is ours. It is the cause of all advanced and progressive mankind." Today they are going away. Many of them, thousands of them, are staying here with the Spanish earth for their shroud, and all Spaniards remember them with the deepest feeling.'

Then she addressed the assembled members of the Brigades.

'Comrades of the International Brigades! Political reasons, reasons of State, the welfare of that same cause for which you offered your blood with boundless generosity, are sending you back, some of you to your own countries and others to forced exile. You can go proudly. You are history. You are legend. You are the heroic example of democracy's solidarity and universality. We shall not forget you, and when the olive tree of peace puts forth its leaves again, mingled with the laurels of the Spanish Republic's victory—come back!'

ACKNOWLEDGEMENTS

The editor and publishers gratefully acknowledge permission to reprint copyright material in the book as follows:

Jay Allen: 'Blood Flows in Badajoz', copyrighted 30 August 1936, Chicago Tribune Co., all rights reserved. Used with permission.

W. H. Auden: 'Spain 1937', copyright 1940 and renewed 1968 by W. H. Auden, 'Impressions of Valencia', copyright © 1977 by Edward Mendelson, William Meredith and Monroe E. Spears, Executors of the Estate of W. H. Auden, both reprinted from *The English Auden: Poems, Essays and Dramatic Writings 1927–1939*, ed. Edward Mendelson, by permission of Faber & Faber Ltd. and Random House Inc. Extract from 'Missing Churches', published first in *Modern Canterbury Pilgrims* (Mowbray 1956) and reprinted by permission of W. H. Auden's Literary Executor, Professor Edward Mendelson.

W. H. Auden and Christopher Isherwood: extract from Valerian's Speech from *On The Frontier* by W. H. Auden and Christopher Isherwood, copyright 1938 by W. H. Auden and Christopher Isherwood. Reprinted by permission of Faber & Faber Ltd., and Curtis Brown Ltd., New York.

From *Authors Take Sides on the Spanish War* (1937), reprinted by permission of Lawrence & Wishart Ltd.

James Barke: from *The Land of Leal* (1939). Reprinted by permission of Collins Publishers.

George Barker: 'Elegy on Spain' reprinted from *Collected Poems 1930–1955* by permission of Faber & Faber Ltd.

Ralph Bates: 'Compañero Sagosta Burns a Church' from *Left Review* II, 13 Oct. 1936, and 'My Friend, Ralph Fox' from *Ralph Fox: Writer in Arms* (1937). Both reprinted by permission of Lawrence & Wishart Ltd.

Julian Bell: 'Letters' reprinted from *Julian Bell: Essays, Poems and Letters*, ed. Quentin Bell, by permission of the Hogarth Press.

Hilaire Belloc: 'The Salvation of Spain' reprinted from *Places* (Cassell, 1942), by permission of A. D. Peters & Co. Ltd.

Georges Bernanos: reprinted from *A Diary of My Times*, trans. Pamela Morris, by permission of The Bodley Head (*Les Grands Cimetières Sous La Lune*, Librairie Plon, Paris, 1938).

Anthony Blunt: two letters to the *Spectator*, 22 Oct. 1937 & 5 Nov. 1937, by permission of the Director, Courtauld Institute of Art: 'Picasso Unfrocked', from the *Spectator*, 8 Oct. 1937, reproduced with permission.

Franz Borkenau: from *The Spanish Cockpit* (Faber 1937). Copyright the Estate of Franz Borkenau.

Roy Campbell: 'Hard Lines, Azaña!'. Reproduced by permission of Francisco Campbell Custódio and Ad. Donker (Pty.) Ltd.

Christopher Caudwell: 'Last Letters of a Hero' from *News Chronicle*, 28 June 1937.

Sir William Coldstream: letter to the *Spectator*, 22 Oct. 1937.

Cyril Connolly: 'The House of Arquebus—1' reprinted from *Night and Day*, 12 Aug. 1937, copyright 1937 by Cyril Connolly, by permission of Deborah Rogers Ltd., Literary Agency; from *Enemies of Promise*, copyright 1938 by Cyril Connolly, reprinted by permission of Deborah Rogers Ltd. and Persea Books; 'Costa Brava', a review of *Volunteer in Spain* from the *New Statesman*, 7 Aug. 1937; 'A Spanish Diary' (review) from the *New Statesman*, 20 Feb. 1937; 'Today the Struggle' (review) from the *New Statesman*, 5 June 1937.

John Cornford: letters to Margot Heinemann; 'To Margot Heinemann' ('Poem') and 'A Letter from Aragon', all reprinted from *John Cornford: A Memoir*, ed. Pat Sloan, by permission of Jonathan Cape Ltd., on behalf of the Estates of Pat Sloan and the author.

Leonard Crome: (letter) 'Julian Bell' from the *New Statesman*, 29 Aug. 1937.

John Dos Passos: reprinted from *Journeys Between Wars* (1938), by permission of Mrs John Dos Passos.

T. S. Eliot: 'A Commentary' (2 extracts) from *The Criterion*, vol. XVI, no. 63, Jan. 1937 and no. 65, July 1937. Reprinted by permission of Faber & Faber Ltd.

Ralph Fox: reprinted from *Ralph Fox: A Writer in Arms*, ed. John Lehmann, T. A. Jackson and C. Day-Lewis (1937), by permission of Lawrence & Wishart Ltd.

Roy Fuller: 'Poem (for M. S. Killed in Spain)', reprinted from *New and Collected Poems 1934–84* by permission of Secker & Warburg Ltd., and the author.

David Gascoyne: reprinted from *Journal 1936–37* (1980), by permission of the author and Enitharmon Press.

Cecil Gerahty: from *The Road to Spain* (Hutchinson 1937).

Nan Green: from *The Road to Spain*, copyright Martin Green. Used with permission.

Graham Greene: extract from *The Confidential Agent*, copyright 1939 by Graham Greene, copyright © renewed 1967 by Graham Greene; 'Alfred Tennyson Intervenes' from the *Spectator*, 10 Dec. 1937, reprinted as 'The Apostles Intervene' in *Collected Essays* by Graham Greene, copyright 1951, © 1966, 1968, 1969 by Graham Greene, copyright renewed © 1979 by Graham Greene. Reprinted by permission of Laurence Pollinger Ltd. and Viking Penguin, Inc.; review of *Last Train from Madrid* from *Night and Day*, 8 July 1937, and War Film Review from the *Spectator*, 29 Sept. 1939, both reprinted in *The Pleasure Dome* and reproduced by permission of Laurence Pollinger Ltd.

Jason Gurney: reprinted from *Crusade in Spain* (1974) by permission of Faber & Faber Ltd.

Bernard Gutteridge: 'Spanish Earth' from *New Writing*, ns iii, Christmas 1939. Copyright © Bernard Gutteridge 1939.

Charlotte Haldane: 'Passionara' from *Left Review*, vol. iii, no. 15, April 1938.

Margot Heinemann: 'For R. J. C. (Summer 1936)' from *New Writing*, Autumn 1937. Reprinted by permission of the author.

Ernest Hemingway: 'The Heat and the Cold: Remembering Turning the Spanish Earth' from *Verve*, vol. i, no. 2, Paris, Spring 1938. Copyright © Ernest Hemingway Inc.

T. A. R. Hyndman: reprinted from *The Distant Drum: Reflections on the Spanish Civil War*, ed. Philip Toynbee, by permission of Sidgwick & Jackson (Publishers).

Randall Jarrell: 'A Poem for Someone Killed in Spain' reprinted from *The Complete Poems*, copyright 1940, copyright renewed © 1968 by Randall Jarrell, by permission of Faber & Faber Ltd, and Farrar Straus & Giroux Inc.

W. E. Johns: extracts from 'The Editor's Cockpit' from *Popular Flying*, vols. vi & vii. Reprinted by permission of A. P. Watt Ltd., on behalf of W. E. Johns (Publications) Ltd.

Lewis Jones: reprinted from *We Live* (1939) by permission of Lawrence & Wishart Ltd.

Arthur Koestler: 'Dialogue with Death' reprinted from *Spanish Testament* (Gollancz) by permission of A. D. Peters & Co. Ltd.

John Langdon-Davies: from a review of *Homage to Catalonia* from the *Daily Worker*, Spain Weekend Supplement, 21 May 1938. Used with permission.

Jef Last: reprinted from *The Spanish Tragedy*, trans. David Haddett (1939), by permission of Routledge & Keagan Paul PLC.

Rosamond Lehmann: (letter), 'Books for Spain' from the *New Statesman*, 21 Aug. 1937. Used with permission.

Arnold Lunn: reprinted from *Come What May: An Autobiography* (1940), by permission of Eyre & Spottiswoode.

Donagh MacDonagh: 'He is dead and gone, Lady' from 'Charles Donnelly', reprinted from *Hungry Grass*, by permission of Faber & Faber Ltd.

Louis MacNeice: 'Autumn Journal—Part VI' from *Collected Poems* (Faber 1949); 'Today in Barcelona' from the *Spectator*, 20 Jan. 1938. Both reprinted by permission of David Higham Associates Ltd.

H. B. Mallalieu: 'Spain' reprinted from *Letter in Wartime & Other Poems* (Fortune Press 1941), by permission of Charles Skilton Ltd.

André Malraux: from *Man's Hope*, trans. Stuart Gilbert and Alastair Macdonald. Translation copyright 1938, renewed 1966 by Random House Inc. Reprinted by the permission of Random House Inc. and Hamish Hamilton Ltd.

Thomas Mann: Epilogue to 'Spain', trans. Thomas Lowe-Porter, published in the UK in *Life and Letters Today*, Summer 1937: collected in the *Complete Works in 13 Volumes: Speeches & Essays*, 4. Used by permission of S. Fisher Verlag GmbH, Frankfurt-am-Main.

Ethel Mannin: reprinted from *Comrade O Comrade* (Jarrolds 1947), by permission of Century Hutchinson Ltd. and the Executors for the Estate of Ethel Mannin.

Carl A. Manzani: 'The Volunteers' from the *Spectator*, 12 Feb. 1937. Used by permission.

George Orwell: 'Spanish Nightmare', two reviews from *Time and Tide*, 31 July 1937; from a letter to Stephen Spender, 2 April 1938; and from a letter to Rayner Heppenstall, 31 July 1937, all reprinted from *Collected Essays, Journalism and Letters*, copyright 1968 by Sonia Brownell Orwell; 'Looking Back on the Spanish Civil War', reprinted in *England Your England* (Secker 1953) and in *Such, Such Were the Joys* (Harcourt, 1953), copyright 1953 by Sonia Brownell Orwell, renewed 1981 by Mrs

George K Perutz, Mrs Miriam Gross, and Dr Michael Dickson, Executors of the Estate of Sonia Brownell Orwell; from *Homage to Catalonia*, copyright 1952, 1980 by Sonia Brownell Orwell. All material reproduced by permission of A. M. Heath & Co. Ltd., and Harcourt Brace Jovanovich Inc.

Roland Penrose: letter to the *Spectator*, 29 Oct. 1937. Copyright © The Estate of Roland Penrose 1986. Used with permission.

Wogan Philipps: 'An Ambulance Man in Spain' from *New Writing*, New Series, Autumn 1938. Reprinted by permission of the author.

Anthony Powell: 'A Reporter in Los Angeles—Hemingway's Spanish Film' from *Night and Day*, 19 Aug. 1937. Reprinted by permission of David Higham Associates Ltd.

V. S. Pritchett: from 'The Spanish Tragedy', a review of *Homage to Catalonia* from the *New Statesman*, 30 April 1938, and from a review of Jef Last's *The Spanish Tragedy* from the *New Statesman*, 11 Nov. 1939.

Herbert Read: 'Bombing Casualties in Spain' reprinted from *Collected Poems* (1966), and 'Picasso Unfrocked', two letters to the *Spectator*, 15 Oct. and 29 Oct. 1937, by permission of David Higham Associates Ltd.

Gustav Regler: reprinted from *The Owl of Minerva*, trans. Norman Denny (1959), by permission of Grafton Books, A Division of the Collins Publishing Group.

Michael Roberts: from *The World and Ourselves* (Epilogue), ed. Laura Riding (Chatto 1938).

Esmond Romilly: from *Boadilla* (Hamish Hamilton 1937).

Antoine de Saint-Exupéry: reprinted from *Wind, Sand and Stars*, trans. Lewis Galantière (1939), copyright 1939 by Antoine de Saint-Exupéry, renewed 1968 by Harcourt Brace Jovanovich Inc., by permission of William Heinemann Ltd., and Harcourt Brace Jovanovich Inc.

Jean-Paul Sartre: 'The Wall', trans. C. A. Whitehouse. Reprinted by permission of the C. W. Daniel Company Ltd.

Claude Simon: trans. John Fletcher from *The Georgics* by Claude Simon, to be published by John Calder (London) and Riverrun Press (New York). Reproduced with permission.

Hugh Slater: 'How Ralph Fox Was Killed' reprinted from *Ralph Fox: Writer in Arms* (1937), by permission of Lawrence & Wishart Ltd.

John Sommerfield: 'To Madrid' from *New Writing* III, Spring 1937, and extract from *Volunteer in Spain* (1937). Both reprinted by permission of Lawrence & Wishart Ltd.

Stephen Spender: 'Ultima Ratio Regum', 'Port Bou', and 'Fall of a City', copyright 1942 and renewed 1970 by Stephen Spender, reprinted from *Collected Poems 1928– 1953*, by permission of Faber & Faber Ltd., and Random House Inc.; 'Pictures in Spain' from the *Spectator*, 30 July 1937 and used by permission of the *Spectator*; 'I Join the Communist Party' from the *Daily Worker*, 19 Feb. 1937 and used with permission; extract from the Introduction to *Poems for Spain*, ed. Stephen Spender & John Lehmann (Hogarth 1939); 'Spain Invites the World's Writers', from *New Writing*, no. iv, Autumn 1937, and Letter to Virginia Woolf, 2 April 1937, Henry W. and Albert A. Berg Collection, the New York Public Library Astor, Lenox and Tuden Foundations. All reproduced by permission of the author. 'War Photograph' from the *New*

Statesman, 5 June 1937, and 'The Bombed Happiness' from the *New Statesman*, 4 Feb. 1939, both reprinted by permission of A. D. Peters & Co. Ltd. Review of *John Cornford: A Memoir* from the *New Statesman*, 12 Nov. 1938, and Picasso's 'Guernica' from the *New Statesman*, 15 Oct. 1938. Reprinted by permission of A. D. Peters & Co. Ltd.

G. L. Steer: 'Guernica', first published in *The London Mercury*, vol. xxxvi. no. 214, Aug. 1937 and reprinted in *The Tree of Gernika* (Hodder 1938). Used by permission of Mrs E. Kenyon Jones, Executor of the Estate of G. L. Steer.

Ruthven Todd: 'Joan Miró' reprinted from *Poets of Tomorrow* (Hogarth 1939), by permission of David Higham Associates Ltd.

Ernst Toller: 'Madrid-Washington' from the *New Statesman*, 8 Oct. 1938.

Miles Tomalin: 'Down the Road', first published in *Volunteer for Liberty*, no. 1 (Jan. 1940). Reprinted by permission of Mrs Miles Tomalin.

Leon Trotsky: 'The Tragedy of Spain' from *The Spanish Revolution (1931–39)* (Pathfinder Press, New York 1973).

Sylvia Townsend Warner: 'Waiting at Cerbère' and 'Benicasim' from *Collected Poems*, ed. Claire Harman (1982), copyright © Susan Pinney and William Maxwell, Executors of The Estate of Sylvia Townsend Warner. Reprinted by permission of Carcanet Press Ltd. 'The Drought Breaks' from *Life and Letters Today*, Summer 1937, and 'What the Soldier Said' from *Time and Tide*, 14 Aug. 1937. Both reprinted by permission of the author's estate and Chatto & Windus.

Evelyn Waugh: (letter) 'Fascist' from the *New Statesman*, 5 March 1938. Reprinted by permission of A. D. Peters & Co. Ltd.

Simone Weil: 'Lettre à Georges Bernanos' from *Écrits Historiques et Politiques* (© Editions Gallimard, Paris, 1960), translation copyright © 1986 Valentine Cunningham. By permission of Editions Gallimard.

Tom Wintringham: 'Monument' from *Left Review* III, no. 9, Oct. 1937. Reprinted by permission of Lawrence & Wishart Ltd.

Virginia Woolf: from *Three Guineas* (1938), copyright 1938 by Harcourt Brace Jovanovich Inc. renewed 1966 by Leonard Woolf, and reprinted by permission of the Hogarth Press, the author's estate and Harcourt Brace Jovanovich Inc. From *Virginia Woolf: A Biography*, by Quentin Bell, copyright 1972 by Quentin Bell and reprinted by permission of the Hogarth Press, and Harcourt Brace Jovanovich Inc.

T. C. Worsley: 'The Flight from Malaga' from *Left Review*, vol. iii, no. 3, 3 April 1937, 'Propaganda in Spain' from a review of *Volunteer in Spain* from *Life and Letters Today*, Autumn 1937. Reprinted by permission of Lawrence & Wishart Ltd.

W. B. Yeats: 'Politics', reprinted from *The Collected Poems of W. B. Yeats*, copyright 1940 by Georgie Yeats, renewed 1968 by Bertha Georgie Yeats, Michael Butler Yeats and Anne Yeats, by permission of A. P. Watt Ltd., on behalf of Michael B. Yeats and Macmillan London Ltd. and Macmillan Publishing Co., New York.

While every effort has been made to secure permission, we have failed in a number of cases to trace the copyright holder.

INDEX OF AUTHORS